Table of Contents

©1993 Donald A. Gardner Architects, Inc.

B. NATHAN

Design HPT300252—see page 255

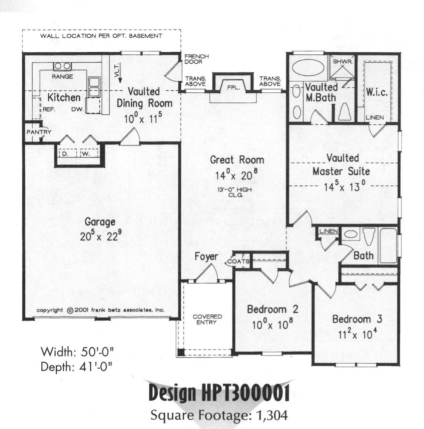

WALL LOCATION PER OPT. BASEMENT

FRENCH DOOR

Kitchen
RANGE
REF. DW.
PANTRY
D. W.

Vaulted Dining Room
10⁰ x 11⁵

VLT.

TRANS. ABOVE
FPL.
TRANS. ABOVE

SHWR.
Vaulted M.Bath
W.i.c.
LINEN

Great Room
14⁰ x 20⁸
13'-0" HIGH CLG.

Vaulted Master Suite
14⁵ x 13⁰

Garage
20⁵ x 22⁹

LINEN

Bath

Foyer
COATS

COVERED ENTRY

Bedroom 2
10⁰ x 10⁸

Bedroom 3
11² x 10⁴

copyright © 2001 frank betz associates, inc.

Width: 50'-0"
Depth: 41'-0"

Design HPT300001
Square Footage: 1,304

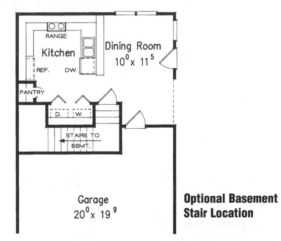

RANGE
Kitchen
REF. DW.
PANTRY

Dining Room
10⁰ x 11⁵

D. W.
STAIRS TO BSMT.

Garage
20⁰ x 19⁹

Optional Basement Stair Location

◆ Country simplicity is the dominant voice of this cottage plan. Horizontal and vertical siding highlight the exterior, while a family-friendly layout is found within. Inside, the foyer opens to the great room, which is warmed by a fireplace. The U-shaped kitchen serves the dining room and features a storage pantry. The vaulted master bedroom enjoys its own vaulted bath and walk-in closet. Two additional bedrooms nearby share a hall bath. A two-car garage completes the plan. Please specify basement or crawlspace foundation when ordering.

ALLEN

ONE-STORY HOMES

SECOND EDITION

© 1995 Donald A. Gardner Architects, Inc.

Design HPT300273—see page 276

B. NATHAN

728.373
Onze

450
Exceptional Home Plans From
810 to 5,400 Square Feet

hanley▲wood
HomePlanners

ONE-STORY HOMES

Published by Home Planners, LLC
3275 W. Ina Road, Suite 220
Tucson, Arizona 85741

DISTRIBUTION CENTER
29333 Lorie Lane
Wixom, Michigan 48393

Chief Financial Officer, Joe Carroll
Vice President, Publishing, Jennifer Pearce
Vice President, General Manager, Marc Wheeler
Executive Editor, Linda Bellamy
National Sales Manager, Book Division, Julie Marshall
Marketing Manager, Julie Turetzky
Director, Online Business, David Gallello
Managing Editor, Jason D. Vaughan
Special Projects Editor, Kristin Schneidler
Editor, Nate Ewell
Director, Plan Products, Matt Higgins
Lead Plans Associate, Morenci C. Clark
Plans Associates, Elizabeth Landry, Nick Nieskes
Proofreader/Copywriter, Douglas Jenness
Technical Specialist, Jay C. Walsh
Lead Data Coordinator, Fran Altemose
Data Coordinators, Misty Boler, Melissa Siewert
Production Director, Sara Lisa
Production Manager, Brenda McClary

BIG DESIGNS, INC.
President, Creative Director, Anthony D'Elia
Vice President, Business Manager, Megan D'Elia
Vice President, Design Director, Chris Bonavita
Editorial Director, John Roach
Assistant Editor, Tricia Starkey
Director of Design and Production, Stephen Reinfurt
Group Art Director, Kevin Limongelli
Photo Editor, Christine DiVuolo
Art Director, Jessica Hagenbuch
Graphic Designer, Mary Ellen Mulshine
Graphic Designer, Lindsey O'Neill-Myers
Graphic Designer, Jacque Young
Assistant Photo Editor, Brian Wilson
Project Director, David Barbella
Assistant Production Manager, Rich Fuentes

PHOTO CREDITS
Front Cover: Design HPT00001 by ©1995 Donald A. Gardner Architects, Inc.
For details, see page 276. Photography courtesy of Donald A. Gardner Architects, Inc.
Back Cover: Design HPT00001 by Design Basics, Inc.
For details, see page 213. Photography courtesy of Design Basics, Inc.

©2002 Home Planners, LLC

10 9 8 7 6 5 4 3

Printed in the United States of America

Library of Congress Control Number: 2003113856

ISBN softcover: 1-931131-07-4

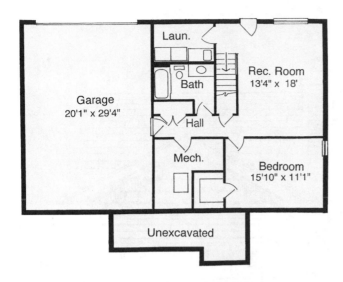

Laun.

Bath

Rec. Room
13'4" x 18'

Garage
20'1" x 29'4"

Hall

Mech.

Bedroom
15'10" x 11'1"

Unexcavated

Design HPT300002
Square Footage: 1,475
Finished Basement: 722 sq. ft.

Width: 48'-8"
Depth: 30'-8"

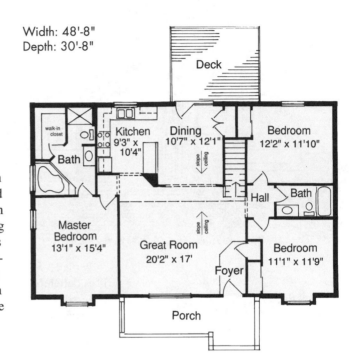

Deck

walk-in closet

Bath

Kitchen
9'3" x 10'4"

Dining
10'7" x 12'1"

Bedroom
12'2" x 11'10"

slope ceiling

Hall

Bath

Master Bedroom
13'1" x 15'4"

slope ceiling

Great Room
20'2" x 17'

Foyer

Bedroom
11'1" x 11'9"

Porch

◆ The mixture of shingles, stone and siding gives this home an eclectic facade. This pleasing cottage would be perfectly accented by trees and flowers. Cool summer evenings are happily spent on the front porch or rear deck. The great room is attached to the dining room for an open family floor plan. The L-shaped kitchen features a peninsula for extra space. The master bedroom contains a luxurious master bath. Two family bedrooms are located on the main floor. In the basement, there is space for another family bedroom along with a spacious recreation room. The laundry room and the garage complete this level.

Design HPT300003

Square Footage: 1,296

◆ Perfect for a starter or empty-nester home, this economical-to-build one-story plan is as delightful on the inside as it is appealing on the outside. Fish-scale siding, a covered porch and window boxes adorn the exterior. Inside, the foyer spills over to a spacious living room with a corner fireplace. The country kitchen across the hall offers a unique U-shaped counter and ample space for a large dining table. Sliding glass doors lead to the rear yard, and a handy service entrance leads past the laundry alcove to the single-car garage. The three bedrooms (or make it two and a den) revolve around the central bath with a soaking tub. The master bedroom has His and Hers entries to the long wall closet.

Width: 48'-0"
Depth: 45'-6"

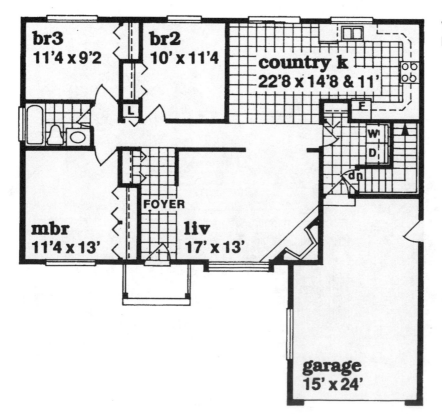

br3
11'4 x 9'2

br2
10' x 11'4

country k
22'8 x 14'8 & 11'

L

E

W
D

dn

FOYER

mbr
11'4 x 13'

liv
17' x 13'

garage
15' x 24'

◆ Meeting the needs of first-time homebuilders, this design is economical to build. Craftsman detailing and a quaint covered porch go a long way to create the charming exterior. Open planning adds to this design's livability. The foyer opens to a hearth-warmed great room. Vaulted ceilings and a half-wall separating the stairs to the basement and the foyer add to the spaciousness. An open island kitchen has an adjoining dining room with sliding glass doors to the deck and box-bay buffet space. The master suite sits adjacent to two family bedrooms and boasts His and Hers wall closets and a full bath with a soaking tub. Two family bedrooms—or make one a den—share a full bath.

Design HPT300004
Square Footage: 1,293

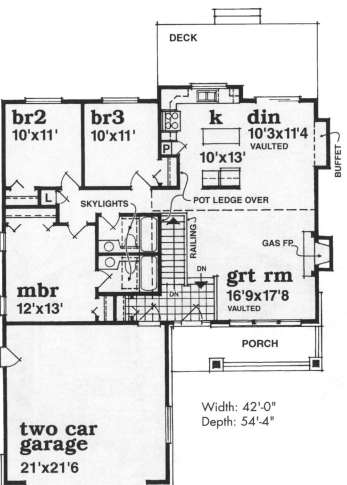

DECK

br2
10'x11'

br3
10'x11'

k

din
10'3x11'4
VAULTED

10'x13'

BUFFET

SKYLIGHTS

POT LEDGE OVER

RAILING

GAS FP.

DN

mbr
12'x13'

DN

grt rm
16'9x17'8
VAULTED

PORCH

two car garage
21'x21'6

Width: 42'-0"
Depth: 54'-4"

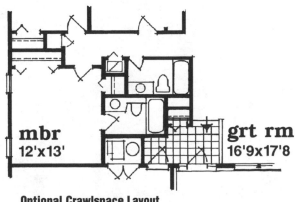

mbr
12'x13'

grt rm
16'9x17'8

Optional Crawlspace Layout

Design HPT300005

Square Footage: 1,253

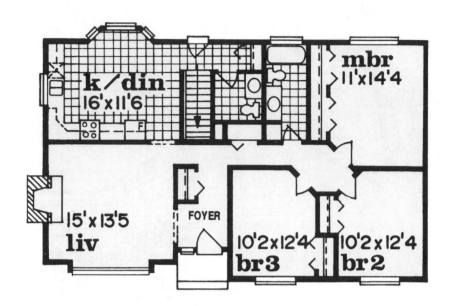

◆ Horizontal siding and quaint window boxes lend a country appeal to the exterior of this design. If you choose this cute one-story home, you'll have the option of a powder room or a laundry room next to the kitchen/dining area. The central foyer leads to a roomy living room with masonry fireplace and a box-bay window. The nearby country kitchen has a long L-shaped counter and a bay-window dining area. A rear door leads to the patio (basement stairs are directly opposite this door). Three bedrooms angle off the central hall. The master bedroom has His and Hers wall closets and a large window overlooking the rear yard. Family bedrooms face to the front of the house.

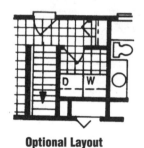

Optional Layout

Width: 46'-0"
Depth: 29'-6"

Design HPT300006
Square Footage: 1,197

◆ This compact three-bedroom design is ideal as a starter or retirement home. Its siding and brick combination and lovely bumped-out windows give it a cozy, rustic feeling. The bedrooms are positioned along the rear of the home for maximum privacy. Each bedroom has a large window overlooking the rear yard; the master bedroom is especially spacious. The entry opens directly to a large living area with a box-bay window and a fireplace. The country kitchen contains long, roomy counters, a convenient serving bar and a breakfast nook with a box-bay window. The side door provides quick, easy access to the kitchen and to the basement. If needed, the basement may be finished for additional living space or bedrooms.

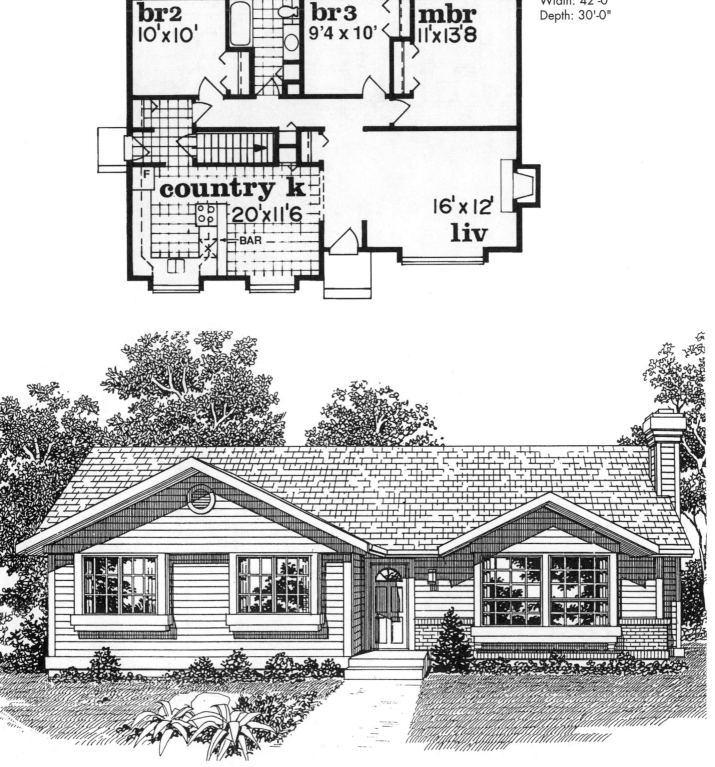

Width: 42'-0"
Depth: 30'-0"

br2
10'x10'

br3
9'4 x 10'

mbr
11'x13'8

country k
20'x11'6

BAR

F

16'x12'
liv

Design HPT300007

Square Footage: 1,319

◆ Charming and economical to build, this brick ranch design is ideal for first-time homeowners or retirement couples. A tiled foyer leads past the open-rail basement stairs to a vaulted great room. Here a gas fireplace warms the living and entertaining area. The dining room has buffet space and sliding glass doors to the rear deck. A nearby L-shaped island kitchen overlooks the rear deck. Sleeping quarters include two family bedrooms that share a full bath. A two-car garage sits in front of the bedrooms to shelter them from street noise.

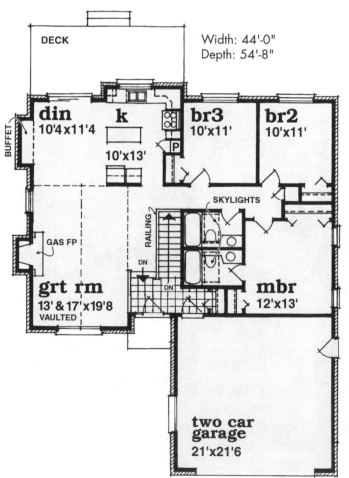

DECK

Width: 44'-0"
Depth: 54'-8"

din 10'4"x11'4"

k 10'x13'

br3 10'x11'

br2 10'x11'

BUFFET

SKYLIGHTS

GAS FP

RAILING

DN

DN

grt rm 13' & 17'x19'8 VAULTED

mbr 12'x13'

two car garage 21'x21'6

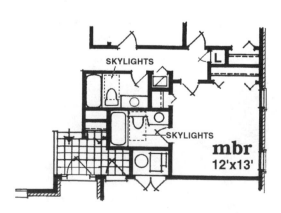

SKYLIGHTS

SKYLIGHTS

L

mbr 12'x13'

Optional Crawlspace Layout

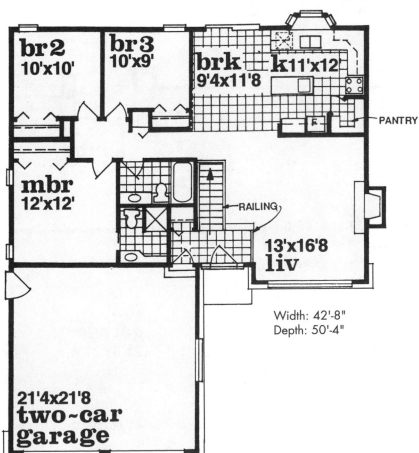

br2
10'x10'

br3
10'x9'

brk
9'4x11'8

k11'x12

PANTRY

mbr
12'x12'

RAILING

13'x16'8
liv

21'4x21'8
two~car
garage

Width: 42'-8"
Depth: 50'-4"

Design HPT300008
Square Footage: 1,204

◆ This attractive siding-and-brick home is not only beautiful, but economical to build as well. The sunken entry steps up to the living room, warmed by a fireplace. An open railing defines the stairway to the basement, enhancing spaciousness and giving this area a feeling of being much larger. A gourmet kitchen offers a walk-in pantry, a center preparation island with a salad sink, and greenhouse windows. Sliding glass doors in the breakfast nook lead to the backyard. The master bedroom has a roomy wall closet and a private bath with a shower. Two secondary bedrooms share a bath that includes a soaking tub. A two-car garage sits to the front of the plan, creating privacy and quiet for the bedrooms.

Design HPT300009
Square Footage: 1,253

◆ A multi-pane bay window, nestled in a gabled roof, adds charm to this bungalow and gives it a touch of elegance. Once inside, a large living/dining area is to the left. The living room has a gas fireplace and a bay window; the dining room features a buffet alcove. The kitchen is conveniently located to serve the dining room and enjoys a view over the sink to the rear yard. A master bedroom and two family bedrooms reside on the right side of the plan. The master suite contains a private bath, while the family bedrooms share a full bath that includes a skylight. A two-car garage sits to the front of the plan to help shield the bedrooms from street noise.

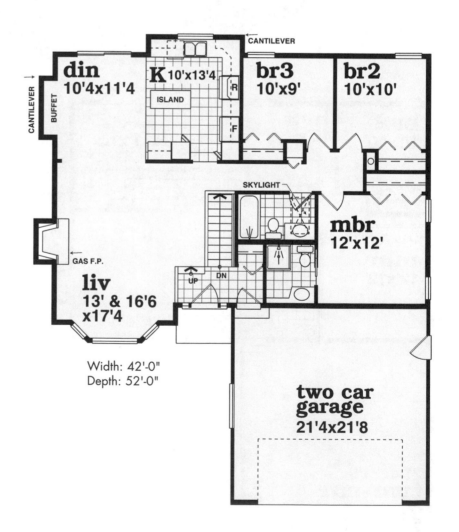

Width: 42'-0"
Depth: 52'-0"

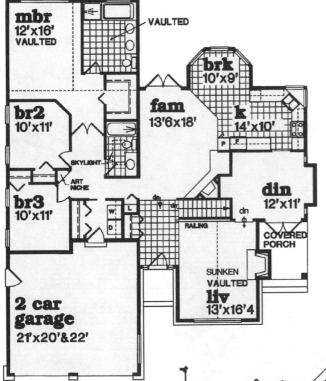

mbr
12'x16'
VAULTED

VAULTED

br2
10'x11'

SKYLIGHT

ART NICHE

br3
10'x11'

2 car garage
21'x20'&22'

brk
10'x9'

fam
13'6x18'

k
14'x10'

din
12'x11'

COVERED PORCH

RAILING

W D

L

SUNKEN VAULTED

liv
13'x16'4

Width: 50'-0"
Depth: 62'-10"

Design HPT300010
Square Footage: 1,879

◆ The same floor plan offers two exterior elevations—each perfect in its own way. One is a contemporary stucco version with keystone and brick detailing. The other is traditional brick throughout. The floor plan begins with a welcoming foyer, brightly lit by an abundance of natural light from gabled windows above. The living room has a cozy fireplace; the dining room is graced by double doors to the side porch. The adjoining family room has a corner fireplace and a media center, plus double doors to the rear patio. The master suite offers a walk-in closet and a vaulted bath with His and Hers vanities, a whirlpool spa and a separate shower.

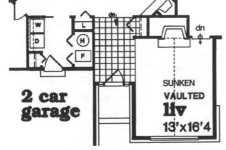

2 car garage

W D

L

H

F

SUNKEN VAULTED

liv
13'x16'4

Optional Crawlspace Layout

Alternate Elevation

Design HPT300011
Square Footage: 1,479

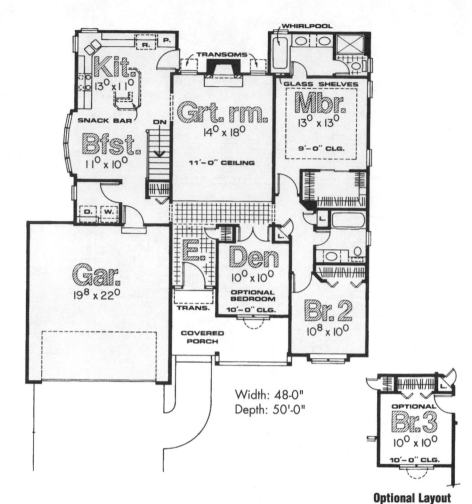

◆ A covered porch and interesting window treatments add charisma to this cheerful bungalow home. The entry opens to a sunny great room with a center fireplace framed by transom windows. Nearby, an efficient kitchen is highlighted by an island snack bar, a corner sink flanked with windows, and access to the backyard. The spacious master suite features a walk-in closet and a pampering master bath with a whirlpool tub and a compartmented toilet and shower area. Two secondary bedrooms—one an optional den designed with French doors—share a full hall bath.

Width: 48-0"
Depth: 50'-0"

Optional Layout

14

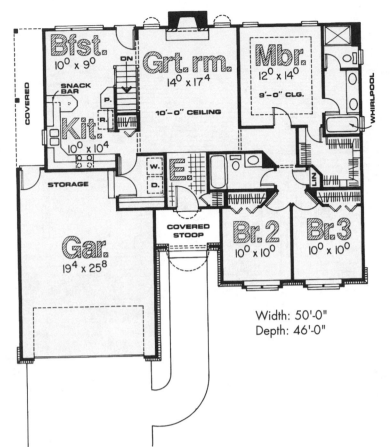

Bfst.
10⁰ x 9⁰

SNACK BAR

Kit
10⁰ x 10⁴

DN

P.

R.

Grt. rm.
14⁰ x 17⁴

10'-0" CEILING

Mbr.
12⁰ x 14⁰

9'-0" CLG.

WHIRLPOOL

W. D.

E

LIN

STORAGE

Gar.
19⁴ x 25⁸

COVERED STOOP

Br. 2
10⁰ x 10⁰

Br. 3
10⁰ x 10⁰

Width: 50'-0"
Depth: 46'-0"

Design HPT300012
Square Footage: 1,339

◆ This home's arched entry complements a brick and siding elevation. The great room features arched windows. In the kitchen, a snack bar and convenient access to a utility room are fine attributes. The great room sports a centered fireplace and access to the breakfast area. Secondary bedrooms share a hall bath while the master bedroom contains its own bath with a whirlpool tub and a compartmented toilet and shower.

Design HPT300013
Square Footage: 1,432

◆ This comfortable home functions as either a three-bedroom home or a two-bedroom with a den design. The living room, with a fireplace, rests in a prominent carousel bay and is warmed by a fireplace. The dining room—open to the living room—is decorated with a bumped-out area flanked by windows. The spacious country kitchen, with abundant counter space, conveniently serves the dining room. Access the rear patio through a door in the kitchen. The main hall has a feeling of spaciousness due to an open-railed staircase leading to the basement. The master suite features a walk-in closet and a bath with His and Hers vanities. Family bedrooms share a main bath that includes a soaking tub. An alcove laundry sits near the bedrooms for convenience.

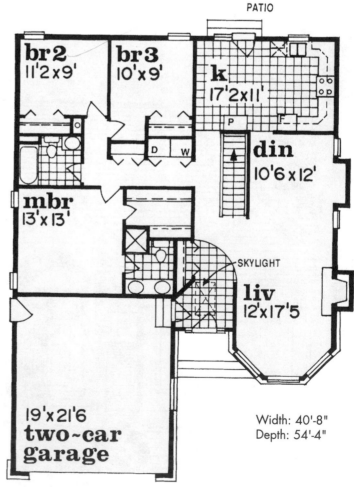

PATIO

br2
11'2 x 9'

br3
10' x 9'

k
17'2 x 11'

P

D W

din
10'6 x 12'

mbr
13' x 13'

SKYLIGHT

liv
12' x 17'5

19' x 21'6
two~car garage

Width: 40'-8"
Depth: 54'-4"

Design HPT300014
Square Footage: 1,486

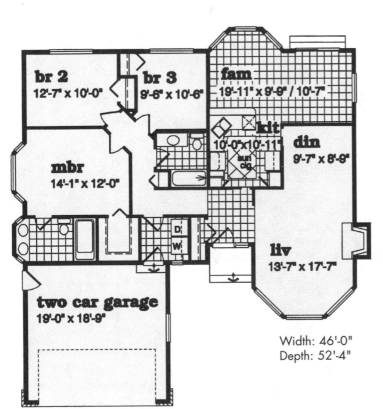

br 2
12'-7" x 10'-0"

br 3
9'-6" x 10'-6"

fam
19'-11" x 9'-9" / 10'-7"

mbr
14'-1" x 12'-0"

kit
10'-0" x 10'-11"

din
9'-7" x 8'-9"

liv
13'-7" x 17'-7"

two car garage
19'-0" x 18'-9"

Width: 46'-0"
Depth: 52'-4"

◆ This contemporary design with board-and-batten siding and brick accents has great curb appeal. This is further enhanced by the carousel living room with its fireplace and attached dining area. A step-saving galley kitchen has a sunshine ceiling and adjoins the rear-facing family room with its breakfast bay. Sliding glass doors here lead to the rear yard. Three bedrooms include a master suite with a large walk-in closet, charming bay window, and bath with His and Hers vanities. Another bath is shared by the two additional rear-facing bedrooms. A two-car garage connects to the house at a service entry that contains a laundry alcove. The basement option for this home adds 1,566 square feet.

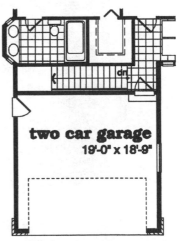

two car garage
19'-0" x 18'-9"

Optional Basement Stair Location

Design HPT300015
Square Footage: 1,295

◆ Special exterior details make this smaller one-story home more than just a plain rectangular box. The bay-window pop-out in the dining room and the covered entryway with a walled garden area are appealing adornments. A volume roofline gives spaciousness to the foyer and great room in the form of ten-foot ceilings. A unique angled counter that separates the great room and kitchen is accented with columns and holds a cooktop for convenience. The den may serve as a guest room when needed and shares a bath with one family bedroom. Note the appointments in the master suite: sliding glass doors to a rear patio, a walk-in closet and a large bath with a linen closet. Space for a washer and dryer is conveniently located near the bedrooms.

Width: 40'-0"
Depth: 52'-0"

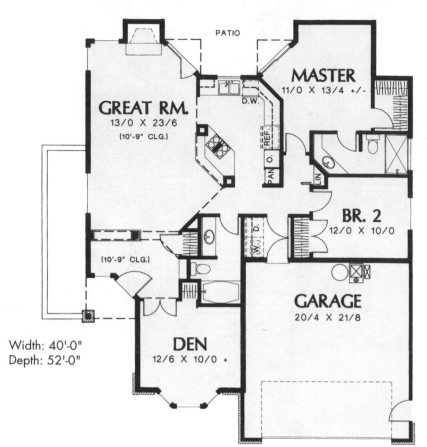

PATIO

GREAT RM.
13/0 X 23/6
(10'-9" CLG.)

MASTER
11/0 X 13/4 +/-

D.W.

PAN. O.

REF.

LIN.

(10'-9" CLG.)

W./ D.

BR. 2
12/0 X 10/0

DEN
12/6 X 10/0 +

GARAGE
20/4 X 21/8

Design HPT300016
Square Footage: 1,271

◆ Spaciousness is the key to this charming three-bedroom home. The decorative columns that define the formal dining room create an open living area at the center of this floor plan. Intimate dining is enjoyed in the breakfast nook, which is nestled between the galley kitchen and the utility closet. The great room boasts an elegant fireplace flanked by radius windows. The sleeping quarters are found on the left where two family bedrooms share a full bath. The master suite pampers with a large walk-in closet and a lavish private bath—note the tray ceiling in the master bedroom. Please specify basement or crawlspace foundation when ordering.

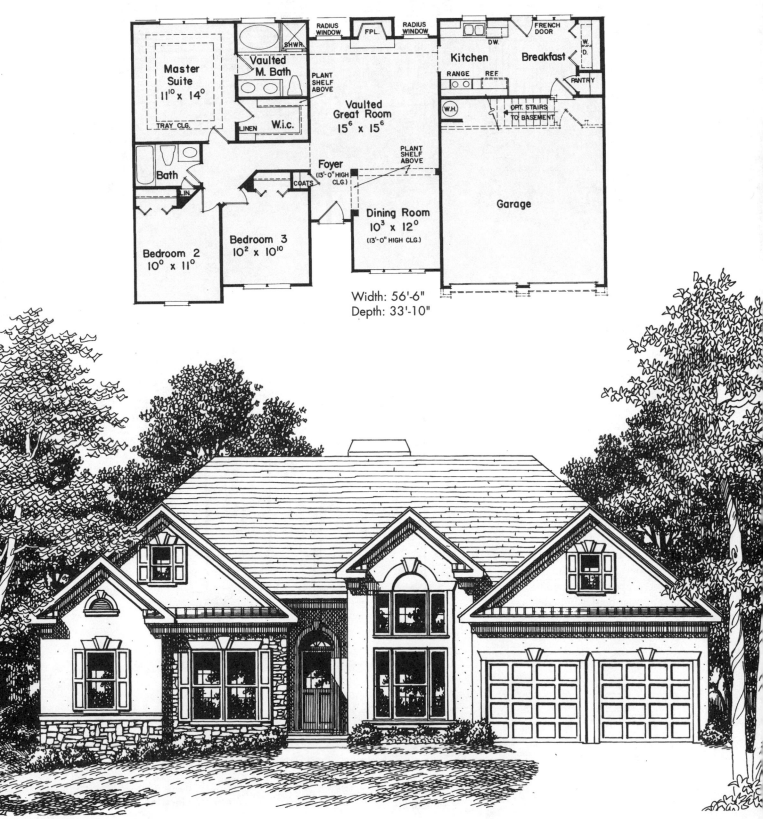

Design HPT300017

Square Footage: 1,366

L D

◆ This design offers you a choice of three distinctively different exteriors. Blueprints show details for all three optional elevations. A study of the floor plan reveals a fine measure of livability. In less than 1,400 square feet, you'll find amenities often found in much larger homes. In addition to the two eating areas and the open planning of the gathering room, the indoor/outdoor relationships are of great interest. The basement may be developed at a later date for recreational activities.

Width: 65'-0"
Depth: 37'-4"

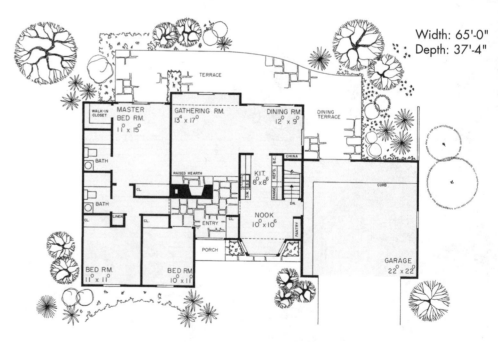

Alternate Elevation

Alternate Elevation

Design HPT300018
Square Footage: 1,196

◆ Offering unique design features, this cozy bungalow is charming with horizontal siding, shuttered windows and multi-paned glass. The foyer leads to a spacious living room with a warming fireplace and huge picture window. The dining room has a buffet alcove, providing extra space for entertaining. The nearby kitchen is well appointed with an angled sink and a walk-in pantry. A short flight of stairs leads to a landing with side-door access and then on to the basement. The master bedroom offers a full wall closet and private bath. Two additional bedrooms share the main bathroom that includes a soaking tub. Blueprints include plans for an optional single-car garage.

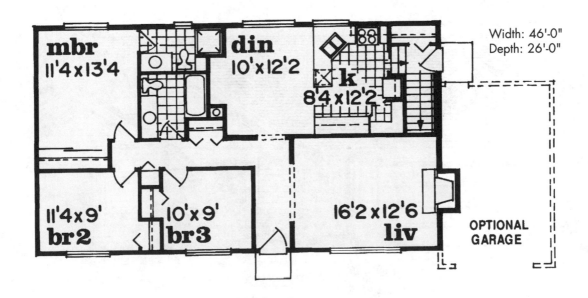

mbr
11'4 x 13'4

din
10' x 12'2

k
8'4 x 12'2

Width: 46'-0"
Depth: 26'-0"

br2
11'4 x 9'

br3
10' x 9'

liv
16'2 x 12'6

OPTIONAL GARAGE

Design HPT300019
Square Footage: 1,467

◆ Vaulted ceilings across the rooms at the rear of this home add spaciousness to the dining room, living room and master bedroom. The kitchen is open to the dining area and has an island cooktop and corner sink. A service entry leads to the two-car garage and holds the laundry alcove and a storage closet. The master suite is as gracious as those found in much larger homes, with a walk-in closet and a bath with a spa tub, separate shower and double sinks.

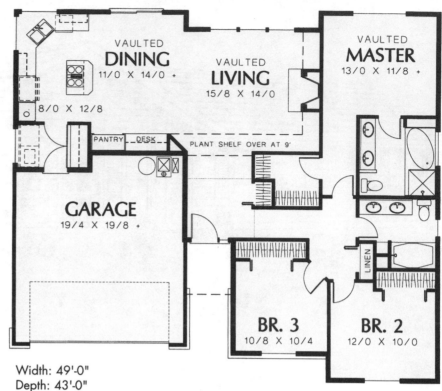

VAULTED
DINING
11/0 X 14/0 +

VAULTED
LIVING
15/8 X 14/0

VAULTED
MASTER
13/0 X 11/8 +

8/0 X 12/8

PANTRY DESK

PLANT SHELF OVER AT 9'

GARAGE
19/4 X 19/8 +

LINEN

BR. 3
10/8 X 10/4

BR. 2
12/0 X 10/0

Width: 49'-0"
Depth: 43'-0"

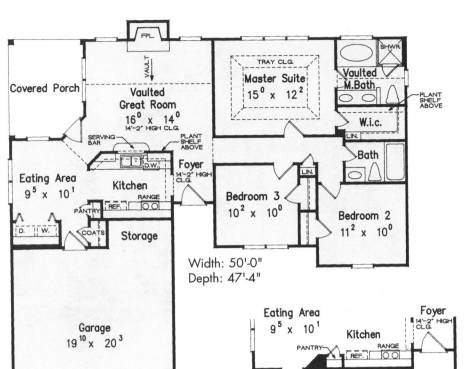

Design HPT302001
Square Footage: 1,185

Covered Porch

FPL.

VAULT

Vaulted
Great Room
16⁰ x 14⁰
14'-2" HIGH CLG.

TRAY CLG.

Master Suite
15⁰ x 12²

Vaulted
M.Bath

SHWR.

PLANT
SHELF
ABOVE

W.i.c.

LIN.

SERVING
BAR

D.W.

PLANT
SHELF
ABOVE

Foyer
14'-2" HIGH CLG.

Bath

LIN.

Eating Area
9⁵ x 10¹

Kitchen

RANGE

REF.

Bedroom 3
10² x 10⁰

Bedroom 2
11² x 10⁰

PANTRY

D. W.

COATS

Storage

Width: 50'-0"
Depth: 47'-4"

Garage
19¹⁰ x 20³

copyright © 1994 frank betz associates, inc.

GARAGE LOCATION WITH BASEMENT

Eating Area
9⁵ x 10¹

Kitchen

Foyer
14'-2" HIGH CLG.

PANTRY

RANGE

REF.

STAIRS
DN.

W.

Laund.

D.

COATS

Storage

Garage
19¹⁰ x 20⁰

Optional Basement Stair Location

◆ This attractive smaller home is perfect for a couple planning for retirement or a small family building a first home, and it boasts many extras you'd expect only in a much larger home. The impressive foyer, with its fourteen-foot ceiling, offers access to both the kitchen and the vaulted great room. The efficient kitchen opens to a sunny eating area, with a pantry, closet and laundry space nearby. Providing access to a rear covered porch, the great room is enhanced by a fireplace, a serving bar from the kitchen, and a plant shelf. The master bedroom features a tray ceiling and a vaulted master bath with a separate tub, double-bowl vanity and large walk-in closet. Two family bedrooms share a full hall bath.

Design HPT300021
Square Footage: 1,489

◆ This tidy design is accented with brick veneer and a lovely bay window in the living room. The foyer opens to a hallway that leads, through an arch to the dining room, or through another arch to the living room. The kitchen, just beyond the dining room, is large enough for a breakfast nook and island work space. Sliding glass doors in the dining room open to a rear patio and the yard; additional sliding glass doors in the breakfast area do the same. The master bedroom is graced with a walk-in closet and a full bath. Two family bedrooms share a hall bath. If you choose, make one of these bedrooms a den or home office. A single-car garage accesses the house through the laundry area.

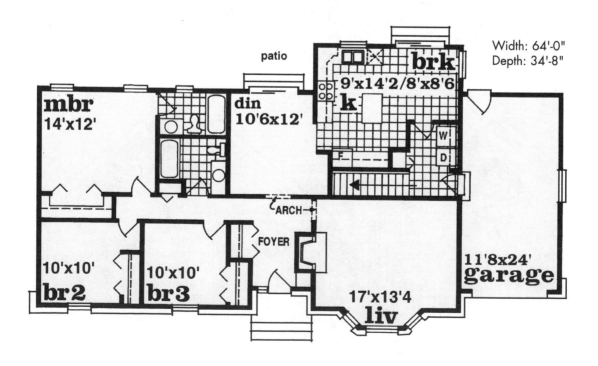

Width: 64'-0"
Depth: 34'-8"

patio

mbr
14'x12'

din
10'6x12'

brk
9'x14'2/8'x8'6
k

W
D

ARCH

FOYER

10'x10'
br2

10'x10'
br3

11'8x24'
garage

17'x13'4
liv

Design HPT300022

Square Footage: 1,332

◆ Brick veneer and siding provide an attractive, low-maintenance option for this ranch home. A weather-protected entry opens to a spacious foyer with a living room on the right and the dining room straight ahead. The living room sports a fireplace and bay window, while the dining room has built-in china cabinet space. The U-shaped kitchen easily serves the dining room and has ample counters. Sliding glass doors in the dining room lead to a rear patio and the yard beyond. The master suite has a walk-in closet and a private bath with a corner shower. Two additional bedrooms share a hall bath. The single-car garage allows room for a workbench. Note the laundry area that connects the garage to the main house.

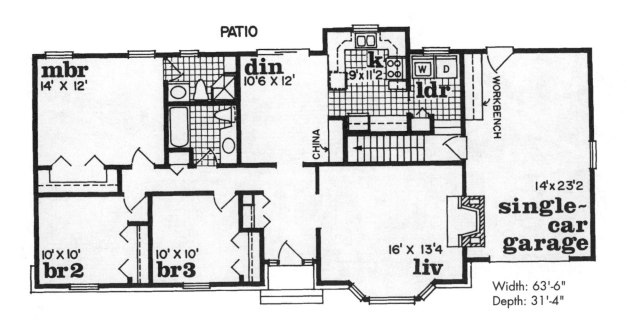

PATIO

mbr
14' X 12'

din
10'6 X 12'

k
9'x11'2

W D

ldr

WORKBENCH

CHINA

br2
10' X 10'

br3
10' X 10'

liv
16' X 13'4

14'x23'2
single-
car
garage

Width: 63'-6"
Depth: 31'-4"

Design HPT300023
Square Footage: 1,295

◆ This affordable three-bedroom home is not only attractive, but offers all the conveniences. The country kitchen, for example, offers abundant U-shaped counters, a desk/organizer area, a pantry and an eating bar. Sliding glass doors in the country kitchen open to a covered patio—ideal for outdoor entertaining. The living room shares the see-through fireplace with the kitchen and also offers a large window overlooking the rear yard. Direct access from the two-car garage through the laundry room to the kitchen is convenient for the family shopper. The master suite offers a full wall closet and a private bath with a soaking tub. Two additional bedrooms include one that might make the perfect office or guest room.

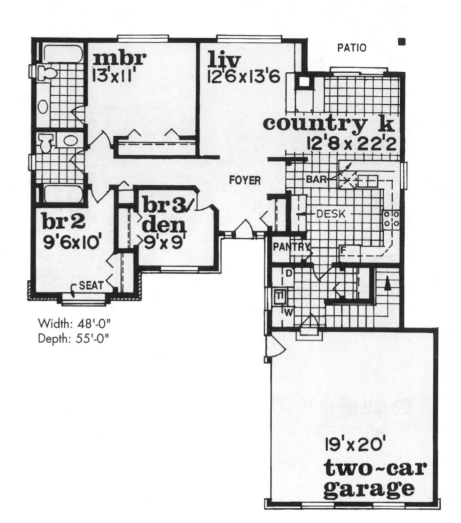

mbr
13'x11'

liv
12'6x13'6

PATIO

country k
12'8 x 22'2

FOYER

BAR

br2
9'6x10'

br3/
den
9'x9'

DESK

PANTRY

F

D

W

SEAT

Width: 48'-0"
Depth: 55'-0"

19'x20'
two~car
garage

Design HPT300024
Square Footage: 1,499

L

◆ This modest-sized house with its 1,499 square feet could hardly offer more in the way of exterior charm and interior livability. Measuring only 60 feet in width means it will not require a huge, expensive piece of property. The orientation of the garage and the front drive court are features which promote an attractive courtyard entry. In addition to the separate formal living and dining rooms, there is the informal kitchen/family room area. Note the beam ceiling, fireplace, sliding glass doors and eating area in the family room.

Width: 60'-0"
Depth: 58'-0"

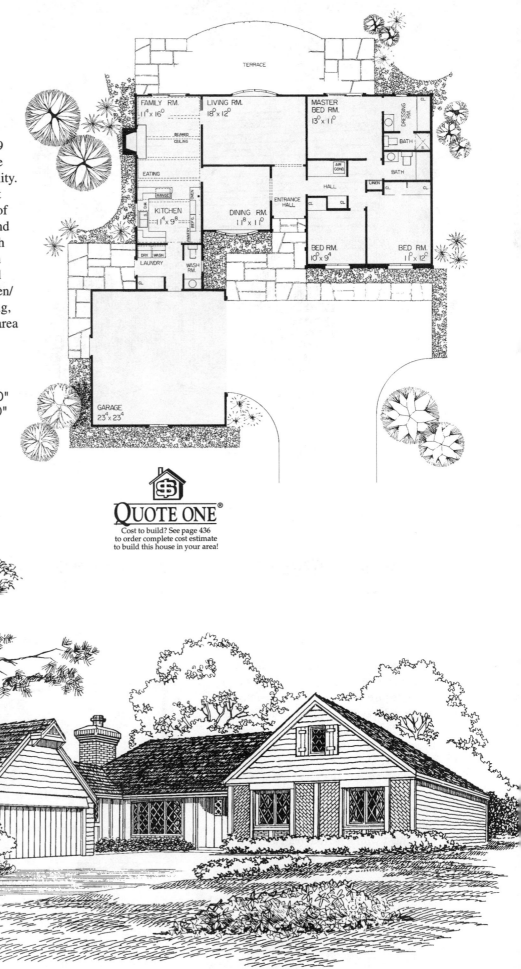

OPTIONAL BASEMENT

Quote One®

Cost to build? See page 436 to order complete cost estimate to build this house in your area!

Design HPT300025

Square Footage: 1,422

◆ Homeowners can wait out rainy days on the front covered porch of this home and likewise enjoy sunny afternoons on the rear deck. They'll find spacious shelter inside in the large great room, easily accessible from the kitchen with a breakfast nook. With a corner fireplace and rear deck access, the great room will be buzzing with activity. Two secondary bedrooms—make one a library—share a full hall bath. The master suite is graciously appointed with a private bath and walk-in closet.

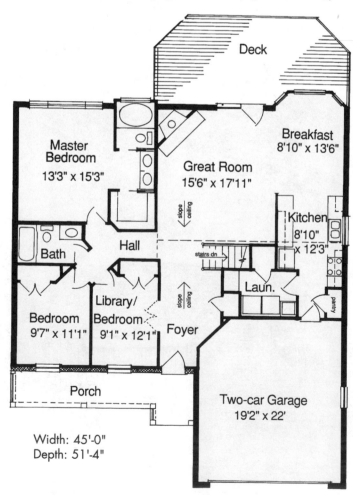

Master Bedroom
13'3" x 15'3"

Deck

Great Room
15'6" x 17'11"

Breakfast
8'10" x 13'6"

Kitchen
8'10" x 12'3"

Bath

Hall

stairs dn

slope ceiling

slope ceiling

Laun.

pantry

Bedroom
9'7" x 11'1"

Library/ Bedroom
9'1" x 12'1"

Foyer

Porch

Two-car Garage
19'2" x 22'

Width: 45'-0"
Depth: 51'-4"

© 1998   Donald A Gardner, Inc.

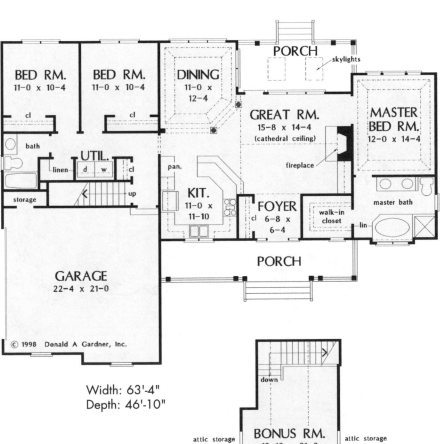

© 1998 Donald A Gardner, Inc.

Width: 63'-4"
Depth: 46'-10"

Design HPT300026
Square Footage: 1,476
Bonus Room: 340 sq. ft.

◆ This country plan begins with crisp horizontal wood siding and an arched entry with sidelights. The foyer opens to a great room with a fireplace and cathedral ceiling. A door in the great room leads out to a covered porch with skylights. Columns and a tray ceiling define the dining room, while the peninsula kitchen sits nearby. The master suite features a tray ceiling, plus a bath with a walk-in closet, double sinks and a separate tub and shower. Note the bonus room over the garage, which is reached via a staircase behind the utility room.

Design HPT300027

Square Footage: 1,425
Bonus Room: 424 sq. ft.

◆ This beautiful country house features light-filled dormers and varied rooflines. A family can appreciate and enjoy the front and rear covered porches in which they can sit and enjoy the view. The great room, dining room and kitchen comprise one large open area—the great room boasts a cathedral ceiling, a fireplace and built-in shelves. The luxurious master suite includes a walk-in closet, private bath and over-sized tub. A cathedral ceiling also graces the front bedroom.

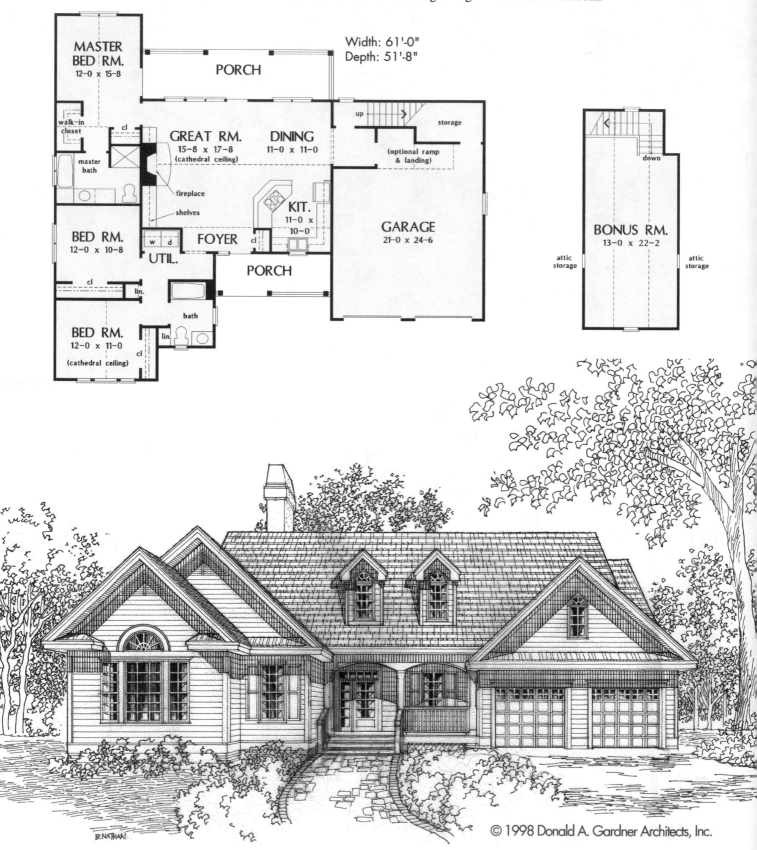

Width: 61'-0"
Depth: 51'-8"

B. NATHAN

© 1998 Donald A. Gardner Architects, Inc.

Design HPT300028
Square Footage: 1,357

◆ Victorian appointments enhance the facade of this one-story home: horizontal siding, fish-scale details in the gable fronts, and simple millwork pieces. The main living area is graced by a vaulted ceiling, a built-in media center and a three-sided fireplace that separates the living area from the country kitchen. The dining space features sliding glass doors to the rear deck. Family bedrooms share a full hall bath that includes a skylight; the master suite has a private bath. If you choose the crawlspace option, you'll gain buffet space in the country kitchen and extra storage space beyond the laundry room.

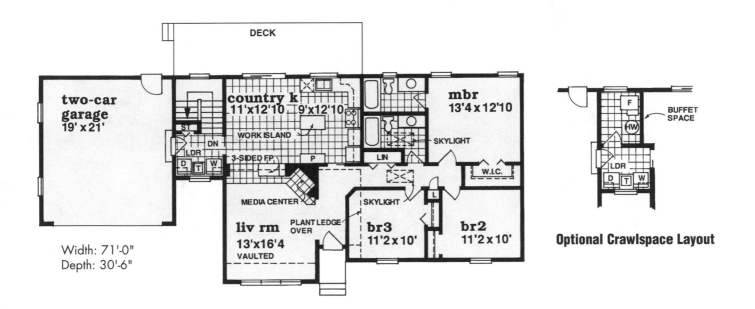

Width: 71'-0"
Depth: 30'-6"

Optional Crawlspace Layout

Design HPT3030001
Square Footage: 1,487

◆ A stone-and-siding facade—ornamented by a flower box and country-style shutters—gives a French Country feel to this farmhouse. The elegant interior offers plenty of amenities. The dining room, great room, and master bedroom all feature stepped ceilings, and sliding glass doors in the great room open to the rear porch. The breakfast nook, near the well-planned kitchen, provides a bay window that overlooks the porch. Family sleeping quarters to the left include two family bedrooms that share a full bath; the master suite, to the right of the plan, boasts a dual-vanity bath with a large walk-in closet and separate shower and tub. The two-car garage includes a work bench.

Porch
25'-5" x 9'-6"

Nook
10'-8" x 8'-10"
9'-0" Flat Clg.

Bedroom 3
11'-8" x 11'-4"
9'-0" Flat Clg.

Great Room
14'-2' x 17'-0"
Stepped Clg.

Master Suite
11'-10" x 15'-6"
Stepped Clg.

Kitchen
9'-0" x 10'-10"

P.

Bath 2

Foyer

Dining
11'-0" x 9'-6"
Stepped Clg.

WIC

Utility
5'-4" x
8'-6"

M. Bath

Bedroom 2
11'-8" x 12'-0"
9'-0" Flat Clg.

Porch
16'-4" x 4'-6"

work bench

Width: 52'-6"
Depth: 66'-0"

2 Car Garage
21'-0" x 25'-0"

© 1994 Donald A. Gardner Architects, Inc.

B. NATHAN

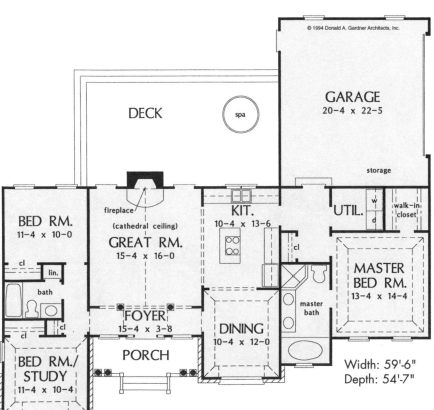

© 1994 Donald A. Gardner Architects, Inc.

GARAGE
20-4 x 22-5

storage

DECK

spa

fireplace
(cathedral ceiling)

KIT.
10-4 x 13-6

UTIL.

w
d

walk-in
closet

BED RM.
11-4 x 10-0

cl

lin.

bath

cl

GREAT RM.
15-4 x 16-0

cl

master
bath

MASTER
BED RM.
13-4 x 14-4

cl

FOYER
15-4 x 3-8

DINING
10-4 x 12-0

BED RM./
STUDY
11-4 x 10-4

PORCH

Width: 59'-6"
Depth: 54'-7"

Design HPT300030
Square Footage: 1,475

◆ This design exhibits timeless appeal.
The front porch leads to the columned
foyer. A cathedral ceiling in the great room
lends height and a feeling of openness. A
fireplace is framed by doors leading to a
rear deck with a spa. The kitchen easily
serves an elegant dining room. In the
quiet master bedroom, a tiered ceiling,
lavish bath and walk-in closet are appreciated features. Two secondary bedrooms
are located on the left side of the plan and
share a full hall bath. The two-car garage
is positioned at the rear of the plan.

Design HPT300031
Square Footage: 1,233

◆ A low-budget home can be a showplace, too. Exquisite site proportion, fine detailing, projected wings and interesting rooflines help provide the appeal of this modest one-story. Each of the bedrooms has excellent wall space and wardrobe storage potential. The master bath features a vanity, twin lavatories, a stall shower and a whirlpool tub. Another full bath is strategically located to serve the second bedroom as well as other areas of the house. Open planning results in a spacious gathering/dining area with a fireplace and access to the outdoor terraces. Two kitchen layouts make the plan versatile.

Width: 50'-0"
Depth: 47'-8"

Optional Layout

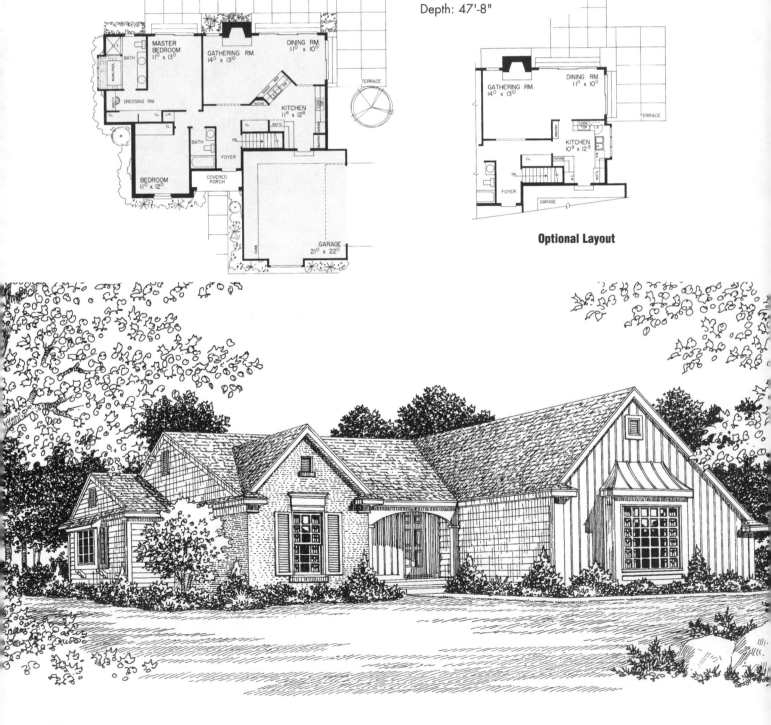

Traditional One-Story Homes
from 1,501-2,000 square feet

Design HPT300032
Square Footage: 1,756

◆ A brick exterior and circle-top windows give this home a rich, solid look. The formal dining room is visually open to the great room, creating a combination of rooms that feels and looks extra large and spacious. Located a few steps away is the well-equipped kitchen featuring a counter/bar that serves the great room. The breakfast bay is surrounded by windows and enables the family to enjoy the outdoors in any weather. Access to the deck through the great room easily expands the entertainment area to the rear yard. The master suite, with its sloped ceiling and ultra-lavish bath, offers the size and luxurious amenities found in today's fashionable homes.

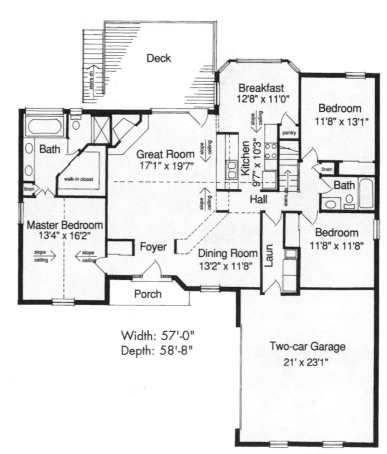

Deck

Breakfast
12'8" x 11'0"

Bedroom
11'8" x 13'1"

pantry

Bath

Great Room
17'1" x 19'7"

Kitchen
9'7" x 10'3"

linen

walk-in closet

Bath

linen

Hall

Master Bedroom
13'4" x 16'2"

Foyer

Dining Room
13'2" x 11'8"

Laun

Bedroom
11'8" x 11'8"

slope ceiling

slope ceiling

Porch

Width: 57'-0"
Depth: 58'-8"

Two-car Garage
21' x 23'1"

Design HPT300033
Square Footage: 1,566

◆ This simple country one-story plan presents decorative touches at its entry, including a planter box and a columned front porch. The foyer introduces additional touches such as a coat closet with a plant ledge above and another plant ledge in the hall. The vaulted living room contains a warming fireplace. Both the kitchen and dining area are also vaulted; the dining room includes sliding glass doors to the rear yard. A roomy wall closet is found in the master bedroom, which also boasts a private bath. Family bedrooms share a bath that contains a linen closet.

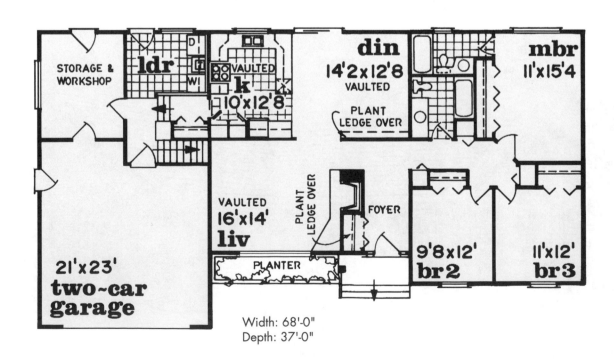

STORAGE & WORKSHOP

ldr

VAULTED

k
10'x12'8

din
14'2x12'8
VAULTED

PLANT LEDGE OVER

mbr
11'x15'4

VAULTED
16'x14'
liv

PLANT LEDGE OVER

FOYER

PLANTER

9'8x12'
br2

11'x12'
br3

21'x23'
two-car garage

Width: 68'-0"
Depth: 37'-0"

Design HPT300034
Square Footage: 1,577

◆ Circle-head windows lend character to the exterior of this three-bedroom country home. The skylit entry foyer leads to a vaulted great room with a centrally located see-through fireplace that's open to the kitchen and breakfast nook. The formal dining room is also vaulted and has sliding glass doors to the rear deck and to a screened porch. Both entries to the kitchen/breakfast area are accented—one by an arch and one with a plant ledge. The master bedroom features three wall closets and a private bath with a separate tub and shower and double vanities. Family bedrooms have the use of a full bath with a skylight.

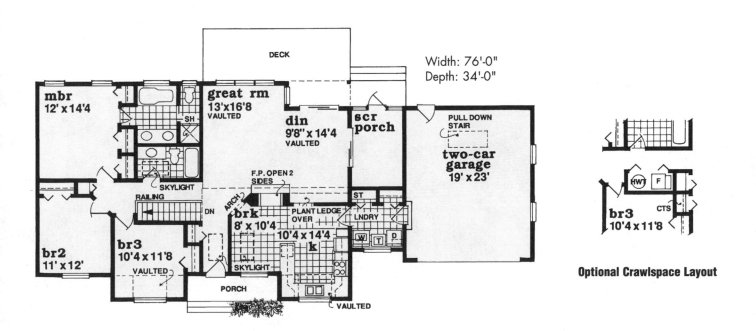

Width: 76'-0"
Depth: 34'-0"

DECK

mbr
12' x 14'4

great rm
13'x16'8
VAULTED

din
9'8" x 14'4
VAULTED

scr
porch

PULL DOWN
STAIR

two-car
garage
19' x 23'

SH

SKYLIGHT

RAILING

F.P. OPEN 2
SIDES

DN

ARCH

ST

brk
8' x 10'4

PLANT LEDGE
OVER

LNDRY

br3
10'4 x 11'8
VAULTED

10'4 x 14'4
k

W   T   D

br2
11' x 12'

SKYLIGHT

PORCH

VAULTED

Optional Crawlspace Layout

HWT   F

br3
10'4 x 11'8

CTS

37

Design HPT300035

Square Footage: 1,679

L D

◆ Housed in varying facades, this floor plan is very efficient. The front foyer leads to each of the living areas. Sized to accommodate large gatherings, the family room is warmed by a fireplace and a wall of windows. A U-shaped kitchen separates the box-bay breakfast room—perfect for casual meals—from the formal dining room. The sleeping area of three bedrooms—or two and a study—is ready to serve the family.

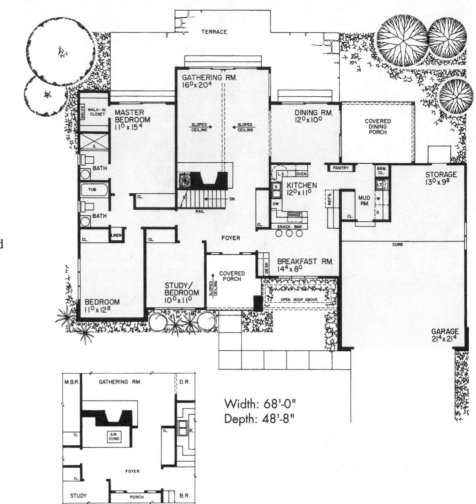

Width: 68'-0"
Depth: 48'-8"

Optional Crawlspace Layout

Width: 60'-0"
Depth: 55'-0"

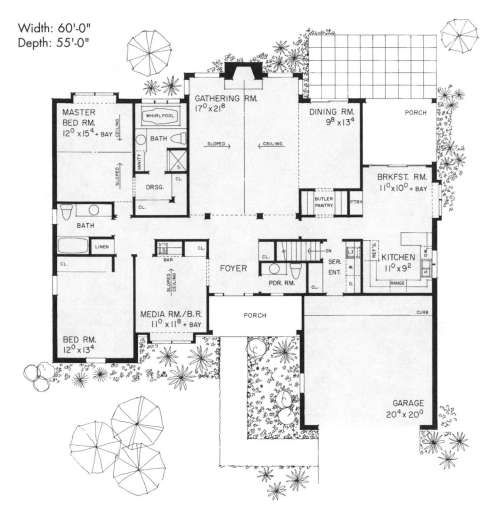

MASTER BED RM.
12⁰ x 15⁴ + BAY

WHIRLPOOL

BATH

GATHERING RM.
17⁰ x 21⁸

SLOPED   CEILING

DINING RM.
9⁸ x 13⁴

PORCH

VANITY

DRSG.

CL.

CL.

BUTLER PANTRY

P'TRY

BRKFST. RM.
11⁰ x 10⁰ + BAY

BATH

LINEN

CL.

CL.

S
BAR

SLOPED CEILING

FOYER

CL.

DN
SER. ENT.

CL.

PDR. RM.

REF'G.

KITCHEN
11⁰ x 9²

RANGE

MEDIA RM./B.R.
11⁰ x 11⁸ + BAY

BED RM.
12⁰ x 13⁴

PORCH

CURB

GARAGE
20⁴ x 20⁰

Design HPT300036
Square Footage: 1,999

L D

◆ Small families will appreciate the layout of this traditional ranch home. The foyer opens to the gathering room with a fireplace and sloped ceiling. The dining room, in turn, leads to the gathering room for entertaining ease and offers sliding glass doors to a rear terrace. The breakfast room also provides access to a covered porch for dining outdoors. The media room to the left of the home offers a bay window and a wet bar.

QUOTE ONE®
Cost to build? See page 436
to order complete cost estimate
to build this house in your area!

Design HPT300037
Square Footage: 1,834

D

◆ This contemporary exterior features vertical siding and a wide-overhanging roof with exposed rafter ends. The spacious foyer highlights a sloped ceiling and a dramatic open staircase to the basement recreation area. Other ceilings in the house are also sloped. The breakfast, dining and media rooms all offer great views of the outside. Other excellent amenities include the laundry, the efficient kitchen, the snack bar and the master bath.

Quote One®
Cost to build? See page 436 to order complete cost estimate to build this house in your area!

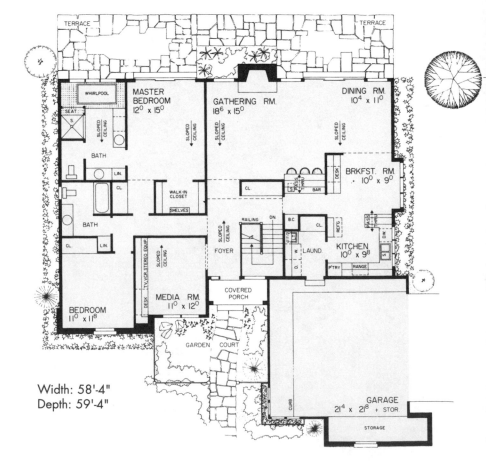

Width: 58'-4"
Depth: 59'-4"

Design HPT300038
Square Footage: 1,746

◆ Special detailing, low-maintenance brick and shuttered windows add a traditional touch to this home. The skylit foyer opens to a sunken living room with sliding glass doors to the rear yard. The dining room shares a through-fireplace with the living room and enjoys a bay window for the view. Just beyond, the U-shaped kitchen uses a large breakfast room for casual meals. The master suite is the picture of luxury with loads of windows and a bath with a raised whirlpool tub, separate shower and double vanity. Family bedrooms share a full hall bath.

Width: 77'-4"
Depth: 42'-8"

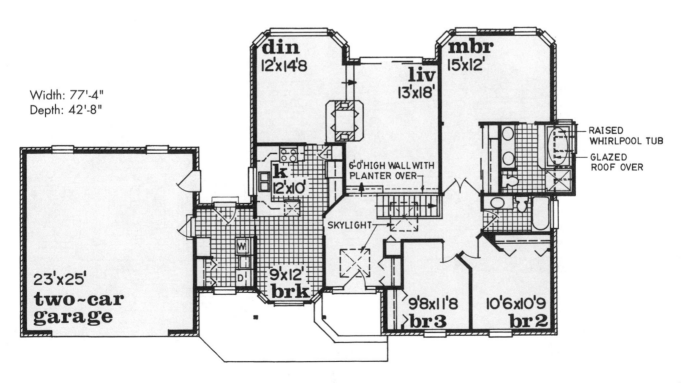

Design HPT300039
Square Footage: 1,588

◆ The columned front porch of this home conceals a recessed entry that opens to a foyer leading directly into the vaulted great room and dining room. The country kitchen is easily accessed from all the main areas of the home. It features a work island and a vaulted ceiling. Down a skylit hall the bedrooms include a master suite with a walk-in closet and a bath with a double vanity and a soaking tub. The family bedrooms share the use of a full bath.

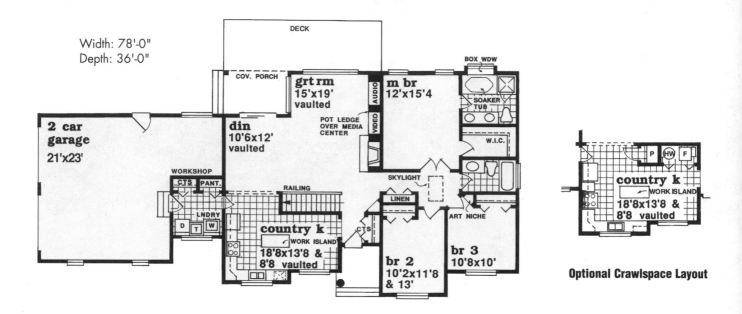

Width: 78'-0"
Depth: 36'-0"

DECK

COV. PORCH

grt rm
15'x19'
vaulted

m br
12'x15'4

BOX WDW

2 car
garage
21'x23'

din
10'6x12'
vaulted

POT LEDGE
OVER MEDIA
CENTER

AUDIO

VIDEO

SOAKER
TUB

W.I.C.

WORKSHOP

CTS. PANT.

RAILING

SKYLIGHT

LNDRY

D T W

country k
WORK ISLAND
18'8x13'8 &
8'8 vaulted

LINEN

CTS

ART NICHE

br 2
10'2x11'8
& 13'

br 3
10'8x10'

country k
WORK ISLAND
18'8x13'8 &
8'8 vaulted

P HW F

Optional Crawlspace Layout

Design HPT300040
Square Footage: 1,759

◆ With its brick facade and gables, this home brings great curb appeal to any neighborhood. This one-story home features a great room with a cozy fireplace, a laundry room tucked away from the spacious kitchen, and a breakfast area accessing the screened porch. Completing this design are two family bedrooms and an elegant master bedroom suite featuring an ample walk-in closet. A dressing area in the master bathroom is shared by a dual vanity and a step-up tub.

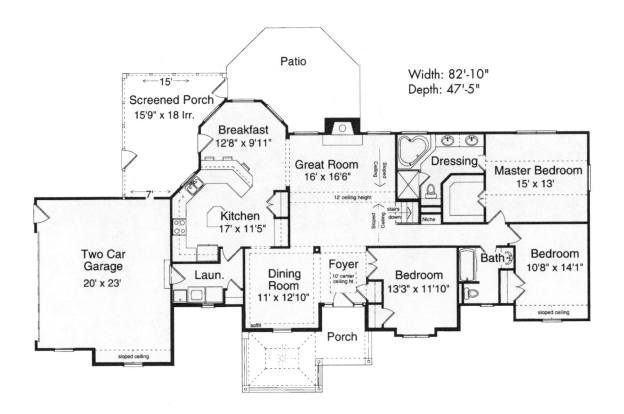

Patio

Width: 82'-10"
Depth: 47'-5"

Screened Porch
15'9" x 18 Irr.

Breakfast
12'8" x 9'11"

Great Room
16' x 16'6"

Dressing

Master Bedroom
15' x 13'

12' ceiling height

Kitchen
17' x 11'5"

Niche

stairs down

Two Car Garage
20' x 23'

Laun.

Dining Room
11' x 12'10"

Foyer
10' center ceiling ht.

Bedroom
13'3" x 11'10"

Bath

Bedroom
10'8" x 14'1"

sloped ceiling

soffit

Porch

sloped ceiling

Design HPT300041

Square Footage: 1,674

L D

◆ Stuccoed arches, multi-paned windows and a gracefully sloped roof accent the exterior of this Spanish-inspired design. The front foyer leads to each of the living areas: a sloped-ceiling gathering room, a study (or optional bedroom), a formal dining room and the light-filled breakfast room. Bedrooms are in a wing to the left and feature a master suite with a walk-in closet and terrace access. A covered porch opens off the dining room for private outdoor meals. The two-car garage is made even more useful with a large storage area—or use it for workshop space.

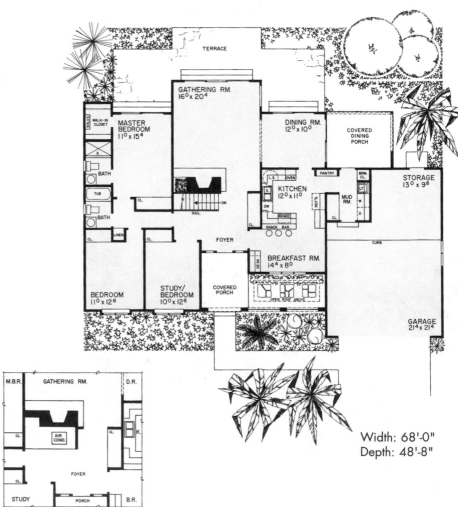

Width: 68'-0"
Depth: 48'-8"

Optional Crawlspace Layout

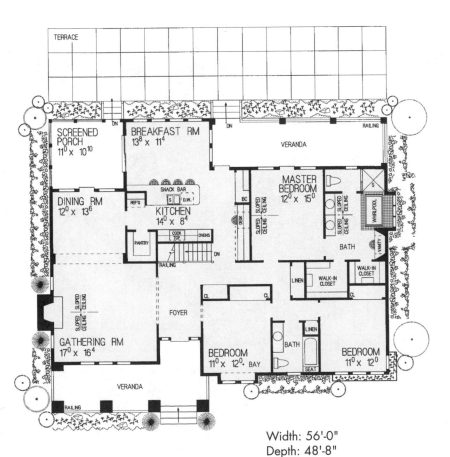

TERRACE

SCREENED PORCH
11⁰ x 10¹⁰

BREAKFAST RM
13⁸ x 11⁴

VERANDA

RAILING

DINING RM
12⁰ x 13⁶

SNACK BAR
D.W.
REF'G

KITCHEN
14⁰ x 8⁴

MASTER BEDROOM
12⁰ x 15⁰

WHIRLPOOL

BC

SLOPED CEILING

SLOPED CEILING

COOK TOP

OVENS

PANTRY

DESK

BATH

VANITY

LINEN

WALK-IN CLOSET

WALK-IN CLOSET

CL

CL

DN

RAILING

SLOPED CEILING

SLOPED CEILING

FOYER

GATHERING RM
17⁰ x 16⁴

BEDROOM
11⁰ x 12⁰, BAY

LINEN

BATH

SEAT

BEDROOM
11⁰ x 12⁰

VERANDA

RAILING

Width: 56'-0"
Depth: 48'-8"

Design HPT300042
Square Footage: 1,951

L

◆ The formal living areas in this plan are joined by a three-bedroom sleeping wing. One bedroom, with foyer access, could function as a study. Two verandas and a screened porch enlarge the plan and enhance indoor/outdoor livability. Notice the added extras: abundant storage space, walk-in pantry, built-in planning desk, whirlpool tub and pass-through snack bar. The sloped ceiling in the gathering room gives this area an open, airy quality. The breakfast room, with its wealth of windows, will be a cheerful and bright space to enjoy a cup of morning coffee.

QUOTE ONE®
Cost to build? See page 436
to order complete cost estimate
to build this house in your area!

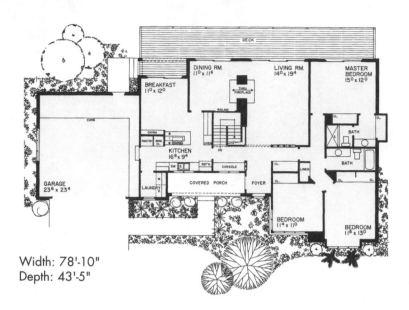

Design HPT300043

Main Level: 1,874 sq. ft.
Lower Level: 1,131 sq. ft.
Total: 3,005 sq. ft.

L

QUOTE ONE®
Cost to build? See page 436
to order complete cost estimate
to build this house in your area!

Width: 78'-10"
Depth: 43'-5"

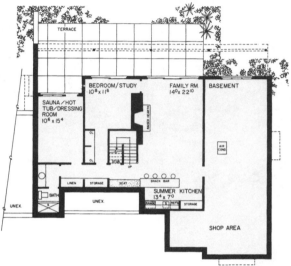

◆ Think Tudors are only two stories? Think again. This is a magnificent hillside plan, complete with a main-level fireplace, easy-to-reach rear deck (four different rooms lead to it), and plenty of storage space. The lower level is a delight. Note the fireplace, second kitchen with a snack bar, rear terrace, space for an extra bedroom (or two), built-ins galore, and lots of bonus space that could easily be a workroom, exercise room or both.

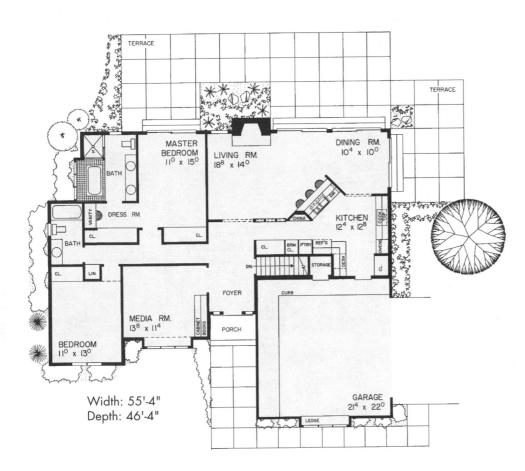

TERRACE

TERRACE

MASTER BEDROOM
11⁰ x 15⁰

BATH

VANITY

DRESS. RM.

BATH

CL.

CL.

LIN.

CL.

LIVING RM.
18⁸ x 14⁰

DINING RM.
10⁴ x 10⁰

CHINA

KITCHEN
12⁴ x 12⁸

COOK

OVENS

CL.

CL.

BRM CL.

PTRY

REF'G

DESK

STORAGE

DN.

FOYER

CURB

MEDIA RM.
13⁸ x 11⁴

CABINET BOOKS

PORCH

BEDROOM
11⁰ x 13⁰

GARAGE
21⁴ x 22⁰

LEDGE

Width: 55'-4"
Depth: 46'-4"

Design HPT300044
Square Footage: 1,608

◆ This cozy Tudor features a very contemporary interior for convenience and practicality. The floor plan features a strategically located kitchen handy to the garage, dining room and dining terrace. The spacious living area has a dramatic fireplace and opens to the rear terrace. A favorite spot is the media room with space for a TV, VCR and stereo system. The large master bedroom contains plenty of wardrobe storage. The extra guest room, or nursery, includes a full bath.

◆ This attractive plan displays an effective use of half-timbered stucco and brick as well as an authentic bay window to create an elegant Tudor elevation. The covered porch serves as a fitting introduction to all the inside amenities. The gathering room will be a favorite place for friends and family with its rustic appeal and rear terrace doors. A full-sized kitchen with a snack bar and breakfast room is well suited for the gourmet. The master bedroom includes a large walk-in closet, private bath and doors to the terrace. Two additional bedrooms share a hall bath. A large storage area or shop space is available in the two-car garage.

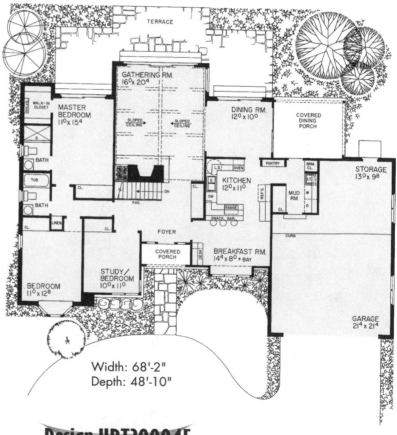

Width: 68'-2"
Depth: 48'-10"

Design HPT300045
Square Footage: 1,729

Optional Crawlspace Layout

Design HPT300046
Square Footage: 1,584

L D

◆ The living/dining room of this home features a sloped ceiling and direct access to the covered porch with skylights. A breakfast room overlooks the covered porch. A desk, snack bar and mudroom with laundry facilities are near the U-shaped kitchen. The master bedroom features a private bath and a walk-in closet. The large front bedroom has a box-bay window, while a third bedroom may alternate as a study or media room.

Width: 58'-10"
Depth: 50'-10"

COVERED PORCH

SKYLIGHT | SLOPED CEILING | SKYLIGHT | SKYLIGHT

BRKFST. RM.
13⁴ x 11¹⁰

LIVING RM.
13⁴ x 17²

DINING RM.
8⁰ x 9¹⁰

DESK

SLOPED CEILING

DN

CL.

MUD RM.

STORAGE

SNACK BAR

DW. | S.

KITCHEN
13⁴ x 9⁶

RANGE

LT | W. | D.

CURB

RAILING

PANT.

SLOPED CEILING

OVEN | REF'G.

DN

FOYER

TV/STUDY
BEDROOM
10⁰ x 10⁴

S.

BATH

BATH

WALK-IN CLOSET | LIN.

CL.

COVERED PORCH

CL.

GARAGE
19⁸ x 19⁰ + STOR.

MASTER BEDROOM
13⁶ x 12⁰

CL.

BEDROOM
13⁶ x 10⁸

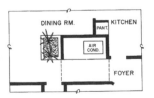

DINING RM. | KITCHEN

PANT.

AIR COND.

FOYER

Optional Crawlspace Layout

49

Design HPT300047
Square Footage: 1,687

L

◆ Intriguing rooflines create an attractive exterior for this home. The interior floor plan is equally lovely. Toward the rear, a wide archway forms the entrance to the spacious family living area, with its centrally placed fireplace and bay-windowed nook. An island counter, mitered corner window and nearby pantry complete the efficient kitchen. This home also boasts a terrific master suite complete with a walk-in wardrobe, a spa tub with corner windows, and a compartmented shower and toilet area. Two family bedrooms share a hall bath.

FAMILY
13/0 X 17/0

MASTER
12/0 X 15/0

SPA

10/0 X 13/0

PANTRY

LINEN

13/4 X 10/0

BR. 2
12/0 X 10/0

SKYLITE

LIVING
13/4 X 14/0

BR. 3
10/10 X 12/0 +

GARAGE
19/2 X 21/8

Width: 50'-0"
Depth: 52'-0"

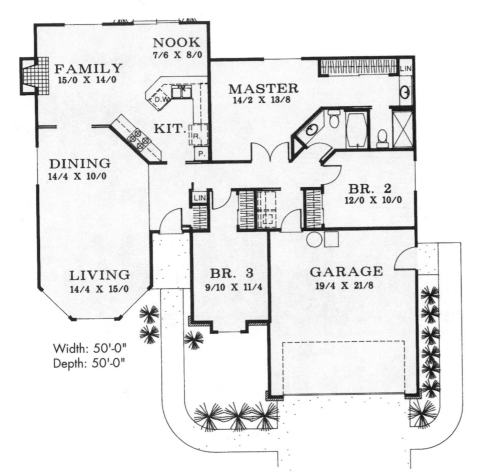

NOOK
7/6 X 8/0

FAMILY
15/0 X 14/0

MASTER
14/2 X 13/8

KIT.

DINING
14/4 X 10/0

BR. 2
12/0 X 10/0

LIVING
14/4 X 15/0

BR. 3
9/10 X 11/4

GARAGE
19/4 X 21/8

Width: 50'-0"
Depth: 50'-0"

Design HPT300048
Square Footage: 1,546

L

◆ Highlighting the exterior of this home are brick accents and a variety of interesting lines and angles. This design exudes a sense of space that far exceeds its actual square footage. Inside, the floor plan offers a number of amenities. Featured in the living room is an immense bay window that encloses the entire end of the room in glass. A pair of doors opens to the large master suite with a compartmented shower and a large closet with space-expanding mirrored doors. Two family bedrooms and another full bath round out this unique plan.

Design HPT300049
Square Footage: 1,860

◆ Traditional symmetry graces the facade of this charming brick home. The covered entry announces the foyer which in turn opens to the great room with its vaulted ceiling and corner fireplace. To the right of the foyer is the spacious living/dining room. The island kitchen, with its convenient snack bar, is situated between the dining room and the sunny breakfast bay. Access to the rear porch and the garage as well as the utility room are found just to the right of this area. The left wing holds the master suite, two family bedrooms and a shared full bath.

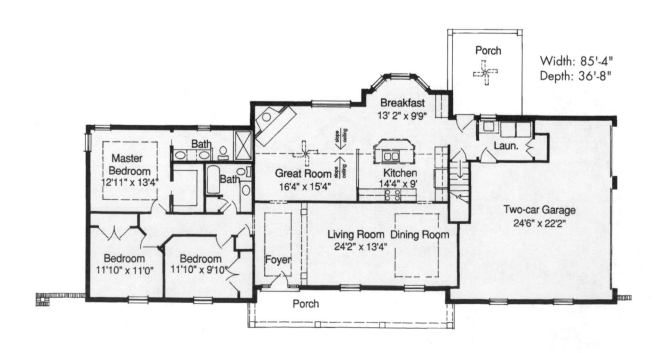

Width: 85'-4"
Depth: 36'-8"

Width: 65'-8"
Depth: 55'-0"

Laundry
9-0x5-8

Stor.
4-8x3-6

Basement Stair
Location

Design HPT300050
Square Footage: 1,836

◆ Pillars, beautiful transoms and sidelights set off the entry door and draw attention to this comfortable home. The foyer leads to a formal dining room and a great room with a ribbon of windows pouring in light. To the left of the kitchen is a roomy laundry area, with lots of storage space for those extra household supplies. Privacy is assured with a master suite—a large walk-in closet and a full bath with a separate shower and large tub add to the pleasure of this wing. Two family bedrooms occupy the right side of the design and share a full bath. Please specify basement, crawlspace or slab foundation when ordering.

Master Bedroom
13-0x15-2

Bath
8-0x13-7

Storage
8-0x3-8

Laundry
9-0x9-6

Breakfast
10-0x10-0

Porch
19-0x9-0

Bedroom
11-3x11-3

Greatroom
16-6x16-6

Bath

Kitchen
12-6x11-3

Garage
21-5x21-8

Storage
8-3x6-6

Dining
13-8x13-6

Foyer

Bedroom
11-3x13-6

Porch
35-0x8-0

Design HPT300051

Square Footage: 1,792

◆ The classic style of this family home provides timeless elegance and symmetry. The covered front porch opens to the foyer, which leads to the spacious great room. Family bedrooms are found to the left, while the kitchen and dining area sit to the right. The master suite features its own private bath and walk-in closet. The two family bedrooms share a full hall bath. The rear porch expands to a courtyard, overlooked by the master suite. A garage with optional storage and a laundry room complete this floor plan. Please specify basement, crawlspace or slab foundation when ordering.

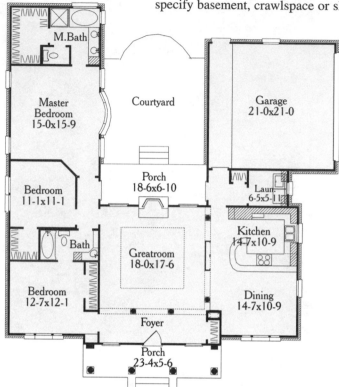

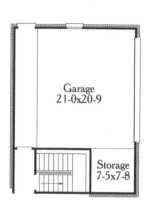

Optional Basement Stair Location

Width: 56'-0"
Depth: 62'-10"

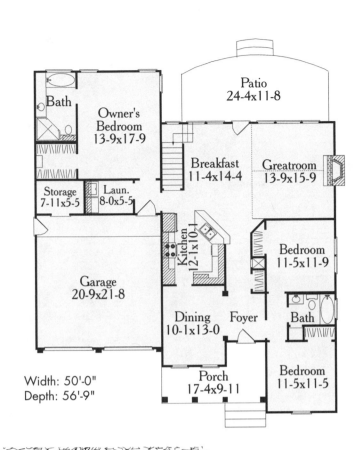

Bath

Owner's
Bedroom
13-9x17-9

Storage
7-11x5-5

Laun.
8-0x5-5

Garage
20-9x21-8

Patio
24-4x11-8

Breakfast
11-4x14-4

Greatroom
13-9x15-9

Kitchen
12-1x10-1

Bedroom
11-5x11-9

Dining
10-1x13-0

Foyer

Bath

Porch
17-4x9-11

Bedroom
11-5x11-5

Width: 50'-0"
Depth: 56'-9"

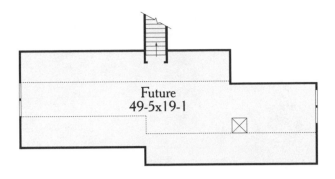

Future
49-5x19-1

Design HPT300052

Square Footage: 1,689
Bonus Room: 830 sq. ft.

◆ Traditional accents and natural materials create an inviting home that's perfect for the countryside. A petite covered front porch introduces you to a foyer flanked by two family bedrooms and a dining room. The great room with a fireplace is open to the breakfast room, and the kitchen is just a few steps away. The master bedroom is secluded behind the garage and laundry room, and includes a private bath, along with a walk-in closet. Please specify basement, crawlspace or slab foundation when ordering.

Design HPT300053
Square Footage: 1,800

◆ Neoclassic style emerges with columns and a pediment at the porch of this lovely one-story home. An arched transom over the front door lights the foyer—perfect for family photos displayed along the hall. To the right is a cozy living room with a large picture window and fireplace. A bay window gives a backyard view to the dining room. The L-shaped island kitchen adjoins the light-filled dining area. This split-bedroom floor plan includes two family bedrooms sharing a bath. The master suite provides a walk-in closet and two-vanity bath.Please specify basement, crawlspace or slab foundation when ordering.

Width: 65'-0"
Depth: 66'-0"

Storage
19-6x8-6

Laundry
9-8x5-10

Basement
Stair Location

Carport
21-10x21-2

Patio
23-9x21-0

Kitchen
11-0x16-0

Dining
12-9x16-0

Master
Bedroom
17-6x13-6

Laundry
9-8x9-3

Bath

Bedroom
13-8x11-7

Bedroom
12-9x11-3

Foyer

Living Room
15-1x13-6

M.Bath
11-8x11-7

Planter Box

Stoop

Planter Box

Storage
17-4x5-8

Garage
20-4x21-4

Width: 56'-4"
Depth: 67'-4"

Porch
17-4x10-0

Master
Bedroom
17-4x13-6

Laundry
7-4x6-3

1/2 Bath

Greatroom
17-4x17-4

Bath

Bath

Pantry

Kitchen/
Breakfast
13-3x20-5

Dining
11-3x13-4

Foyer

Bedroom
11-3x10-1

Bedroom
11-4x11-4

Porch
31-0x8-0

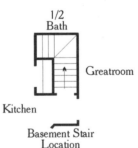

1/2
Bath

Greatroom

Kitchen

Basement Stair
Location

Design HPT300054
Square Footage: 1,955

◆ Double pillars, beautiful transoms and side-lights set off the entry door and draw attention to this comfortable home. The foyer leads to a formal dining room and a great room with two pairs of French doors framing a warming fire-place. The kitchen enjoys a large island/snack bar and a walk-in pantry. Privacy is assured in the master suite—a large walk-in closet and full bath with a separate shower and large tub add to the pleasure of this wing. Two family bedrooms share a full bath at the front of the design. Please specify basement, crawlspace or slab foundation when ordering.

Design HPT300055

Square Footage: 1,819
Bonus Room: 797 sq. ft.

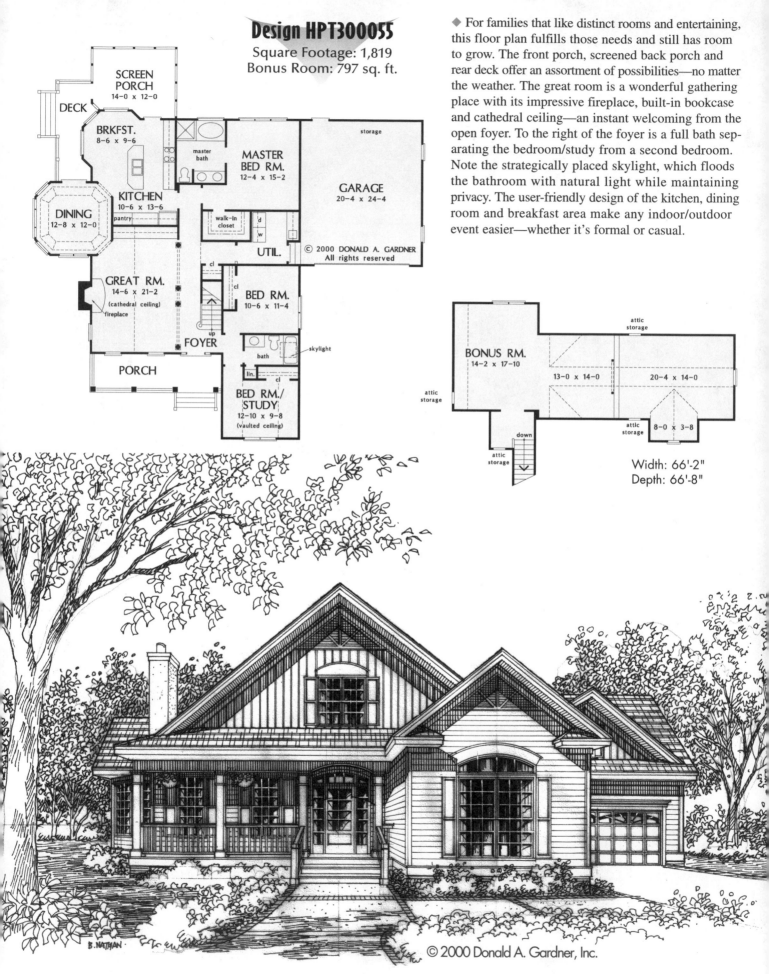

SCREEN PORCH 14-0 x 12-0

DECK

BRKFST. 8-6 x 9-6

master bath

MASTER BED RM. 12-4 x 15-2

storage

GARAGE 20-4 x 24-4

KITCHEN 10-6 x 13-6

pantry

DINING 12-8 x 12-0

walk-in closet

UTIL.

d
w

cl

GREAT RM. 14-6 x 21-2
(cathedral ceiling)
fireplace

cl

BED RM. 10-6 x 11-4

up

FOYER

bath

skylight

PORCH

lin.

cl

BED RM./ STUDY 12-10 x 9-8
(vaulted ceiling)

◆ For families that like distinct rooms and entertaining, this floor plan fulfills those needs and still has room to grow. The front porch, screened back porch and rear deck offer an assortment of possibilities—no matter the weather. The great room is a wonderful gathering place with its impressive fireplace, built-in bookcase and cathedral ceiling—an instant welcoming from the open foyer. To the right of the foyer is a full bath separating the bedroom/study from a second bedroom. Note the strategically placed skylight, which floods the bathroom with natural light while maintaining privacy. The user-friendly design of the kitchen, dining room and breakfast area make any indoor/outdoor event easier—whether it's formal or casual.

BONUS RM. 14-2 x 17-10

attic storage

attic storage

13-0 x 14-0

20-4 x 14-0

attic storage

8-0 x 3-8

down

attic storage

Width: 66'-2"
Depth: 66'-8"

B. NATHAN

© 2000 Donald A. Gardner, Inc.

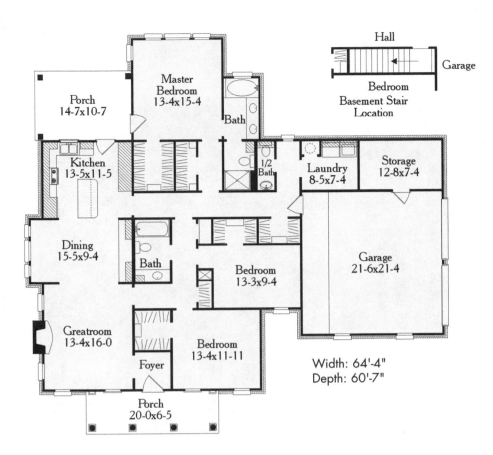

Porch
14-7x10-7

Master
Bedroom
13-4x15-4

Bath

Hall

Garage

Bedroom
Basement Stair
Location

Design HPT300056
Square Footage: 1,854

Kitchen
13-5x11-5

1/2
Bath

Laundry
8-5x7-4

Storage
12-8x7-4

Dining
15-5x9-4

Bath

Bedroom
13-3x9-4

Garage
21-6x21-4

Greatroom
13-4x16-0

Foyer

Bedroom
13-4x11-11

Width: 64'-4"
Depth: 60'-7"

Porch
20-0x6-5

◆ This pleasing roofline provides a pilastered porch set symmetrically on a hipped design. Full-length windows add to the appeal. The great room is just inside the foyer and offers a beautiful fireplace set between two windows. The adjoining dining area features a ribbon of windows to bring in sunlight or moonlight. The L-shaped kitchen enjoys a center island and access to the rear porch—perfect for an outdoor grill. Walk-in closets and extra storage space will provide plenty of room for family treasures. The split-bedroom floor plan allows for privacy. Please specify basement, crawlspace or slab foundation when ordering.

Design HPT300057
Square Footage: 1,989
Bonus Room: 274 sq. ft.

◆ Covered porches both front and back extend the living space of this home to the outdoors. The foyer opens to the great room, with its coffered ceiling and twin sets of French doors, and to the dining room on the right. The angled kitchen is nestled between the dining room and the breakfast bay, serving both with ease and efficiency. The lavish master suite resides on the far right for privacy while the two additional bedrooms are situated on the left. Space is available over the side-loading garage for future development.

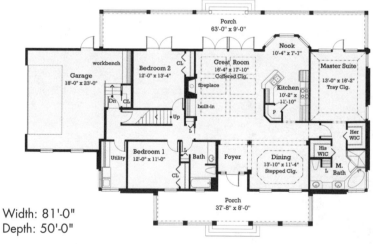

Width: 81'-0"
Depth: 50'-0"

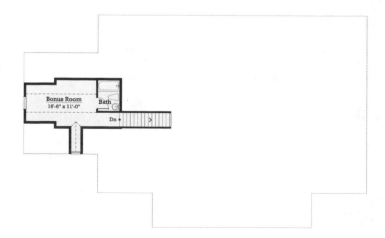

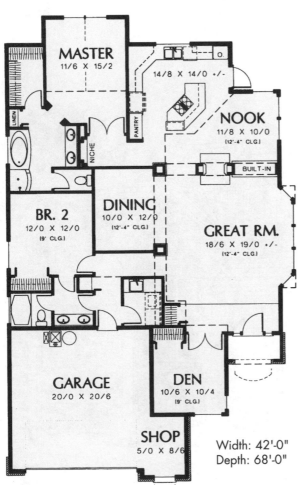

MASTER
11/6 X 15/2

14/8 X 14/0 +/-

NOOK
11/8 X 10/0
(12'-4" CLG.)

BUILT-IN

LINEN

NICHE

PANTRY

DINING
10/0 X 12/0
(12'-4" CLG.)

BR. 2
12/0 X 12/0
(9' CLG.)

GREAT RM.
18/6 X 19/0 +/-
(12'-4" CLG.)

GARAGE
20/0 X 20/6

DEN
10/6 X 10/4
(9' CLG.)

SHOP
5/0 X 8/6

Width: 42'-0"
Depth: 68'-0"

Design HPT300058
Square Footage: 1,864

◆ With an offset front entry and brick-and-siding detail, this home is the model of sheltered style. The entry opens directly into the large great room, but a secluded den is just to the left through double doors. A through-fireplace serves both the great room and the nook; columns separate the formal dining room from the great room. A lovely island kitchen features everything the gourmet might request: pantry, abundant counter space, an over-the-sink window and outdoor access. Both bedrooms have private baths. The master bath is a study in indulgence with a whirlpool tub, separate shower, compartmented toilet, double sink and huge walk-in closet. The two-car garage has space enough for a workshop.

Design HPT300059

Square Footage: 1,995
Bonus Room: 344 sq. ft.

◆ A nested gable, dormers and a wrap-around covered porch lend a country feel to this one-story home. To the left of the foyer is a flexible space that can be developed as a bedroom or a study with optional door and closet placement. The formal dining room sits to the right and leads to the island kitchen. The angled snack bar faces the breakfast nook and the elegant living room. The master suite, with its large walk-in closet and lavish bath, is tucked out of the way for privacy.

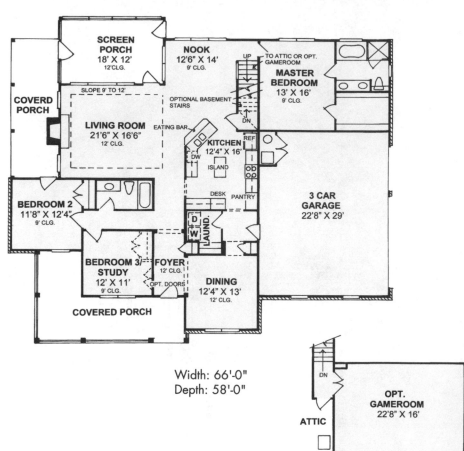

Width: 66'-0"
Depth: 58'-0"

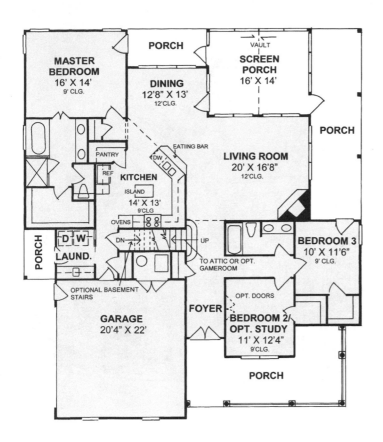

PORCH

MASTER
BEDROOM
16' X 14'
9' CLG.

SCREEN
PORCH
16' X 14'
VAULT

DINING
12'8" X 13'
12' CLG.

PORCH

PANTRY

REF

KITCHEN
14' X 13'
9' CLG.

ISLAND

EATIING BAR

LIVING ROOM
20' X 16'8"
12' CLG.

DW

OVENS

UP

DN

D W

LAUND.

TO ATTIC OR OPT.
GAMEROOM

BEDROOM 3
10' X 11'6"
9' CLG.

OPTIONAL BASEMENT
STAIRS

GARAGE
20'4" X 22'

FOYER

OPT. DOORS

BEDROOM 2/
OPT. STUDY
11' X 12'4"
9' CLG.

PORCH

Design HPT300060

Square Footage: 1,842
Bonus Room: 386 sq. ft.

◆ A wraparound front porch and an interesting roofline add style to this efficient country cottage that boasts a total of four covered porches. The foyer opens to the living room with a corner fireplace and two walls of windows. Just past the snack bar of the island kitchen is the formal dining room with access to the vaulted screened porch. The master suite is tucked behind the kitchen for privacy while two family bedrooms sit to the right of the foyer where they share a full bath.

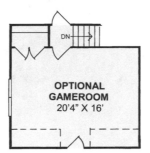

DN

OPTIONAL
GAMEROOM
20'4" X 16'

Width: 54'-0"
Depth: 63'-0"

63

Design HPT300061

Square Footage: 1,838
Bonus Room: 394 sq. ft.

◆ Outdoor enthusiasts will enjoy the outside areas on this home: a wraparound porch, a screened back porch, and two adjoining rear porches. The floor plan inside lends itself to convenience. The third bedroom, to the left of the entry, can be built as a study with an optional door to the foyer. The breakfast nook, living room and dining room radiate around the kitchen. The master suite, with its private bath, walk-in closet and rear exit, is secluded on the far right.

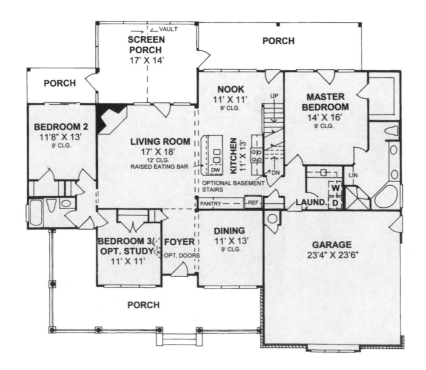

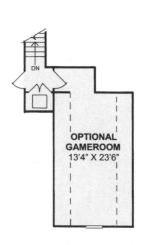

Width: 65'-0"
Depth: 56'-0"

Design HPT300062
Square Footage: 1,604
Bonus Room: 316 sq. ft.

◆ This traditional cottage plan offers a simple one-story design with a bonus room for flexible use. A wrapping front porch welcomes you inside to a formal living room warmed by a fireplace. The island kitchen is open to the dining room. The vaulted screened porch provides space for brisk entertaining at seasonal times of the year. Three family bedrooms and a garage complete the floor plan.

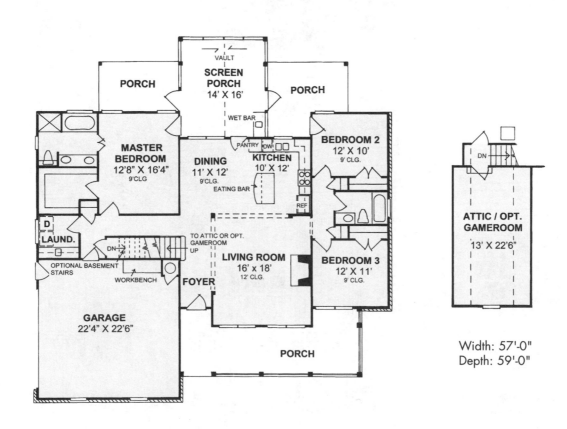

PORCH

VAULT
SCREEN
PORCH
14' X 16'

PORCH

WET BAR

MASTER
BEDROOM
12'8" X 16'4"
9'CLG

DINING
11' X 12'
9'CLG.

PANTRY

KITCHEN
10' X 12'

BEDROOM 2
12' X 10'
9' CLG.

EATING BAR

REF

DN

ATTIC / OPT.
GAMEROOM
13' X 22'6"

D
LAUND.

TO ATTIC OR OPT.
GAMEROOM
UP

OPTIONAL BASEMENT
STAIRS

DN

WORKBENCH

LIVING ROOM
16' x 18'
12' CLG.

FOYER

BEDROOM 3
12' X 11'
9' CLG.

GARAGE
22'4" X 22'6"

PORCH

Width: 57'-0"
Depth: 59'-0"

Design HPT300063

Square Footage: 1,762

◆ A brick-and-siding facade with two quaint dormers and porch columns creates a fresh look for this three-bedroom home. Inside, the foyer leads to the nook on the right and the formal dining room on the left. The island kitchen opens to both the breakfast nook and the hearth-warmed family room. Here, a wall of windows offers a magnificent view as well as access to the rear property. The master suite sits on the right with a tray ceiling, walk-in closet and lavish private bath. Two family bedrooms rest on the left where they share a full bath.

Width: 46'-0"
Depth: 58'-0"

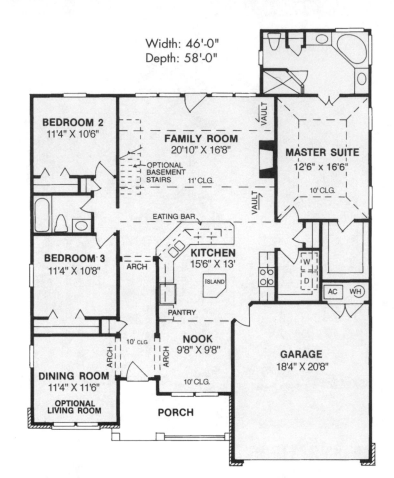

BEDROOM 2
11'4" X 10'6"

FAMILY ROOM
20'10" X 16'8"

VAULT

MASTER SUITE
12'6" x 16'6"

OPTIONAL BASEMENT STAIRS

11' CLG.

10' CLG.

VAULT

EATING BAR

BEDROOM 3
11'4" X 10'8"

ARCH

KITCHEN
15'6" X 13'

ISLAND

W
D

AC   WH

PANTRY

ARCH

NOOK
9'8" X 9'8"

GARAGE
18'4" X 20'8"

10' CLG

ARCH

ARCH

10' CLG.

DINING ROOM
11'4" X 11'6"

OPTIONAL LIVING ROOM

PORCH

Design HPT300064

Square Footage: 1,828
Bonus Room: 352 sq. ft.

◆ A simple footprint and easy roofline make this mid-size home affordable, and families will appreciate its split-bedroom design and stylish exterior. Interior columns and a tray ceiling accent the formal dining room, while a vaulted ceiling enhances the great room, kitchen and breakfast area. A rear clerestory dormer window further embellishes the open great room, which features a cozy fireplace and built-in bookshelves. The adjacent back porch increases living space. The master suite is secluded from the two family bedrooms for privacy. A tray ceiling, back-porch access, a walk-in closet and a whirlpool tub enrich the master suite's luxury.

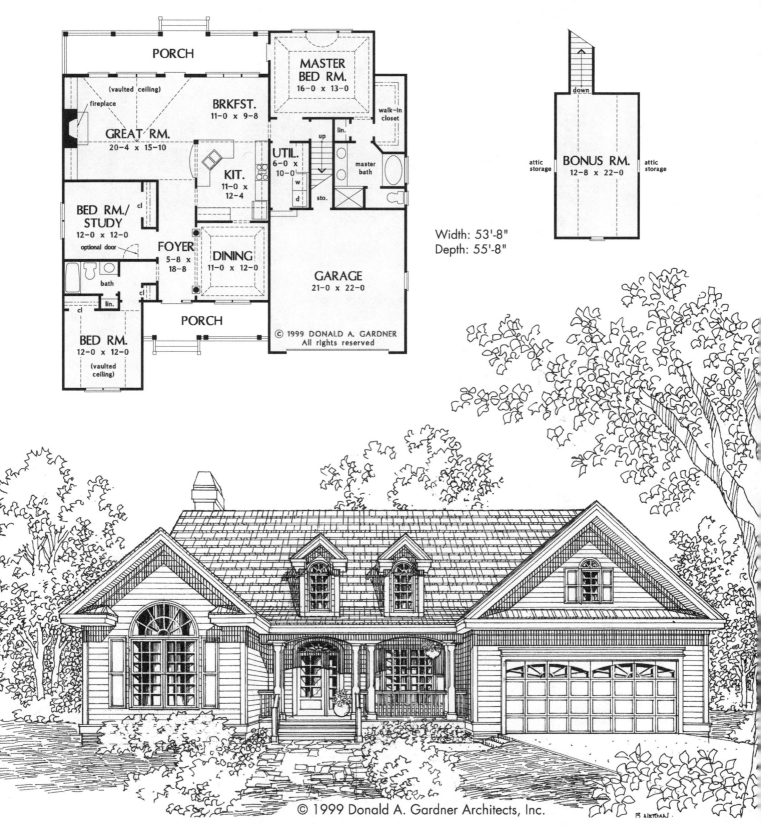

Width: 53'-8"
Depth: 55'-8"

© 1999 Donald A. Gardner Architects, Inc.

Design HPT300065

Square Footage: 1,912
Bonus Room: 398 sq. ft.

◆ An appealing blend of stone, siding and stucco announces a 21st-Century floor plan that invites traditional events as well as cozy family gatherings. A formal dining area defined by decorative columns opens to a grand great room with wide views of the outdoors. The gourmet kitchen overlooks an expansive food-preparation counter to the great room, and enjoys natural light brought in by the bayed breakfast nook. The sleeping wing, to the right of the plan, includes a sumptuous master suite with a tray ceiling, a door to the rear property, and a skylit bath with twin vanities and a walk-in closet. A secluded study neighbors a family bedroom and shares its bath.

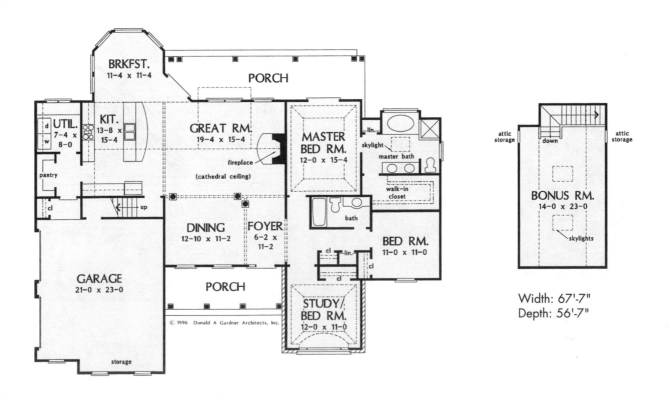

Width: 67'-7"
Depth: 56'-7"

B. NATHAN.

Design HPT300066

Square Footage: 1,972
Bonus Room: 398 sq. ft.

◆ This delightful country-cottage elevation gives way to a modern floor plan. The formal dining room is set off from the expansive great room with decorative columns. Amenities in the nearby kitchen include an abundance of counter and cabinet space, a bi-level island with a snack bar, and a gazebo breakfast nook. The master suite is detailed with a tray ceiling and features a lush private bath with a large walk-in closet. Two additional bedrooms share a full hall bath. A bonus room over the garage can be finished as extra living space.

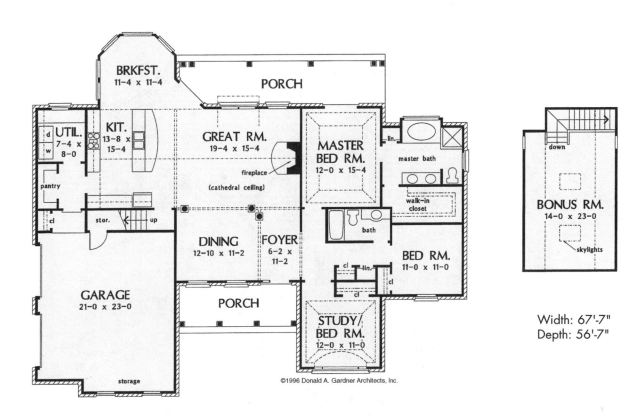

Width: 67'-7"
Depth: 56'-7"

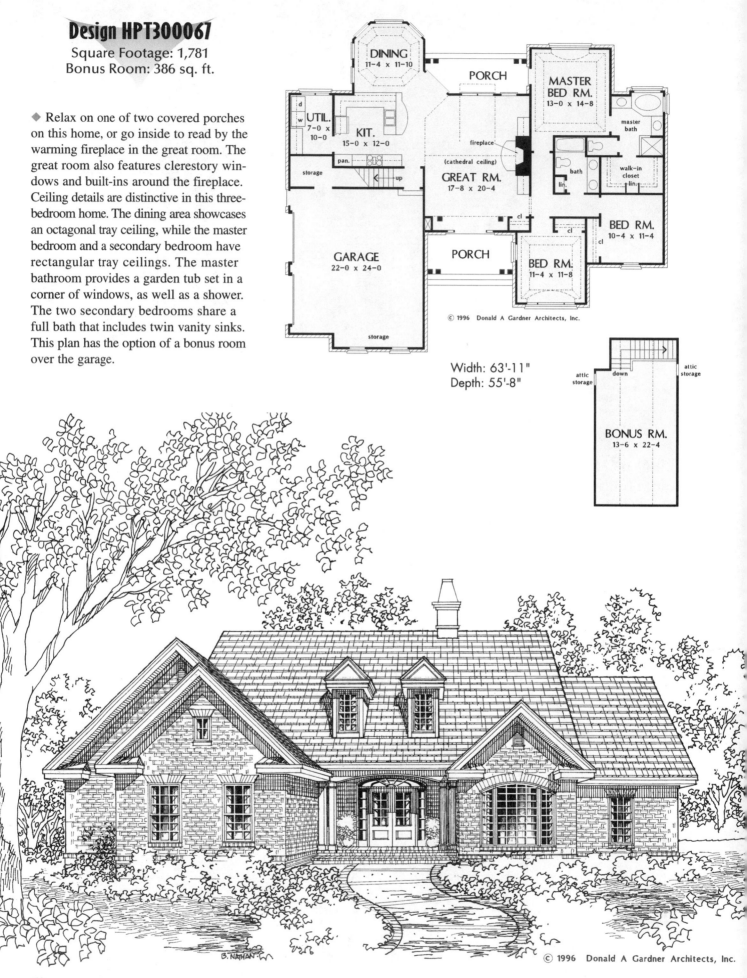

Design HPT300067

Square Footage: 1,781
Bonus Room: 386 sq. ft.

◆ Relax on one of two covered porches on this home, or go inside to read by the warming fireplace in the great room. The great room also features clerestory windows and built-ins around the fireplace. Ceiling details are distinctive in this three-bedroom home. The dining area showcases an octagonal tray ceiling, while the master bedroom and a secondary bedroom have rectangular tray ceilings. The master bathroom provides a garden tub set in a corner of windows, as well as a shower. The two secondary bedrooms share a full bath that includes twin vanity sinks. This plan has the option of a bonus room over the garage.

DINING
11-4 x 11-10

PORCH

MASTER
BED RM.
13-0 x 14-8

master
bath

UTIL.
7-0 x
10-0

KIT.
15-0 x 12-0

pan.

storage

fireplace

(cathedral ceiling)

GREAT RM.
17-8 x 20-4

bath

lin.

walk-in
closet

lin.

up

GARAGE
22-0 x 24-0

PORCH

cl

BED RM.
10-4 x 11-4

cl

storage

PORCH

BED RM.
11-4 x 11-8

cl

© 1996 Donald A Gardner Architects, Inc.

Width: 63'-11"
Depth: 55'-8"

attic
storage

down

attic
storage

BONUS RM.
13-6 x 22-4

B. NATHAN

© 1996 Donald A Gardner Architects, Inc.

Design HPT300068
Square Footage: 1,576

DECK

spa

BED RM.
11-4 x 11-0

cl

bath

cl

BED RM./
STUDY
11-4 x 10-4

fireplace

GREAT RM.
15-4 x 16-10
(cathedral ceiling)

cl

FOYER
8-2 x 5-10

cl

PORCH

BRKFST.
11-4 x 7-8

KITCHEN
11-4 x 10-0

DINING
11-4 x 11-4

MASTER
BED RM.
13-4 x 13-8

master
bath

skylights

w
d

walk-in
closet

storage

GARAGE
20-0 x 19-8

Width: 66'-0"
Depth: 43'-3"

◆ This stately three-bedroom, one-story home exhibits sheer elegance with its large arched windows, corner quoins, round columns, covered porch and brick veneer. In the foyer, natural light enters through arched windows in clerestory dormers. The European-style silhouette is interrupted by country dormers overlooking the front yard—this detail lends a more cottage feel to the overall plan. A formal front porch, flanked by columns, welcomes you into the entry foyer. In the great room, a dramatic cathedral ceiling and a fireplace set the mood. The kitchen and breakfast rooms open through gracious, round columns.

B. NATHAN.

Design HPT300069
Square Footage: 1,725

◆ Twin dormers and double gables adorn the exterior of this pleasing three-bedroom home. The foyer opens to the formal dining area and arches leading to the great room, which offers a warming corner fireplace. Add the optional greenhouse to the kitchen-sink window for a beautiful glass display or herb garden location. Keep household records and dry goods well organized with the desk and pantry room just off the galley kitchen. The vaulted breakfast room is brightened by three lovely windows. A lovely master retreat features a whirlpool tub, separate shower and knee-space vanity. Two additional bedrooms share a full bath. Please specify crawlspace or slab foundation when ordering.

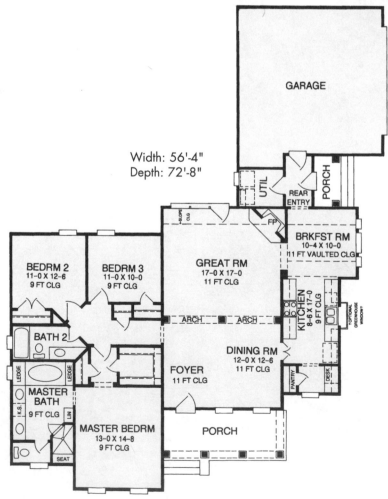

Width: 56'-4"
Depth: 72'-8"

GARAGE

Width: 54'-10"
Depth: 69'-10"

STORAGE

UTILITY

B/C

FP

GREAT ROOM
17-8x16-0
11 FT CLG

BRKFST
11-0x10-6
9 FT CLG

BDRM 2
10-8x13-8
9 FT CLG

BDRM 3
11-0x10-0
9 FT CLG

42" LEDGE

BATH 2

HALL
9 FT CLG

KITCH
12-6x
13-8
9 FT CLG

LIN

FOYER
11 FT
CLG

DINING
12-4x13-8
11 FT CLG

MSTR
BATH
9 FT CLG

PANTRY

MSTR BDRM
12-4x16-8
10 FT CLG

PORCH

SEAT

Design HPT300070
Square Footage: 1,654

◆ Twin dormers perch above a welcoming covered front porch in this three-bedroom home. Inside, a formal dining room on the right is defined by pillars, while the spacious great room lies directly ahead. This room is enhanced by a fireplace, plenty of windows, access to the rear yard, and a forty-two-inch ledge looking into the angular kitchen. Nearby, a bayed breakfast room awaits casual mealtimes. The sleeping zone consists of two family bedrooms sharing a full hall bath and a luxurious master bedroom suite with a huge walk-in closet and a sumptuous private bath. Please specify crawlspace or slab foundation when ordering.

Design HPT300071
Square Footage: 1,808

◆ Discriminating buyers will love the refined yet inviting look of this three-bedroom home plan. A tiled entry with a ten-foot ceiling leads into the spacious great room with a large bay window. An open-hearth fireplace warms both the great room and the kitchen. The sleeping area features a spacious master suite with a dramatic arched window and a bath with a whirlpool tub, twin vanities and a walk-in closet. Two secondary bedrooms each have private access to the shared bath. Don't miss the storage space in the oversized garage.

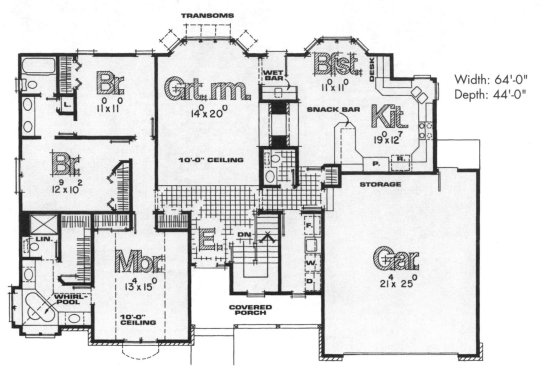

Width: 64'-0"
Depth: 44'-0"

74

SEAT. LIN.

WHIRLPOOL

SCREEN PORCH

Grt. rm.
14⁴ x 20¹⁰

10'-0" CEILING

Din.
10⁴ x 11⁰

Mbr.
13⁰ x 13⁰

9'-0" CEILING

Bfst.
10⁰ x 14³

SNACK BAR

Kit.
9⁴ x 13⁰

DESK

P.

LIN.

ON

R.

SHELVES

D. W.

Br.3
10⁰ x 11⁰

Br.2
10⁴ x 11⁰

OPTIONAL DEN

9'-0" CEILING

TRANS.
COVERED
STOOP

Gar.
19³ x 22⁴

Width: 48'-0"
Depth: 60'-0"

Den
10⁴ x 13⁴

9'-0" CEILING

Optional Layout

Design HPT300072
Square Footage: 1,580

◆ Brick wing walls give a visually expansive front elevation to this charming home. From the entry, traffic flows into the bright great room that has an impressive two-sided fireplace. The dining room opens to the great room, offering a view of the fireplace. French doors off the entry lead to the kitchen. Here, a large pantry, planning desk and snack bar are appreciated amenities. The breakfast nook accesses a large, comfortable screened porch. The laundry room is strategically located off the kitchen and provides direct access to the garage. The master suite features a formal ceiling, French doors and a pampering bath. Two secondary bedrooms and a full hall bath complete the sleeping wing.

G. MacDONALD

Design HPT300073

Square Footage: 1,911

◆ Horizontal wood siding graces the exterior of this quaint one-story home. Enter through double doors to an entry where a skylight spills its brightness into the living and dining area. The living space has a vaulted ceiling over a full-height window wall and a warming fireplace. The open kitchen and its attached family room are ideal for a casual gathering spot. The kitchen features a spacious work island, a pantry and a breakfast nook. In the master suite are a walk-in closet and a bath with His and Hers vanities, a corner shower and whirlpool spa. The family bedrooms share a skylit main bath.

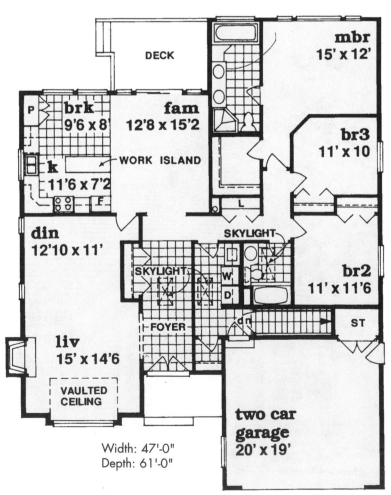

Width: 47'-0"
Depth: 61'-0"

Floor Plan

SITTING AREA

COFFERED CEILING

mbr
13' x 14'

COFFERED CEILING

PATIO

DECK

fam
13' x 12'4

GAS F.P.

liv
13'4 x 16'
VAULTED

brk

k
14'6 x 10'

PLANT SHELF OVER

P.

WHIRLPOOL TUB

SH.

L

F.
W.H.

COFFERED CEILING

W
T
D

br2
9'2 x 11'

din
10'1 x 11'8

br3
13' x 10'

PLANTERS

two-car garage
19'4 x 20'4

Width: 47'-0"
Depth: 72'-0"

Design HPT300074
Square Footage: 1,936

◆ Two elevations—a Prairie style and a Sun country facade—create a home that is well suited to any neighborhood. A transom window over the entry and the living room accentuates the vaulted ceiling, which stretches throughout the home. A pair of fluted columns accents the entrance to the living room, and there's also a bridging plant shelf. A glass-walled fireplace shares space with both the living room and the breakfast room. The L-shaped kitchen features a pantry and island cooktop. Bedrooms include a master suite with a sitting bay.

Alternate Elevation

Width: 57'-0"
Depth: 58'-0"

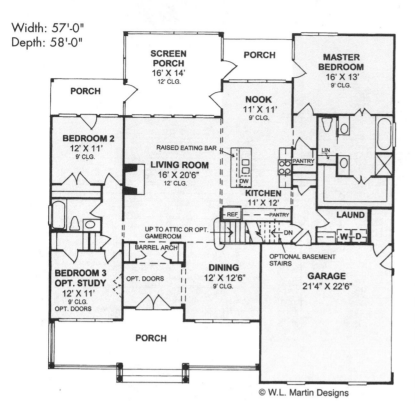

PORCH

SCREEN PORCH
16' X 14'
12' CLG.

PORCH

MASTER BEDROOM
16' X 13'
9' CLG.

BEDROOM 2
12' X 11'
9' CLG.

NOOK
11' X 11'
9' CLG.

RAISED EATING BAR

LIVING ROOM
16' X 20'6"
12' CLG.

KITCHEN
11' X 12'

PANTRY

LIN

DW

REF

PANTRY

LAUND

W D

UP TO ATTIC OR OPT. GAMEROOM

DN

BARREL ARCH

OPTIONAL BASEMENT STAIRS

BEDROOM 3 OPT. STUDY
12' X 11'
9' CLG.
OPT. DOORS

OPT. DOORS

DINING
12' X 12'6"
9' CLG.

GARAGE
21'4" X 22'6"

PORCH

© W.L. Martin Designs

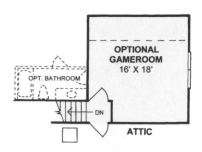

OPTIONAL GAMEROOM
16' X 18'

OPT. BATHROOM

DN

ATTIC

Design HPT300075

Square Footage: 1,915
Bonus Room: 308 sq. ft.

◆ A smattering of gables creates interest that would enhance any neighborhood. The formal dining room and study/bedroom flank the barrel-arched foyer, which opens to the living room with a window wall. To the right is the efficient island kitchen with the adjoining sunny breakfast nook. The master suite sits in the rear behind the laundry and the garage. Bedroom 2, on the far left, accesses a rear porch, as does the master bedroom and the breakfast nook.

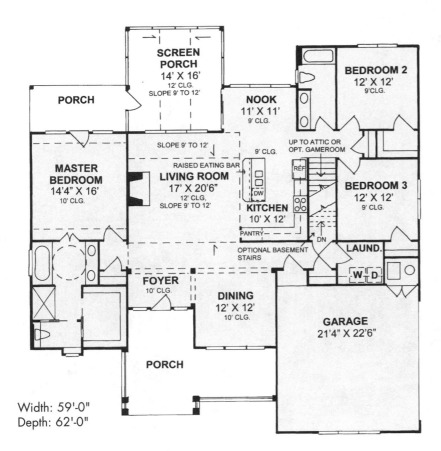

SCREEN
PORCH
14' X 16'
12' CLG.
SLOPE 9' TO 12'

PORCH

BEDROOM 2
12' X 12'
9' CLG.

NOOK
11' X 11'
9' CLG.

SLOPE 9' TO 12'

RAISED EATING BAR

MASTER
BEDROOM
14'4" X 16'
10' CLG.

LIVING ROOM
17' X 20'6"
12' CLG,
SLOPE 9' TO 12'

9' CLG.

REF.

UP TO ATTIC OR
OPT. GAMEROOM

DW

KITCHEN
10' X 12'

BEDROOM 3
12' X 12'
9' CLG.

PANTRY

OPTIONAL BASEMENT
STAIRS

FOYER
10' CLG.

DINING
12' X 12'
10' CLG.

DN

LAUND.

W D

GARAGE
21'4" X 22'6"

PORCH

Width: 59'-0"
Depth: 62'-0"

ATTIC

OPTIONAL
GAMEROOM/
BEDROOM 4
12' X 19'

DN

Design HPT300076
Square Footage: 1,958
Bonus Room: 276 sq. ft.

◆ This compact plan packs a punch with a
screened porch, two covered porches and a
bonus room, for future expansion, over the
garage. Decorative columns allow freedom of
movement between the dining room, foyer and
living room. A sloped ceiling adds to the spacious feel of the living room, which flows easily
into the kitchen and breakfast nook. A short
hall off the kitchen leads to the two family
bedrooms while the master suite is situated
on the left with its lavish private bath.

Design HPT300077

Square Footage: 1,537

◆ The intricate window treatment and stately columns give this home magnificent curb appeal. Inside, the columns continue from the foyer into the spacious great room. A fireplace is flanked by windows with a view to the rear deck and the spa. The great room opens to the large island kitchen and the formal dining room. The master suite is to the left of the foyer. The remaining bedrooms, a shared full bath and a conveniently placed utility room are located in the right wing of the house.

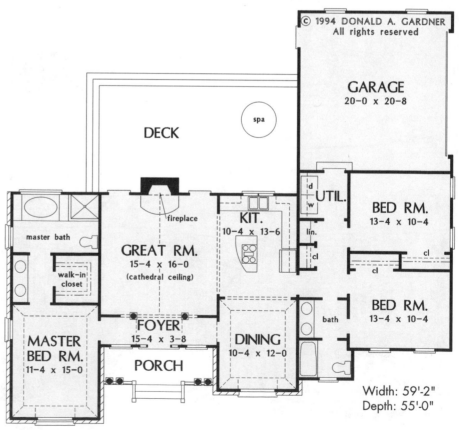

DECK

spa

GARAGE
20-0 x 20-8

fireplace

master bath

KIT.
10-4 x 13-6

UTIL.

BED RM.
13-4 x 10-4

GREAT RM.
15-4 x 16-0
(cathedral ceiling)

walk-in closet

lin.

cl

cl

BED RM.
13-4 x 10-4

FOYER
15-4 x 3-8

DINING
10-4 x 12-0

bath

MASTER
BED RM.
11-4 x 15-0

PORCH

Width: 59'-2"
Depth: 55'-0"

© 1994 Donald A. Gardner Architects, Inc.

seat

spa

DECK

SCREEN PORCH
16-0 x 11-0
skylights
wet bar

MASTER BED RM.
13-4 x 18-8

skylights
master bath

walk-in closet

UTIL.
d w
lin.
storage

BED RM.
12-4 x 11-8
cl
lin.
bath
cl

GREAT RM.
16-0 x 17-4
fireplace
cabinets

BRKFST.
12-0 x 8-6

KITCHEN
12-0 x 12-8

up

GARAGE
22-0 x 20-4

FOYER
12-4 x 5-6

cl

© 1994 Donald A. Gardner Architects, Inc.

BED RM./ STUDY
12-0 x 12-0

PORCH

DINING
12-0 x 13-8

storage

attic storage

skylights

BONUS RM.
18-0 x 19-0

down

Width: 69'-8"
Depth: 59'-6"

QUOTE ONE®
Cost to build? See page 436
to order complete cost estimate
to build this house in your area!

Design HPT300078
Square Footage: 1,977
Bonus Room: 430 sq. ft.

◆ A two-story foyer with a Palladian window above sets the tone for this sun-lit home. Columns mark the passage from the foyer to the great room, where a centered fireplace and built-in cabinets are found. A screened porch with four skylights above and a wet bar provides a pleasant place to start the day or wind down after work. The kitchen is flanked by the formal dining room and the breakfast room, which provides sliding glass doors to the large rear deck. Hidden quietly in the rear, the master suite includes a bath with dual vanities and skylights. Two family bedrooms (one an optional study) share a bath that has twin sinks.

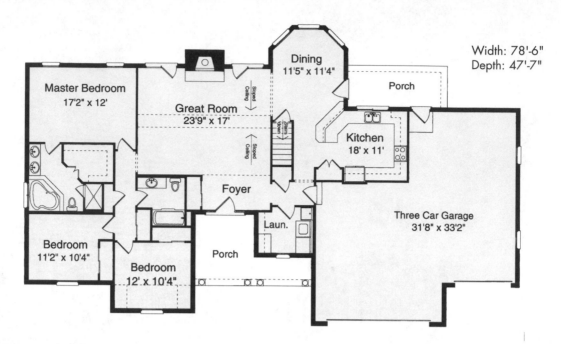

Width: 78'-6"
Depth: 47'-7"

Master Bedroom
17'2" x 12'

Great Room
23'9" x 17'

Dining
11'5" x 11'4"

Porch

Kitchen
18' x 11'

Foyer

Bedroom
11'2" x 10'4"

Bedroom
12' x 10'4"

Porch

Laun.

Three Car Garage
31'8" x 33'2"

Design HPT300079
Square Footage: 1,755

◆ A sunburst window set within a brick exterior and multi-gabled roof lends a vibrant aura to this three-bedroom home. The slope-ceilinged great room features a fireplace with French doors at each side. The nearby bay-windowed dining room accesses the rear porch—a perfect place for a barbecue grill. Conveniently placed near the garage for fast unloading, the U-shaped kitchen is sure to please. The master suite enjoys a walk-in closet and a luxurious bath, which includes a separate shower, whirlpool tub and twin-sink vanity. The two family bedrooms benefit from front-facing windows and share a full bath.

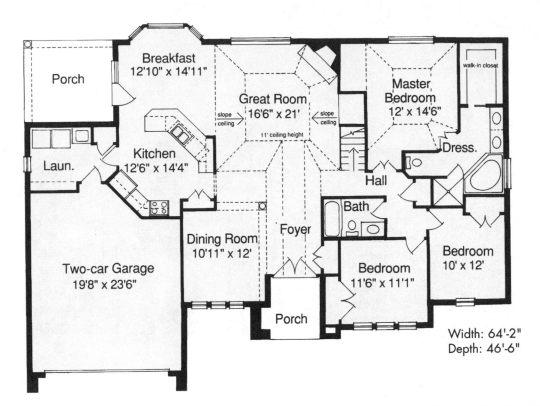

Porch

Breakfast
12'10" x 14'11"

Great Room
16'6" x 21'

slope ceiling   slope ceiling

11' ceiling height

Master Bedroom
12' x 14'6"

walk-in closet

Kitchen
12'6" x 14'4"

Dress.

Laun.

Hall

Bath

Foyer

Dining Room
10'11" x 12'

Bedroom
10' x 12'

Two-car Garage
19'8" x 23'6"

Bedroom
11'6" x 11'1"

Porch

Width: 64'-2"
Depth: 46'-6"

Design HPT300080
Square Footage: 1,860

◆ This exciting three-bedroom, one-story home offers an open floor plan with sloped ceilings and formal dining. The roomy kitchen includes a pantry and easy access to the large laundry room. With a serving bar for the great room and breakfast area, the angled kitchen counter provides extra seating. The corner fireplace adds warmth to the living area and the eleven-foot ceiling height adds excitement for entertaining formal or informal gatherings. For outdoor enjoyment, a porch is conveniently located off the breakfast area. To pamper the homeowner, the private master bedroom suite offers a ten-foot ceiling height and a deluxe bath with a whirlpool tub.

Design HPT300081
Square Footage: 1,807

◆ The striking European facade of this home presents a beautiful stone exterior, complete with stone quoins, a shingled rooftop and French-style shutters on the front windows. Step inside the great room where a ten-foot ceiling and fireplace will greet you. A large island in the kitchen provides plenty of much-needed counter space for the cook of the family. An element of privacy is observed, with the master suite separated from the other two bedrooms, which share a full bath. An oversized two-car garage and a covered patio are just some of the added amenities.

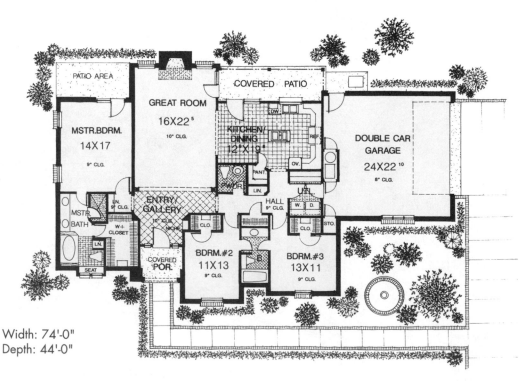

Width: 74'-0"
Depth: 44'-0"

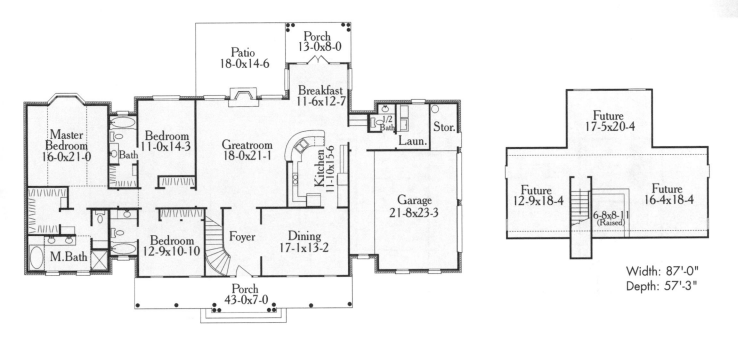

Master Bedroom
16-0x21-0

Bath

M.Bath

Bedroom
11-0x14-3

Bedroom
12-9x10-10

Foyer

Greatroom
18-0x21-1

Kitchen
11-10x15-6

Dining
17-1x13-2

Patio
18-0x14-6

Porch
13-0x8-0

Breakfast
11-6x12-7

1/2 Bath

Laun.

Stor.

Garage
21-8x23-3

Porch
43-0x7-0

Future
17-5x20-4

Future
12-9x18-4

Future
16-4x18-4

6-8x8-11
(Raised)

Width: 87'-0"
Depth: 57'-3"

Design HPT300082
Square Footage: 2,497
Bonus Space: 966 sq. ft.

◆ This elegant symmetrical home features a gabled porch complemented by columns. The breakfast room, adjacent to the kitchen, opens to a rear porch. The spacious great room provides a fireplace and a view of the patio. A lovely bayed window brightens the master suite, which includes a walk-in closet and a bath with a garden tub and a separate shower. Two secondary bedrooms each offer a private bath. A winding staircase leads to second-level future space. Please specify basement, crawlspace or slab foundation when ordering.

Design HPT300083

Square Footage: 2,258
Bonus Space: 441 sq. ft.

◆ This charming cottage design offers rustic character and traditional simplicity. The quaint covered porch welcomes you inside to a foyer flanked on either side by the formal dining room and the study. The kitchen serves the breakfast room, which accesses the rear yard through a French door. Two family bedrooms that share a hall bath are located to the left side of the plan. The secluded master suite is on the opposite side of the home and is enhanced by a sitting room, vaulted master bath and walk-in closet. Upstairs, the optional bonus room features a bath and a walk-in closet—great for a private home office or guest suite. Please specify basement or crawlspace foundation when ordering.

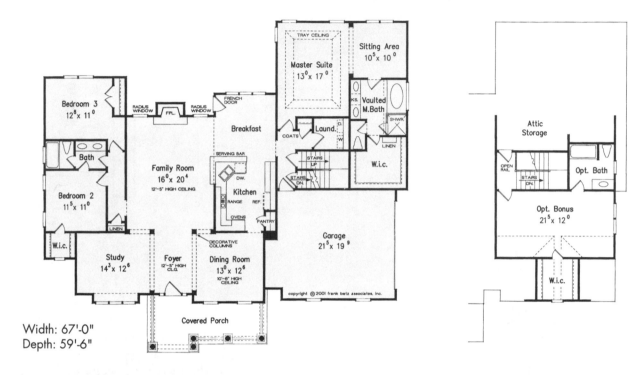

Width: 67'-0"
Depth: 59'-6"

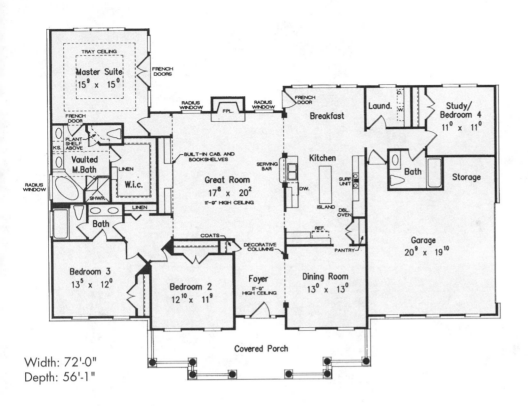

TRAY CEILING

Master Suite
15⁹ x 15⁰

FRENCH DOORS

RADIUS WINDOW   FPL.   RADIUS WINDOW

FRENCH DOOR

Breakfast

Laund.   W   D

Study/
Bedroom 4
11⁰ x 11⁰

FRENCH DOOR

PLANT SHELF ABOVE   KS.

Vaulted
M.Bath

LINEN

W.i.c.

BUILT-IN CAB. AND BOOKSHELVES

Kitchen

SERVING BAR

Bath

Storage

RADIUS WINDOW

Great Room
17⁸ x 20²
11'-9" HIGH CEILING

SURF UNIT

ISLAND

DW.

DBL. OVEN

SHWR.

LINEN

Bath

COATS

DECORATIVE COLUMNS

REF.

PANTRY

Garage
20⁹ x 19¹⁰

Bedroom 3
13⁵ x 12⁰

Bedroom 2
12¹⁰ x 11⁹

Foyer
11'-9" HIGH CEILING

Dining Room
13⁰ x 13⁰

Covered Porch

Width: 72'-0"
Depth: 56'-1"

LINEN

W.i.c.

STAIRS DN

LINEN

Great Room

Optional Basement Stair Location

Design HPT300084
Square Footage: 2,306

◆ A covered porch, columns, twin dormers and many windows provide a grand facade for this lovely home. Inside, the great room enjoys a fireplace and radius windows along with built-in bookshelves. The island kitchen is flanked by the breakfast area and the formal dining room. The master suite features a tray ceiling, access to the rear through French doors, and a bath with a vaulted ceiling. Please specify basement or crawlspace foundation when ordering.

Design HPT300085
Square Footage: 2,170

◆ This classic cottage features a stone and wooden exterior with an arch-detailed porch and a box-bay window. From a hallway off the foyer, double doors open to the den with built-in bookcases and a fireplace. A full bath is situated next to the den, allowing for an optional guest room. The family room is centrally located, just beyond the foyer. Its hearth is framed by windows overlooking the porch at the rear of the home. A breakfast area complements the attractive and efficiently designed kitchen. The master bedroom includes a private bath with a large walk-in closet, double vanities, a corner tub and separate shower. Two secondary bedrooms with large closets share a full bath featuring double vanities. This home is designed with a walkout basement foundation.

QUOTE ONE®
Cost to build? See page 436
to order complete cost estimate
to build this house in your area!

BEDROOM NO. 3
11'-6" X 11'-0"

BATH

BEDROOM NO. 2
11'-4" X 11'-0"

SUN ROOM
12'-0" X 13'-8"

PORCH

MASTER
BATH

W.I.C.

PORCH

BREAKFAST
10'-0" X 9'-0"

FAMILY ROOM
18'-0" X 14'-0"

MASTER BEDROOM
13'-4" X 15'-6"

LAUNDRY

KITCHEN
12'-0" X 13'-2"

BATH

STORAGE

DN

DINING ROOM
11'-4" X 11'-4"

FOYER
6'-8" X 11'-10"

TWO CAR GARAGE
20'-4" X 19'-8"

PORCH

DEN/GUEST
BEDROOM
11'-4" X 14'-0"

Width: 62'-0"
Depth: 61'-6"

QUOTE ONE®
Cost to build? See page 436 to order complete cost estimate to build this house in your area!

Width: 61'-0"
Depth: 70'-6"

PORCH

MASTER BATH

MASTER BEDROOM
16'-4" X 13'-6"

BEDROOM/ OFFICE
10'-4" X 11'-0"

BREAKFAST
13'-4" X 9'-0"

GREAT ROOM
17'-0" X 17'-8"

KITCHEN
13'-4" X 10'-6"

BEDROOM NO. 2
10'-4" X 12'-0"

BATH

LAUNDRY

DN.

BATH

TWO CAR GARAGE
20'-6" X 19'-6"

DINING ROOM
11'-4" X 12'-10"

FOYER
5'-4" X 12'-10"

BEDROOM/ STUDY
11'-2" X 12'-0"

PORCH

Design HPT300086
Square Footage: 2,090

◆ This traditional home features board-and-batten and cedar shingles in an attractively proportioned exterior. Finishing touches include a covered entrance and porch with column detailing and an arched transom, flower boxes and shuttered windows. The foyer opens to both the dining room and the great room beyond with French doors leading to the porch. To the right of the foyer is the combination bedroom/study. A short hallway leads to a full bath and a secondary bedroom with ample closet space. The spacious master bedroom offers walk-in closets on both sides of the entrance to the master bath. This home is designed with a walkout basement foundation.

Design HPT300087
Square Footage: 2,296
Bonus Room: 286 sq. ft.

◆ With the grand room as the hub, the floor plan of this home includes formal and informal spaces. The master suite includes a vaulted bath with a separate tub and shower. Family bedrooms each contain a walk-in closet. The second floor can be developed into an additional bedroom. Please specify basement or crawlspace foundation when ordering.

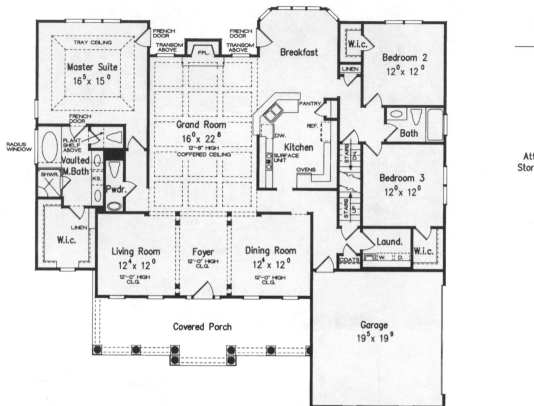

OPT. SECOND FLOOR PLAN

Width: 61'-0"
Depth: 58'-6"

Design HPT300088
Square Footage: 2,144

BEDROOM 3
10'6" X 11'6"
9' CLG

BEDROOM 2
10'10" X 11'6"
9' CLG

NOOK
10'6" X 11'6"

PORCH

SITTING

KITCHEN
14'4" X 12'

VAULTED

MASTER SUITE
13'4" X 15'6"
10' CLG

PANTRY

EATING BAR

LIVING ROOM
16' X 19'4"

14' CLG

BEDROOM 4
10'6" X 11'6"
9' CLG

VAULTED

BARREL ARCH

VAULTED

D | W

AC

K DN

OPTIONAL BASEMENT STAIRS

DINING ROOM
10'8" X 11'8"

ARCH   ARCH

11' CLG

OPTIONAL DOOR

STUDY
10'4" X 11'8"

11' CLG

GARAGE
20'4" X 23'8"

PORCH
11' CLG

Width: 67'-0"
Depth: 52'-0"

◆ An eyebrow dormer beckons to passers-by from over the columned porch of this four-bedroom home. Inside, a barrel arch leads from the entry to the hearth-warmed living room where magnificent views of the rear property are enjoyed via the stunning window wall. The island kitchen is situated between the formal dining room and the sunny breakfast nook. The master suite, on the right, enjoys a naturally lit sitting area that opens, like the breakfast nook, to the rear porch. Three bedrooms, a shared full bath and the utility room are on the left, nestled behind the garage.

Design HPT300089
Square Footage: 2,404

◆ This great ranch-style home features a low-maintenence brick finish, shuttered windows and a covered porch surrounded by decorative pillars. Directly in view of the skylit foyer is a spacious family room with twin skylights. The living room features a tray ceiling and a fireplace and opens from the foyer, across from the formal dining room. A gourmet kitchen features a center prep island, long pantry, breakfast room and built-in desk. Bedrooms are positioned away from the living areas for privacy.

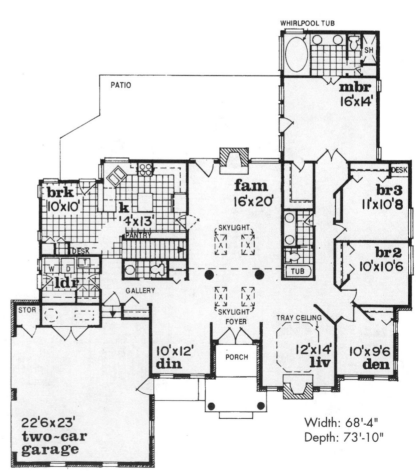

WHIRLPOOL TUB

PATIO

mbr
16'x14'

SH

brk
10'x10'

k
14'x13'

fam
16'x20'

DESK

br3
11'x10'8

PANTRY

DESK

SKYLIGHT

br2
10'x10'6

W D

ldr

TUB

STOR

GALLERY

SKYLIGHT

FOYER

TRAY CEILING

10'x12'
din

PORCH

12'x14'
liv

10'x9'6
den

22'6x23'
two-car
garage

Width: 68'-4"
Depth: 73'-10"

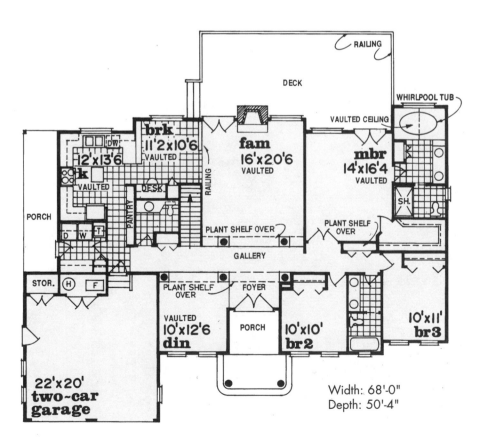

Width: 68'-0"
Depth: 50'-4"

Design HPT300090
Square Footage: 2,021

◆ This beautiful design is enhanced by brick siding and decorative wood columns at the entry. Plant ledges, which encompass the colonnaded foyer, and high vaulted ceilings throughout adorn the interior. The fireplace in the family room also warms the breakfast nook—the two are separated only by a low railing. A gourmet kitchen offers a center preparation island, a long pantry and a built-in desk. A formal dining room is also defined by columns and sits just across the hall from the family room. The master suite opens to the rear deck through double doors and contains a large walk-in closet, a whirlpool spa, His and Hers vanities and a separate shower.

Design HPT300091

Square Footage: 2,424

L

◆ This unique one-story plan seems tailor-made for a small family or for empty-nesters. Formal areas are situated well for entertaining—living room to the right and formal dining room to the left. A large family room to the rear accesses a rear wood deck and is warmed in the cold months by a welcome hearth. The U-shaped kitchen features an attached morning room for casual meals near the laundry and a washroom. The master suite sits to the right of the plan and has a walk-in closet and a fine bath. A nearby den opens to a private porch. Two family bedrooms on the other side of the home share a full bath.

Width: 68'-0"
Depth: 64'-0"

QUOTE ONE®
Cost to build? See page 436
to order complete cost estimate
to build this house in your area!

Design HPT300092

Square Footage: 2,407

L

◆ A projecting portico with an archway supported by two sets of twin columns provides shelter, as well as an appealing front entrance for this home. The dramatic central foyer has a high ceiling and an abundance of natural light. At the center of the plan is the family room with its sloped ceiling, raised-hearth fireplace and entertainment center. This room also looks over a low wall into the kitchen and nearby snack bar. French doors open to the covered patio. There are two bedrooms and a bath for the children. At the opposite end of the plan is the master suite, where the focal point is the three-sided, raised-hearth fireplace, which can be enjoyed from the whirlpool tub.

Width: 65'-4"
Depth: 55'-0"

QUOTE ONE®
Cost to build? See page 436 to order complete cost estimate to build this house in your area!

Floor plan labels:
COVERED PORCH · BRKFST 11⁰ x 9⁶ · LAUNDRY ROOM · COVERED PATIO SLOPED CEILING · SITTING/EXERCISE · MASTER BATH · SHWR · SEAT · WHIRLPOOL · RAISED HEARTH · KIT 11⁰ x 13 · SNACK BAR · PANTRY · LINEN · WALK-IN CLOSET · BEDRM 13² x 12⁰ · FAMILY RM 16⁰ x 18⁸ SLOPED CEILING · ENT. CENTER · MORNING BAR · RAISED HEARTH · MASTER SUITE 16⁶ x 15⁰ · HALLWAY · BATH · WALK-IN CLOSET · BEDRM 11⁴ x 13⁴ · ARCH · CHINA · SHELF · FOYER 11'-0" CEILING · SHELF · BOOKSHELF · POWDER · WALK-IN CLOSET · DINING RM 10⁴ x 12² · LIVING RM 15⁴ x 12² 11'-0" CEILING · COVERED PORCH · RAILING

95

Design HPT300093

Square Footage: 2,006

L D

◆ Many years of delightful living will
surely be enjoyed in this one-story traditional home. The covered front porch adds
charm to the exterior as do the multi-pane
windows. Easy living centers around the
large gathering room with a raised-hearth
fireplace and sliding glass doors to the
rear terrace. The dining room is set off
just enough to accommodate more formal
dinners and is easily accessible from the
eat-in kitchen. Kitchen amenities include
a cooktop island, an abundance of cabinet
and counter space and an adjoining utility
room. The master bedroom has private
patio access, a large walk-in closet and a
compartmented bath. A study, a secondary
bedroom and a full hall bath complete
the plan. Extra storage space is available
in the two-car garage.

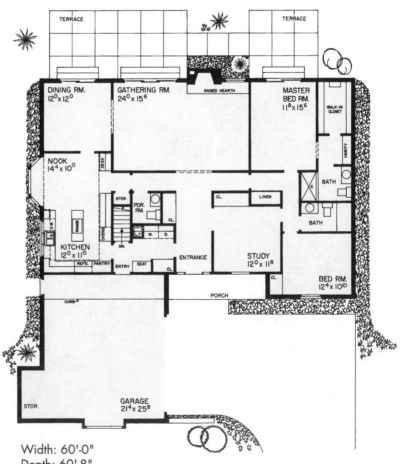

Width: 60'-0"
Depth: 60'-8"

Design HPT300094
Square Footage: 2,203

L

◆ Nothing completes a traditional-style home quite as well as a country kitchen with a fireplace and built-in wood box. Notice also the second fireplace (with its raised hearth) and the sloped ceiling in the living room. The nearby dining room has an attached porch and separate dining terrace. Aside from two family bedrooms with a shared full bath, there is also a marvelous master suite with rear-terrace access, a walk-in closet, whirlpool tub and double vanities. A handy washroom is near the laundry, just off the two-car garage.

Width: 77'-2"
Depth: 46'-6"

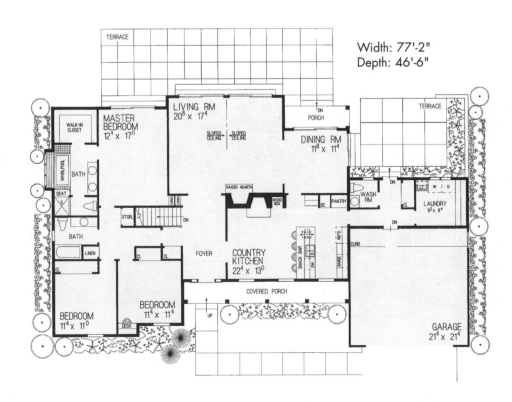

Design HPT300095

Square Footage: 2,032

L

◆ This home boasts a delightful Tudor exterior with a terrific interior floor plan. Though compact, there's plenty of living space: a large study with a fireplace, a gathering room, a formal dining room and a breakfast room. The master bedroom is enhanced with His and Hers walk-in closets and a relaxing private bath with a soothing whirlpool tub. An additional bedroom with a full bath nearby completes the sleeping quarters. A laundry room connects to the two-car garage.

QUOTE ONE®

Cost to build? See page 436
to order complete cost estimate
to build this house in your area!

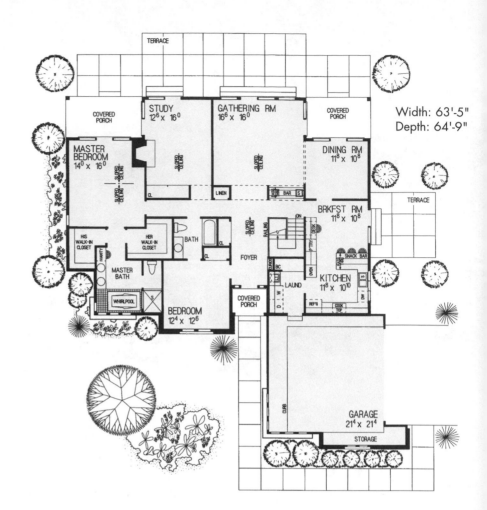

Width: 63'-5"
Depth: 64'-9"

TERRACE

STUDY
12⁶ x 16⁰

GATHERING RM
16⁶ x 16⁰

COVERED PORCH

COVERED PORCH

MASTER BEDROOM
14⁰ x 16⁰

DINING RM
11⁸ x 10⁸

TERRACE

LINEN

BRKFST RM
11⁸ x 10⁸

HIS WALK-IN CLOSET

HER WALK-IN CLOSET

BATH

FOYER

SNACK BAR

MASTER BATH

WHIRLPOOL

BEDROOM
12⁴ x 12⁶

COVERED PORCH

LAUND

KITCHEN
11⁸ x 10¹⁰

COOK TOP

GARAGE
21⁴ x 21⁴

STORAGE

Design HPT300096
Square Footage: 2,112

◆ A Tudor exterior with an efficient floor plan is favored by many. Each of the three main living zones in this plan are within a few steps of the foyer for easy traffic flow. Open planning and plenty of glass create a bright environment for the living/dining areas. The L-shaped kitchen with an island range and a work surface is open to the large breakfast room. Nearby is the step-saving laundry. The sleeping zone has the flexibility of functioning as a two- or three-bedroom area.

Width: 63'-4"
Depth: 54'-10"

Cost to build? See page 436 to order complete cost estimate to build this house in your area!

Design HPT300097
Square Footage: 2,022

L

◆ You'll love this compact and comfortable three-bedroom plan! It is a good building candidate for a small family or for empty-nester retirees. Of special interest are the covered eating porch and the sloped ceilings in the gathering room and the master bedroom. The kitchen offers new angles on your favorite amenities and also enjoys the companionship of an attached breakfast room. In the master suite, a full bath with a whirlpool tub, dual lavatories and a compartmented commode is sure to delight. A hall bath serves the two secondary bedrooms.

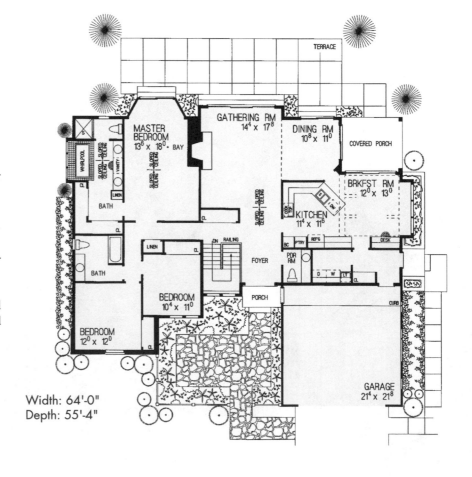

Width: 64'-0"
Depth: 55'-4"

PATIO

MASTER BEDRM
17⁴ x 14⁰

LIVING RM
17⁰ x 15⁴

DINING RM
10⁰ x 12⁶

BEDRM
14⁴ x 12⁰

WALK-IN CLOSET

LINEN

BC

LINEN

BATH

SNACK BAR

DW SINK

RANGE

FOYER

KIT
19⁰ x 11²

PANTRY

REF

MASTER BATH

D

W

LT

SHOWER

GARDEN TUB

LAUNDRY

BEDRM
14⁴ x 14⁴

COVERED PORCH

RAILING

GARAGE
21⁴ x 20⁴

Width: 64'-8"
Depth: 54'-7"

Design HPT300098
Square Footage: 2,076

L D

◆ Multi-pane windows, mock shutters and a covered front porch exhibit the charm of this home's facade. Inside, the foyer is flanked by a spacious, efficient kitchen to the right and a large convenient laundry room to the left. The living room features a warming fireplace. To the right of the living room is the formal dining room; both rooms share a snack bar and direct access to the kitchen. Sleeping quarters are split, with two family bedrooms and a full bath on the right side of the plan and the deluxe master suite on the left. The private master bath offers such luxuries as a walk-in closet, twin vanities, a garden tub and a separate shower.

Design HPT300099
Square Footage: 2,217

L D

◆ This Tudor design provides a handsome exterior complemented by a spacious and modern floor plan. The sleeping area is positioned to the left side of the home. The master bedroom features an elegant bath with a whirlpool tub, a shower, dual lavs and a separate vanity area. Two family bedrooms share a full bath. A media room exhibits the TV, VCR and stereo. The enormous gathering room is set off by columns and contains a fireplace and sliding doors to the rear terrace. The dining room and breakfast room each feature a box-bay window.

QUOTE ONE®
Cost to build? See page 436
to order complete cost estimate
to build this house in your area!

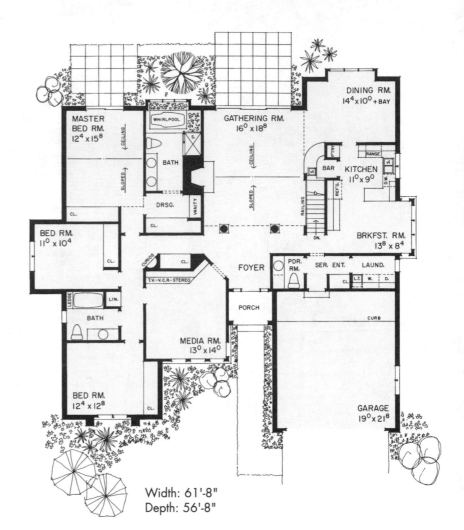

Width: 61'-8"
Depth: 56'-8"

Design HPT300100
Square Footage: 2,211
Bonus Room: 408 sq. ft.

◆ This home is built for entertaining. The large great room is perfect for parties and the kitchen, with sunny skylights and an adjoining dining room, creates a cozy breakfast buffet. Access from both rooms to the expansive deck completes the picture perfectly. The location of the master bedroom and the other bedrooms allows for quiet comfort. You'll love the bonus room, which can be made into a game room or a study.

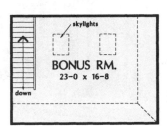

skylights

BONUS RM.
23-0 x 16-8

down

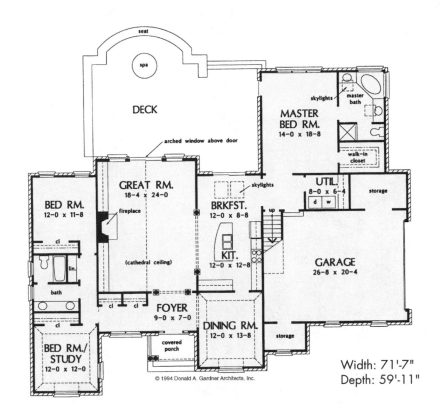

seat

spa

DECK

skylights

master bath

MASTER BED RM.
14-0 x 18-8

walk-in closet

arched window above door

GREAT RM.
18-4 x 24-0

fireplace

skylights

BRKFST.
12-0 x 8-8

up

UTIL.
8-0 x 6-4

d | w

storage

BED RM.
12-0 x 11-8

cl

lin.

bath

(cathedral ceiling)

KIT.
12-0 x 12-8

GARAGE
26-8 x 20-4

cl

cl

cl

FOYER
9-0 x 7-0

BED RM./ STUDY
12-0 x 12-0

covered porch

DINING RM.
12-0 x 13-8

storage

© 1994 Donald A. Gardner Architects, Inc.

Width: 71'-7"
Depth: 59'-11"

B. NATHAN

Design HPT300101

Square Footage: 2,135
Bonus Room: 315 sq. ft.

◆ The pediment over the front entry, flanked by twin dormers, adds a hint of Southern hospitality to this three-bedroom home. The island kitchen is conveniently located to serve any occassion—hors d'oeuvres in the living room, brunch in the breakfast nook or dinner in the formal dining room. The screened porch connects the two covered porches at the rear. The bedrooms are split for privacy, putting the lavish master suite on the left with access to the rear. An optional game room is available for future development.

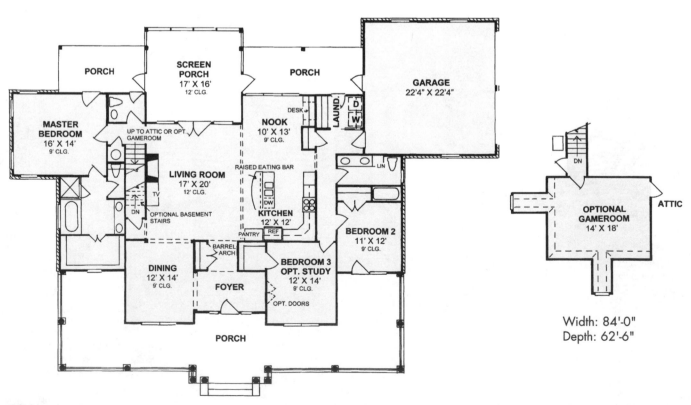

Width: 84'-0"
Depth: 62'-6"

104

Design HPT300102

Square Footage: 2,184
Bonus Room: 436 sq. ft.

◆ Inspired by Southern farmhouses, this home boasts a full-width covered front porch as well as a screened porch in the rear flanked by two additional porches. In true Southern style, the kitchen opens to the outdoors, in this case, the front porch. The breakfast nook is to the rear near the laundry area and a short hall that leads to the garage. The living room boasts a warming fireplace. Two bedrooms, a full bath and the master suite sit on the left. An optional game room is available for future development.

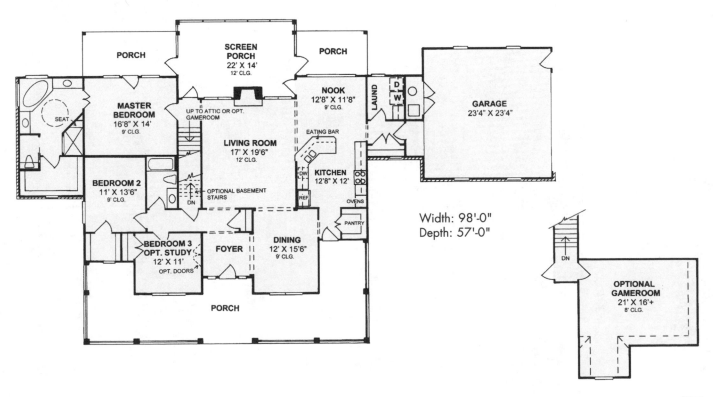

PORCH

SCREEN PORCH
22' X 14'
12' CLG.

PORCH

MASTER BEDROOM
16'8" X 14'
9' CLG.

SEAT

UP TO ATTIC OR OPT. GAMEROOM

LIVING ROOM
17' X 19'6"
12' CLG.

EATING BAR

NOOK
12'8" X 11'8"
9' CLG.

LAUND

D W
D W

GARAGE
23'4" X 23'4"

BEDROOM 2
11' X 13'6"
9' CLG.

OPTIONAL BASEMENT STAIRS

DN

KITCHEN
12'8" X 12'

DW

REF

OVENS

PANTRY

BEDROOM 3
OPT. STUDY
12' X 11'
OPT. DOORS

FOYER

DINING
12' X 15'6"
9' CLG.

PORCH

Width: 98'-0"
Depth: 57'-0"

DN

OPTIONAL GAMEROOM
21' X 16'+
8' CLG.

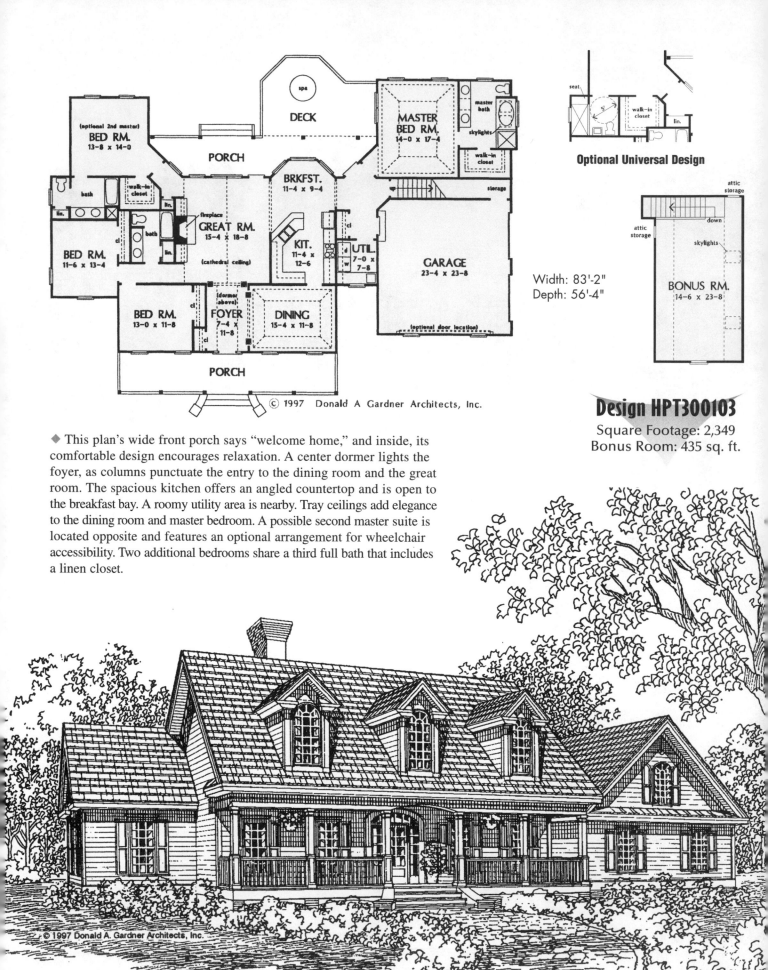

Optional Universal Design

Width: 83'-2"
Depth: 56'-4"

© 1997 Donald A Gardner Architects, Inc.

BONUS RM.
14-6 x 23-8

Design HPT300103
Square Footage: 2,349
Bonus Room: 435 sq. ft.

◆ This plan's wide front porch says "welcome home," and inside, its comfortable design encourages relaxation. A center dormer lights the foyer, as columns punctuate the entry to the dining room and the great room. The spacious kitchen offers an angled countertop and is open to the breakfast bay. A roomy utility area is nearby. Tray ceilings add elegance to the dining room and master bedroom. A possible second master suite is located opposite and features an optional arrangement for wheelchair accessibility. Two additional bedrooms share a third full bath that includes a linen closet.

Design HPT300104

Square Footage: 2,487

◆ A trio of dormers and a front porch adorn the facade of this sprawling four-bedroom country home. Illuminated by the center dormer, the vaulted foyer gives way to the dining room with a tray ceiling and the spacious great room with a cathedral ceiling, a fireplace and built-in shelves. A split-bedroom layout provides privacy for the homeowners in a xreside on the opposite side of the home.

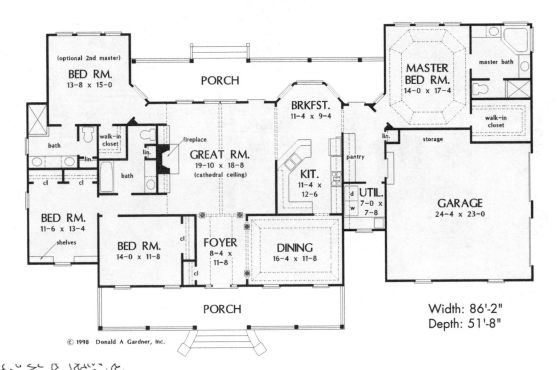

Width: 86'-2"
Depth: 51'-8"

© 1998 Donald A Gardner, Inc.

© 1998 Donald A Gardner, Inc.

107

© 1997 Donald A. Gardner Architects, Inc.   B. NATHAN

Design HPT300105
Square Footage: 2,273
Bonus Room: 342 sq. ft.

◆ With an exciting blend of styles, this home features the wrapping porch of a country farmhouse with a brick-and-siding exterior for a uniquely pleasing effect. The great room shares its cathedral ceiling with an open kitchen, while the octagonal dining room is complemented by a tray ceiling. Built-ins flank the great room's fireplace for added convenience. The master suite features a full bath, a walk-in closet and access to the rear porch. Two additional bedrooms share a full hall bath, while a third bedroom can be converted into a study. Skylit bonus space is available above the garage, which is connected to the home by a covered breezeway.

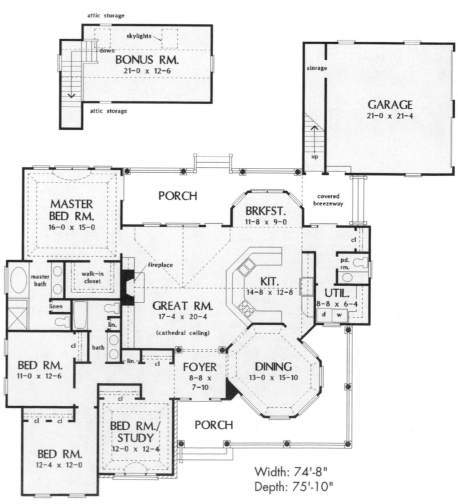

Width: 74'-8"
Depth: 75'-10"

©1999 Donald A. Gardner, Inc.

B. NATHAN

attic storage

down

BONUS RM.
21-0 x 12-0

attic storage

storage

GARAGE
21-0 x 21-0

up

Design HPT300106
Square Footage: 2,078
Bonus Room: 339 sq. ft.

PORCH

covered breezeway

**MASTER
BED RM.**
16-0 x 16-0

(cathedral ceiling)

skylights

fireplace

walk-in closet

master bath

cl

BRKFST.
11-0 x 9-0

GREAT RM.
21-0 x 18-0

(cathedral ceiling)

KITCHEN
13-0 x 11-0

pd. rm.

UTIL.

d   w

lin.   lin.

cl

FOYER
8-4 x 8-4

DINING
13-0 x 12-0

bath

cl

BED RM.
12-0 x 12-0

BED RM.
11-0 x 13-0

(cathedral ceiling)

PORCH

©1999 Donald A. Gardner, Inc.

Width: 62'-2"
Depth: 47'-8"

◆ An enchanting L-shaped front porch lends charm and grace to this country home with dual dormers and gables. Bay windows expand both of the home's dining areas, while the great room and kitchen are amplified by a shared cathedral ceiling. The generous great room features a fireplace with flanking built-ins, skylights and access to a marvelous back porch. A cathedral ceiling enhances the master suite, which enjoys a large walk-in closet and a luxurious bath. Two more bedrooms, one with a cathedral ceiling, share a generous hall bath that has a dual-sink vanity.

Design HPT300107

Square Footage: 2,099

◆ This enchanting design incorporates the best in floor planning all on one amenity-filled level. Large arched windows and corner quoins lend a distinctly European flavor to this brick home. The central great room is the hub of the plan, from which all other rooms radiate. It is highlighted with a fireplace and cathedral ceiling. Nearby is a skylit sun room with sliding glass doors to the rear deck and a built-in wet bar. The master suite is split from the family bedrooms and accesses the rear deck. The pampering master bath offers a whirlpool tub, separate shower and twin vanities. Family bedrooms share a full hall bath.

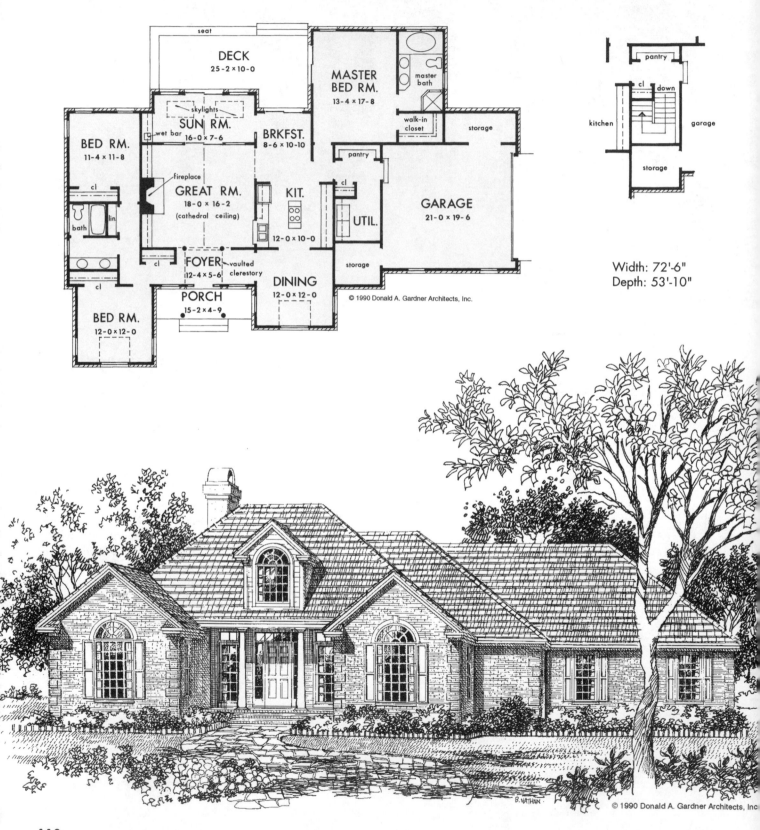

DECK
25-2 × 10-0

MASTER
BED RM.
13-4 × 17-8

master
bath

SUN RM.
16-0 × 7-6

wet bar

skylights

BRKFST.
8-6 × 10-10

walk-in
closet

storage

BED RM.
11-4 × 11-8

cl

fireplace

GREAT RM.
18-0 × 16-2
(cathedral ceiling)

KIT.
12-0 × 10-0

pantry

cl

GARAGE
21-0 × 19-6

bath

lin

cl

UTIL.

FOYER
12-4 × 5-6

vaulted
clerestory

storage

DINING
12-0 × 12-0

PORCH
15-2 × 4-9

BED RM.
12-0 × 12-0

© 1990 Donald A. Gardner Architects, Inc.

pantry

cl

down

kitchen

garage

storage

Width: 72'-6"
Depth: 53'-10"

B. NATHAN

© 1990 Donald A. Gardner Architects, Inc

© 1990 Donald A. Gardner Architects, Inc.

GARAGE
20-4 x 20-4

Width: 68'-9"
Depth: 68'-7"

DECK
43-0 x 10-0

covered breezeway

◆ Multi-pane windows, dormers, copper-covered bay windows, a covered porch with round columns, and brick siding help to emphasize the sophisticated appearance of this three-bedroom home. An added special feature to this plan is the sun room with a hot tub that's accessible to both the master bath and the great room. The great room has a fireplace, cathedral ceiling and sliding glass doors with an arched window above to allow plenty of natural light. The spacious master bedroom contains a walk-in closet and a bath with a double-bowl vanity, shower and garden tub. Two family bedrooms are located at the opposite end of the house for privacy.

skylights

hot tub

SUN RM.
15-8 x 7-10

fireplace

GREAT RM.
20-0 x 15-6
(cathedral ceiling)

UTILITY
8-10 x 5-4

bath

cl

BED RM.
11-4 x 13-8

powder rm.

lin.

master bath

walk-in closet

FOYER
4-6 x 12-4

DINING
12-0 x 12-0

KITCHEN
14-4 x 12-0

cl

cl

BED RM.
14-8 x 11-0

MASTER BED RM.
13-4 x 16-8

cl

PORCH
18-10 x 5-1

BRKFST.
13-4 x 7-8

B. NATHAN

© 1990 Donald A. Gardner Architects, Inc.

© 2000 Donald A. Gardner, Inc.

B. NATHAN

Design HPT300109
Square Footage: 2,184

◆ The country look of this classic cottage home is appealing to families and vacationers alike. A petite covered porch welcomes you into a foyer flanked by family bedrooms on the right and the kitchen area on the left. The master suite is truly pampering with a lavish private bath and huge walk-in closet. The family bedrooms share a full hall bath nearby. One family bedroom can double as a study. The kitchen/breakfast area is conveniently placed between the garage and formal dining room. The great room, which includes a warming fireplace, overlooks the rear porch.

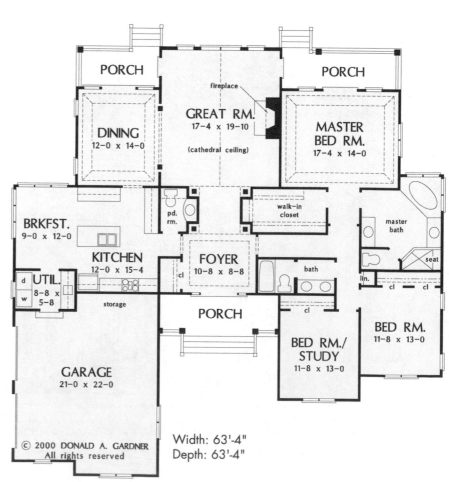

PORCH

GREAT RM.
17-4 x 19-10
(cathedral ceiling)

fireplace

PORCH

DINING
12-0 x 14-0

MASTER
BED RM.
17-4 x 14-0

BRKFST.
9-0 x 12-0

pd. rm.

walk-in closet

master bath

seat

KITCHEN
12-0 x 15-4

FOYER
10-8 x 8-8

bath

lin.

cl

cl

d w

UTIL.
8-8 x 5-8

storage

cl

BED RM.
11-8 x 13-0

PORCH

cl

GARAGE
21-0 x 22-0

BED RM./
STUDY
11-8 x 13-0

Width: 63'-4"
Depth: 63'-4"

© 1990 Donald A. Gardner Architects, I

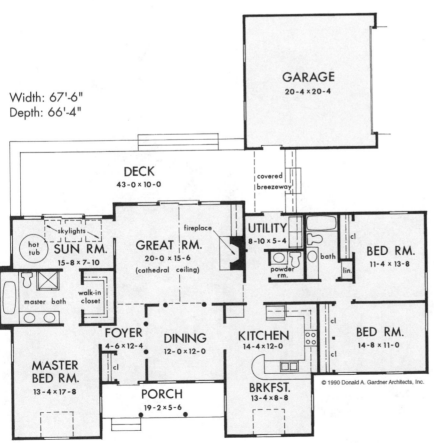

Width: 67'-6"
Depth: 66'-4"

GARAGE
20-4 × 20-4

DECK
43-0 × 10-0

covered
breezeway

skylights

hot
tub

SUN RM.
15-8 × 7-10

fireplace

GREAT RM.
20-0 × 15-6
(cathedral ceiling)

UTILITY
8-10 × 5-4

bath

cl

BED RM.
11-4 × 13-8

powder
rm.

lin.

master bath

walk-in
closet

FOYER
4-6 × 12-4

DINING
12-0 × 12-0

KITCHEN
14-4 × 12-0

cl

cl

BED RM.
14-8 × 11-0

MASTER
BED RM.
13-4 × 17-8

cl

PORCH
19-2 × 5-6

BRKFST.
13-4 × 8-8

© 1990 Donald A. Gardner Architects, Inc.

Design HPT300110
Square Footage: 2,032

◆ Simplicity embraces elegance in this three-bedroom home: a low-maintenance stucco exterior is complemented by decorative columns, arched windows and copper dormers. A split-bedroom plan allows privacy for the sensational master suite, which opens to a skylit sun room with hot tub. Guests may enjoy the sun room from the expansive great room with a cathedral ceiling and fireplace. The thoroughly modern kitchen joins a breakfast area with a vaulted ceiling. Two family bedrooms to the right of the plan share a full bath.

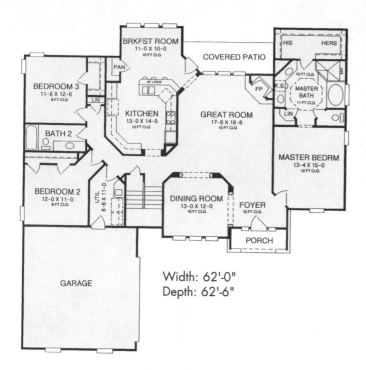

BRKFST ROOM
11-0 X 10-0
10 FT CLG

COVERED PATIO

HIS   HERS

PAN

BEDROOM 3
11-6 X 12-6
8 FT CLG

LIN

10 FT CLG

KITCHEN
13-0 X 14-0
10 FT CLG

42" LEDGE

FP

K.S.

MASTER
BATH
11 FT CLG

GREAT ROOM
17-6 X 18-6
10 FT CLG

BATH 2

LIN

BEDROOM 2
12-0 X 11-0
8 FT CLG

UTIL
6-6 X 11-0

MASTER BEDRM
13-4 15-0
10 FT CLG

DINING ROOM
13-0 X 12-0
10 FT CLG

FOYER
10 FT CLG

PORCH

GARAGE

Width: 62'-0"
Depth: 62'-6"

Design HPT300111
Square Footage: 2,127
Bonus Room: 338 sq. ft.

◆ Three arched windows provide just the right touch of elegance and give this home a picturesque appeal. The great room with a corner fireplace is located near the breakfast area and kitchen. Ten-foot ceilings in all major living areas give the plan an open, spacious feel. The master suite includes a luxury bath with a coffered ceiling, large His and Hers closets, a whirlpool tub, a shower with a seat, and twin vanities. A stair leads to an expandable area on the second floor. Please specify crawlspace or slab foundation when ordering.

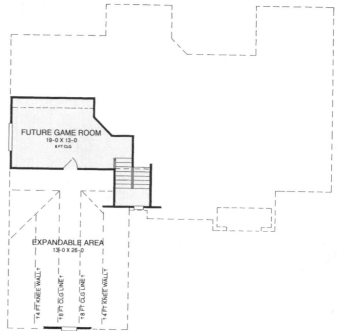

FUTURE GAME ROOM
19-0 X 13-0
8 FT CLG

EXPANDABLE AREA
13-0 X 26-0

↑4 FT KNEE WALL↑   ↑8 FT CLG LINE↑   ↑8 FT CLG LINE↑   ↑4 FT KNEE WALL↑

Width: 65'-9"
Depth: 60'-5"

SCREEN PORCH
24-6 x 8-6

BRKFST.
11-8 x 8-6
(cathedral ceiling)

(cathedral ceiling)

fireplace

KIT.
11-8 x 12-10

bath

BED RM.
11-0 x 12-0

MASTER BED RM.
16-2 x 14-0

GREAT RM.
19-0 x 15-8

cl

cl

master bath

lin.

FOYER
6-0 x 9-0

pd. rm.

DINING
11-8 x 12-0

UTIL
6-0 x 10-4

w d

up

BED RM.
11-8 x 11-8

walk-in closet

cl

BED RM./ STUDY
11-4 x 12-0
(cathedral ceiling)

PORCH

GARAGE
21-8 x 21-0

© 1999 Donald A. Gardner, Inc.

storage

BONUS RM.
14-0 x 21-0

down

attic storage

attic storage

cl

(optional full bath)

Design HPT3030002

Square Footage: 2,151
Bonus Room: 354 sq. ft.

◆ Graceful arches complement the front porch and echo the elegant arched windows on the facade of this four-bedroom brick home. Stunning cathedral ceilings enhance the great room, kitchen, breakfast room, and bedroom/study; the dining room and master bedroom enjoy distinctive tray ceilings. A fireplace flanked by built-in shelves and cabinets creates warmth and interest in the great room, which opens to a generous screened porch. Also boasting access to the porch, the master suite features a well-appointed bath and walk-in closet. The versatile bedroom/study has a single-door option for enlarging the adjacent powder room into a full bath.

B. NATHAN

© 1999 Donald A. Gardner, Inc.

115

Design HPT300113
Square Footage: 2,047

◆ This handsome home features brick siding and wood railings on a lovely covered porch. Inside, the plan allows for a private den off the entry to be converted to a third bedroom, if preferred. Ten-foot ceilings in the dining room and the great room add depth and sophistication. The great room features a fireplace flanked by transom windows; the dining room has hutch space. The U-shaped kitchen is made for the gourmet cook, with a pantry and loads of counter space. Accessed by French doors, the master bedroom is indulgent with a walk-in closet and a bath with a corner whirlpool tub, double vanity and separate shower with a seat.

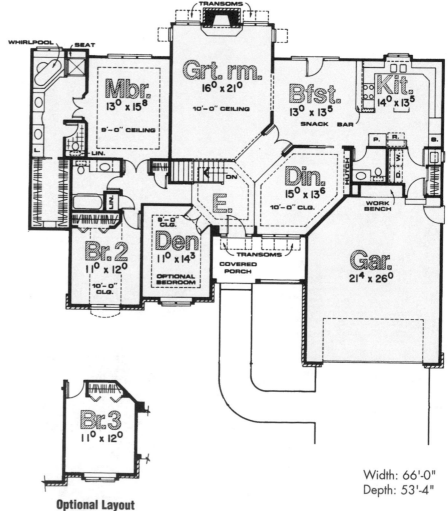

Optional Layout

Width: 66'-0"
Depth: 53'-4"

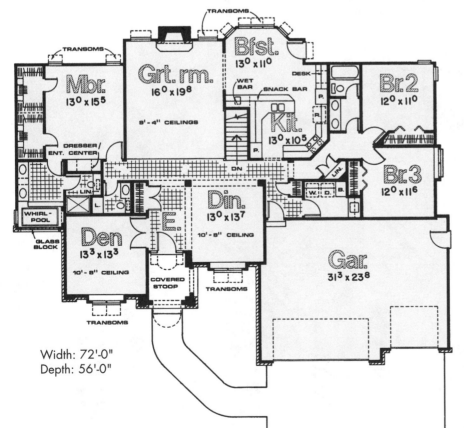

TRANSOMS

Mbr.
13⁰ x 15⁵

Grt. rm.
16⁰ x 19⁸

9'-4" CEILINGS

Bfst.
13⁰ x 11⁰

DESK

WET BAR

SNACK BAR

Kit.
13⁰ x 10⁵

Br. 2
12⁰ x 11⁰

Br. 3
12⁰ x 11⁶

DRESSER / ENT. CENTER

LIN

DN

LIN

W.D.

WHIRL-POOL

GLASS BLOCK

Den
13³ x 13³
10'-8" CEILING

Din.
13⁰ x 13⁷
10'-8" CEILING

Gar.
31³ x 23⁸

COVERED STOOP

TRANSOMS

TRANSOMS

Width: 72'-0"
Depth: 56'-0"

Design HPT300114
Square Footage: 2,276

◆ Drama and harmony are expressed in this plan by utilizing a variety of elegant exterior materials. The great room with a window-framed fireplace is conveniently located next to the eat-in kitchen with a bayed breakfast area. Two secluded secondary bedrooms enjoy easy access to a compartmented bath with twin vanities. His and Hers closets and a built-in armoire grace the master suite where a private bath features glass blocks over the whirlpool tub, double sinks and an extra linen storage cabinet. An alternate elevation is provided at no extra cost.

Alternate Elevation

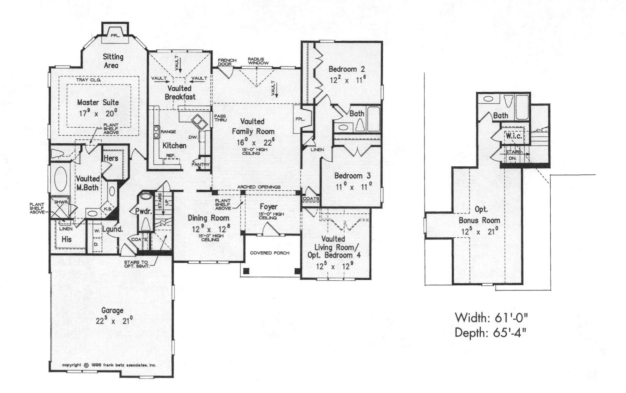

FPL.

Sitting Area

VAULT

VAULT VAULT

FRENCH DOOR

RADIUS WINDOW

TRAY CLG.

Vaulted Breakfast

Master Suite
17⁹ x 20⁰

VAULT

Bedroom 2
12² x 11⁶

PLANT SHELF ABOVE

RANGE

DW.

PASS THRU

Vaulted Family Room
16⁰ x 22⁶
15'-0" HIGH CEILING

FPL.

Bath

Kitchen

Hers

REF.

PANTRY

LINEN

Vaulted M.Bath

Bedroom 3
11⁰ x 11⁰

PLANT SHELF ABOVE

SHWR.

STAIRS

UP

ARCHED OPENINGS

PLANT SHELF ABOVE

COATS

LINEN

K.S.

Pwdr.

Foyer
15'-0" CEILING

His

Laund.

w.

Dining Room
12⁹ x 12⁸
15'-0" CEILING

D.

COATS

STAIRS TO OPT. BSMT.

COVERED PORCH

Vaulted Living Room/ Opt. Bedroom 4
12⁵ x 12⁸

Garage
22⁵ x 21⁰

copyright © 1996 frank betz associates, inc.

Bath

W.i.c.

STAIRS DN.

Opt. Bonus Room
12⁵ x 21⁰

Width: 61'-0"
Depth: 65'-4"

Design HPT300115
Square Footage: 2,311
Bonus Room: 425 sq. ft.

◆ With elegant hipped rooflines, stucco-and-brick detailing, arched windows and gabled roofs, this home presents its European heritage with pride. The covered entryway leads to a formal dining room defined by graceful columns and arched openings. Columns and arched openings also lead into the vaulted family room, where a welcoming fireplace waits to warm cool evenings, while radius windows flood the room with light. The kitchen is sure to please with its angled counter and accessibility to the vaulted breakfast nook. Two family bedrooms are to the right of the design while the master suite is to the left. Please specify basement, crawlspace, or slab foundation when ordering.

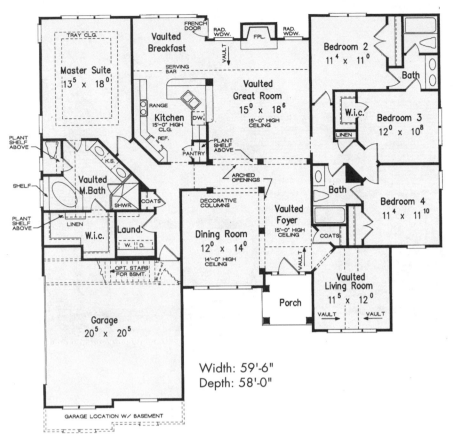

TRAY CLG.

Master Suite
13⁵ x 18⁰

Vaulted Breakfast

FRENCH DOOR

RAD. WDW.

FPL.

RAD. WDW.

Bedroom 2
11⁴ x 11⁰

Bath

SERVING BAR

Vaulted Great Room
15⁰ x 18⁶
15'-0" HIGH CEILING

W.i.c.

LINEN

Bedroom 3
12⁰ x 10⁸

RANGE

Kitchen
15'-0" HIGH CLG.

DW.

REF.

PANTRY

PLANT SHELF ABOVE

PLANT SHELF ABOVE

PLANT SHELF ABOVE

SHELF

K.S.

Vaulted M.Bath

SHWR

COATS

ARCHED OPENINGS

Bath

Bedroom 4
11⁴ x 11¹⁰

LINEN

W.i.c.

Laund.

W. D.

DECORATIVE COLUMNS

Vaulted Foyer
15'-0" HIGH CEILING

COATS

Dining Room
12⁰ x 14⁰
14'-0" HIGH CEILING

OPT. STAIRS FOR BSMT.

VAULT

Garage
20⁵ x 20⁵

Porch

Vaulted Living Room
11⁵ x 12⁰

VAULT

VAULT

GARAGE LOCATION W/ BASEMENT

Width: 59'-6"
Depth: 58'-0"

Design HPT300116
Square Footage: 2,279

◆ Spacious quarters for a large family are found in this four-bedroom traditional one-story design with country French accents. The master suite occupies the left side of the plan, while the right side contains family bedrooms and a vaulted living room. The hub of this home is the vaulted great room with a fireplace. The kitchen, breakfast nook and dining room are nearby. Please specify basement or crawlspace foundation when ordering.

Design HPT300117
Square Footage: 2,149

◆ Beautiful and accommodating, this traditional home features open-entry views into formal rooms plus volume ceilings in major living spaces. The beam-ceilinged family room offers a cozy fireplace. The kitchen is equipped with a snack bar that's open to the breakfast area, as well as a built-in desk and a pantry. Sleeping areas are comprised of three bedrooms, including a master suite with a walk-in closet, double vanity and whirlpool tub. Two additional family bedrooms share a private bath. Bedroom 3 may be used as a den with French doors to the hall.

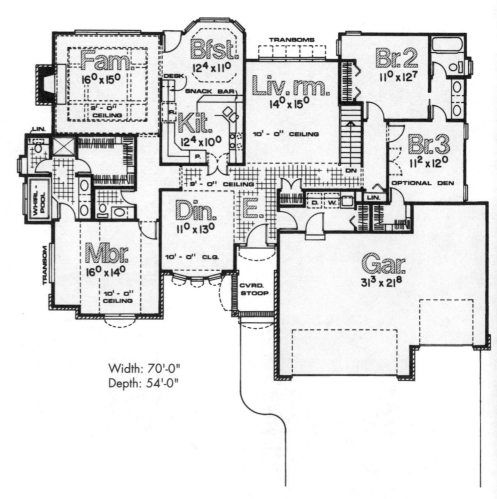

Width: 70'-0"
Depth: 54'-0"

Design HPT300118
Square Footage: 2,512
Bonus Room: 360 sq. ft.

◆ Spacious luxury is evident in this delightful Southern farmhouse where extensive outdoor living is inviting with both a screened porch and several covered porches. The foyer is flanked by the dining room and a study/Bedroom 4. Beyond the staircase that leads to the bonus space lies the living room with a grand fireplace set off by a window wall accessing the screened porch through French doors. Two family bedrooms, a full bath and the laundry area reside on the right. The master suite, with its luxurious private bath and walk-in closet/dressing area rests on the left.

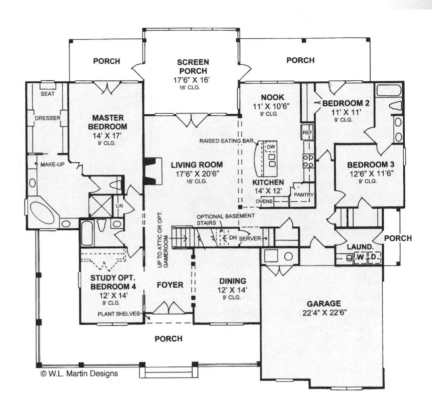

PORCH
SCREEN PORCH 17'6" X 16' 16' CLG.
PORCH
SEAT
DRESSER
NOOK 11' X 10'6" 9' CLG.
BEDROOM 2 11' X 11' 9' CLG.
MASTER BEDROOM 14' X 17' 9' CLG.
RAISED EATING BAR
REF
MAKE-UP
LIVING ROOM 17'6" X 20'6" 16' CLG.
DW
BEDROOM 3 12'6" X 11'6" 9' CLG.
KITCHEN 14' X 12'
OVENS
PANTRY
LIN
UP TO ATTIC OR OPT. GAMEROOM
OPTIONAL BASEMENT STAIRS
DN SERVER
PORCH
LAUND. W D
STUDY OPT. BEDROOM 4 12' X 14' 9' CLG.
FOYER
DINING 12' X 14' 9' CLG.
GARAGE 22'4" X 22'6"
PLANT SHELVES
PORCH
© W.L. Martin Designs

Width: 71'-0"
Depth: 67'-0"

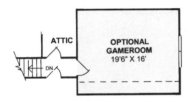

ATTIC
OPTIONAL GAMEROOM 19'6" X 16'
DN

Design HPT300119
Square Footage: 2,595
Bonus Space: 1,480 sq. ft.

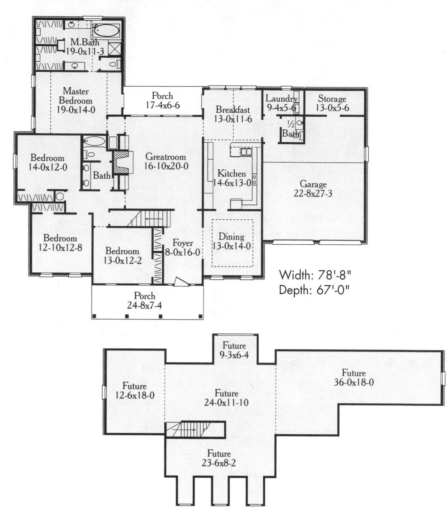

Width: 78'-8"
Depth: 67'-0"

◆ This home has a touch of modernism with all the comforts of country style. The pillared front porch allows for summer evening relaxation. The foyer extends into the bright great room equipped with a fireplace. The large kitchen is stationed between the vaulted dining room and the airy breakfast nook. Two walk-in closets, dual vanities and a spacious bath complement the master suite. Each of the three family bedrooms features abundant closet space. The entire second floor is left for future development, whether it be a guest room, rec room, study or all three.

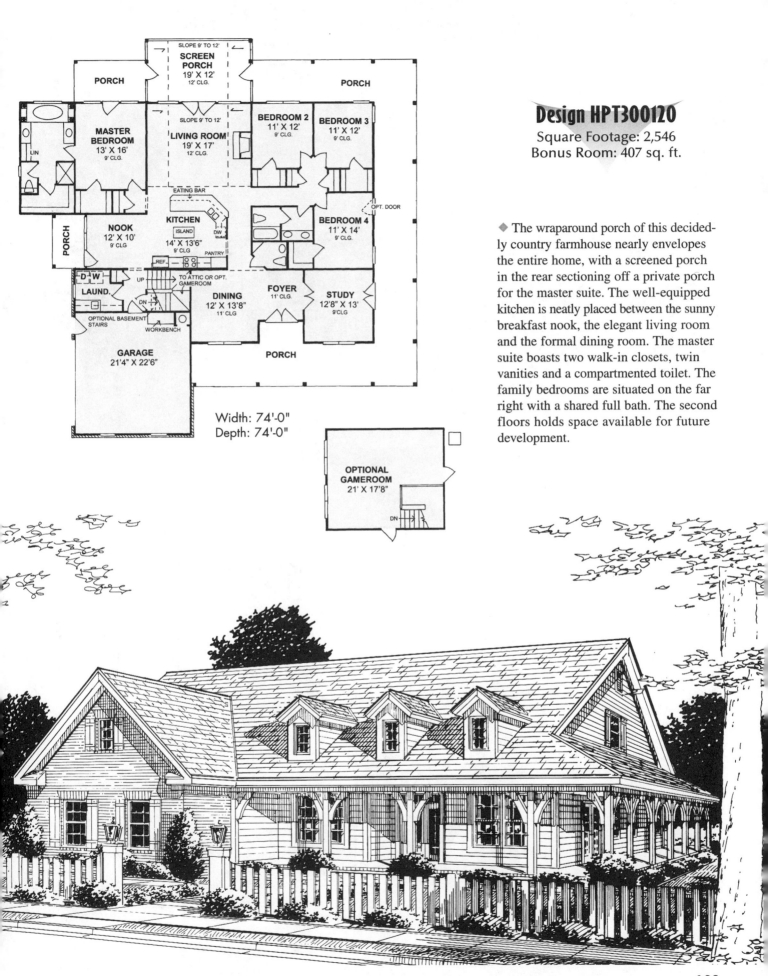

SLOPE 9' TO 12'

SCREEN PORCH
19' X 12'
12' CLG.

PORCH

PORCH

SLOPE 9' TO 12'

MASTER BEDROOM
13' X 16'
9' CLG.

LIN

LIVING ROOM
19' X 17'
12' CLG.

BEDROOM 2
11' X 12'
9' CLG.

BEDROOM 3
11' X 12'
9' CLG.

EATING BAR

OPT. DOOR

PORCH

NOOK
12' X 10'
9' CLG

KITCHEN
14' X 13'6"
9' CLG

ISLAND

DW

PANTRY

BEDROOM 4
11' X 14'
9' CLG.

REF.

D W

UP

TO ATTIC OR OPT. GAMEROOM

LAUND.

DN

FOYER
11' CLG.

STUDY
12'8" X 13'
9'CLG

OPTIONAL BASEMENT STAIRS

WORKBENCH

DINING
12' X 13'8"
11' CLG

GARAGE
21'4" X 22'6"

PORCH

Width: 74'-0"
Depth: 74'-0"

OPTIONAL GAMEROOM
21' X 17'8"

DN

Design HPT300120
Square Footage: 2,546
Bonus Room: 407 sq. ft.

◆ The wraparound porch of this decidedly country farmhouse nearly envelopes the entire home, with a screened porch in the rear sectioning off a private porch for the master suite. The well-equipped kitchen is neatly placed between the sunny breakfast nook, the elegant living room and the formal dining room. The master suite boasts two walk-in closets, twin vanities and a compartmented toilet. The family bedrooms are situated on the far right with a shared full bath. The second floors holds space available for future development.

Design HPT300121

Square Footage: 2,648
Bonus Room: 293 sq. ft.

◆ This Southern-raised elevation looks cozy but lives large, with an interior layout and amenities preferred by today's homeowners. Inside, twelve-foot ceilings and graceful columns and arches lend an aura of hospitality throughout the formal rooms and the living space in the great room. Double doors open to the gourmet kitchen, which offers a built-in desk, a snack counter for easy meals, and a breakfast room with a picture window. The secluded master suite features His and Hers walk-in closets, a whirlpool tub and a knee-space vanity. Please specify basement, crawlspace or slab foundation when ordering.

Width: 68'-10"
Depth: 77'-10"

Width: 83'-0"
Depth: 76'-2"

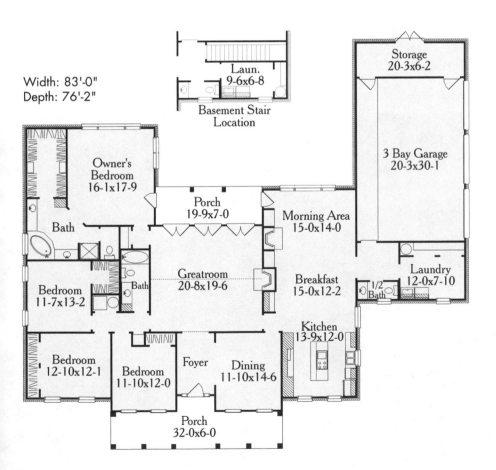

Storage
20-3x6-2

3 Bay Garage
20-3x30-1

Laun.
9-6x6-8

Basement Stair
Location

Owner's
Bedroom
16-1x17-9

Bath

Porch
19-9x7-0

Morning Area
15-0x14-0

Bedroom
11-7x13-2

Bath

Greatroom
20-8x19-6

Breakfast
15-0x12-2

Laundry
12-0x7-10

1/2
Bath

Kitchen
13-9x12-0

Bedroom
12-10x12-1

Bedroom
11-10x12-0

Foyer

Dining
11-10x14-6

Porch
32-0x6-0

Design HPT300122
Square Footage: 2,925

◆ Symmetry and style color the facade of this four-bedroom Cape Cod home. Magnificent views beyond the triplet of French doors in the great room are visible upon entering the foyer. The formal dining room is conveniently situated near the galley kitchen that adjoins the breakfast area. Both the morning area and the great room enjoy the warmth of a fireplace. Three bedrooms on the left share a full bath. The master suite boasts a sun-filled bedroom, a lavish bath and a large walk-in closet. The massive three-car garage includes compartmented storage space. Please specify basement, crawlspace or slab foundation when ordering.

Design HPT300123
Square Footage: 2,585

◆ Classical columns give the entrance of this floor plan a graceful appeal. The great room leads through two sets of double doors to the rear porch. This porch can also be accessed by a door connected to the garage and by another private door from the master bedroom. The master suite is brilliantly lit by multiple window views to the outdoors. Three additional bedrooms complete the family sleeping quarters. Please specify basement, crawlspace or slab foundation when ordering.

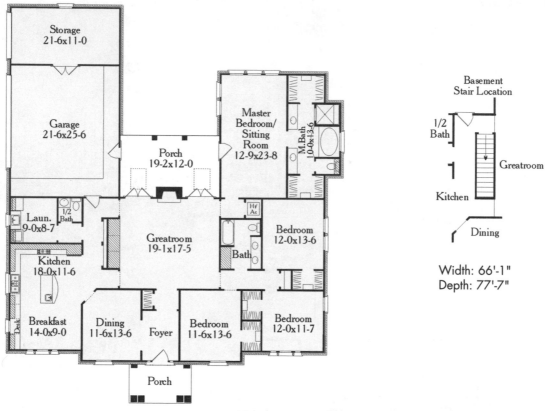

Storage
21-6x11-0

Garage
21-6x25-6

Porch
19-2x12-0

Master
Bedroom/
Sitting
Room
12-9x23-8

M.Bath
10-0x13-6

Laun.
9-0x8-7

1/2
Bath

H/
Ac

Bedroom
12-0x13-6

Greatroom
19-1x17-5

Bath

Kitchen
18-0x11-6

Breakfast
14-0x9-0

Dining
11-6x13-6

Foyer

Bedroom
11-6x13-6

Bedroom
12-0x11-7

Porch

Basement
Stair Location

1/2
Bath

Greatroom

Kitchen

Dining

Width: 66'-1"
Depth: 77'-7"

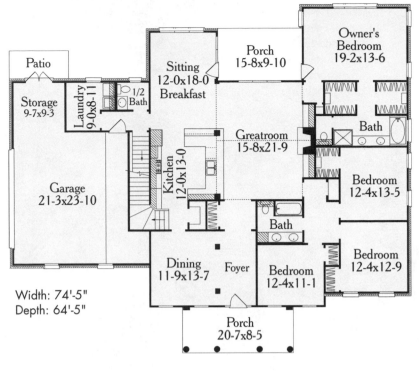

Patio

Storage
9-7x9-3

Laundry
9-0x8-11

1/2 Bath

Garage
21-3x23-10

Width: 74'-5"
Depth: 64'-5"

Sitting
12-0x18-0
Breakfast

Porch
15-8x9-10

Owner's
Bedroom
19-2x13-6

Bath

Greatroom
15-8x21-9

Kitchen
12-0x13-0

Bedroom
12-4x13-5

Bath

Dining
11-9x13-7

Foyer

Bedroom
12-4x11-1

Bedroom
12-4x12-9

Porch
20-7x8-5

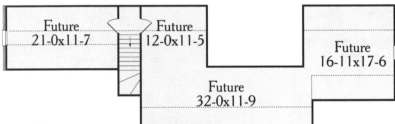

Future
21-0x11-7

Future
12-0x11-5

Future
16-11x17-6

Future
32-0x11-9

Design HPT300124

Square Footage: 2,636
Bonus Space: 1,132 sq. ft.

◆ This 1½-story Colonial Revival home begins with a pedimented porch from the Georgian era for a stately effect. The side-loading garage keeps the facade fresh and symmetrical. Columns define the formal dining room while a butler's pantry connects it to the expansive kitchen. The sunny sitting room/breakfast nook lies at the opposite end of the kitchen. The generous great room delights with a window wall, a fireplace and built-ins. The master suite sits at the back with twin walk-in closets leading to the lavish bath. A wealth of undeveloped space is available on the second floor for future use. Please specify basement, crawlspace or slab foundation when ordering.

Design HPT300125
Square Footage: 2,540

L

◆ A gabled stucco archway with over-sized columns emphasizes the arched glass entry of this winsome one-story brick home. Arched windows on either side of the front door add symmetry and style to this pleasing exterior. An arched passage leads to the three family bedrooms and is flanked by twin bookcases and a plant ledge. A large, efficient kitchen shares space with an octagonal breakfast area and a family room with a fireplace. Enter the master bedroom through angled double doors and view the cathedral ceiling. Attention centers immediately on the arched entry to the relaxing master bath and its central whirlpool tub. Please specify crawlspace or slab foundation when ordering.

Width: 70'-0"
Depth: 65'-0"

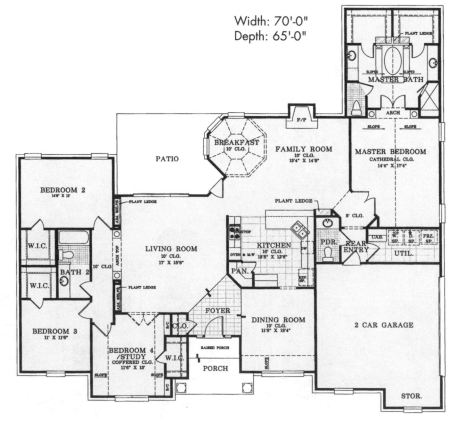

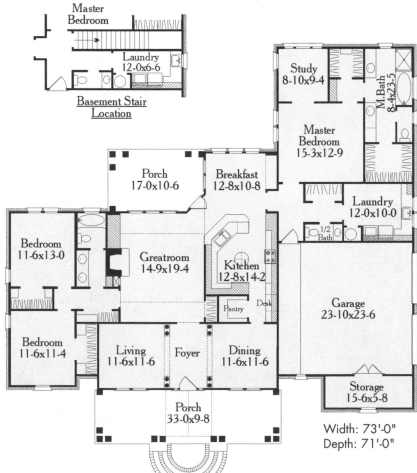

Master
Bedroom

Laundry
12-0x6-6

Basement Stair
Location

Study
8-10x9-4

M.Bath
8-4x23-5

Master
Bedroom
15-3x12-9

Laundry
12-0x10-0

Porch
17-0x10-6

Breakfast
12-8x10-8

1/2
Bath

Bedroom
11-6x13-0

Greatroom
14-9x19-4

Kitchen
12-8x14-2

Garage
23-10x23-6

Pantry

Desk

Bedroom
11-6x11-4

Living
11-6x11-6

Foyer

Dining
11-6x11-6

Storage
15-6x5-8

Porch
33-0x9-8

Width: 73'-0"
Depth: 71'-0"

Design HPT300126
Square Footage: 2,570

◆ European charm cleverly frames this home with keystone lintels, columns on the porch, and a sunburst transom over the door. The columned foyer radiates to the living, dining and great rooms. A fireplace with built-ins sets off the great room. Ribbon windows in the great room, breakfast area and study take full advantage of a backyard view. The master bedroom includes a lavish bath, walk-in closets and a private study. The kitchen is full of helpful amenities, such as a built-in desk, large pantry and snack bar. Two family bedrooms sharing a full compartmented bath finish the plan. Please specify basement, crawlspace or slab foundation when ordering.

Design HPT300127
Square Footage: 2,747

L D

◆ A natty Tudor ranch, this plan combines wood, brick and stucco to create an elegantly appealing exterior. Inside is a thoroughly contemporary floor plan. The open living room and dining area, with more than 410 square feet, features a fireplace, a wall of built-in shelves and a clear view to the outside through diagonally shaped windowpanes. Other highlights include a family room with a raised-hearth fireplace, the U-shaped kitchen and adjacent breakfast nook, an optional bedroom, study or office, and a four-bedroom sleeping wing including a master suite with access to a private terrace.

Width: 91'-4"
Depth: 47'-0"

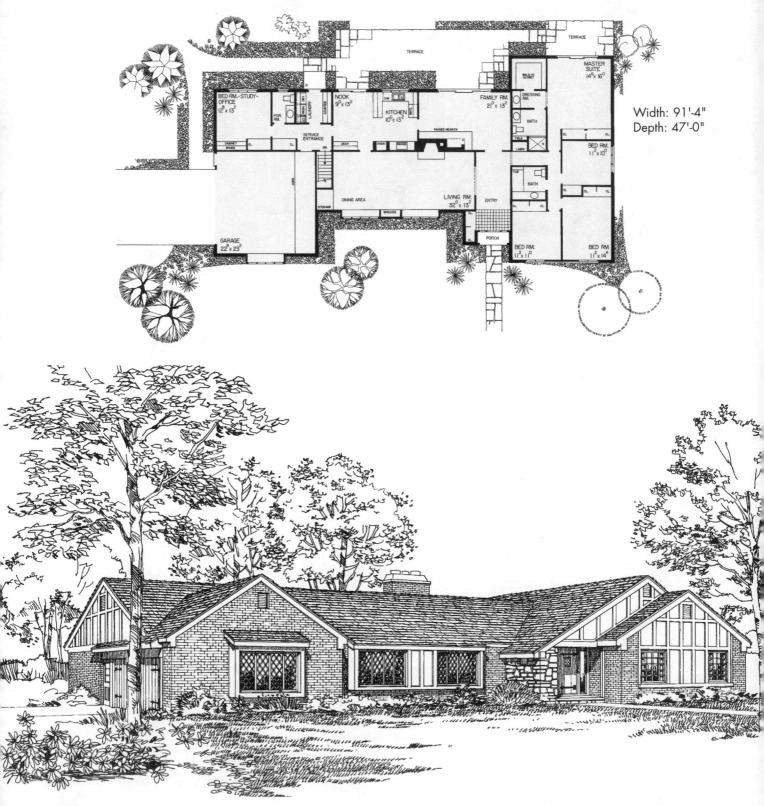

Floor Plan Labels

TERRACE

COUNTRY KITCHEN
14⁰x24⁸

DINING RM.
11⁴x11⁸

LIVING RM.
16⁰x13⁸

MASTER BEDROOM
12⁰x19⁸

HER WALK-IN CLOSET

WHIRLPOOL

VANITY

BATH

GREENHOUSE
7⁰x18⁰

EATING

SLOPED CEILING

HIS WALK-IN CLOSET

SHLV'S

BATH

SNACK BAR

TV, STEREO/VCR EQUIPMENT SPEAKERS, ECT.

SLOPED CEILING

FOYER

CL.

PDR. RM.

CL.

LINEN

POTTING

TOOL BENCH

COOK TOP

REF'S.

WORK ISLAND

PANTRY

WASH RM.

MEDIA RM.
13⁰x15⁴

COVERED PORCH

SEAT

BEDROOM
11⁰x13⁰

BEDROOM
11⁰x12⁸

CLUTTER RM.
13⁰x13⁴

SEWING

CL.

GARAGE
23²x23⁸

STORAGE

FLOWER BOX

Width: 81'-4"
Depth: 76'-0"

QUOTE ONE®
Cost to build? See page 436
to order complete cost estimate
to build this house in your area!

Design HPT300128
Square Footage: 2,758

L D

◆ This comfortable traditional home offers plenty of modern livability. A clutter room off the two-car garage is an ideal space for a workbench, sewing or hobbies. Across the hall, a media room is the perfect place for a stereo, DVD and more. A spacious country kitchen to the right of the greenhouse (great for fresh herbs) is a cozy gathering place for family and friends. Both the formal living room, with its friendly fireplace, and the dining room provide access to the rear grounds. A spacious, amenity-filled master suite features His and Hers walk-in closets, a relaxing whirlpool tub and access to the rear terrace. Two large secondary bedrooms share a full bath.

Design HPT300129
Square Footage: 2,846

L

◆ This Southern Colonial home is distinguished by its columned porch and double dormers. Inside, columns and connecting arches define the angled foyer. The master suite is located away from the other bedrooms for privacy and includes a large master bath and a walk-in closet. Three additional bedrooms are located adjacent to the family room. The kitchen, breakfast area and family room are open—perfect for informal entertaining and family gatherings. The foyer, living room and dining room have twelve-foot ceilings. Ten-foot ceilings are used in the family room, kitchen, breakfast area and master suite to give this home an open, spacious feeling. Please specify crawlspace or slab foundation when ordering.

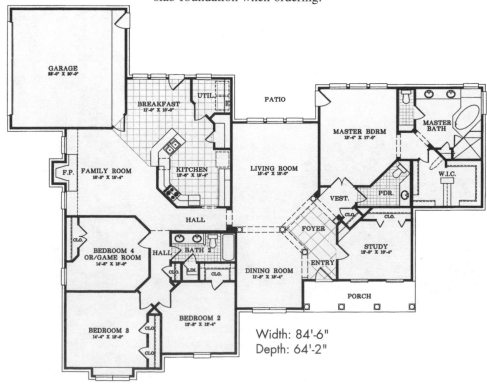

Width: 84'-6"
Depth: 64'-2"

DECK

BREAKFAST
12'-0"x 13'-6"

DN.

KITCHEN
14'-3"x 13'-6"

LAUNDRY
9'-0" X 8'-6"

STORAGE

TWO CAR GARAGE
21'-6"x 27'-6"

GREAT ROOM
20'-6"x 18'-6"

DINING ROOM
13'-6" X 14'-6"

FOYER

STOOP

SITTING
12'-0"x 12'-0"

W.I.C.

MASTER BATH

MASTER SUITE
16'-6"x 15'-0"

W.I.C.

POWDER

BEDROOM NO.3
12'-0"x 12'-0"

BEDROOM NO.2
12'-3"x 14'-0"

BATH

Width: 73'-6"
Depth: 78'-0"

Design HPT300130
Square Footage: 2,770

◆ This English cottage with a cedar shake exterior displays the best qualities of a traditional design. With a window and recessed entry, visitors will feel warmly welcomed. The foyer opens to both the dining room and the great room with its fireplace and built-in cabinetry. Surrounded by windows, the breakfast room opens to a gourmet kitchen and a laundry room conveniently located near the garage entrance. Through double doors at the end of a short hall, the master suite awaits with a tray ceiling and an adjoining sunlit sitting room. The master bath features His and Hers closets, separate vanities, an individual shower and a garden tub with a bay window. This home is designed with a walkout basement foundation.

Design HPT300131

Square Footage: 2,757

Width: 69'-6"
Depth: 68'-8"

◆ French country appointments lend an elegant Old World look to this design. The foyer opens to the well-proportioned dining room, which boasts a twelve-foot ceiling. Two sets of French double doors with transoms open off the living room to the rear porch. The kitchen, breakfast room and family room are open to one another. The fireplace is visible from all these areas and provides a lovely focal point for the room. The master suite features a tray ceiling and a luxury master bath. Please specify basement, crawlspace or slab foundation when ordering.

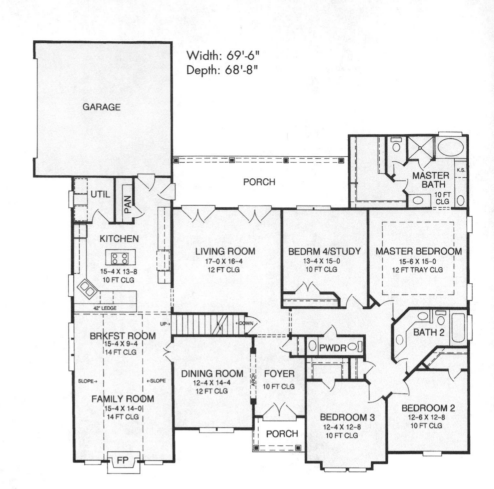

GARAGE

PORCH

MASTER BATH
10 FT CLG
K.S.

UTIL

PAN

KITCHEN
15-4 X 13-8
10 FT CLG

LIVING ROOM
17-0 X 16-4
12 FT CLG

BEDRM 4/STUDY
13-4 X 15-0
10 FT CLG

MASTER BEDROOM
15-6 X 15-0
12 FT TRAY CLG

42" LEDGE

UP

DOWN

BATH 2

BRKFST ROOM
15-4 X 9-4
14 FT CLG

PWDR

SLOPE

SLOPE

FAMILY ROOM
15-4 X 14-0
14 FT CLG

DINING ROOM
12-4 X 14-4
12 FT CLG

FOYER
10 FT CLG

BEDROOM 3
12-4 X 12-8
10 FT CLG

BEDROOM 2
12-6 X 12-8
10 FT CLG

PORCH

FP

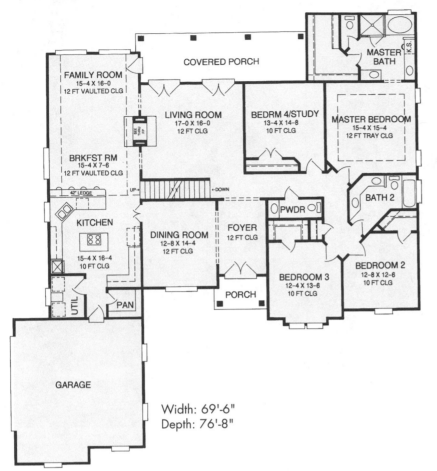

Design HPT300132
Square Footage: 2,745

FAMILY ROOM
15-4 X 16-0
12 FT VAULTED CLG

COVERED PORCH

MASTER
BATH

LIVING ROOM
17-0 X 16-0
12 FT CLG

BEDRM 4/STUDY
13-4 X 14-8
10 FT CLG

MASTER BEDROOM
15-4 X 15-4
12 FT TRAY CLG

BRKFST RM
15-4 X 7-6
12 FT VAULTED CLG

SEE THRU FP

UP

DOWN

42" LEDGE

KITCHEN

15-4 X 16-4
10 FT CLG

PWDR

BATH 2

DINING ROOM
12-8 X 14-4
12 FT CLG

FOYER
12 FT CLG

UTIL

PAN

PORCH

BEDROOM 3
12-4 X 13-6
10 FT CLG

BEDROOM 2
12-8 X 12-6
10 FT CLG

GARAGE

Width: 69'-6"
Depth: 76'-8"

◆ A gentle European charm flavors the facade of this ultra-modern home. The foyer opens to a formal dining room, which leads to the kitchen through privacy doors. Here, a center cooktop island complements wrapping counter space, a walk-in pantry and a snack counter. Casual living space shares a through-fireplace with the formal living room and provides its own access to the rear porch. Clustered sleeping quarters include a well-appointed master suite, two family bedrooms and an additional bedroom which could double as a study. Please specify basement, crawlspace or slab foundation when ordering.

©1993 Donald A. Gardner Architects, Inc. Photography courtesy of Donald A. Gardner Architects, Inc.

Design HPT300133
Square Footage: 2,663
Bonus Room: 653 sq. ft.

◆ This home features large arched windows, round columns, a covered porch and brick veneer siding. The arched window in the clerestory above the entrance provides natural light to the interior. The great room boasts a cathedral ceiling, a fireplace and built-in cabinets and bookshelves. Sliding glass doors lead to the sun room. The L-shaped kitchen serves the dining room, the breakfast area and the great room. The master suite, with a fireplace, uses a private passage to the deck and its spa. Three additional bedrooms—one could serve as a study—are at the other end of the house for privacy.

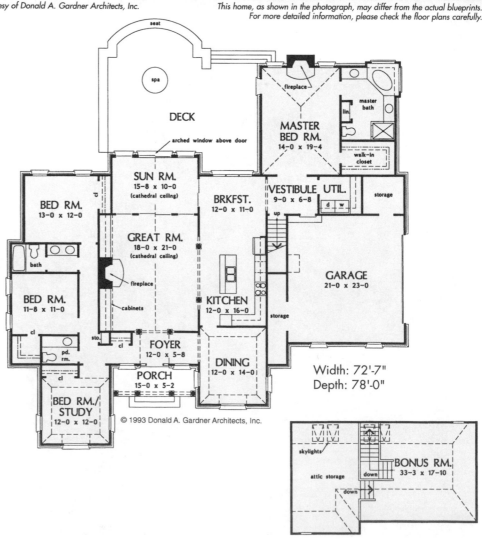

© 1993 Donald A. Gardner Architects, Inc.

Width: 72'-7"
Depth: 78'-0"

DECK

seat

spa

SUN RM.
15-8 × 10-0
(cathedral ceiling)

BRKFST.
12-0 × 12-0

MASTER BED RM.
14-0 × 19-4

fireplace

master bath

walk-in closet

storage

BED RM.
13-0 × 11-0

cl

cabinets

fireplace

bath

BED RM.
11-10 × 10-0

GREAT RM.
18-0 × 19-0
(cathedral ceiling)

KITCHEN
12-0 × 12-8

UTIL.
6-6 × 8-0

d
w

GARAGE
22-2 × 21-0

closet

pd. rm.

cl

lin

cl

FOYER
11-8 × 5-8

storage

cl

BED RM./
STUDY
12-0 × 11-0

PORCH

DINING
12-0 × 13-2

Width: 76'-11"
Depth: 71'-7"

master bedroom

down   cl

kitchen

storage

garage

storage

Basment Stair Option

Design HPT300134
Square Footage: 2,526

◆ A covered front porch, an arched-window dormer and brick detailing all combine to give this home plenty of curb appeal. A cozy fireplace and built-in cabinets accent the great room. The island kitchen is partially open to the great room, maintaining a spacious feeling. The sun room and breakfast area will surely brighten each day. The lovely master suite has a romantic fireplace and a pampering bath. Three bedrooms—or two with a study—one full bath and a powder room complete the plan.

Design HPT300135

Square Footage: 2,517

L

Width: 69'-0"
Depth: 63'-6"

◆ A graceful stucco arch supported by columns gives this home instant curb appeal. Stucco quoins are used to further accent its traditional brick finish. Inside, the angled foyer steps down into the living room. Step down again to enter the formal dining room. The kitchen features a coffered ceiling and is conveniently grouped with a bayed breakfast room and the family room, the perfect place for informal gatherings. Upon entering the master suite, the master bath becomes the focal point. Columns flank the entry to this luxurious bath with a whirlpool tub as its centerpiece, as well as His and Hers walk-in closets, a separate shower and twin vanities. Please specify crawlspace or slab foundation when ordering.

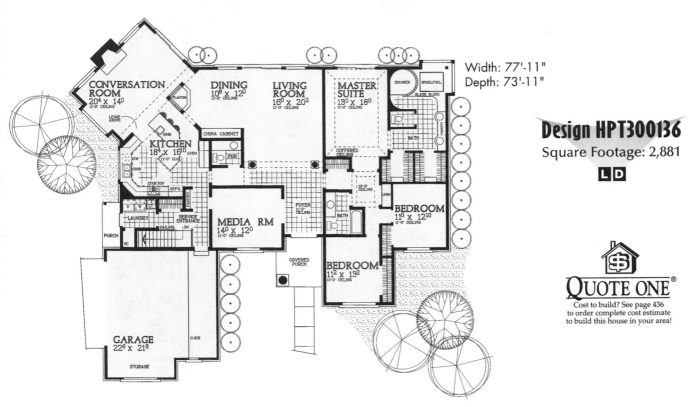

CONVERSATION
ROOM
20⁴ x 14⁰
11'-0" CEILING

LEDGE
ABOVE

PLANTER

DINING
10⁸ x 12⁰
11'-0" CEILING

LIVING
ROOM
16⁰ x 20²
11'-0" CEILING

MASTER
SUITE
13⁰ x 18⁰
11'-0" CEILING

SHOWER
WHIRLPOOL
GLASS BLOCK

BATH
VANITY

KITCHEN
18⁴ x 16¹⁰

CHINA CABINET

OVEN

SINK

PDR

COFFERED
CEILING

COOKTOP

REFG

PLANTER

DW W T
SINK

LAUNDRY

SERVICE
ENTRANCE

MEDIA RM
14⁰ x 12⁰
11'-0" CEILING

FOYER
11'-0"
CEILING

10'-0"
CEILING

BATH

BEDROOM
11⁰ x 12¹⁰
11'-0" CEILING

PORCH

SC

RAILING

DN

COVERED
PORCH

BEDROOM
11² x 13²
11'-0" CEILING

GARAGE
22⁶ x 21⁸

CURB

STORAGE

Width: 77'-11"
Depth: 73'-11"

Design HPT300136
Square Footage: 2,881

L D

QUOTE ONE®
Cost to build? See page 436
to order complete cost estimate
to build this house in your area!

◆ The high, massive hipped roof of this home creates an impressive facade, while varying roof planes and projecting gables further enhance appeal. A central foyer routes traffic efficiently to the sleeping, formal and informal zones of the house. Note the sliding glass doors that provide access to outdoor living facilities. A built-in china cabinet and planter unit are fine decor features. In the angular kitchen, a high ceiling and efficient work patterning set the pace. The conversation room may act as a multi-purpose room. Sleeping quarters take off in the spacious master suite, with a tray ceiling and sliding doors to the rear yard. Two sizable bedrooms accommodate family members or guests.

Design HPT300137
Square Footage: 2,670

◆ The lovely brick facade of this comforting cottage is decorated with shutters, arched and straight lintels, and a transom with sidelights on the entry. At the center of the house, the great room holds a fireplace with built-ins and a ribbon of bright windows. The French doors in the breakfast nook open to the rear porch—perfect for an outdoor barbecue! A roomy master suite includes a walk-in closet over seventeen feet in length, a garden tub, twin vanity sinks and a compartmented shower and toilet. Three secondary bedrooms and lots of storage give this house long-lasting appeal with any family. Please specify crawlspace or slab foundation when ordering.

Width: 70'-6"
Depth: 72'-4"

Porch
13-0x10-0

Breakfast
11-5x14-0

Storage
8-2x9-10

Laun.
7-5x9-10

1/2
Bath

Kitchen
11-5x12-0

Greatroom
17-3x19-6

Garage
21-0x26-0

Dining
11-5x15-2

Foyer

Bedroom
11-5x13-6

Walk-in Closet

M.Bath

Master
Bedroom
17-10x15-6

Bedroom
15-6x11-6

Bath

Bedroom
11-7x13-6

Design HPT300138
Square Footage: 2,547

◆ A brick exterior, with traditional arch details and elegant rooflines, defines this stately home. Formal dining and living rooms open through arches from the front entry foyer. Chefs can utilize their talents in the spacious kitchen with its center island cooktop, abundant counter space and light-filled breakfast nook. The family room is separated from the kitchen by a snack counter. The private master suite is separated from family bedrooms and offers a walk-in closet and luxurious bath with a whirlpool spa, oversized shower, twin vanities and a compartmented toilet. Three additional bedrooms allow design flexibility—use one as a guest room, den or home office.

Width: 74'-8"
Depth: 56'-8"

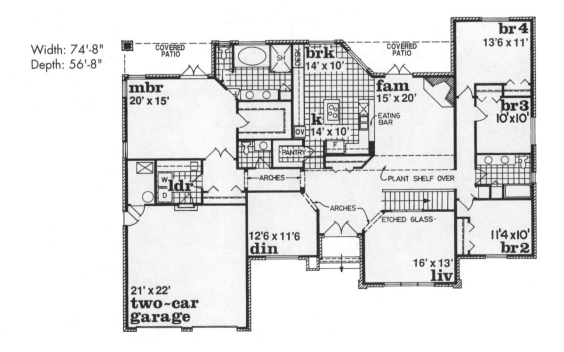

Design HPT300139
Square Footage: 2,502

◆ Cottage quaintness and Victorian accents lend a timeless style to this family design. The covered front entry porch welcomes you inside to a foyer open to a combined living room/dining area, defined by columns. Two sets of double doors lead to the expansive rear porch. The kitchen, open to the dining room, features an island workstation and a casual breakfast nook. Two family bedrooms share a hall bath with the quiet office/study. The master suite provides private access to the rear porch, His and Hers walk-in closets and a spacious bath.

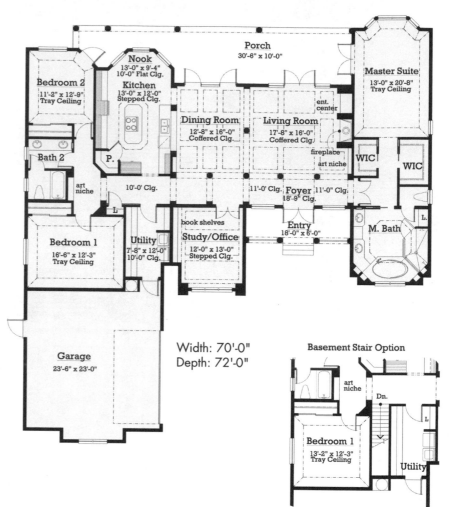

Width: 70'-0"
Depth: 72'-0"

Contemporary One-Story Homes

Design HPT300140
Square Footage: 3,110

◆ If you have an active growing family, chances are that they will want their new home to relate to the outdoors. This distinctive design puts a premium on private outdoor living. And you don't have to install a swimming pool to get the most enjoyment from this home. Note the fine zoning of the plan—each area has sliding glass doors to provide an unrestricted view. Three bedrooms plus a study are serviced by three baths. The family and gathering rooms provide two great living areas and the kitchen is most efficient. Of special note is the master suite with dressing room, two sinks and linen closet.

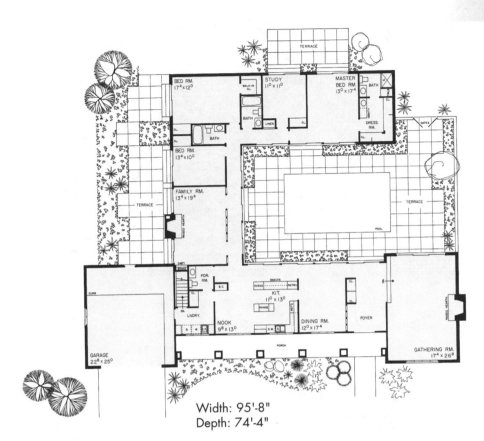

Width: 95'-8"
Depth: 74'-4"

Design HPT300141
Square Footage: 2,626

L

◆ Frank Lloyd Wright had a knack for enhancing the environment with the homes he designed. This adaptation reflects his purest Prairie style complemented by a brick exterior, a multitude of windows and a low-slung hip roof. The foyer introduces a gallery wall to display your artwork. To the right, an archway leads to a formal dining room lined with a wall of windows. Nearby, the spacious kitchen features an island snack bar. The two-story family/great room provides an ideal setting for formal or informal gatherings. If philosophical discussions heat up, they can be continued in the open courtyard. The left wing contains the sleeping quarters and an office/den. The private master suite includes a sitting area, a walk-in closet and a lavish master bath.

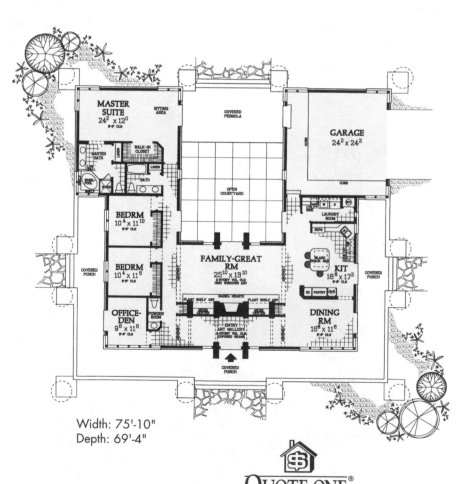

Width: 75'-10"
Depth: 69'-4"

QUOTE ONE®
Cost to build? See page 436
to order complete cost estimate
to build this house in your area!

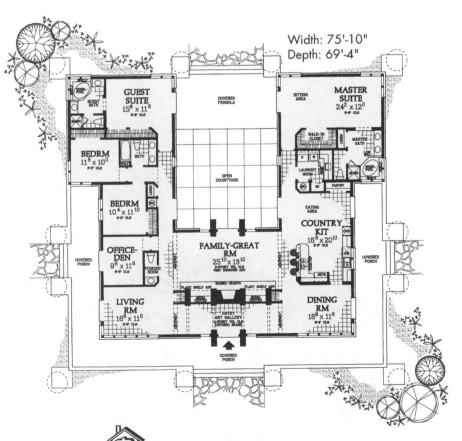

Width: 75'-10"
Depth: 69'-4"

GUEST SUITE
15⁸ x 11⁶

BEDRM
11⁸ x 10⁰

BEDRM
10⁴ x 11¹⁰

OFFICE-DEN
9⁶ x 11⁶

LIVING RM
18⁸ x 11⁶

COVERED PORCH

COVERED PERGOLA

OPEN COURTYARD

FAMILY-GREAT RM
25¹⁰ x 13¹⁰
2-STORY VOL. CLG.
HIGH WINDOWS ABV.

RAISED HEARTH

ENTRY
1-STORY VOL. CLG.
EXPOSED BEAMS

ART GALLERY

COVERED PORCH

SITTING AREA

MASTER SUITE
24² x 12⁰

WALK-IN CLOSET

MASTER BATH

LAUNDRY ROOM

PANTRY

EATING AREA

COUNTRY KIT
16⁸ x 20¹⁰

DINING RM
18⁸ x 11⁶

COVERED PORCH

Design HPT300142
Square Footage: 3,278

L

◆ Form follows function as dual gallery halls lead from formal areas to split sleeping quarters in this Prairie adaptation. At the heart of the plan, the grand-scale great room offers a raised-hearth fireplace framed by built-in cabinetry and plant shelves. Open planning combines the country kitchen with an informal dining space, and adds an island counter with snack bar. A lavish master suite harbors a sitting area with private access to the covered pergola. The secondary sleeping wing includes a spacious guest suite. A fifth bedroom or home office offers its own door to the wraparound porch.

QUOTE ONE®
Cost to build? See page 436
to order complete cost estimate
to build this house in your area!

145

Design HPT300143
Square Footage: 1,835

D

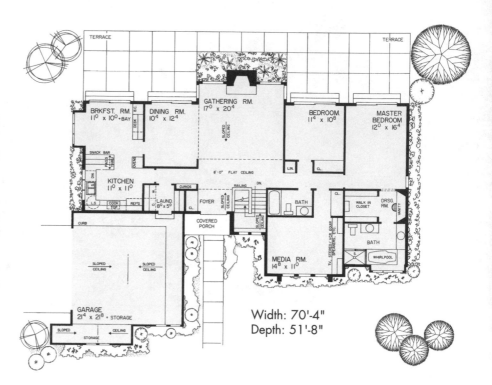

◆ This smart design features a multi-gabled roof and vertical windows. A covered porch leads through a foyer to a gathering room with a fireplace, a sloped ceiling and access to the rear terrace. A modern kitchen with a snack bar features a pass-through to the breakfast room. The dining room is nearby. A media room in the bedroom wing offers a quiet, private area for enjoying music or surfing the Internet. The master suite includes its own dressing area and a whirlpool tub. A large garage includes an extra storage room.

Width: 70'-4"
Depth: 51'-8"

◆ This elegant one-story contemporary is designed for sites that slope slightly to the front. As a consequence, the major rooms of the home are sunken just a few steps from the grand entry foyer. The large gathering room is in line with the entry doors and has sliding glass doors to the terrace and a through fireplace to the study. The dining room is nearby, with sliding glass doors to a covered porch. The L-shaped kitchen and breakfast nook share the use of a patio just outside the nook. For real convenience, the study has built-ins and a powder room close at hand. Amenities in the master suite include a walk-in closet, spa tub and double sinks. Family bedrooms share a full bath with garden tub and double sinks.

Width: 85'-10"
Depth: 72'-4"

Design HPT300145
Square Footage: 2,231

◆ This sun-oriented design was created to face the south, allowing the morning sun to brighten the living and dining rooms and the adjacent terrace. During the winter, a glass roof and walls on the garden room will provide solar heat—and relief from high energy bills. Solar shades allow you to adjust the amount of light allowed in. The kitchen has a snack bar and a serving counter to the dining room. The breakfast room and laundry area are convenient to the kitchen. The master bath includes a skylight, garden tub and separate shower. Two nearby family bedrooms share a full bath.

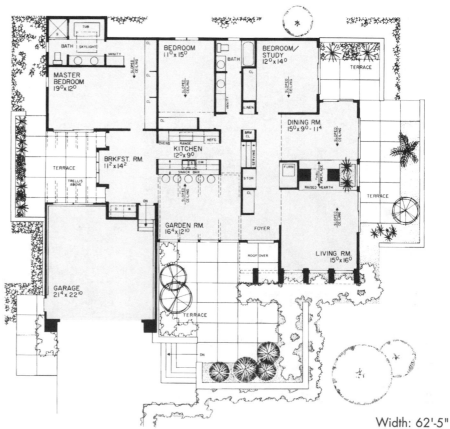

Width: 62'-5"
Depth: 62'-0"

Design HPT300146

Square Footage: 1,824

D

◆ A greenhouse area off the dining room and living room provides a cheerful focal point for this comfortable three-bedroom home. The spacious living room features a cozy fireplace and a sloped ceiling. In addition to the dining room, there's a less formal breakfast room just off the modern kitchen. The kitchen and breakfast area look out onto a front terrace. Stairs just off the foyer lead down to a recreation room in the basement. The master bedroom suite opens to a terrace. A mudroom and a washroom off the garage allow rear entry to the house during inclement weather.

Width: 80'-4"
Depth: 43'-0"

QUOTE ONE®
Cost to build? See page 436
to order complete cost estimate
to build this house in your area!

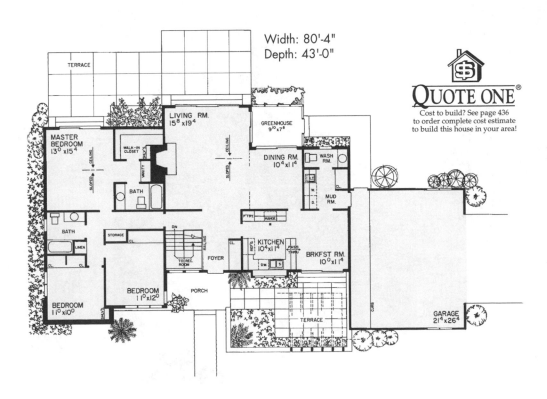

Design HPT300147
Square Footage: 2,459

◆ Indoor-outdoor living will be enjoyed to its fullest in this rambling one-story contemporary plan. Each of the rear rooms in this design, excluding the study, has access to a terrace or porch. Even the front breakfast room has access to a private dining patio. The covered porch off the family, dining and living rooms has a sloped ceiling and skylights. A built-in barbecue and storage room is found on the second covered porch. Inside, there is exceptional livability. The master suite is especially nice, with a huge walk-in closet and grand bath. Note the through-fireplace that the living room shares with the study. A built-in etagere is nearby. There is even extra storage in the three-car garage.

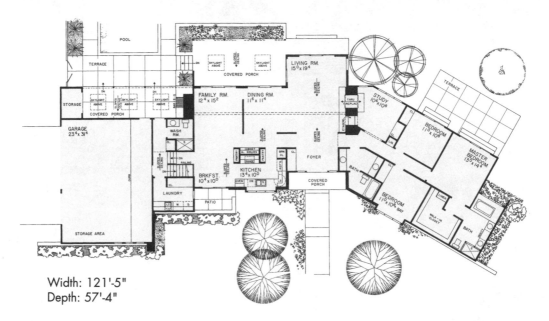

Width: 121'-5"
Depth: 57'-4"

Design HPT300148
Square Footage: 2,133

◆ The diagonal nature of this contemporary design makes it a versatile choice for a variety of lot arrangements. Inside, it is quite open visually. From the entry are exquisite views of the great room, with its fireplace flanked by windows, and of the stunning dining room. An island kitchen, with a snack bar, planning desk and walk-in pantry, adjoins the breakfast area. In the sleeping wing, a romantic master suite is accented with yard access, a whirlpool tub and a tiered ceiling. Two family bedrooms share a full hall bath. The three-car garage holds extra storage space and allows access to the house through the mud/laundry room.

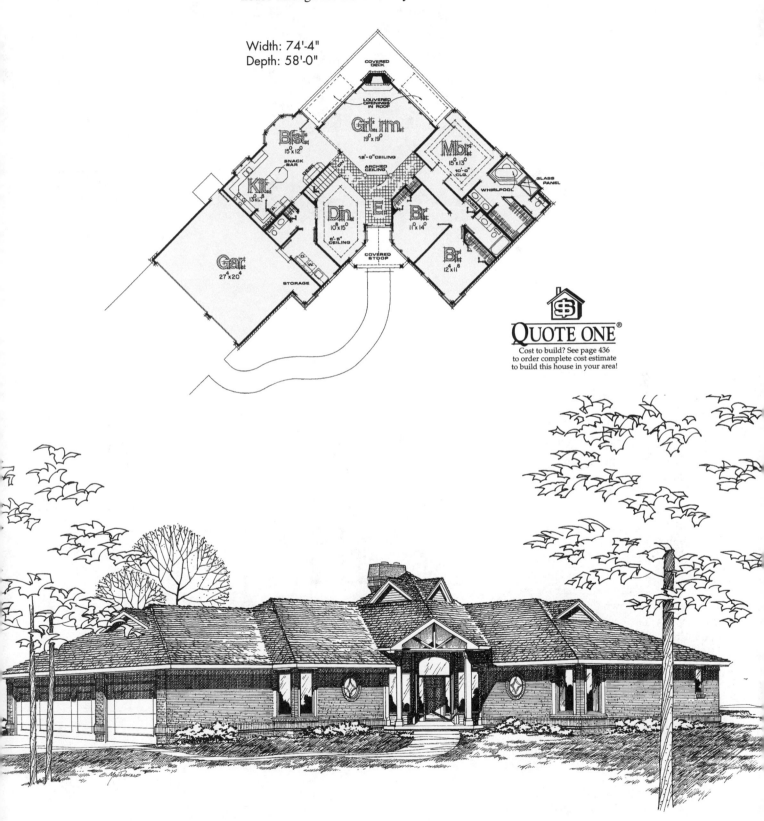

Width: 74'-4"
Depth: 58'-0"

QUOTE ONE®
Cost to build? See page 436
to order complete cost estimate
to build this house in your area!

Design HPT300149
Square Footage: 2,734

L D

◆ Clean, contemporary lines define this grand one-story home. Double doors open onto a sunlit foyer that leads to a sunken gathering room straight ahead. Thoughtful planning allows a see-through fireplace to share its warmth with the nearby study. Adjoining the gathering room is a dining room that opens onto a covered porch, perfect for dining alfresco. The master bedroom is located to the rear for privacy and opens to its own private terrace. Two walk-in closets, sized for frequent shoppers, share space with a master bath designed for pampering. Here, a bumped-out whirlpool tub invites relaxation. Other amenities include dual sinks, a separate shower and a compartmented toilet. Two family bedrooms located to the front of the plan share a full bath.

Width: 82'-6"
Depth: 81'-10"

QUOTE ONE®
Cost to build? See page 436
to order complete cost estimate
to build this house in your area!

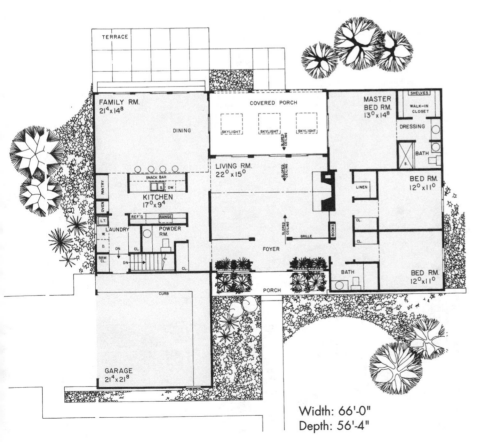

TERRACE

FAMILY RM.
21⁴x14⁸

COVERED PORCH

MASTER
BED RM.
13⁰x14⁸

SHELVES

WALK-IN
CLOSET

DRESSING

BATH

DINING

SKYLIGHT   SKYLIGHT   SKYLIGHT

SNACK BAR

LIVING RM.
22⁰x15⁰

BED RM.
12⁰x11⁰

LINEN

KITCHEN
17⁰x9⁴

OVEN

REF'G   RANGE

LAUNDRY

POWDER
RM.

FOYER

BOOKS

GRILLE

CL

CL

BATH

BED RM.
12⁰x11⁰

DN

DN

CURB

PORCH

GARAGE
21⁴x21⁸

Width: 66'-0"
Depth: 56'-4"

Design HPT300150
Square Footage: 2,075

◆ Enter this hip-roofed contemporary home through the double doors and you'll immediately appreciate the sloped-ceilinged living room with fireplace. It has sliding glass doors to the covered porch at the rear, brightened by skylights above. The family room also has sliding glass doors—they lead to a rear terrace. A galley-style kitchen has a snack bar to share with the family room and its dining space. Sleeping quarters consist of two family bedrooms and a master suite. The master bath features a walk-in closet and bath with dressing area. Family bedrooms share a full bath—note the walk-in linen closet. A two-car garage is accessed through the service area near the kitchen.

Design HPT300151

Square Footage: 1,566

L D

◆ This outstanding contemporary design features a recessed front entry with a covered front porch. The rear gathering room has a sloped ceiling, a raised-hearth fireplace, sliding glass doors to the terrace and a snack bar with a pass-through to the kitchen. The formal dining room is convenient to the kitchen. Three bedrooms and two closely located baths are in the sleeping wing. This plan includes details for the construction of an optional basement.

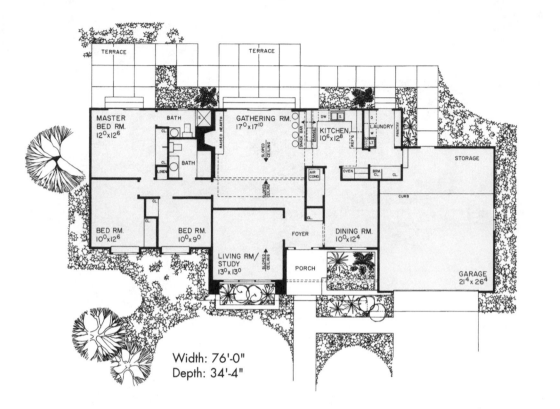

Width: 76'-0"
Depth: 34'-4"

OPTIONAL BASEMENT PLAN

QUOTE ONE®

Cost to build? See page 436
to order complete cost estimate
to build this house in your area!

Design HPT300152

Square Footage: 1,089

◆ Brick and wood siding work in combination on the exterior of this cozy one-story home. The entry is protected by a covered porch and opens to a foyer with a half-wall separating it from the living room, which features a large window overlooking the front porch. A fireplace warms this gathering space in cold weather. The U-shaped kitchen has abundant counter space and is adjacent to the dining room for convenience. Down a few steps is the handy laundry area with stairs to the basement and access to the single-car garage. Three bedrooms share a bath that includes a soaking tub. The basement may be developed in the future to add more bedrooms or to create additional gathering space.

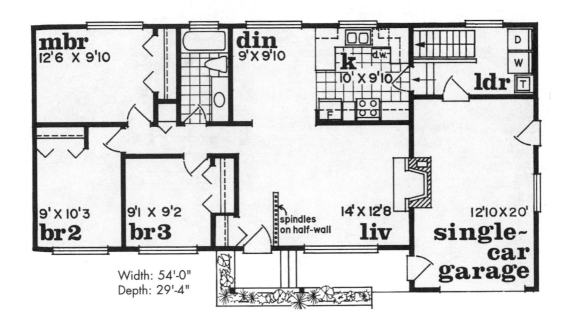

mbr
12'6 X 9'10

din
9' X 9'10

k
10' X 9'10

D
W
ldr
T

br2
9' X 10'3

br3
9'1 X 9'2

spindles on half-wall

liv
14 X 12'8

single-car garage
12'10 X 20'

Width: 54'-0"
Depth: 29'-4"

Design HPT300153
Square Footage: 2,652

L **D**

◆ This impressive one-story home has numerous fine features that will assure the best in contemporary living. The sunken gathering room and dining room share an impressive sloped ceiling; a series of three sliding glass doors provide access to the terrace. The family room, with a cozy fireplace, is ideal for informal entertaining. The kitchen features an efficient work island, pantry and built-in desk. The master suite opens to the rear terrace and the bath offers a separate step-up tub and shower. Two additional bedrooms are located at the front of the home.

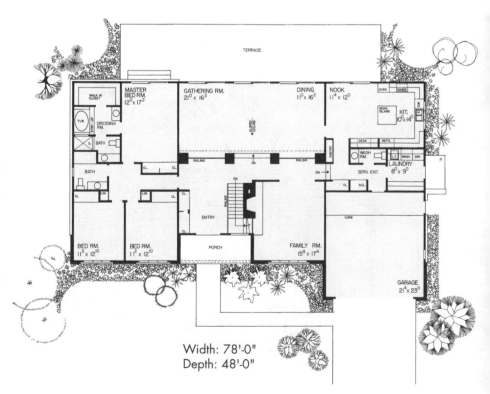

Width: 78'-0"
Depth: 48'-0"

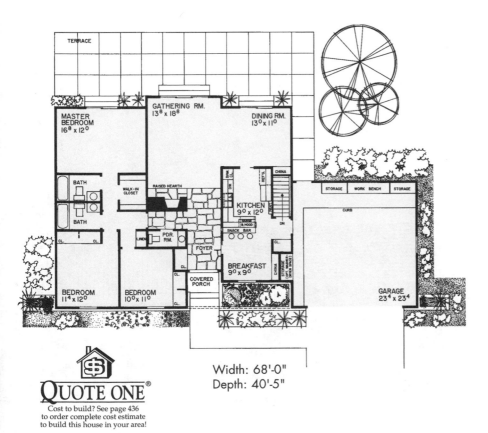

TERRACE

MASTER BEDROOM 16⁸ x 12⁰

GATHERING RM. 13⁸ x 18⁶

DINING RM. 13⁰ x 11⁰

BATH

WALK-IN CLOSET

RAISED HEARTH

CHINA

KITCHEN 9⁰ x 12⁰

BATH

CL. CL.

LINEN

POR. RM.

FOYER

SNACK BAR

CL.

STORAGE WORK BENCH STORAGE

CURB

BREAKFAST 9⁰ x 9⁰

CHINA

STORAGE (OPT. WASHER-DRYER SPACE)

BEDROOM 11⁴ x 12⁰

BEDROOM 10⁰ x 11⁰

COVERED PORCH

CL.

GARAGE 23⁴ x 23⁴

Width: 68'-0"
Depth: 40'-5"

QUOTE ONE®
Cost to build? See page 436
to order complete cost estimate
to build this house in your area!

Design HPT300154
Square Footage: 1,589

L D

◆ The rustic exterior of this one-story home features vertical wood siding. The entry foyer is floored with flagstone and leads to the three areas of the plan: the sleeping area, the living area and the work center. The sleeping area features three bedrooms. The master bedroom utilizes sliding glass doors to the rear terrace. The living area, consisting of the gathering room and a dining room, also enjoys access to the terrace. The work center is efficiently planned. It houses the kitchen with a snack bar, the breakfast room with a built-in china cabinet and stairs to the basement. This is a very livable plan exemplified by such special amenities as a raised-hearth fireplace and a walk-in closet in the master bedroom.

Design HPT300155
Square Footage: 1,298

◆ Traditional charm with an outstanding layout describes this low-cost, one-story ranch home. A covered front porch welcomes visitors. Three bedrooms or two bedrooms and a study are accompanied by two full baths. An expansive living room, a formal dining room and an eat-in kitchen make up the living area of this home. Livability may be enhanced by the completion of an optional standard or double-size deck, a fireplace in the living room, and a two-car garage.

Width: 52'-0"
Depth: 44'-5"

Basic Plan

Enhanced Plan

◆ This three-bedroom ranch home contains many spacious features. It includes a full-size bath in the master bedroom and a shared bath for the secondary bedrooms. The dining room and living room combine to create a spacious formal or informal gathering area. A two-car garage, a standard deck, decorative louvers and a centrally located fireplace are optional. The blueprints for this home show how to build both the basic version and the enhanced, upgraded version.

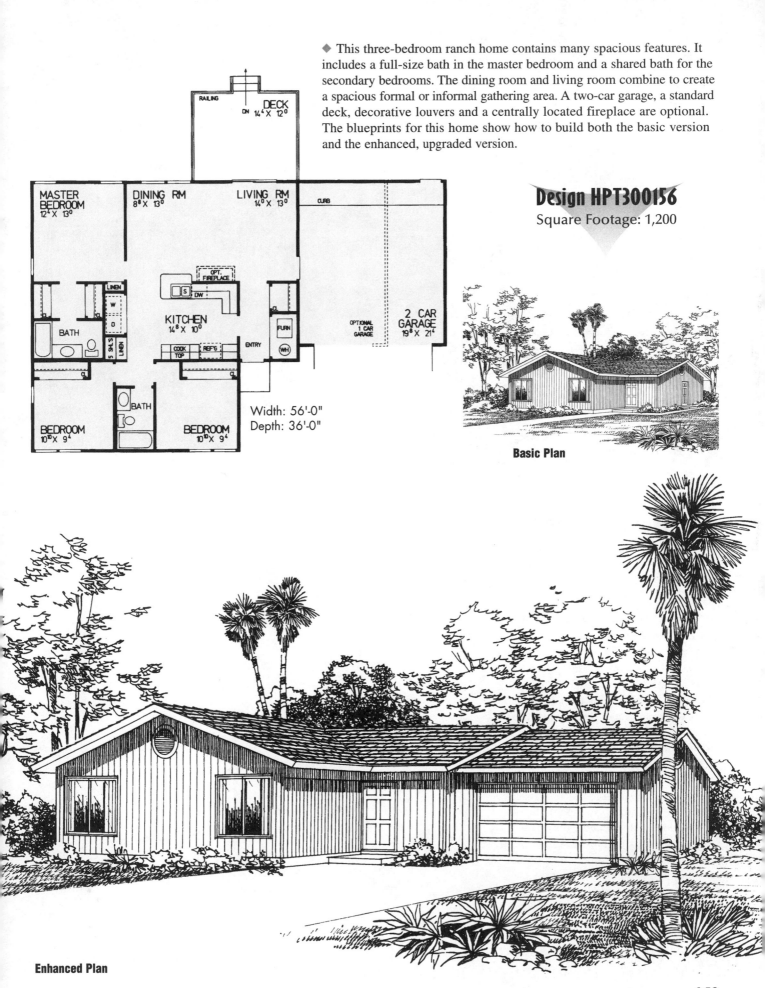

RAILING

DECK
DN 14⁴ X 12⁰

MASTER
BEDROOM
12⁴ X 13⁰

DINING RM
8⁸ X 13⁰

LIVING RM
14⁰ X 13⁰

CURB

LINEN

W
D

BATH

S SHLS LINEN

OPT.
FIREPLACE

S DW

KITCHEN
14⁸ X 10⁰

CL

FURN

OPTIONAL
1 CAR
GARAGE

2 CAR
GARAGE
19⁸ X 21⁴

COOK
TOP

REF'G

ENTRY

WH

BATH

BEDROOM
10¹⁰ X 9⁴

BEDROOM
10¹⁰ X 9⁴

Width: 56'-0"
Depth: 36'-0"

Design HPT300156
Square Footage: 1,200

Basic Plan

Enhanced Plan

Design HPT300157
Square Footage: 1,862

◆ The extension of the wide overhanging roof of this distinctive home provides shelter for the walkway to the front door. A raised brick planter adds appeal to the outstanding exterior design. The living patterns offered by this plan are delightfully different, yet extremely practical. Notice the separation of the master bedroom from the other two bedrooms. While assuring an extra measure of quiet privacy for the parents, this master bedroom location may be ideal for a live-in relative. Locating the kitchen in the middle of the plan frees up valuable outside wall space and leads to interesting planning. The front living room is sunken for dramatic appeal and need not have any cross-room traffic. The utility room houses the laundry and the heating and cooling equipment.

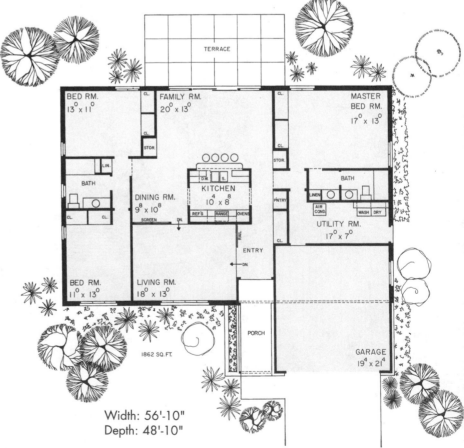

TERRACE

BED RM. 13⁰ x 11⁰

FAMILY RM. 20⁰ x 13⁰

MASTER BED RM. 17⁰ x 13⁰

BATH

KITCHEN 10⁸ x 8⁴

BATH

DINING RM. 9⁸ x 10⁸

UTILITY RM. 17⁰ x 7⁰

BED RM. 11⁰ x 13⁰

LIVING RM. 18⁰ x 13⁰

ENTRY

PORCH

GARAGE 19⁴ x 21⁴

1862 SQ. FT.

Width: 56'-10"
Depth: 48'-10"

Design HPT300158
Square Footage: 2,739

L

◆ This spacious one-story home has a classic French country hip roof. Beyond the covered porch is an octagonal foyer. All of the living areas overlook the rear yard. Features include a fireplace in the living room, a skylight in the dining room and a second set of sliding glass doors in the family room leading to a covered porch. An island cooktop and other built-ins are featured in the roomy kitchen. Adjacent is the breakfast room which can be used for informal dining. The four bedrooms and the baths are clustered in one wing. Bay windows brighten the master bedroom, the breakfast room and the three-car garage.

Width: 91'-8"
Depth: 52'-0"

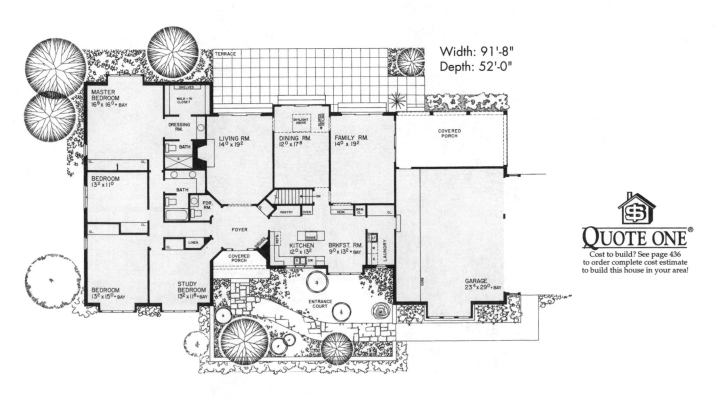

QUOTE ONE®
Cost to build? See page 436
to order complete cost estimate
to build this house in your area!

161

Design HPT300159
Square Footage: 1,530

LD

◆ This charming one-story traditional design offers plenty of livability in a compact size. Thoughtful zoning puts all sleeping areas to one side of the house, away from household activity in the living and service areas. The home includes a spacious gathering room with a sloped ceiling, in addition to a formal dining room and a separate breakfast room. There's also a handy pass-through between the breakfast room and the large, efficient kitchen. The laundry room is strategically located adjacent to the garage and the breakfast/kitchen areas for handy access. The master bedroom enjoys a private bath and a walk-in closet. A third bedroom just off the foyer can double as a sizable study.

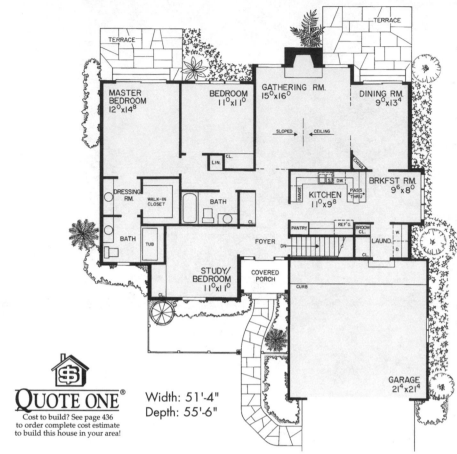

QUOTE ONE®
Cost to build? See page 436 to order complete cost estimate to build this house in your area!

Width: 51'-4"
Depth: 55'-6"

Design HPT300160

Square Footage: 1,754

D

◆ This inviting U-shaped western ranch adaptation offers outstanding living potential behind its double front doors. In only 1,754 square feet there are three bedrooms and 2½ baths. The formal living room is open to the dining area and offers a raised-hearth fireplace and a sloped ceiling. The functional kitchen features an adjacent breakfast nook and has easy access to the informal family room. A rear terrace stretches the width of the home and is accessible from the master bedroom, living room and family room. Stairs lead to a basement which may be developed at a later time.

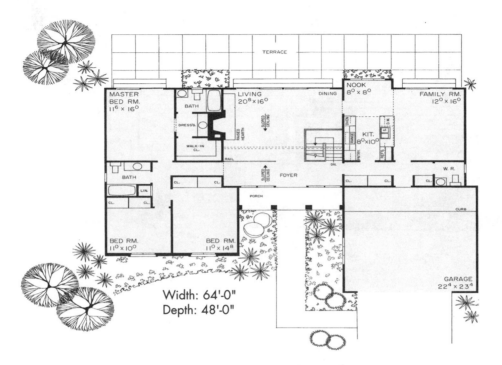

Width: 64'-0"
Depth: 48'-0"

Design HPT300161

Square Footage: 1,632

L

◆ A sun space highlights this passive solar design. It features access from the kitchen, the dining room and the garage. It will be a great place to enjoy meals because of its location. Three skylights highlight the interior—in the kitchen, laundry and master bath. An air-locked vestibule helps this design's energy efficiency. Interior livability is excellent. The living/dining room rises with a sloped ceiling and enjoys a fireplace and two sets of sliding glass doors to the terrace. Three bedrooms are in the sleeping wing. The master bedroom will delight with its private bath with a luxurious whirlpool tub.

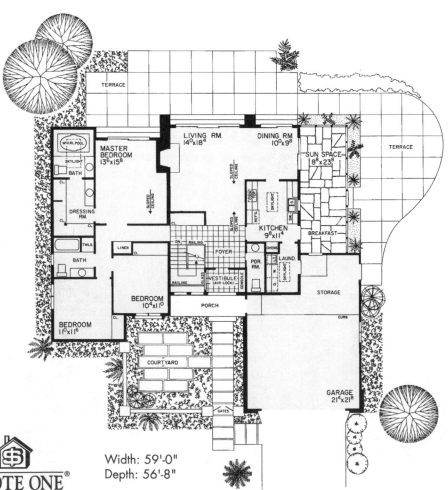

Width: 59'-0"
Depth: 56'-8"

Width: 56'-0"
Depth: 72'-0"

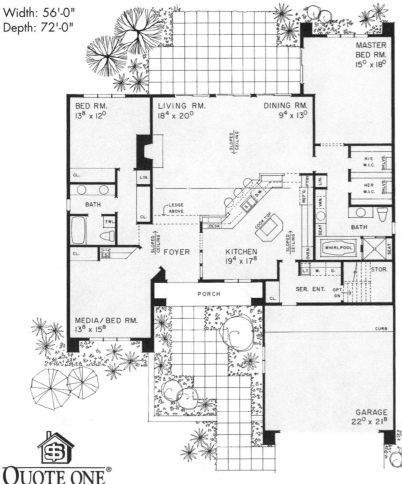

BED RM.
13⁸ x 12⁰

LIVING RM.
18⁴ x 20⁰

DINING RM.
9⁴ x 13⁰

MASTER
BED RM.
15⁰ x 18⁰

CL.

LIN.

SLOPED CEILING

HIS
W.I.C.

SHLVS.

HER
W.I.C.

SHLVS.

BATH

CL.

LEDGE
ABOVE

CL.

REF.

PTRY.

LIN.

VAN.

SEAT

BATH

TWL.

SLOPED CEILING

DESK

COOK TOP

SLOPED CEILING

OVEN

WHIRLPOOL

WHIRLPOOL

SEAT

CL.

FOYER

KITCHEN
19⁴ x 17⁸

LT.

W.

D.

STOR.

SEAT

MEDIA/BED RM.
13⁸ x 15⁸

PORCH

CL.

SER. ENT.

OPT.
DN

CURB

GARAGE
22⁰ x 21⁸

Design HPT300162
Square Footage: 2,189

L

◆ Simplicity is the key to the stylish good looks of this home's facade. Inside, the kitchen opens directly off the foyer and contains an island counter and a work counter with eating space on the living area side. The master bedroom sports sliding glass doors to the terrace. Its dressing area is enhanced with double walk-in closets and lavatories. A whirlpool tub and seated shower are additional amenities. Two family bedrooms are found on the opposite side of the house.

Design HPT300163

Square Footage: 1,997

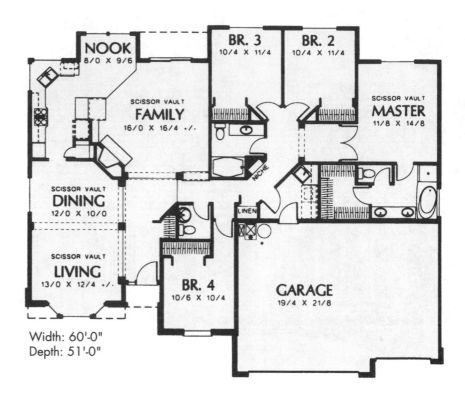

◆ Terrific views and open planning are highlights of this one-story design. Columns take the place of walls to create an open arrangement of the dining, family and living rooms. The angled kitchen is situated on the left, centrally located between the dining room and the sunny breakfast nook. The hallway to the right of the entry leads to the family bedrooms and the master suite. The three family bedrooms share a full bath while the master suite enjoys a lavish private bath.

Width: 60'-0"
Depth: 51'-0"

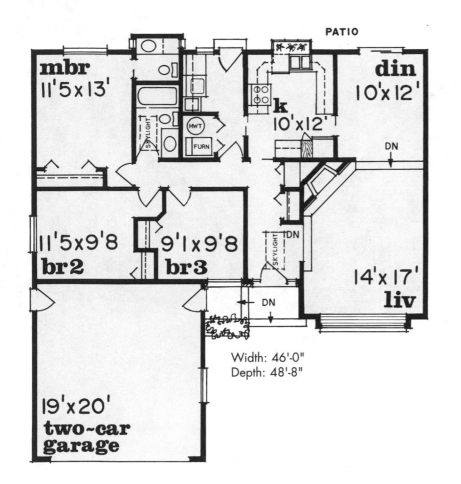

mbr
11'5 x 13'

br2
11'5 x 9'8

br3
9'1 x 9'8

k
10' x 12'

din
10' x 12'

liv
14' x 17'

PATIO

SKYLIGHT

HWT

FURN

DN

DN

DN

SKYLIGHT

**19' x 20'
two-car
garage**

Width: 46'-0"
Depth: 48'-8"

Design HPT300164
Square Footage: 1,289

◆ This contemporary bungalow offers a skylit foyer and leads down a few steps on the right to the sunken living room with corner fireplace. A box-bay window allows for room-enhancing natural light. The nearby dining room is appointed with sliding glass doors to the rear patio. A U-shaped kitchen features a window over the sink and accesses a nearby laundry room. Bedrooms include a master suite with half-bath and two family bedrooms sharing a skylit full bath. A two-car garage sits in front of the bedrooms to shield them from street noise.

Design HPT300165
Square Footage: 2,394

◆ This traditional home is great for any family. Right off the foyer are the open living and dining rooms, defined by columns. French doors open to a nearby den, which can be converted into a small bedroom as well. The island kitchen, with adaptable base cabinets and a pantry, enjoys an open floor plan which features a massive family room with a fireplace and built-ins. An octagonal breakfast nook is surrounded with glass and accesses the rear of the home. The sleeping quarters are found to the far left of the home for extra privacy. Two family bedrooms enjoy walk-in closets and share a full bath. The master suite boasts a vaulted ceiling and a luxurious private bath.

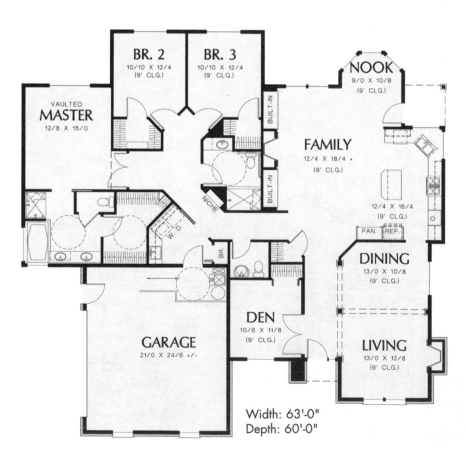

BR. 2
10/10 X 12/4
(9' CLG.)

BR. 3
10/10 X 12/4
(9' CLG.)

NOOK
9/0 X 10/8
(9' CLG.)

VAULTED
MASTER
12/8 X 15/0

FAMILY
12/4 X 18/4 +
(9' CLG.)

BUILT-IN

NICHE

BUILT-IN

12/4 X 16/4
(9' CLG.)

W.D.

PAN. REF.

DINING
13/0 X 10/8
(9' CLG.)

BR.

DEN
10/6 X 11/8
(9' CLG.)

GARAGE
21/0 X 24/6 +/-

LIVING
13/0 X 12/8
(9' CLG.)

Width: 63'-0"
Depth: 60'-0"

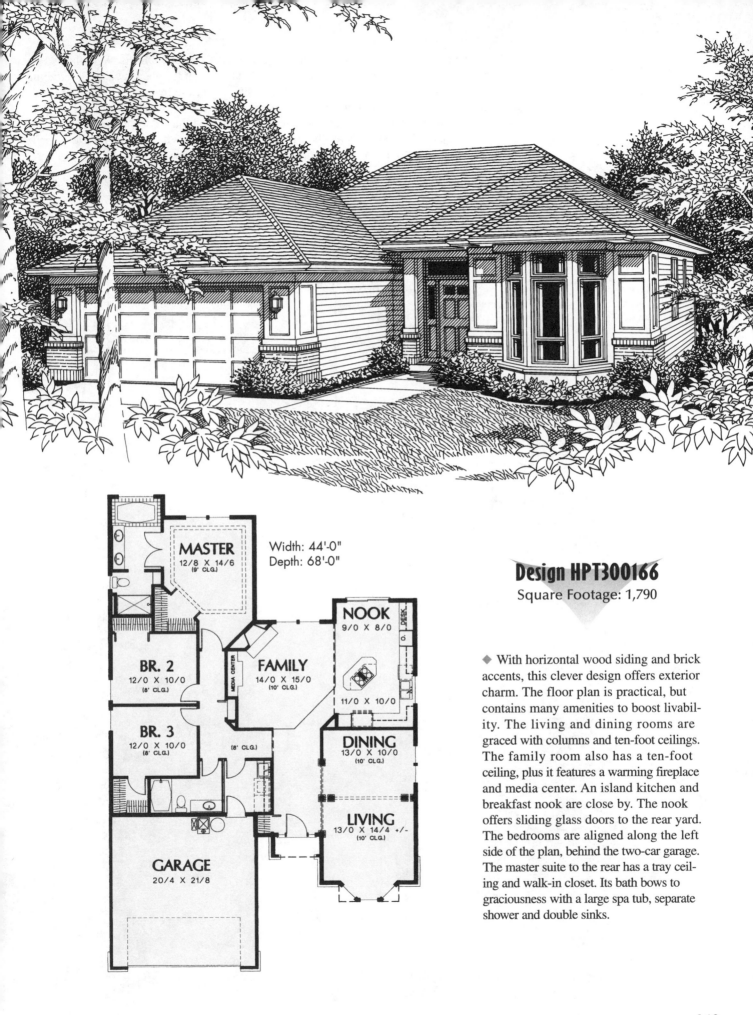

MASTER
12/8 X 14/6
(9' CLG.)

Width: 44'-0"
Depth: 68'-0"

NOOK
9/0 X 8/0

BR. 2
12/0 X 10/0
(8' CLG.)

FAMILY
14/0 X 15/0
(10' CLG.)

11/0 X 10/0

BR. 3
12/0 X 10/0
(8' CLG.)

(8' CLG.)

DINING
13/0 X 10/0
(10' CLG.)

LIVING
13/0 X 14/4 +/-
(10' CLG.)

GARAGE
20/4 X 21/8

Design HPT300166
Square Footage: 1,790

◆ With horizontal wood siding and brick accents, this clever design offers exterior charm. The floor plan is practical, but contains many amenities to boost livability. The living and dining rooms are graced with columns and ten-foot ceilings. The family room also has a ten-foot ceiling, plus it features a warming fireplace and media center. An island kitchen and breakfast nook are close by. The nook offers sliding glass doors to the rear yard. The bedrooms are aligned along the left side of the plan, behind the two-car garage. The master suite to the rear has a tray ceiling and walk-in closet. Its bath bows to graciousness with a large spa tub, separate shower and double sinks.

Design HPT300167

Square Footage: 1,738

◆ The charming brick facade of this home warms any family's heart. Walk through the grand entryway into the great room, where a magnificent fireplace awaits. Entertaining is a delight in this home, with the kitchen easily accessible from the dining room and great room. A rear porch makes warm summer evenings enjoyable. A storage room is conveniently located off the garage. Dual sinks come with the delicate master suite. The additional two bedrooms share a bath and are located on the left of the plan. Please specify basement, crawlspace or slab foundation when ordering.

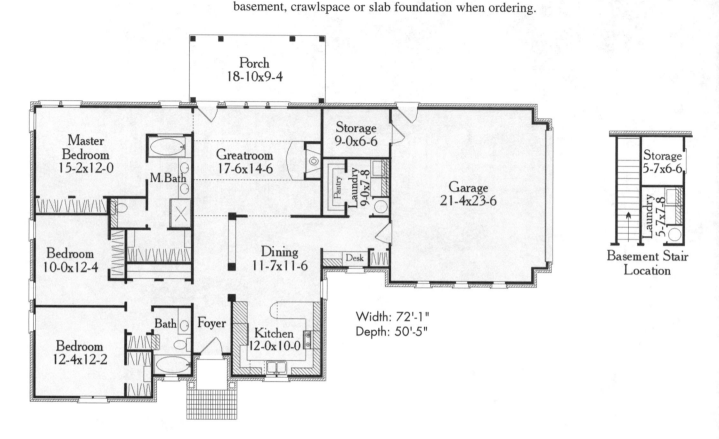

Porch
18-10x9-4

Master Bedroom
15-2x12-0

M.Bath

Greatroom
17-6x14-6

Storage
9-0x6-6

Pantry

Laundry
9-0x7-8

Garage
21-4x23-6

Bedroom
10-0x12-4

Dining
11-7x11-6

Desk

Bath

Foyer

Kitchen
12-0x10-0

Bedroom
12-4x12-2

Width: 72'-1"
Depth: 50'-5"

Storage
5-7x6-6

Laundry
5-7x7-8

Basement Stair Location

Covered Patio

Family Room
20⁰ · 16⁸
10⁰Clg.

fireplace

shelves

Breakfast

Sitting Rm
23⁰ · 15⁰
10⁰Clg.

Bath

Living Room
15⁸ · 13⁴
12⁸Clg.

dw
Kitchen

desk

Bedroom 2
12⁰ · 11⁰
10⁰Clg.

Master
Bedroom

ref

pantry

Bath

lin

Bath

w.i.c.

Den Study
Bedroom 4
11⁰ · 11⁰
10⁰Clg.

Foyer

Dining
11⁸ · 11⁰
14⁰Clg.

linen

Utility
d w

Bedroom 3
12⁰ · 11⁰
10⁰Clg.

ac

ac

wh

ac

Width: 66'-4"
Depth: 74'-4"

Design HPT3030003
Square Footage: 2,660

◆ Circle-top windows are beautifully showcased in this magnificent home. The double-door entry leads into the foyer and welcomes guests into a formal living and dining room area with wonderful views. As you approach the entrance to the master suite, you pass the den/study, which can easily become a guest or bedroom suite. A gently bowed soffit and stepped ceiling treatments add excitement to the master bedroom, with floor-length windows framing the bed. The bay-window sitting area further enhances the opulence of the suite. The master bath comes complete with a double vanity, a make-up area, and a soaking tub balanced by the large shower and private toilet chamber. The walk-in closet caps off this well-appointed space with ample hanging and built-in areas.

Design HPT300169
Square Footage: 2,916

L D

◆ Intricate details make the most of this lovely one-story design. Besides the living room/dining room area to the rear, there is a large conversation area with a fireplace and plenty of windows. The kitchen is separated from living areas by an angled snack-bar counter. Three bedrooms grace the right side of the plan. The master suite features a tray ceiling and sliding glass doors to the rear terrace. The dressing area is graced by His and Hers walk-in closets, a double-bowl vanity and a compartmented toilet. The shower area is highlighted with glass block and is sunken down one step. A garden whirlpool tub finishes off this area.

Width: 77'-10"
Depth: 73'-10"

QUOTE ONE®
Cost to build? See page 436
to order complete cost estimate
to build this house in your area!

Design HPT300170
Square Footage: 2,837

◆ On one lovely level, this brick home offers great livability and an attractive facade. Formal rooms line the foyer on the right side: a living room and a dining room defined by columns. The master suite is found on the left side. On the far right is the more casual area—a family room with a fireplace, an island kitchen and a light-filled nook. Two family bedrooms sharing a bath and a guest bedroom are at the back of the plan. Top the whole thing off with a three-car garage, and you've got a fine family plan.

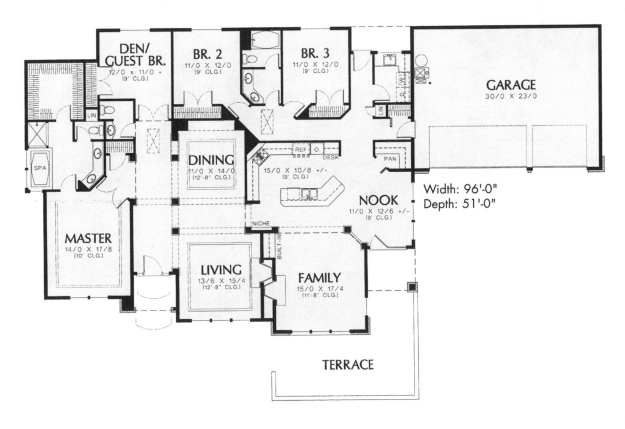

Width: 96'-0"
Depth: 51'-0"

Design HPT300171

Square Footage: 1,593

◆ Multiple gables, a transom over the entry door and a brick-and-stone exterior combine to create an exciting front on this beautiful one-story home. The open foyer offers a view through the great room to the rear yard. A dramatic fireplace and sloped ceiling decorate the fashionable great room. The spacious kitchen and breakfast room feature a favorable indoor/outdoor relationship. The first-floor master bedroom with a tray ceiling, private bath and extra-large walk-in closet pampers homeowners with its size and luxury. Two additional bedrooms complete this spectacular home.

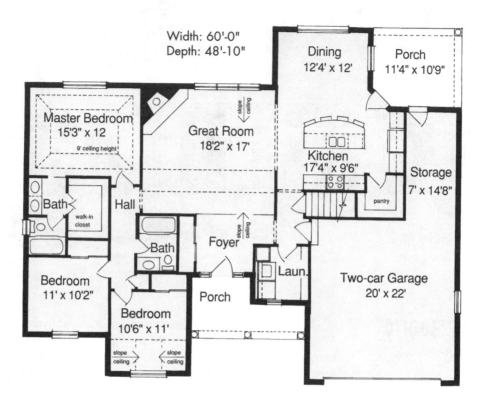

Width: 60'-0"
Depth: 48'-10"

Dining 12'4" x 12'

Porch 11'4" x 10'9"

Master Bedroom 15'3" x 12
9' ceiling height

Great Room 18'2" x 17'
slope ceiling

Kitchen 17'4" x 9'6"

Storage 7' x 14'8"

pantry

Bath

walk-in closet

Hall

Bath

Foyer
slope ceiling

Laun.

Two-car Garage 20' x 22'

Bedroom 11' x 10'2"

Bedroom 10'6" x 11'

Porch

slope ceiling

slope ceiling

Design HPT300172

Square Footage: 2,098
Finished Basement: 1,302 sq. ft.

◆ A solid brick exterior with wood trim and angles gives a strong appearance to this delightful one-story home. A large foyer introduces the open great room, decorated with high windows and a warm fireplace. A grand opening into the dining area visually expands the great room, while a sloped ceiling adds a dramatic effect. A circular island with seating adds a stylish element to the gourmet kitchen. An abundance of counter space, cabinets and a pantry make working in this kitchen a pleasure. A sloped ceiling tops the master bedroom suite, while a whirlpool tub, double-bowl vanity, shower and large walk-in closet provide luxury and comfort for the homeowner. A door to the patio from the master suite is a pleasant surprise. The option of creating a library in the third bedroom, and accessing additional square footage in the walkout basement offers flexibility to this exciting home.

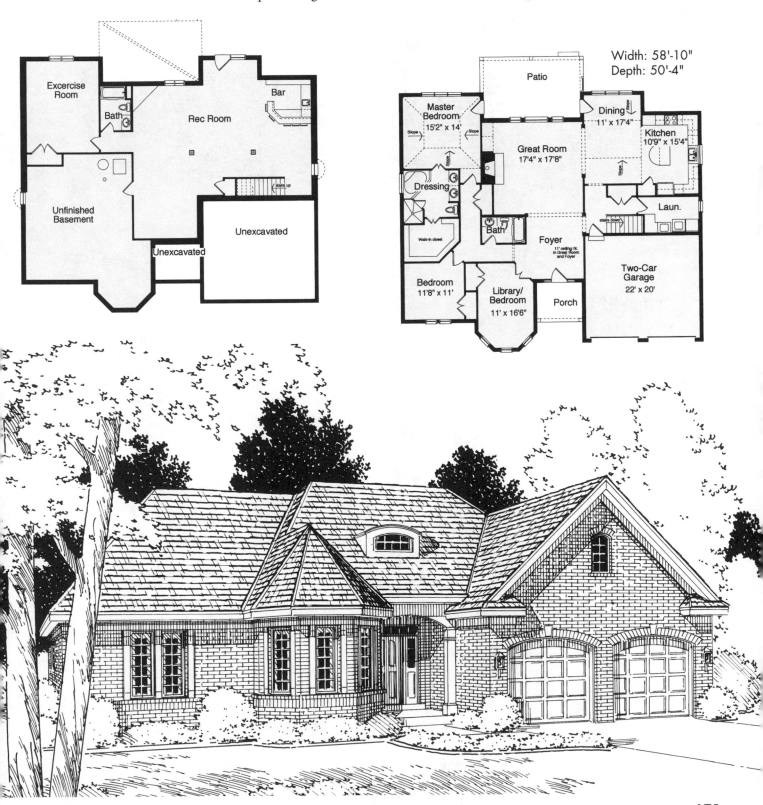

Exercise Room

Bath

Rec Room

Bar

Unfinished Basement

Unexcavated

Unexcavated

stairs up

Width: 58'-10"
Depth: 50'-4"

Patio

Master Bedroom
15'2" x 14'

Slope

Slope

Dining
11' x 17'4"

Slope

Kitchen
10'9" x 15'4"

Great Room
17'4" x 17'8"

Dressing

Slope

Laun.

stairs down

Walk-in closet

Bath

Foyer
11' ceiling ht.
in Great Room and Foyer

Two-Car Garage
22' x 20'

Bedroom
11'8" x 11'

Library/Bedroom
11' x 16'6"

Porch

Design HPT300173
Square Footage: 1,834

◆ This charming home, with its transitional-style facade, creates a grand first impression upon entering. Columns define the great room, while a fireplace and matching windows decorate the rear wall. The seven-foot opening into the dining area creates a spacious effect and the functional kitchen provides an abundance of counter space and a peninsula with seating. A sloped ceiling tops the great room and dining area for a dramatic effect. The luxury of the master suite includes a double-bowl vanity, whirlpool tub, separate shower and large walk-in closet. Storage is abundant with this delightful floor plan and a walkout basement provides additional living space.

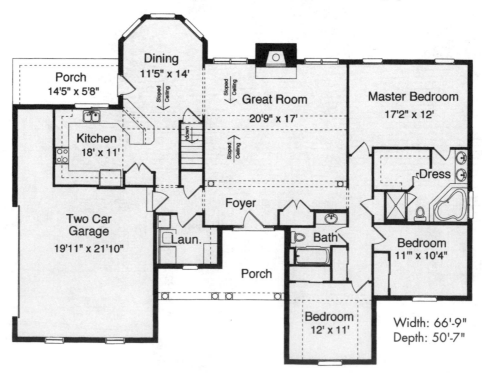

Porch
14'5" x 5'8"

Dining
11'5" x 14'

Great Room
20'9" x 17'

Master Bedroom
17'2" x 12'

Kitchen
18' x 11'

Dress

Two Car Garage
19'11" x 21'10"

Foyer

Laun.

Bath

Bedroom
11'" x 10'4"

Porch

Bedroom
12' x 11'

Width: 66'-9"
Depth: 50'-7"

Design HPT300174
Square Footage: 1,860

◆ This smart-looking starter home features traditional accents and an amenity-filled interior. Inside, the kitchen easily serves the formal dining room and the casual breakfast nook. A porch just outside the breakfast room is perfect for seasonal outdoor grilling. The great room is spacious and open and is warmed by a corner fireplace. The master bedroom is enhanced by a pampering bath and walk-in closet. Two family bedrooms share a hall bath. The laundry room accesses the two-car garage.

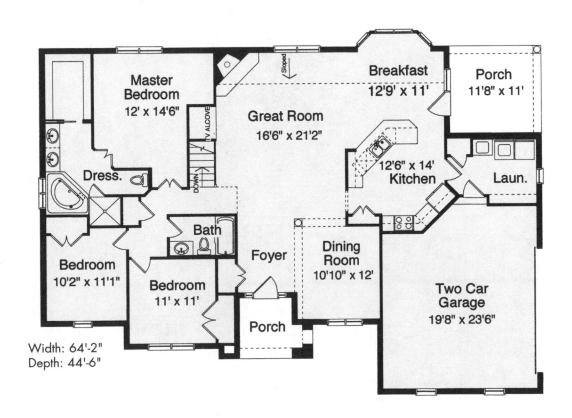

Master Bedroom
12' x 14'6"

Breakfast
12'9' x 11'

Porch
11'8" x 11'

Great Room
16'6" x 21'2"

TV ALCOVE

DOWN

Dress.

Kitchen
12'6" x 14'

Laun.

Bath

Bedroom
10'2" x 11'1"

Bedroom
11' x 11'

Foyer

Dining Room
10'10" x 12'

Two Car Garage
19'8" x 23'6"

Porch

Width: 64'-2"
Depth: 44'-6"

Design HPT300175
Square Footage: 1,611

◆ This three-bedroom brick home pampers the homeowner with its charming exterior and efficient floor plan. Columns define the great room while dual windows and a gas fireplace on the rear wall offer an attractive first impression. The spacious kitchen and dining area with bar seating and a bayed window create an expansive yet comfortable center for preparing meals and for enjoying the formal, as well as informal, dining experience. Introducing a delightful screened porch are sliding doors from the dining area. Providing a luxurious retreat, the master suite showcases a tray ceiling and a lavishly equipped dressing room. Two additional bedrooms—one with a sloped ceiling—complete this wonderful one-story home.

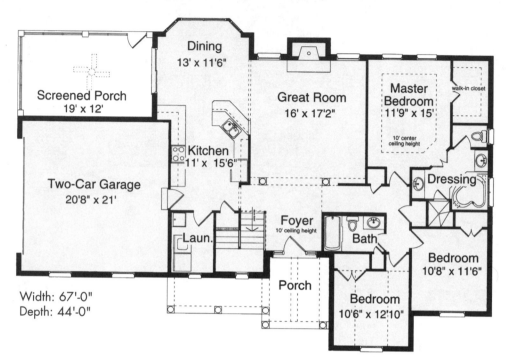

Screened Porch
19' x 12'

Dining
13' x 11'6"

Great Room
16' x 17'2"

Master Bedroom
11'9" x 15'

walk-in closet

10' center ceiling height

Two-Car Garage
20'8" x 21'

Kitchen
11' x 15'6"

Dressing

Laun.

Foyer
10' ceiling height

Bath

Bedroom
10'8" x 11'6"

Porch

Bedroom
10'6" x 12'10"

Width: 67'-0"
Depth: 44'-0"

Design HPT300176

Square Footage: 1,611

◆ A stone-and-siding exterior easily combines with the front covered porch on this three-bedroom ranch home. Inside, columns define the great room, which holds a warming fireplace framed by windows. The bay window in the dining room pours light into the nearby kitchen. Access the screened porch via the dining room to expand the possible living space. The master suite enjoys a walk-in closet and a luxurious bath, including a separate shower and whirlpool tub. Two family bedrooms share a full bath and views of the front yard. Note the two-car, side-access garage—perfect for a corner lot.

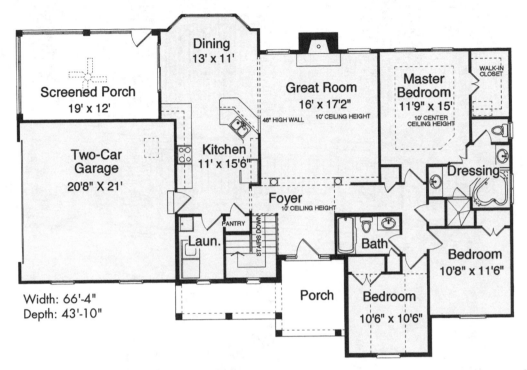

Screened Porch
19' x 12'

Dining
13' x 11'

Great Room
16' x 17'2"
10' CEILING HEIGHT

48" HIGH WALL

WALK-IN CLOSET

Master Bedroom
11'9" x 15'
10' CENTER CEILING HEIGHT

Two-Car Garage
20'8" X 21'

Kitchen
11' x 15'6"

Foyer
10' CEILING HEIGHT

Dressing

PANTRY

STAIRS DOWN

Laun.

Bath

Bedroom
10'8" x 11'6"

Width: 66'-4"
Depth: 43'-10"

Porch

Bedroom
10'6" x 10'6"

Design HPT300177
Square Footage: 2,514

◆ The angled footprint of this brick and stone home adds visual interest to the neighborhood. Beyond the foyer, the heart of the home opens to include the dining room, great room, kitchen and breakfast nook. The library/bedroom and breakfast nook access the screened porch at the rear. The master suite boasts a walk-in closet and a private bath with a dual-sink vanity.

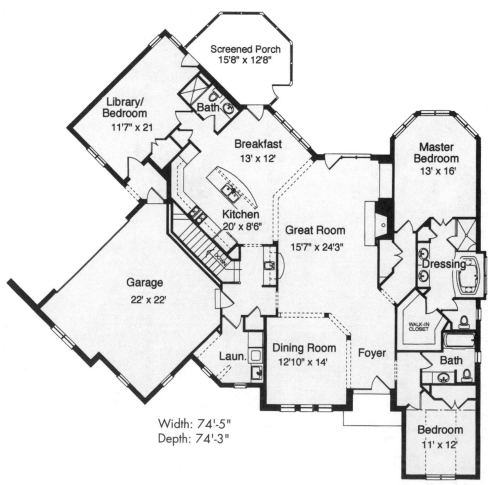

Screened Porch
15'8" x 12'8"

Library/
Bedroom
11'7" x 21

Bath

Breakfast
13' x 12'

Master
Bedroom
13' x 16'

Kitchen
20' x 8'6"

Great Room
15'7" x 24'3"

Dressing

Garage
22' x 22'

WALK-IN
CLOSET

Laun.

Dining Room
12'10" x 14'

Foyer

Bath

Width: 74'-5"
Depth: 74'-3"

Bedroom
11' x 12'

Design HPT300178
Square Footage: 2,393
Bonus Room: 222 sq. ft.

◆ Multiple gables and French doors adorn the facade of this three-bedroom home. Columns define the dining room from the entry, and a through-fireplace sets off the family room. The study and the master bedroom reside to the left of the plan while two family bedrooms share a full bath to the right.

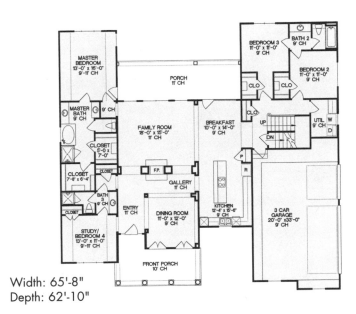

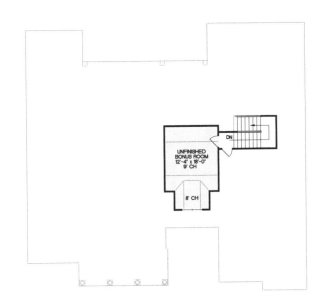

Width: 65'-8"
Depth: 62'-10"

Design HPT300179
Square Footage: 1,852

◆ Shingles-and-vertical siding combine with multiple rooflines and gables on a hipped roof to create an eye-catching appeal for this three-bedroom home. All on one floor, this home provides plenty of room with ease of accessibility. Just inside the entry, the great room features a warming fireplace and a built-in media center. The dining room and island kitchen have an excellent view of this focal point in the great room. The master suite and a den fill the left side of the plan, while two family bedrooms share a full bath to the right. Note the shop area or third-car parking within the garage.

Width: 70'-0"
Depth: 45'-0"

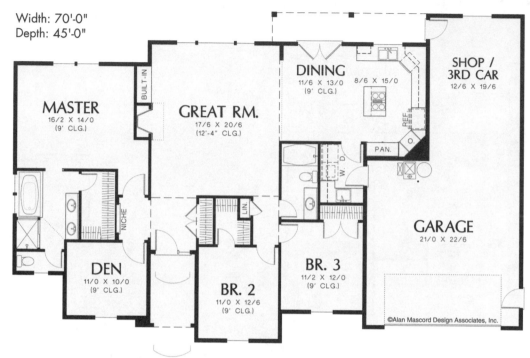

MASTER
16/2 X 14/0
(9' CLG.)

BUILT-IN

GREAT RM.
17/6 X 20/6
(12'-4" CLG.)

DINING
11/6 X 13/0
(9' CLG.)

8/6 X 15/0

SHOP /
3RD CAR
12/6 X 19/6

REF.

O.

PAN.

W. D.

NICHE

LIN.

GARAGE
21/0 X 22/6

DEN
11/0 X 10/0
(9' CLG.)

BR. 2
11/0 X 12/6
(9' CLG.)

BR. 3
11/2 X 12/0
(9' CLG.)

©Alan Mascord Design Associates, Inc.

Design HPT3030004
Square Footage: 2,590

◆ With a solid exterior of rough cedar and stone, this new French Country design will stand the test of time. A wood-paneled study in the front features a large bay window. The heart of the house is found in a large open great room with a built-in entertainment center. The spacious master bedroom features a corner reading area and access to an adjacent covered patio. A three-car garage and three additional bedrooms complete this generous family home.

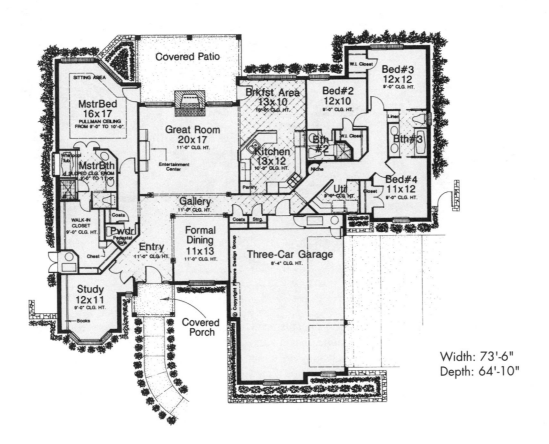

Covered Patio

SITTING AREA

MstrBed
16x17
PULLMAN CEILING
FROM 9'-0" TO 10'-0"

Brkfst Area
13x10
10'-0" CLG. HT.

Bed#2
12x10
9'-0" CLG. HT.

W.I. Closet

Bed#3
12x12
9'-0" CLG. HT.

Great Room
20x17
11'-0" CLG. HT.

Entertainment
Center

Kitchen
13x12
10'-0" CLG. HT.

Bth
#2

W.I. Closet

Liner

Bth#3

Whirlpool
Tub

MstrBth
SLOPED CEILING FROM
8'-6" TO 11'-0"

Niche

Pantry

Uti.
9'-0" CLG. HT.

Bed#4
11x12
9'-0" CLG. HT.

Coats

WALK-IN
CLOSET
9'-0" CLG. HT.

Gallery
11'-0" CLG. HT.

Coats   Strg.

Chest

Pwdr
Pedestal
Sink

Entry
11'-0" CLG. HT.

Formal
Dining
11x13
11'-0" CLG. HT.

Three-Car Garage
8'-4" CLG. HT.

Study
12x11
9'-0" CLG. HT.

Books

Covered
Porch

Copyright Fillmore Design Group

Width: 73'-6"
Depth: 64'-10"

Design HPT300181
Square Footage: 2,517

◆ This European stucco home is a well-designed one-story villa. Turrets top identical bayed rooms that are enclosed behind double doors just off the entry. The formal dining room and study are situated in the window-filled turrets. The family room is a spacious entertaining area with a fireplace and built-ins. An efficiently laidout kitchen is uniquely designed with its island and angular shape. The split-bedroom floor plan places the master suite away from the two family bedrooms.

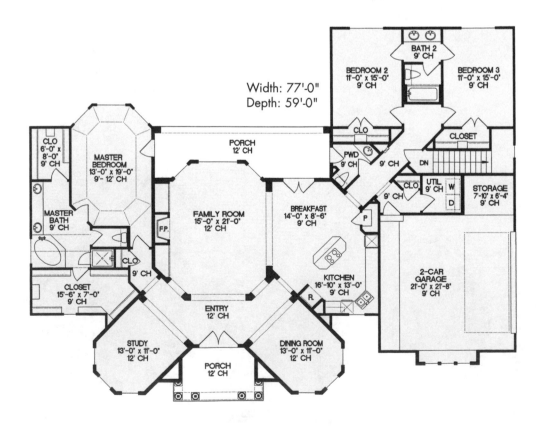

Width: 77'-0"
Depth: 59'-0"

Design HPT300182
Square Footage: 2,331

◆ Traditional good looks and fine window details make this design a neighborhood winner. Perfect for today's families, this fine home offers split-bedroom planning that keeps the formal and casual spaces as buffer zones between bedrooms. A separate study is available for a home office, while the angled kitchen easily works with the octagonal family room. A wall of windows in the dining/living room offers a view to the rear porch. Two garages—one a two-car and the other a one-car—finish this home off nicely.

BATH 2

BEDROOM 2
11'-0" x 16'-0"
9' CH

CLOSET

BEDROOM 3
11'-0" x 11'-0"
9' CH

CLO

FAMILY ROOM
15'-0" x 15'-0"
9'-11" CH

FP

CLO
9' CH

9' CH

BRKFST
6'-6" x 11'-0"
9' CH

PORCH
11' CH

MASTER BEDROOM
14'-0" x 15'-0"
9'-10" CH

MSTR. BATH
9' CH

FP

1-CAR GARAGE
11'-0" x 22'-0"
9' CH

UTIL
6'-4" x 8'-0"
9' CH

D
W

KITCHEN
14'-7" x 14'-0"
11' CH

R DN CLO

9' CH

DINING/ LIVING ROOM
18'-9" x 13'-0"
11' CH

CLO PDR
9' CH

CLO
6'-0" x 12'-0"

ENTRY
11' CH

P

2-CAR GARAGE
22' x 23'-8"
9' CH

PORCH
11' CH

STUDY
13'-0" x 13'-0"
9' CH

Width: 74'-11"
Depth: 68'-9"

Design HPT300183
Square Footage: 1,594

◆ This impressive home has an array of special features, yet it's cost-effective and easy-to-build for those on a limited budget. Tray ceilings elevate the bedroom/study, dining room and master bedroom. Turret bays illuminate the formal dining room and study. The great room features a cathedral ceiling and a striking fireplace. A smart angled counter is all that separates the great room, kitchen and bayed breakfast area. The master bedroom suite remains a private getaway from the rest of the home. Note the tub, large separate shower and double vanity.

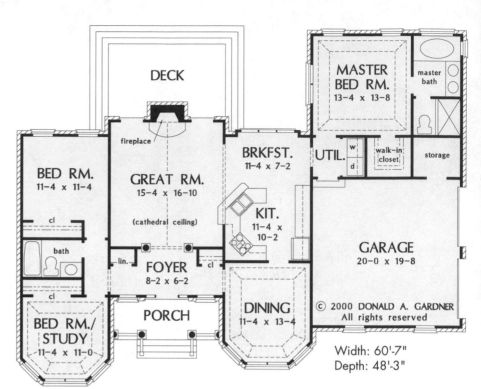

DECK

fireplace

BED RM.
11-4 x 11-4

GREAT RM.
15-4 x 16-10

(cathedral ceiling)

BRKFST.
11-4 x 7-2

KIT.
11-4 x 10-2

MASTER BED RM.
13-4 x 13-8

master bath

UTIL.

walk-in closet

storage

cl

bath

lin.

FOYER
8-2 x 6-2

cl

GARAGE
20-0 x 19-8

BED RM./
STUDY
11-4 x 11-0

PORCH

DINING
11-4 x 13-4

Width: 60'-7"
Depth: 48'-3"

B. NATHAN

GARAGE
24–8 x 21–4

Width: 55'-2"
Depth: 50'-5"

PORCH

skylights

BRKFST.
10–6 x 8–6

MASTER
BED RM.
14–8 x 15–4
(cathedral ceiling)

GREAT RM.
17–4 x 19–0
(cathedral ceiling)

KIT.
11–8 x
10–6

UTIL.
8–8 x
11–0

w
d

cl

master
bath

walk-in
closet

fireplace

PORCH

linen

bath

sto.   cl

DINING
11–4 x 12–8

cl

FOYER
8–8 x 8–0

cl

BED RM.
12–2 x 12–4

BED RM.
10–10 x 12–4
(cathedral ceiling)

PORCH

Design HPT300184
Square Footage: 1,904

◆ Columns and hipped rooflines give this traditional home a taste of Colonial style. Flanked right off the foyer are two family bedrooms to the left while a formal dining room is to the right. The great room enjoys a cathedral ceiling and a fireplace and is open to the breakfast area with a bay window and the gourmet kitchen. The utility room is conveniently secluded away from the sleeping quarters. The fabulous master bedroom boasts a cathedral ceiling with lots of space to move around and relax. Included in this retreat is a deluxe private bath and a large walk-in closet.

B. NATHAN.

Design HPT300185

Square Footage: 1,930

◆ Economical and builder-friendly, this graceful home incorporates a lot of space and amenities into its footage. Elegant tray ceilings accent the foyer and the dining room, while vaulted ceilings crown the study/bedroom and master bedroom. Adorning the great room is the fireplace embraced by built-ins, and across from the fireplace is the kitchen's handy pass-through. The spacious kitchen contains a convenient island counter and ample cabinets. The master bath is equipped with a garden tub, double vanity, shower and compartmented toilet. Note the spacious utility room.

Width: 46'-7"
Depth: 70'-3"

(vaulted ceiling)

MASTER BED RM.
13-0 x 16-0

Width: 54'-11"
Depth: 65'-9"

walk-in closet

walk-in closet

BRKFST.
9-0 x 9-0

PORCH
skylights

BED RM.
11-0 x 13-0

cl

bath

lin.

UTILITY
10-8 x 6-0

KIT.
11-4 x 14-4

GREAT RM.
19-4 x 16-0

fireplace

d w

cl

FOYER
5-8 x 8-8 cl

DINING
11-0 x 13-0

BED RM.
11-0 x 13-0

GARAGE
22-4 x 21-2

PORCH

storage

Design HPT300186
Square Footage: 1,966

◆ Old World charm mingles and merges with traditional detailings upon the facade of this three-bedroom home. The covered entry opens to the foyer where open planning allows views through the stately great room and out beyond the skylit rear porch. The formal dining room enjoys a tray ceiling, the master bedroom has a vaulted ceiling and the great room boasts a stepped ceiling treatment. The angled kitchen adjoins the sunny breakfast nook while being out of sight, but not out of reach of the dining room. On the right, the full bath lends privacy to the two family bedrooms.

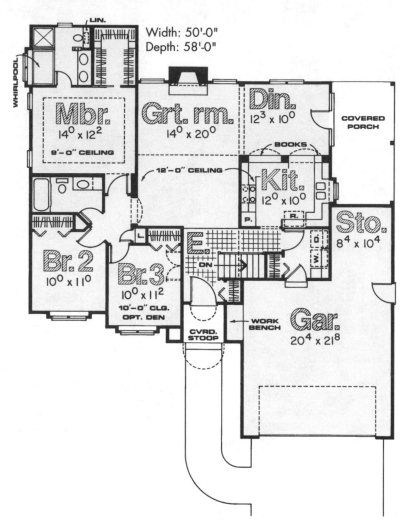

Width: 50'-0"
Depth: 58'-0"

Design HPT300187
Square Footage: 1,422

◆ This small efficient home makes a grand statement with its prominent entrance. Once inside, the tiled flooring leads either to the kitchen to the right or the great room straight ahead. The kitchen features a plant shelf above the upper cabinets and easily serves the nearby dining room. The master suite contains a whirlpool bath and a walk-in closet. Bedroom 3 easily converts to a den and shares a full hall bath with Bedroom 2.

Width: 55'-4"
Depth: 56'-0"

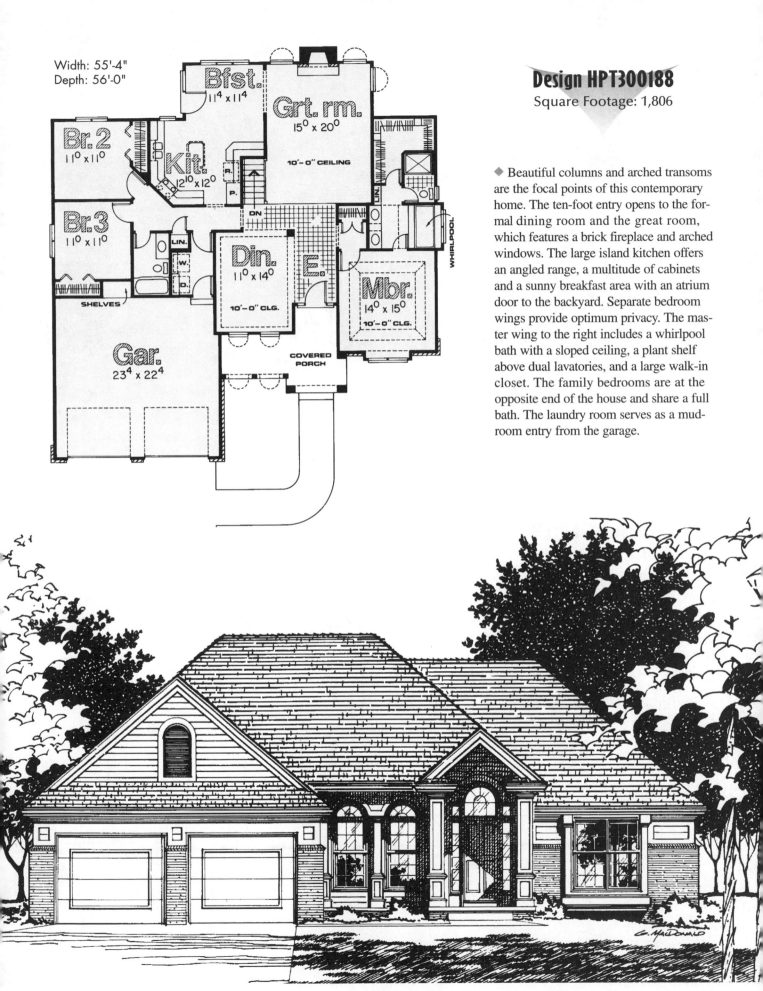

Br. 2
11⁰ x 11⁰

Bfst.
11⁴ x 11⁴

Grt. rm.
15⁰ x 20⁰

10'-0" CEILING

Kit.
12¹⁰ x 12⁰

R.

P.

DN

Br. 3
11⁰ x 11⁰

LIN.

W.

D.

SHELVES

Din.
11⁰ x 14⁰

10'-0" CLG.

E.

Mbr.
14⁰ x 15⁰

10'-0" CLG.

WHIRLPOOL

Gar.
23⁴ x 22⁴

COVERED
PORCH

Design HPT300188
Square Footage: 1,806

◆ Beautiful columns and arched transoms are the focal points of this contemporary home. The ten-foot entry opens to the formal dining room and the great room, which features a brick fireplace and arched windows. The large island kitchen offers an angled range, a multitude of cabinets and a sunny breakfast area with an atrium door to the backyard. Separate bedroom wings provide optimum privacy. The master wing to the right includes a whirlpool bath with a sloped ceiling, a plant shelf above dual lavatories, and a large walk-in closet. The family bedrooms are at the opposite end of the house and share a full bath. The laundry room serves as a mudroom entry from the garage.

Design HPT300189
Square Footage: 2,197

◆ Corner quoins, a Palladian window, open gables and a hipped roof embellish this traditional design. The open foyer introduces the dining room on the right, accented by columns, and a private den on the left. The great room repeats the open style with smooth interaction to the breakfast nook and kitchen. The secluded master suite enjoys its own bath and elegant Palladian window. To the left are two secondary bedrooms with private access to a shared bathroom. A three-car garage completes this design.

Width: 60'-0"
Depth: 64'-0"

MASTER
15/0 X 16/0
(11'-6" CLG.)

SPA

NOOK
10/0 X 10/0 +/-
(9' CLG.)

GREAT RM.
15/0 X 17/6 +
(11'-6" CLG.)

BR. 3
10/10 X 12/0
(9' CLG.)

BUILT-IN

D.W.

REF

LINEN

BR. 2
11/8 X 13/0 +/-
(9' CLG.)

DEN
10/0 X 11/4
(11'-6" CLG.)

DINING
10/4 X 12/0
(11'-6" CLG.)

PAN

GARAGE
19/0 X 21/6

Design HPT300190
Square Footage: 1,500

◆ A spacious interior is implied from the curb with the lofty hipped rooflines of this economical family home. From the entry, the large living room is fully visible, as is the rear yard, through windows flanking the fireplace. The kitchen is partially open to the living room via a snack bar and offers full access to the breakfast room. A formal dining room just off the kitchen will serve entertaining needs with style. Please specify crawlspace or slab foundation when ordering.

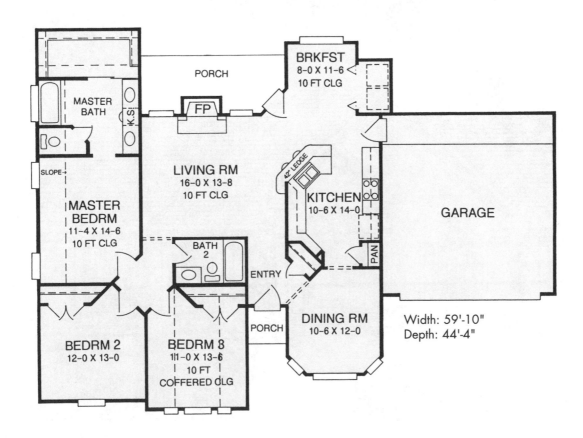

PORCH

BRKFST
8-0 X 11-6
10 FT CLG

MASTER
BATH

W.I.C.

FP

LIVING RM
16-0 X 13-8
10 FT CLG

42 LEDGE

KITCHEN
10-6 X 14-0

GARAGE

SLOPE →

MASTER
BEDRM
11-4 X 14-6
10 FT CLG

BATH
2

PAN

ENTRY →

BEDRM 2
12-0 X 13-0

BEDRM 8
11-0 X 13-6
10 FT
COFFERED CLG

PORCH

DINING RM
10-6 X 12-0

Width: 59'-10"
Depth: 44'-4"

Design HPT300191

Square Footage: 2,678

Width: 70'-2"
Depth: 67'-9"

◆ Split sleeping arrangements enhance this lovely home. Two family bedrooms off a hallway in the left wing have walk-in closets and share a bath that features a double-bowl vanity. The study or extra bedroom also opens off the hall. In the opposite wing, the master suite opens through French doors from a private hallway. The family room, kitchen and breakfast room comprise one open area with access to two rear porches. Please specify slab or crawlspace foundation when ordering.

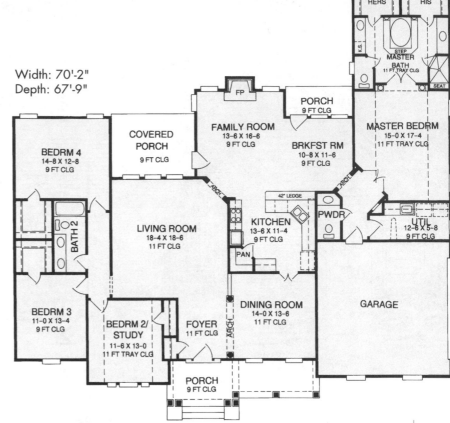

194

Design HPT300192
Square Footage: 2,010

◆ An arched entrance, a sunburst and sidelights around the four-panel door provide a touch of class to this European-style home. An angled bar opens the kitchen and breakfast room to the living room with bookcases and a fireplace. The master suite boasts a sloped ceiling and private bath with a five-foot turning radius, dual vanity, and a separate tub and shower. Two family bedrooms provide ample closet space and share a full hall bath and linen closet. Don't miss the two-car garage located to the far right of the plan.

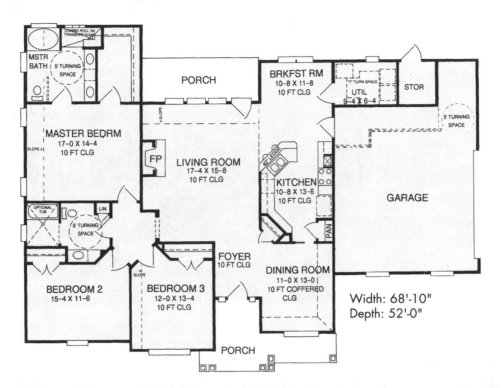

Width: 68'-10"
Depth: 52'-0"

Design HPT3030005

Square Footage: 1,884

◆ Arched openings, decorative columns, and elegant ceiling details throughout highlight this livable floor plan. The country kitchen includes a spacious work area, preparation island, serving bar to the great room, and a breakfast nook with a tray ceiling. Set to the rear for gracious entertaining, the dining room opens to the great room. Note the warming fireplace and French-door access to the backyard in the great room. The master suite is beautifully appointed with a tray ceiling, bay window, compartmented bath, and walk-in closet. Two family bedrooms, a laundry room, and a powder room complete this gracious design. Please specify basement, crawlspace, or slab foundation when ordering.

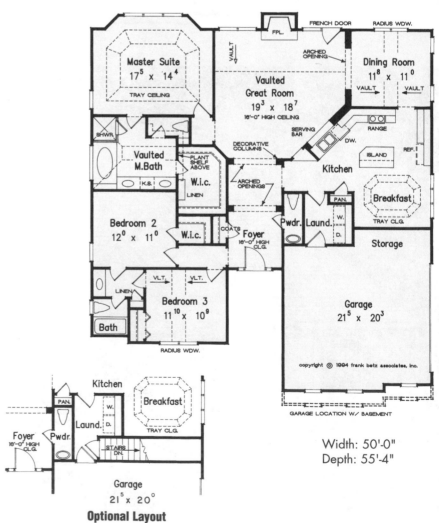

Width: 50'-0"
Depth: 55'-4"

Optional Layout

Width: 57'-0"
Depth: 56'-4"

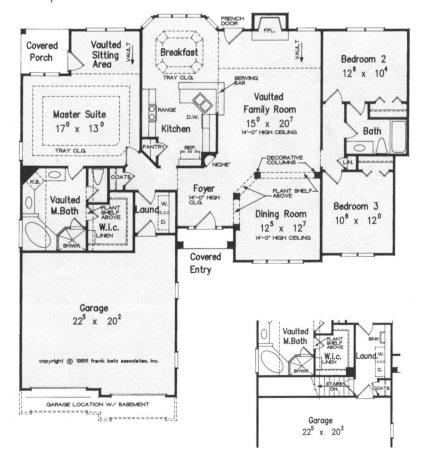

Optional Layout

Design HPT3030006
Square Footage: 1,779

◆ European style shines from this home's facade in the form of its stucco detailing, hipped rooflines, fancy windows, and elegant entryway. Inside, decorative columns and a plant shelf define the formal dining room, which works well with the vaulted family room. The efficient kitchen offers a serving bar to both the family room and the deluxe breakfast room. Located apart from the family bedrooms for privacy, the master suite is sure to please with its many amenities, including a vaulted sitting area and a private covered porch. The two secondary bedrooms share a full hall bath. Please specify basement, crawlspace or slab foundation when ordering.

Design HPT3030007

Square Footage: 1,715

◆ A grand double bank of windows looking in on the formal dining room mirrors the lofty elegance of the extra-tall vaulted ceiling inside. From the foyer, an arched entrance to the great room visually frames the fireplace on the back wall. The wraparound kitchen has plenty of counter and cabinet space, along with a handy serving bar. The luxurious master suite features a front sitting room for quiet times and a large spa-style bath. Two family bedrooms share a hall bath. Please specify basement, crawlspace or slab foundation when ordering.

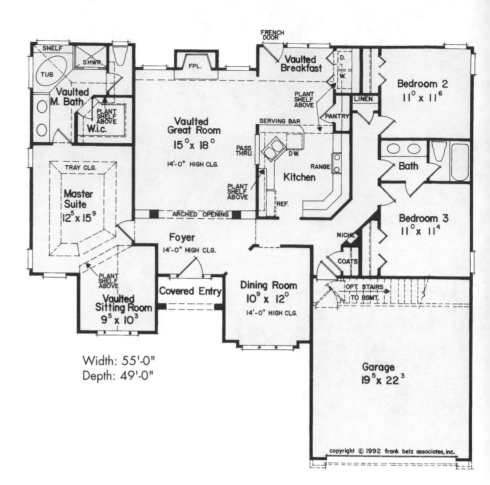

Width: 55'-0"
Depth: 49'-0"

Design HPT3030008

Square Footage: 1,429

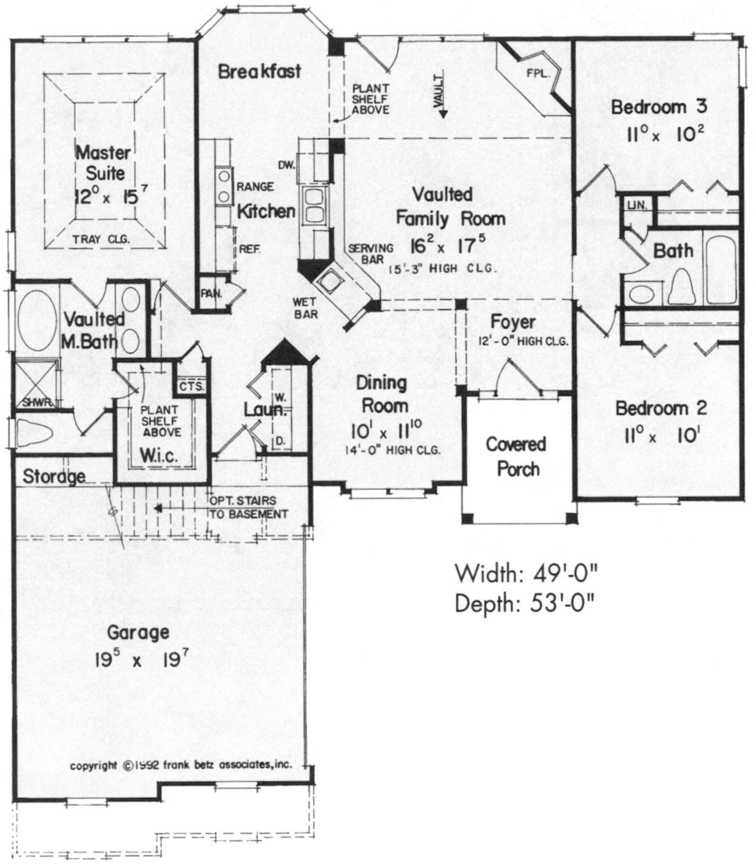

Floor Plan Labels:

- Breakfast
- PLANT SHELF ABOVE
- VAULT
- FPL.
- Bedroom 3 — 11⁰ x 10²
- Master Suite — 12⁰ x 15⁷ — TRAY CLG.
- DW.
- RANGE
- Kitchen
- REF.
- Vaulted Family Room — 16² x 17⁵ — SERVING BAR — 15'-3" HIGH CLG.
- LIN.
- Bath
- PAN.
- WET BAR
- Foyer — 12'-0" HIGH CLG.
- Vaulted M.Bath
- SHWR.
- CTS.
- PLANT SHELF ABOVE
- W.i.c.
- Laun.
- W.
- D.
- Dining Room — 10¹ x 11¹⁰ — 14'-0" HIGH CLG.
- Bedroom 2 — 11⁰ x 10¹
- Covered Porch
- Storage
- OPT. STAIRS TO BASEMENT
- Garage — 19⁵ x 19⁷
- copyright ©1992 frank betz associates, inc.

Width: 49'-0"
Depth: 53'-0"

◆ This home's gracious exterior is indicative of the elegant, yet extremely livable floor plan inside. Volume ceilings that crown the family living areas combine with an open floor plan to give the modest square footage a more spacious feel. The formal dining room is set off from the foyer and vaulted family room with stately columns. The spacious family room has a corner fireplace, rear-yard door, and serving bar from the open galley kitchen. A bay-windowed breakfast nook flanks the kitchen on one end, and a laundry center and wet bar/serving pantry lead to the dining room on the other. The split-bedroom plan allows the amenity-rich master suite maximum privacy. A pocket door off the family room leads to the hall housing the two family bedrooms and a full bath. Please specify basement, crawlspace or slab foundation when ordering.

Width: 40'-0"
Depth: 78'-11"

m ba

mbr
16' X 12'

porch

study
9'-3" X 8'

family
16'-8" X 16'-6"

dining
10'-1" X 13'-4"

pwdr

foyer

kit
13' X 8'-10"

laundry

br 2
12' X 11'

storage

garage
23'-4" X 19'-2"

Design HPT3030009
Square Footage: 1,535

◆ A seemingly compact facade reveals a spacious layout within. Double doors lead through the foyer straight to the family room, which includes a cozy fireplace and is open to the elegant dining room—French doors can be accessed from the dining room to the rear porch. The L-shaped kitchen is a dream of efficiency and is convenient to a laundry room and powder room just steps away. To the left of the home a family bedroom and a study share a hall bath. The spacious master bedroom is complete with a large walk-in closet and lavish private bath.

Design HPT3030010
Square Footage: 2,454
Bonus Room: 256 sq. ft.

◆ A neat row of classic front-porch pillars opens this beautiful one-story plan. The bay window in the master suite offers a front-row seat to views. Favorite foods will be the order of the day in the step-saving kitchen, with a central island in a unique diamond shape. The pentagonal dining room is large enough for special occasions. A double-sided fireplace lights the great room and adjacent study. To the right of the entry is an angled hallway that leads to two bedrooms and a hall bath. A bonus room with a full bath sits above the double garage.

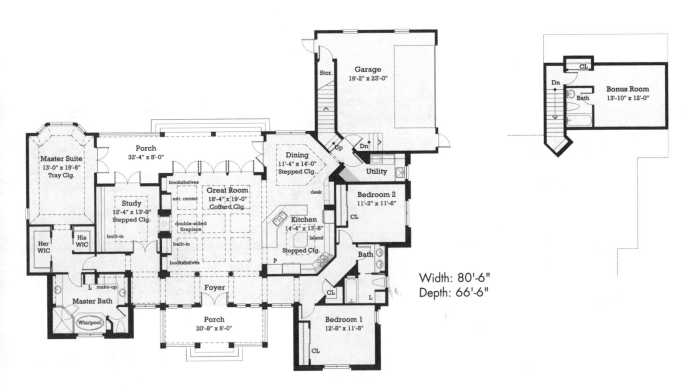

Width: 80'-6"
Depth: 66'-6"

Design HPT3030011

Square Footage: 3,424
Bonus Room: 507 sq. ft.

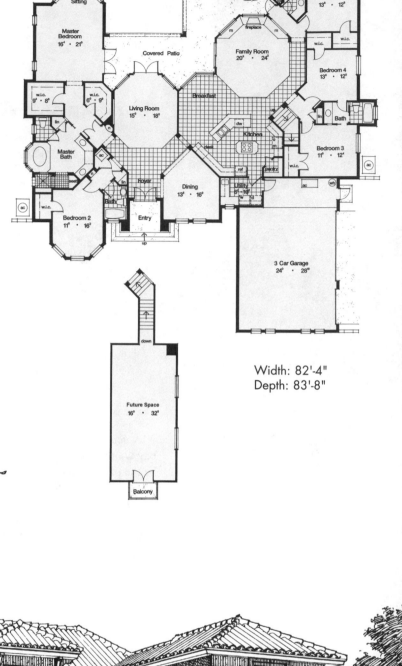

◆ This lovely five-bedroom home exudes the beauty and warmth of a Mediterranean villa. The foyer views explode in all directions with the dominant use of octagonal shapes throughout. Double doors lead to the master wing, which abounds with niches. The sitting area of the master bedroom has a commanding view of the rear gardens. A bedroom just off the master suite is perfect for a guest room or office. The formal living and dining rooms share expansive glass walls and marble or tile pathways. The mitered glass wall of the breakfast nook can be viewed from the huge island kitchen. Two secondary bedrooms share the convenience of a Pullman-style bath. An additional rear bedroom completes this design.

Width: 82'-4"
Depth: 83'-8"

Design HPT3030012

Square Footage: 3,064
Bonus Room: 366 sq. ft.

Floor Plan Labels

Lanai

Pool

Family Rm.
19⁰ • 19⁰

Nook
11⁰ • 10⁴

Bedroom 3
11⁴ • 15⁰

Kitchen

Living
14⁴ • 16⁰

Master Suite
15⁰ • 17⁴

Pool Bath

Bath 2

Bedroom 2
11⁴ • 15⁰

Laun.

storage

Dining
11⁰ • 13⁰

Foyer

Den
13⁰ • 12⁰

Master Bath

Entry

w.i.c.

3 Car Garage
20⁰ • 31⁴

Width: 79'-6"
Depth: 91'-0"

Bath 3

Bonus Rm.
12⁰ • 18⁰

◆ From a more graceful era, this estate evokes the sense of quiet refinement. Exquisite exterior detailing makes it a one-of-a-kind. Inside are distinctive treatments that make the floor plan unique and functional. The central foyer is enhanced with columns that define the dining room and formal living room. A beam ceiling complements the den. An indulgent master suite includes a private garden with a fountain, pool access, a large walk-in closet, and a fireplace to the outdoor spa. Family bedrooms share an unusual compartmented bath. The kitchen and family room are completed with a breakfast nook. Pool access and a lanai with a summer kitchen make this area a natural for casual lifestyles. A bonus area over the garage can become a home office or game room.

Design HPT300201

Square Footage: 1,604

◆ A thoughtful arrangement makes this uncomplicated three-bedroom plan comfortable. The living and working areas are grouped together for convenience—a great room with cathedral ceiling, dining room with wet bar pass-through and kitchen with breakfast room. The sleeping area features a spacious master suite with a skylit bath, whirlpool tub and large walk-in closet. Two smaller bedrooms accommodate the rest of the family. An alternate elevation is available at no extra cost.

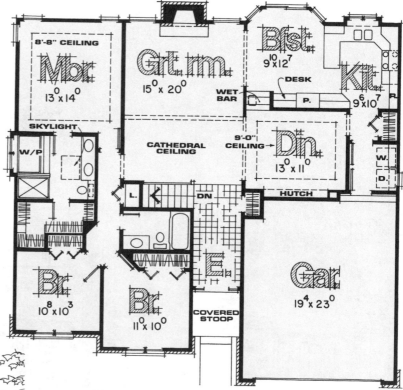

Width: 48'-8"
Depth: 48'-0"

Cost to build? See page 436 to order complete cost estimate to build this house in your area!

Alternate Elevation

TRANSOMS

Width: 64'-0"
Depth: 50'-0"

Bfst.
13⁸ x 12⁰
10'-0" CEILING

SNACK BAR

Grt. rm.
16⁷ x 18⁹
10'-0" CEILING

DESK

BOOKS

Mbr.
15² x 13⁶
10'-0" CEILING

Kit.
13⁸ x 9⁰

R.

DN

12'-0"
CLG.
SKYLIGHT

W/P
L.

D. W.

LAUNDRY

9'-0"
CLG.

TANDEM
DRIVE-THRU

HUTCH

Dn.
12 x 13⁰
11'-0"
CEILING

E.

OPT. BEDROOM

Br.
11⁸ x 12⁰

Gar.
20⁰ x 42⁰

CVRD.
STOOP

Liv. rm.
13⁴ x 13⁸
10'-0"
CEILING

Design HPT300202
Square Footage: 1,996

◆ Practical, yet equipped with a variety of popular amenities, this pleasant ranch home is an excellent choice for empty-nesters or small families. The front living room can become a third bedroom if you choose. The great room with a dramatic fireplace serves as the main living area. A luxurious master suite features a ten-foot tray ceiling and a large bath with a whirl-pool tub, skylight, plant ledge and twin vanities. The kitchen with a breakfast room serves both the dining and great rooms. A tandem drive-through garage holds space for a third car or extra storage.

Design HPT300203
Square Footage: 1,911

◆ This sophisticated design shows off its facade with fanlights and elegant arches. Grace pervades the interior, starting with the formal dining room with a twelve-foot coffered ceiling and an arched window. An extensive great room shares a through-fireplace with a bayed hearth room. The well-planned kitchen features a spacious work area and a snack-bar pass-through to the breakfast area. The secluded master suite offers a coffered ceiling, corner windows, a whirlpool tub and a skylight. On the opposite side of the plan, two family bedrooms—or one bedroom and a den—share a hall bath that has a skylight.

QUOTE ONE®
Cost to build? See page 436
to order complete cost estimate
to build this house in your area!

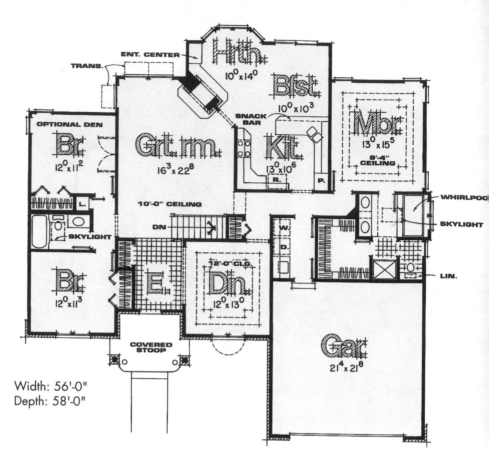

OPTIONAL DEN

Br
12⁰ x 11²

Grt. rm.
16³ x 22⁸

10'-0" CEILING

SKYLIGHT

Br
12⁰ x 11³

ENT. CENTER

TRANS.

Hrth.
10⁰ x 14⁰

Brkst.
10⁰ x 10³

SNACK BAR

Kit
13⁰ x 10⁶

R.

P.

Mbr
13⁰ x 15⁵

9'-4" CEILING

WHIRLPOOL

SKYLIGHT

LIN.

DN

W. D.

12'-0" CLG.

Dn
12⁰ x 13⁰

COVERED STOOP

Gar
21⁴ x 21⁸

Width: 56'-0"
Depth: 58'-0"

Design HPT300204
Square Footage: 2,538

WHIRLPOOL

GLASS BLOCK

L

BUILT-IN DRESSERS

Mbr.
13⁰ x 20⁴
9'-0" CEILING

TRANS

Bfst.
12⁴ x 12⁰
9'-0" CLG.

Fam. rm.
19⁰ x 17⁴

CATHEDRAL CEILING

TRANSOMS

Din.
16⁰ x 13⁰
12'-0" CEILING

SNACK BAR

P.

Kit.
14⁰ x 14⁸

D.W.

COVERED PORCH

P.

ON

SHELVES

LIN

Br. 2
13⁰ x 11⁰
OPTIONAL DEN
10'-0" CEILING

E.

Liv. rm.
13⁴ x 16⁰
10'-0" CEILING

P.

Gar.
22⁴ x 31⁴

Br. 3
11⁰ x 13⁰

TRANSOMS

COVERED PORCH

TRANSOMS

Width: 68'-8"
Depth: 64'-8"

◆ The grand front porch gives this home unique style and majestic curb appeal. Inside, the entry centers on the stately dining room with its bowed window. Both the living room and the second bedroom—which can be converted into a den—have ten-foot ceilings. The island kitchen features abundant storage space, a lazy Susan and a snack bar. A sun-filled breakfast area opens to the large family room with its cathedral ceiling and central fireplace. The private bedroom wing offers two secondary bedrooms and a luxurious master suite featuring a spacious walk-in closet with built-in dressers, and private access to the backyard. The master bath includes a vaulted ceiling, a corner whirlpool and His and Hers vanities.

Design HPT300205
Square Footage: 1,347

◆ From the high ceiling in the entry and great room to the snack bar in the open kitchen, there's a great deal to enjoy with this home. The great room features a fireplace, transoms and great views to the rear property. This area provides plenty of space for entertaining guests or enjoying casual family time. The kitchen flows into the breakfast room and shares a snack bar. Two family bedrooms are to the left of the entry, and share a full bath. One of the bedrooms could serve as a den with French doors off the entry. The opulent master suite features a double-sink vanity, walk-in closet, box-bay window and tiered ceiling.

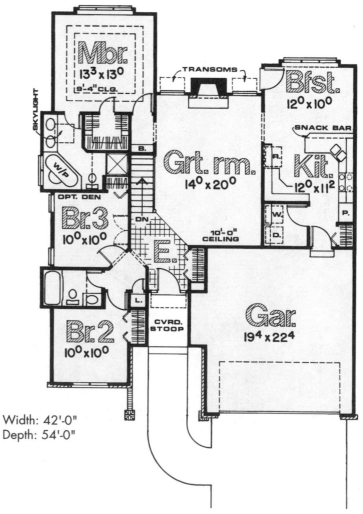

Width: 42'-0"
Depth: 54'-0"

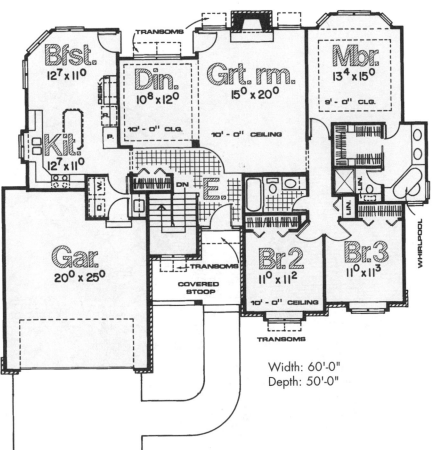

Width: 60'-0"
Depth: 50'-0"

Design HPT300206
Square Footage: 1,735

◆ A covered porch leads to a tiled foyer within this three-bedroom home. The great room enjoys high ceilings, a central fireplace and natural light from transom windows. To the left of the great room is the formal dining area, which also features transom windows. Access to the island kitchen and breakfast bay is just steps away from the living hub. Private sleeping quarters reside to the right of the plan. An amenity-filled master bath services the master suite. Two family bedrooms share a full hall bath.

Design HPT300207
Square Footage: 1,697

◆ This volume-look home gives the impression of size and scope in just under 1,700 square feet. The large great room with fireplace is perfect for entertaining. Its proximity to the kitchen, with breakfast room, and to the formal dining room ensures easy serving and clean-up. Besides a walk-in closet, other features in the master suite include a whirlpool tub, double vanity, skylit dressing area and convenient linen storage. Two family bedrooms share a full bath—that includes a skylight—and offer ample closet space.

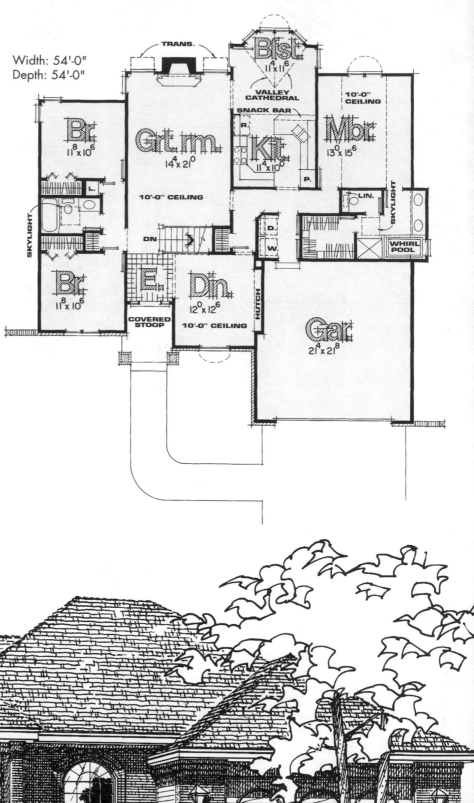

Width: 54'-0"
Depth: 54'-0"

Design HPT300208
Square Footage: 2,498

◆ Elegant arches at the covered entry of this home announce an exquisite floor plan with plenty of bays and niches. The tiled entry opens to the formal living and dining rooms, which enjoy open, soaring space defined by arches and a decorative column. A gourmet kitchen offers an island cooktop counter, and serves a bayed breakfast nook and a convenient snack bar. The sleeping wing includes a master suite with a whirlpool bath, a sizable walk-in closet, two vanities and a box-bay window. Two family bedrooms share a full bath nearby, while a secluded den offers the possibility of a fourth bedroom.

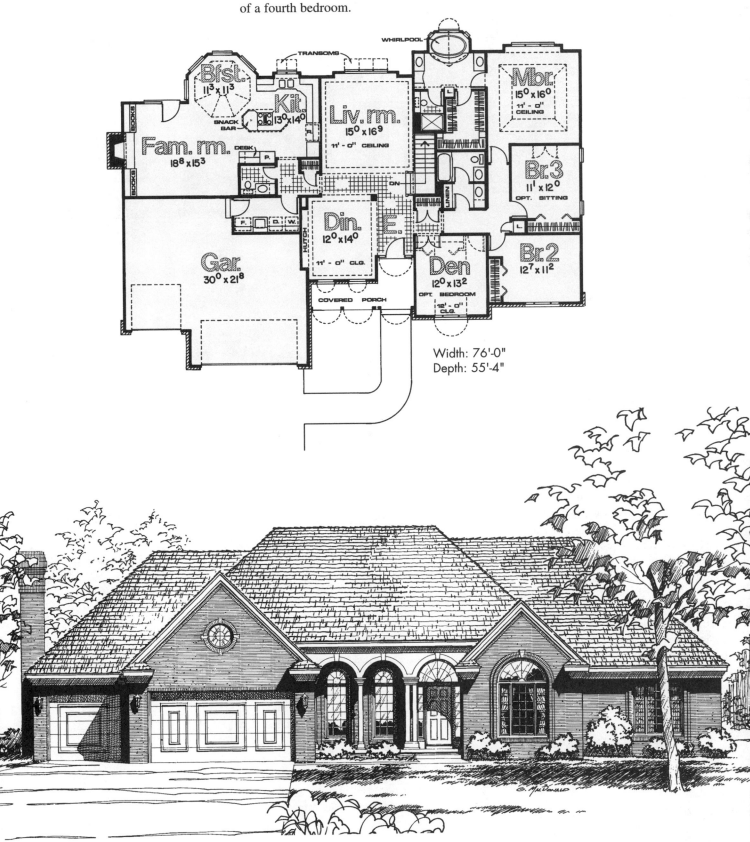

Width: 76'-0"
Depth: 55'-4"

Design HPT300209
Square Footage: 1,666

◆ This delightfully updated European plan displays brick and stucco on the dramatic front elevation, showcased by sleek lines and decorative windows. An inviting entry has a view to the great room and is enhanced by an arched window. Sunny windows with transoms above frame the great room's fireplace. The bay-windowed dining room is nestled between the great room and the superb eat-in kitchen. The secluded master suite features a walk-in closet and a luxurious bath with dual lavatories and a whirlpool tub. Two additional bedrooms share a hall bath.

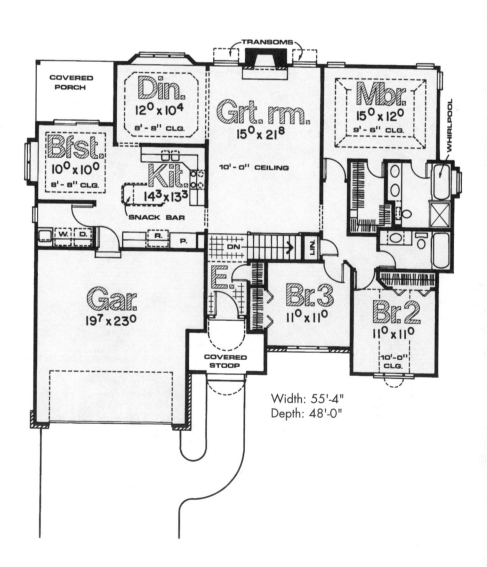

Width: 55'-4"
Depth: 48'-0"

212

Design HPT300210

Square Footage: 2,172

◆ This one-story home with grand rooflines enjoys a convenient floor plan. The great room with a fireplace complements a front-facing living room. The formal dining room with a tray ceiling sits just across the hall from the living room and is also easily accessible to the kitchen. An island, pantry, breakfast room and patio are highlights in the kitchen. A bedroom at this end of the house works fine as an office or guest bedroom. Two additional bedrooms are to the right of the plan: a master suite with a grand bath and an additional family bedroom.

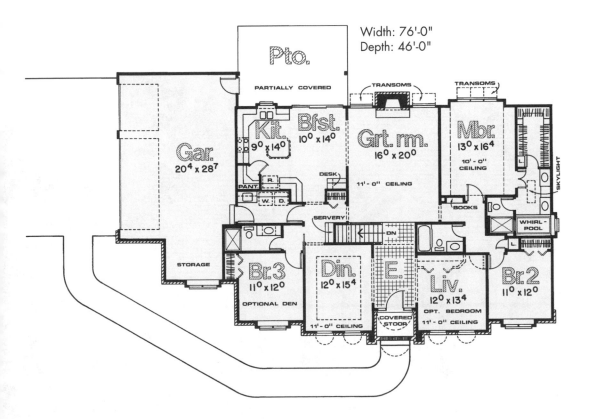

Width: 76'-0"
Depth: 46'-0"

Cost to build? See page 436
to order complete cost estimate
to build this house in your area!

Design HPT300211
Square Footage: 2,456

◆ Gently tapered columns set off an elegant arched entry framed by multipane windows. Inside, an open great room features a wet bar, fireplace, tall transom windows and access to a covered porch with skylights. The gourmet kitchen boasts a food-preparation island and a snack bar, and overlooks the gathering room. Double doors open to the master suite, where French doors lead to a private bath with an angled whirlpool tub and a sizable walk-in closet. One of two nearby family bedrooms could serve as a den, with optional French doors opening from a hall to the sleeping wing.

Width: 66'-0"
Depth: 68'-0"

QUOTE ONE®
Cost to build? See page 436
to order complete cost estimate
to build this house in your area!

PORCH

BREAKFAST
11'-4" X 11'-0"
9' C.H.

MASTER
BEDROOM
13'-4" X 19'-8"
9' C.H.

TV

F.P.

FAMILY ROOM
19'-0" X 20'-8"
11' C.H.

KITCHEN
13'-8" X 15'-4"
9' C.H.

R

PANT

W.I.C.

PWDR

DINING ROOM
16'-0" X 11'-0"
11' C.H.

MASTER
BATH
9' C.H.

11' C.H.

W.I.C.

W
D

UTIL

LIN

DN

BEDROOM 3
12'-0" X 11'-4"
9' C.H.

ENTRY
11' C.H.

UP

2-CAR GARAGE
9' C.H.

PORCH

UP

BEDROOM 2
12'-0" X 13'-0"
11' C.H.

BATH

© CARMICHAEL & DAME DESIGNS, INC.

Design HPT300212
Square Footage: 2,404

◆ A charming facade with a set-back entry creates a cozy look with large livability. Two family bedrooms are found at the front of the plan, sharing a Jack-and-Jill bath. A high-ceilinged portico introduces a formal dining room and the family room to the rear. A built-in entertainment center and fireplace make the family room a comfortable place to entertain or just relax. The kitchen serves up convenience to the bright breakfast area, dining room and family room. The master bedroom is secluded to the rear and features a luxurious bath with all the amenities.

Width: 50'-4"
Depth: 70'-8"

Design HPT300213
Square Footage: 1,875

◆ An oversized picture window gives a cheerful first impression to this well-appointed family home. Boxed columns frame the formal dining room to one side of the foyer. A living room or den is to the other side. A vaulted ceiling soars over the family room. A lovely fireplace flanked by windows and a wraparound serving bar make this room the heart of family gatherings. The kitchen has all the amenities, including a sunny breakfast nook. The master suite is split from the two family bedrooms and features a lush compartmented bath and walk-in closet. Please specify basement, crawlspace or slab foundation when ordering.

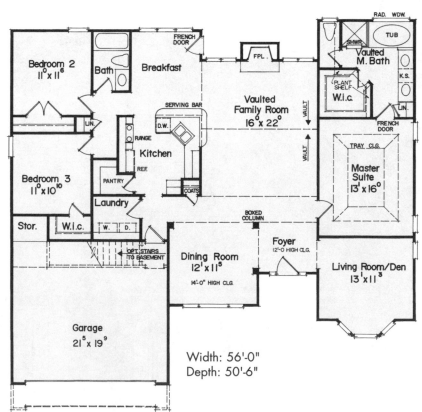

Width: 56'-0"
Depth: 50'-6"

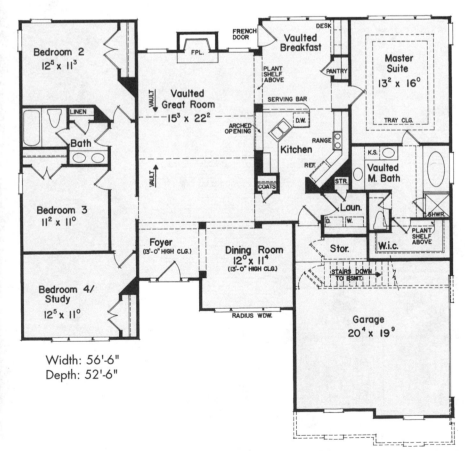

Bedroom 2
12⁵ x 11³

LINEN

Bath

Bedroom 3
11² x 11⁰

Foyer
(13'-0" HIGH CLG.)

Bedroom 4/
Study
12⁵ x 11⁰

Width: 56'-6"
Depth: 52'-6"

VAULT

Vaulted
Great Room
15³ x 22²

VAULT

FPL.

ARCHED
OPENING

COATS

Dining Room
12⁰ x 11⁴
(13'-0" HIGH CLG.)

RADIUS WDW.

FRENCH
DOOR

DESK

Vaulted
Breakfast

PLANT
SHELF
ABOVE

SERVING BAR

D.W.

Kitchen

RANGE

REF.

PANTRY

Master
Suite
13² x 16⁰

TRAY CLG.

K.S.

Vaulted
M. Bath

STR.

Laun.

D. W.

Stor.

STAIRS DOWN
TO BSMT.

T. SHWR.

PLANT
SHELF
ABOVE

W.i.c.

Garage
20⁴ x 19⁹

Design HPT300214
Square Footage: 1,945

◆ Corner quoins and keystones above graceful window treatments have long been a hallmark of elegant European-style exteriors—this home has all that and more. This becomes apparent upon entering the foyer, which is beautifully framed by columns in the dining room and the entrance to the vaulted great room. The left wing holds three secondary bedrooms—one doubles as a study—and a full bath. To the right of the combined kitchen and vaulted breakfast room, you will find the private master suite. A relaxing master bath and a large walk-in closet complete this splendid retreat. Please specify basement or crawlspace foundation when ordering.

Design HPT300215

Square Footage: 2,322

◆ An eclectic mix of building materials—stone, stucco and siding—sing in tune with the European charm of this one-story home. Decorative columns set off the formal dining room and the foyer from the vaulted family room, while the formal living room is quietly tucked behind French doors. The gourmet kitchen provides an angled snack bar and a sunny breakfast room. Two family bedrooms each have a walk-in closet and private access to a shared bath. The master suite holds an elegant tray ceiling, a bay sitting area and a lush bath. Please specify basement, crawlspace or slab foundation when ordering.

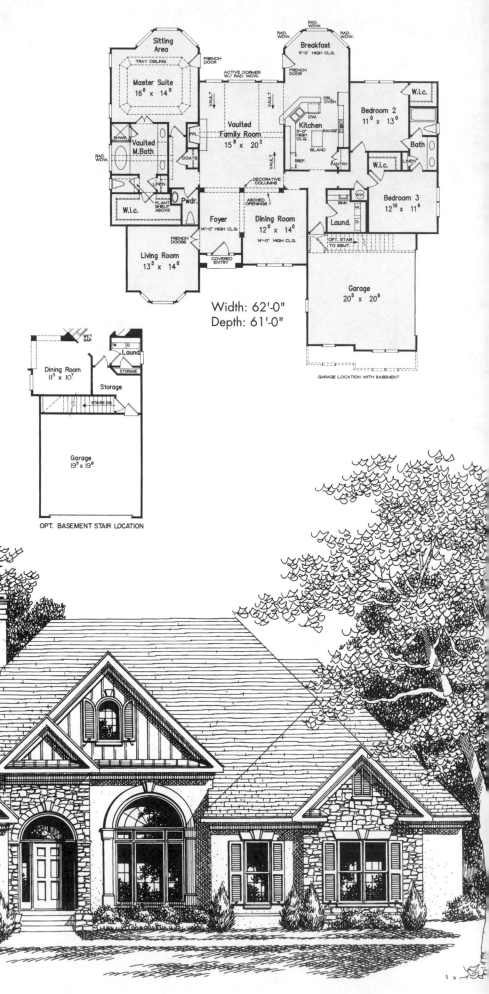

Width: 62'-0"
Depth: 61'-0"

GARAGE LOCATION WITH BASEMENT

OPT. BASEMENT STAIR LOCATION

Floor Plan Labels (Opt. Bonus Room Plan)

W.i.c.

Opt. Bonus
11³ x 12⁰

STAIRS DN

Opt. Bath

LINEN

OPT. BONUS ROOM PLAN

Basement Stair Option

Vaulted
Breakfast
LINEN

Bedroom 2
12⁵ x 11⁰

Kitchen

Bath

Bedroom 3
11³ x 12⁰

STAIRS DN

Pwdr.

STAIRS UP

COATS

Laund.

Basement Stair Option

Main Floor Plan

RADIUS WINDOW

SHWR.

K.S.

Vaulted M.Bath

LINEN

Hers

His

PLANT SHELF ABOVE

RADIUS WINDOWS

BOOKCASE

TRAY CLG.

Master Suite
13¹⁰ x 17⁰

FPL.

BOOKCASE

Family Room
16⁰ x 21⁰
14'-0" HIGH COFFERED CEILING

RADIUS WINDOW

FRENCH DOOR

Vaulted Breakfast

VAULT

VAULT

SERVING BAR

Kitchen

DW.

RANGE

OVEN

PANTRY

REF.

Bedroom 2
12⁵ x 11⁰

Bath

Bedroom 3
11³ x 12⁰

LINEN

WET BAR

COATS

Foyer
14'-0" HIGH CEILING

Dining Room
12⁰ x 14⁰
14'-0" HIGH CEILING

Vaulted Living Room / Opt. Sitting
14⁰ x 12²

VLT.

VLT.

Covered Entry

Pwdr.

WH

STAIRS

Laund.

W.i.c.

SINK

Garage
21¹⁰ x 20⁴

Width: 60'-0"
Depth: 67'-0"

Design HPT300216

Square Footage: 2,403
Bonus Room: 285 sq. ft.

◆ Asymmetrical gables, pediments and tall arch-top windows accent a European-style exterior, while inside, an unrestrained floor plan expresses its independence. A spider-beam ceiling and a centered fireplace framed by shelves redraw the open space of the family room to cozy dimensions. The vaulted breakfast nook enjoys a radius window and a French door that leads outside. Split sleeping quarters lend privacy to the luxurious master suite. Please specify basement, crawlspace, or slab foundation when ordering.

Design HPT300217
Square Footage: 2,193
Bonus Room: 400 sq. ft.

◆ From the hipped and gabled roof to the gracious entryway, class is a common element in the makeup of this home. Inside, the foyer is flanked by a formal living room (or make it a guest bedroom) and a formal dining room, defined by columns. Directly ahead lies the spacious family room, offering a warming fireplace. The sleeping quarters are separated for privacy. The master suite has a lavish bath and tray ceiling. Please specify basement, crawlspace or slab foundation when ordering.

Width: 64'-6"
Depth: 59'-0"

Design HPT300218
Square Footage: 1,832

◆ This compact one-story home has plenty of living in it. The master suite features an optional sun-washed sitting area with views to the rear of the home. A vaulted great room with a fireplace conveniently accesses the kitchen via a serving bar. Meals can also be taken in the cozy breakfast area. For formal occasions the dining room creates opulence with its decorative columns. Two family bedrooms flank the right of the home with a shared bath, linen storage and easy access to laundry facilities. Please specify basement or crawlspace foundation when ordering.

Opt. Sitting Room

Master Suite 13⁵ x 17⁴
TRAY CEILING

Vaulted M.Bath

Pwdr.

SHWR.

LINEN

PLANT SHELF ABOVE

W.i.c.

Foyer 14'-0" HIGH CLG.

Covered Porch

VAULT

VAULT

ARCHED OPENINGS

DECORATIVE COLUMNS

Vaulted Great Room 15⁰ x 20⁰

FPL.

FRENCH DOOR

TRAY CEILING

Breakfast

SERVING BAR

Kitchen

REF.

DW.

RANGE

PANTRY

Dining Room 12⁰ x 12⁰
14'-0" HIGH CLG.

Laund.

D.

W.

COATS

OPT. STAIR TO BSMT.

Bedroom 3 11⁰ x 12⁰

W.i.c.

Bath

LINEN

Bedroom 2 12¹⁰ x 11⁴

Garage 19⁵ x 20⁴

copyright © 1995 frank betz associates, inc.

Width: 59'-6"
Depth: 52'-6"

221

Design HPT300219

Square Footage: 2,032

◆ This stunning design dazzles in stucco and stone accents. A giant front window illuminates the formal dining room accented by arches. The foyer welcomes you into the vaulted great room, warmed by an enormous hearth. The kitchen is set between the dining and breakfast rooms for convenience. The master wing provides a vaulted master bath and huge walk-in closet. On the opposite side of the home, three additional family bedrooms share a hall bath. A handy laundry room completes the floor plan.

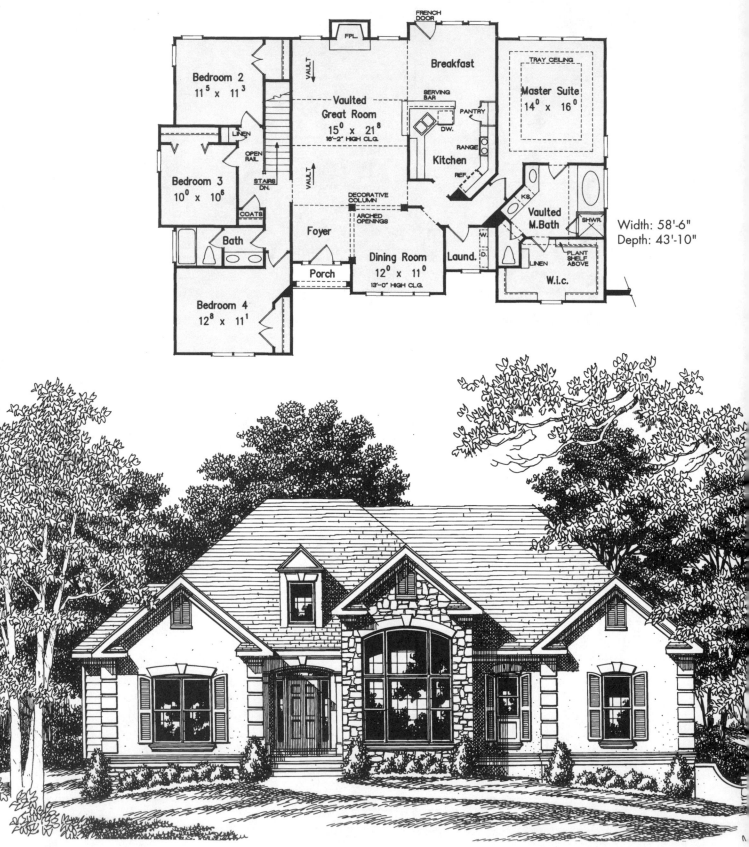

Width: 58'-6"
Depth: 43'-10"

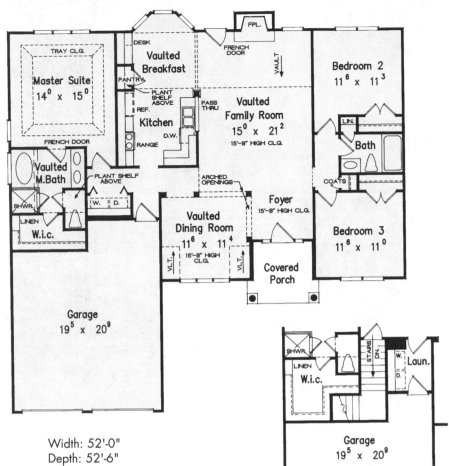

Master Suite
14⁰ x 15⁰
TRAY CLG.

Vaulted Breakfast
DESK

FPL.
FRENCH DOOR

PANTRY
PLANT SHELF ABOVE
REF.
Kitchen
D.W.
RANGE
PASS THRU
VAULT

Vaulted Family Room
15⁰ x 21²
15'-8" HIGH CLG.

Bedroom 2
11⁶ x 11³

LIN.

Bath

COATS

Vaulted M.Bath
SHWR
LINEN
W.i.c.
PLANT SHELF ABOVE
W. D.
FRENCH DOOR

Vaulted Dining Room
11⁶ x 11⁴
15'-8" HIGH CLG.
VLT.
VLT.

ARCHED OPENINGS

Foyer
15'-8" HIGH CLG.

Bedroom 3
11⁶ x 11⁰

Covered Porch

Garage
19⁵ x 20⁹

Width: 52'-0"
Depth: 52'-6"

SHWR
LINEN
W.i.c.
STAIRS DN.
W. D.
W.
Laun.

Garage
19⁵ x 20⁹

Optional Basement Stair Location

Design HPT300220
Square Footage: 1,575

◆ A lovely facade opens this one-story home, with gable ends and dormer windows as decorative features. The interior features vaulted family and dining rooms—a fireplace in the family room offers warmth. Defined by columns, the formal dining experience is enhanced. The kitchen attaches to a bayed breakfast nook with a vaulted ceiling. A split floor plan has the family bedrooms on the right side and the master suite on the left. The master bedroom has a tray ceiling, vaulted bath and walk-in closet. Please specify basement or crawlspace foundation when ordering.

Design HPT300221
Square Footage: 2,431

◆ Hipped rooflines, a projecting bay window and muntin windows are the key structural elements of this stunning home. Inside, the foyer opens to a great room with a built-in entertainment center surrounding a fireplace. An elegant tray ceiling and arches define the formal dining room. The study looks out through a bay window and includes a built-in bookshelf. Arched doorways lead into the island kitchen with a walk-in pantry. Read the morning news in the natural light of the breakfast nook's bay windows or contemplate nature on the covered lanai. Two family bedrooms share a full bath to the right of the plan, while the master suite enjoys many luxuries to the left.

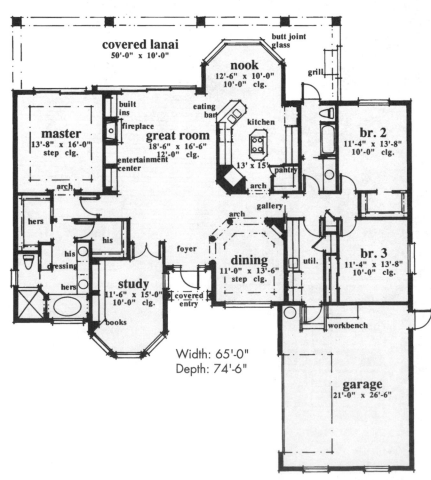

covered lanai
50'-0" x 10'-0"

butt joint glass

nook
12'-6" x 10'-0"
10'-0" clg.

grill

built ins
fireplace

eating bar

kitchen

br. 2
11'-4" x 13'-8"
10'-0" clg.

master
13'-8" x 16'-0"
step clg.

great room
18'-6" x 16'-6"
12'-0" clg.

entertainment center

13' x 15'

pantry

arch

hers

his

arch

gallery

arch

hers
his
dressing

foyer

util.

br. 3
11'-4" x 13'-8"
10'-0" clg.

hers

study
11'-6" x 15'-0"
10'-0" clg.

covered entry

dining
11'-0" x 13'-6"
step clg.

books

workbench

Width: 65'-0"
Depth: 74'-6"

garage
21'-0" x 26'-6"

Design HPT300222
Square Footage: 2,491
Bonus Space: 588 sq. ft.

◆ European details bring charm and a bit of *joie de vivre* to this traditional home, and a thoughtful floor plan warms up to a myriad of lifestyles. Comfortable living space includes a vaulted family room with a centered fireplace and complements the formal dining room, which offers a tray ceiling. A sizable gourmet kitchen contains a walk-in pantry and a center cooktop island counter and overlooks the breakfast area, which opens to a secluded covered porch through a French door. The master suite features a tray ceiling and a private sitting room, bright with windows and a warming hearth. Please specify basement, crawlspace, or slab foundation when ordering.

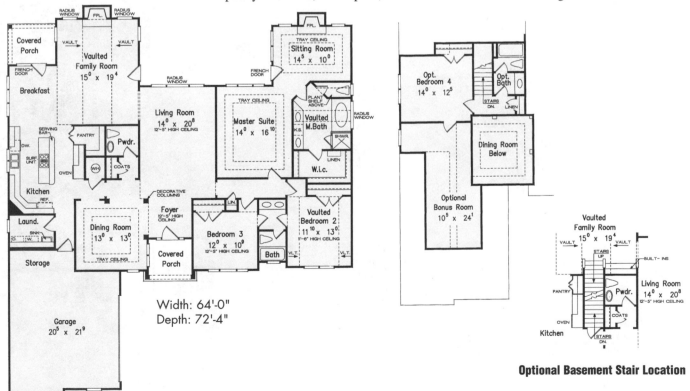

Width: 64'-0"
Depth: 72'-4"

Optional Basement Stair Location

Design HPT300223

Square Footage: 1,815

◆ This stately European home offers an easy-care stucco exterior with finely detailed windows and a majestic front door that furthers a graceful presence. Inside, a grand, columned foyer opens to both the formal dining room and the great room with a vaulted ceiling and a fireplace. The spacious, well-appointed kitchen, open to a breakfast room and adjacent to the formal dining area, makes serving and entertaining easy and delightful work. Nestled away at the opposite end of the home, the master suite combines perfect solitude with elegant luxury. This home is designed with a walkout basement foundation.

PORCH

BREAKFAST
10'-0" X 10'-0"

GREAT ROOM
16'-0" X 18'-0"

MASTER BEDROOM
15'-0" X 14'-0"

W.I.C.

MASTER BATH

POWDER

KITCHEN
14'-0" X 11'-4"

FOYER
5'-0" X 9'-0"

DINING ROOM
10'-6" X 13'-0"

BEDROOM
NO. 3
10'-6" X 10'-0"

BEDROOM NO. 2
11'-2" X 11'-0"

BATH

LAUND
5'-2" X
10'-6"

DN

TWO CAR GARAGE
20'-4" X 19'-4"

Width: 60'-0"
Depth: 58'-6"

QUOTE ONE®
Cost to build? See page 436
to order complete cost estimate
to build this house in your area!

Width: 48'-0"
Depth: 47'-6"

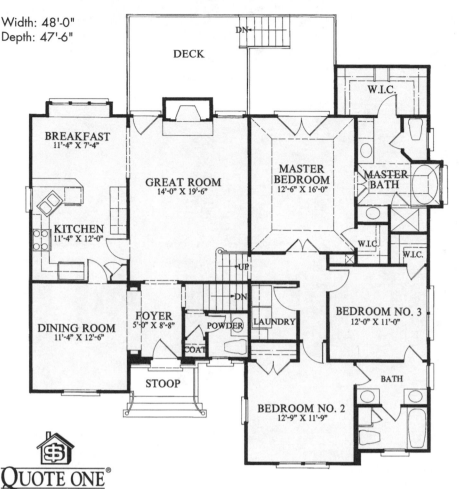

BREAKFAST
11'-4" X 7'-4"

KITCHEN
11'-4" X 12'-0"

DINING ROOM
11'-4" X 12'-6"

DECK

DN

GREAT ROOM
14'-0" X 19'-6"

MASTER
BEDROOM
12'-6" X 16'-0"

W.I.C.

MASTER
BATH

W.I.C.

W.I.C.

UP

DN

FOYER
5'-0" X 8'-8"

POWDER

COAT

LAUNDRY

BEDROOM NO. 3
12'-0" X 11'-0"

BATH

STOOP

BEDROOM NO. 2
12'-9" X 11'-9"

Design HPT300224
Square Footage: 1,770

◆ Perfect for a sloping lot, this European one-story home includes living areas on one level and bedrooms on another. The great room contains a fireplace and access to the rear deck. Close by are the U-shaped kitchen and breakfast room with a boxed window. The formal dining room completes the living area and is open to the entry foyer. Bedrooms are a few steps up from the living areas. The master suite enjoys two walk-in closets and a sumptuous bath with a compartmented toilet. Secondary bedrooms share a full bath that includes a double-bowl vanity. On the lower level is garage space and bonus space that may be used later for additional bedrooms or casual gathering areas. This home is designed with a walk-out basement foundation.

Design HPT300225

Square Footage: 2,295

◆ The abundance of details in this plan makes it the finest in one-story living. The great room and formal dining room are loosely defined by a simple column at the entry foyer, allowing for an open, dramatic sense of space. The kitchen with a prep island shares the right side of the plan with a bayed breakfast area and a keeping room with a fireplace. Sleeping accommodations to the left of the plan include a master suite with a sitting area, two closets and a separate tub and shower. Two family bedrooms share a full bath. Additional living and sleeping space can be developed in the walkout basement.

Width: 69'-0"
Depth: 49'-6"

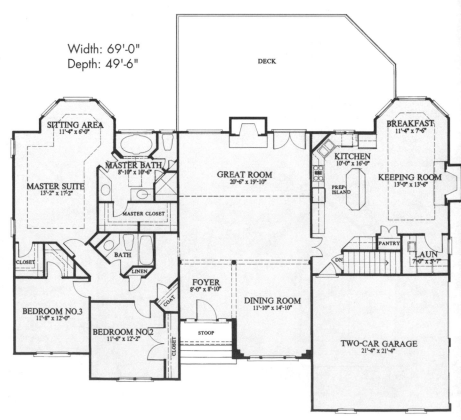

DECK

BREAKFAST
11'-4" X 8'-6"

BEDROOM NO. 3
11'-6" X 11'-0"

GREAT ROOM
14'-0" X 17'-6"

KITCHEN
11'-4" X 10'-0"

MASTER
BEDROOM
12'-4" X 15'-6"

BATH

HIS

DN.

PWDR.

MASTER
BATH

FOYER
6'-6" X 6'-6"

BEDROOM NO. 2
11'-0" X 14'-8"

DINING ROOM
11'-4" X 10'-6"

HERS

LAUNDRY

TWO-CAR GARAGE
20'-4" X 19'-4"

Width: 55'-6"
Depth: 57'-6"

Quote One®

Cost to build? See page 436
to order complete cost estimate
to build this house in your area!

Design HPT300226
Square Footage: 1,733

◆ Delightfully different, this brick one-story home has everything for the active family. The entry foyer opens to a formal dining room, accented with four columns, and a great room with a fireplace and French doors to the rear deck. The efficient kitchen has an attached, light-filled breakfast nook. The master bath features a tray ceiling, His and Hers walk-in closets, a double vanity and a huge garden tub. This home is designed with a walkout basement foundation.

Width: 65'-0"
Depth: 55'-11"

Design HPT300227
Square Footage: 2,095

◆ Inside this home, the foyer opens to the living room—defined through carefully placed openings—and the dining room, accented by dramatic window details. The open family room displays a fireplace and built-in cabinetry. In the master suite, a large bath with dual vanities, a whirlpool tub and a separate shower is complete with a spacious walk-in closet. Two additional bedrooms sit on the opposite side of the home. This home is designed with a walkout basement foundation.

QUOTE ONE®
Cost to build? See page 436
to order complete cost estimate
to build this house in your area!

Width: 71'-3"
Depth: 66'-3"

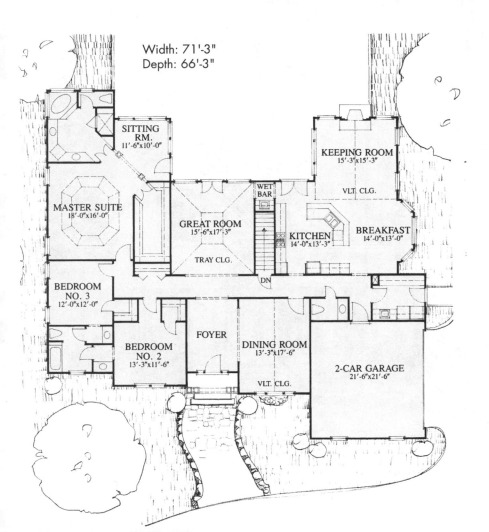

SITTING RM.
11'-6"x10'-0"

KEEPING ROOM
15'-3"x15'-3"

VLT. CLG.

WET BAR

MASTER SUITE
18'-0"x16'-0"

GREAT ROOM
15'-6"x17'-3"

TRAY CLG.

KITCHEN
14'-0"x13'-3"

BREAKFAST
14'-0"x13'-0"

DN

BEDROOM NO. 3
12'-0"x12'-0"

BEDROOM NO. 2
13'-3"x11'-6"

FOYER

DINING ROOM
13'-3"x17'-6"

2-CAR GARAGE
21'-6"x21'-6"

VLT. CLG.

Design HPT300228
Square Footage: 2,902

◆ Arches, transoms and sweeping roof-lines blend artfully to highlight this French exterior. The state-of-the-art interior starts with a great room that features a tray ceiling, a wet bar and French doors to the outside. Adjoining the kitchen and breakfast room, the spacious keeping room provides a fireplace and lots of windows to let in natural light. The master suite offers a sitting room and a sumptuous bath, while two family bedrooms share a connecting bath. This home is designed with a walkout basement foundation.

QUOTE ONE®
Cost to build? See page 436
to order complete cost estimate
to build this house in your area!

231

Design HPT300229
Square Footage: 2,090

◆ This home's European styling will work well in a variety of environments. As for livability, this plan has it all. Begin with the front door which opens into the dining and great rooms—the latter complete with fireplace and doors that open onto the back porch. The kitchen combines with the breakfast nook to create ample space for meals. This plan incorporates four bedrooms; you may want to use one bedroom as an office and another as a study. The master bedroom houses a fabulous bath with twin walk-in closets and a spa tub. This home is designed with a walkout basement foundation.

Quote One®
Cost to build? See page 436 to order complete cost estimate to build this house in your area!

Width: 61'-0"
Depth: 72'-0"

Design HPT300230
Square Footage: 2,150

◆ From the arched covered entry to the jack-arch window, this house retains the distinction of a much larger home. From the foyer and across the spacious great room, French doors and large side windows give a generous view of the covered rear porch. The dining room is subtly defined by the use of columns and a large triple window. The kitchen has a generous work island and breakfast area and joins the cozy keeping room. Two family bedrooms share a private bath. The home is completed by a quiet master suite located at the rear. It contains a bay window, a garden tub and His and Hers vanities. This home is designed with a walkout basement foundation.

Floor plan labels:

KEEPING ROOM 13'-4" X 13'-8"

PORCH

MASTER BEDROOOM 13'-4" X 15'-6"

W.I.C.

DN.

BREAKFAST 11'-4" X 10'-0"

DINING ROOM 11'-6" X 13'-0"

GREAT ROOM 16'-4" X 15'-4"

MASTER BATH

PANTRY

KITCHEN 14'-8" X 11'-0"

LAUNDRY 8'-6" X 5'-4"

PWDR.

BEDROOM NO. 3 11'-8" X 12'-0"

FOYER 8'-0" X 13'-8"

BEDROOM NO. 2/ STUDY 11'-4" X 12'-0"

STOOP

BATH

TWO CAR GARAGE 21'-4" X 21'-8"

Width: 64'-0"
Depth: 60'-4"

QUOTE ONE®
Cost to build? See page 436
to order complete cost estimate
to build this house in your area!

233

Design HPT300231

Square Footage: 2,095

◆ This special cottage design carries a fully modern floor plan. The entry leads to open living areas with a dining room and a living room flanking the foyer. The family room—with a fireplace and built-in bookcases—is nearby the bright breakfast room with deck access. The efficiently patterned kitchen provides a helpful lead-in to the dining room. Two secondary bedrooms make up the left side of the plan. A full compartmented bath connects them. The master bedroom suite pampers with a tiered ceiling and a bath with dual vanities, a whirlpool tub, a separate shower, a compartmented toilet and a walk-in closet. This home is designed with a walkout basement foundation.

Width: 65'-0"
Depth: 55'-6"

Design HPT300232

Square Footage: 1,684

◆ Charming and compact, this home is as beautiful as it is practical. The impressive arch over the double front door is repeated with an arched window in the formal dining room. This room opens to a spacious great room with a fireplace and is near the kitchen and bayed breakfast area. Split sleeping arrangements put the master suite at the right of the plan and two family bedrooms at the left. This home is designed with a walkout basement foundation.

DECK

BREAKFAST
11'-4" X 8'-6"

BEDROOM NO. 3
11'-6" X 11'-0"

GREAT ROOM
14'-0" X 17'-6"

KITCHEN
11'-4" X 10'-0"

MASTER
BEDROOM
12'-4" X 15'-6"

BATH

DN.

HIS

FOYER
6'-6" X 5'-0"

PWDR

MASTER
BATH

BEDROOM NO. 2
11'-0" X 12'-2"

DINING ROOM
11'-4" X 10'-6"

HERS

STOOP

LAUNDRY

Width: 55'-6"
Depth: 57'-6"

TWO-CAR GARAGE
20'-4" X 19'-4"

QUOTE ONE®

Cost to build? See page 436
to order complete cost estimate
to build this house in your area!

Design HPT300233
Square Footage: 2,377

Width: 69'-0"
Depth: 49'-6"

◆ One-story living takes a lovely traditional turn in this brick home. The entry foyer opens to the formal dining room and the great room through graceful columned archways. The open gourmet kitchen, bayed breakfast nook and keeping room with a fireplace will be a magnet for family activity. Sleeping quarters offer two family bedrooms and a hall bath and a rambling master suite with a bayed sitting area and a sensuous bath. This home is designed with a walkout basement foundation.

SITTING
14'-0" X 12'-0"

HIS

MASTER BATH

MASTER SUITE
16'-6" X 15'-6"

HERS

POWDER

BREAKFAST
12'-0" X 13'-6"

DN.

GREAT ROOM
20'-6" X 18'-6"

BEDROOM NO. 3
12'-0" X 12'-0"

KITCHEN
14'-3" X 13'-6"

FOYER

LAUNDRY

DINING ROOM
13'-6" X 14'-6"

BATH

STOOP

BEDROOM NO. 2
12'-3" X 14'-0"

STORAGE

2-CAR GARAGE
21'-6" X 27'-6"

Width: 74'-0"
Depth: 79'-0"

Design HPT300234
Square Footage: 2,770

◆ The European-inspired excitement of this stucco home can be seen in its use of large, abundant windows. Inside, the spacious foyer leads directly to a large great room with a massive fireplace. The banquet-sized dining room receives light from the triple window and features a dramatic vaulted ceiling. The master suite features a separate sitting area with a cathedral ceiling and access to the patio. The two additional bedrooms each have their own vanity within a shared bath. This home is designed with a walkout basement foundation.

Design HPT300235
Square Footage: 2,697

Width: 65'-3"
Depth: 67'-3"

◆ Dual chimneys (one a false chimney created to enhance the aesthetic effect) and a double stairway to the covered entry of this home create a balanced architectural statement. The sunlit foyer leads straight into the spacious great room, where French doors provide a generous view of the covered veranda in back. The great room features a tray ceiling and a fireplace, bordered by twin bookcases. Another great view is offered from the spacious kitchen with a breakfast bar and a roomy work island. The master suite provides a large balanced bath and a spacious closet. This home is designed with a walkout basement foundation.

QUOTE ONE®
Cost to build? See page 436 to order complete cost estimate to build this house in your area!

2-CAR GARAGE
21'-6" X 21'-0"

LAUNDRY

STORAGE

VERANDA

MASTER BATH

BREAKFAST
13'-6" X 10'-0"

MASTER SUITE
15'-9" X 16'-0"

W.I.C.

UP

GREAT ROOM
20'-6" X 17'-6"

KITCHEN
16'-0" X 13'-6"

DN.

BEDROOM NO. 3
12'-0" X 13'-3"

POWDER

PANTRY

DINING ROOM
13'-3" X 14'-9"

FOYER

BEDROOM NO. 2
12'-6" X 13'-3"

BATH

PORTICO

© American Home Gallery, Ltd.

BREAKFAST
11'-6" X 9'-2"

BEDROOM NO. 3
10'-6" X 12'-6"

KITCHEN
11'-6" X 11'-0"

BATH

GREAT ROOM
14'-0" X 17'-10"

DECK

MASTER BEDROOM
12'-4" X 14'-8"

MASTER BATH

BEDROOM NO. 2
12'-0" X 11'-2"

LAUNDRY

DN

FOYER
5'-4" X 8'-0"

POWDER

W.I.C.

DINING ROOM
12'-0" X 11'-0"

STOOP

TWO-CAR GARAGE
20'-4" X 20'-4"

Width: 54'-0"
Depth: 52'-0"

DesignHPT300236
Square Footage: 1,800

◆ This European-inspired cottage contains one of the most efficient floor plans available. From the formal dining room at the front of the plan to the commodious great room at the rear, it accommodates various lifestyles in less than 2,000 square feet. An opulent master suite with deck access and grand bath dominates the right wing of the house. Two family bedrooms and a full bath are found to the left. There's even a powder room for guests. The gourmet-style kitchen has an attached breakfast area with a glassed bay for sunny brunches. Bonus space in the basement allows for future development.

Design HPT300237

Square Footage: 2,120

◆ Arch-top windows act as graceful accents for this wonderful design. Inside, the floor plan is compact but commodious. The family room serves as the center of activity. It provides a fireplace and connects to a lovely sun room with rear-porch access. A private den opens off the foyer with double doors and boasts its own cozy fireplace. The kitchen area opens to the sun room and contains an island work counter. Bedrooms are split, with the master suite to the right side of the design. This home is designed with a walkout basement foundation.

Width: 62'-0"
Depth: 62'-6"

BATH

BEDROOM NO. 3
11'-6" X 11'-0"

BEDROOM NO. 2
11'-4" X 11'-0"

SUN ROOM
12'-0" X 13'-9"

PORCH

MASTER BATH

W.I.C.

MASTER BEDROOM
13'-4" X 15'-8"

BREAKFAST
10'-0" X 9'-0"

FAMILY ROOM
18'-0" X 14'-0"

LAUNDRY

KITCHEN
12'-0" X 13'-9"

BATH

DN.

TWO CAR GARAGE
20'-4" X 20'-8"

DINING ROOM
10'-6" X 13'-6"

FOYER

DEN
11'-4" X 12'-6"

STOOP

Design HPT300238
Square Footage: 3,613
Bonus Room: 590 sq. ft.

◆ A grand brick exterior with a hipped roof and impressive gables creates a striking impact for this luxurious estate home. Elegant tray ceilings enhance several of the home's key rooms: the foyer, dining room, sun room/breakfast area, bedroom/study and master bedroom and bath. A cathedral ceiling with a rear clerestory dormer augments the large central great room. Note this home's many extras: built-in cabinetry in the great room and bedroom/study, a generous walk-in pantry, fireplaces in the great room and master bedroom, and a three-car garage. The master suite enjoys rear-deck access, His and Hers walk-in closets and a spacious bath. Both secondary bedrooms feature private baths and walk-in closets.

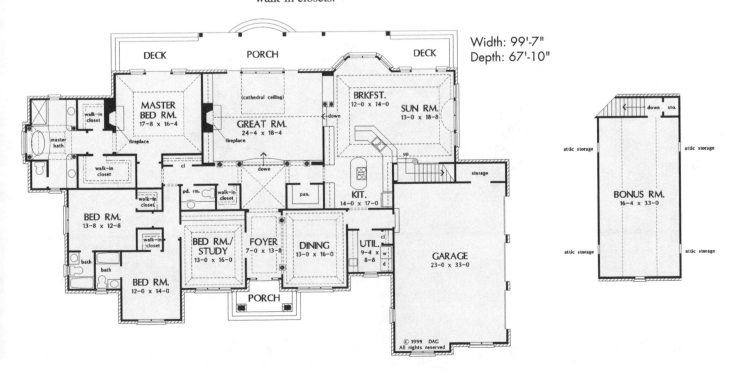

Width: 99'-7"
Depth: 67'-10"

◆ Some of the pleasures of this traditional home are the muntin windows with lintels, the gables, and the arched entrance, but most of all, its brick facade makes the exterior even more enjoyable—note that all three porches are adorned by columns. The foyer is adorned with elegant columns leading to the massive great room, which boasts a cathedral ceiling, a fireplace with built-in shelves, and dormer windows. Sleeping quarters to the right of the home include two family bedrooms sharing a dual-vanity bath. The inviting master bedroom enjoys a tray ceiling, lots of closet space and a private bath with a pampering tub and dual vanities.

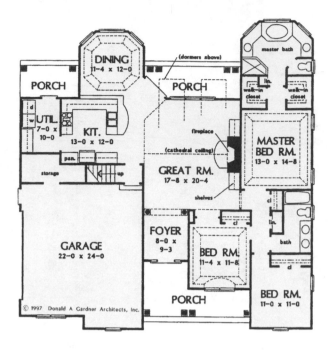

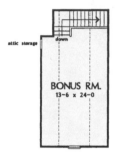

Width: 54'-0"
Depth: 57'-8"

Design HPT302002
Square Footage: 1,770
Bonus Room: 401 sq. ft.

DECK

seat

SCREEN PORCH
16-0 x 12-0
skylights
(cathedral ceiling)

BED RM.
12-4 x 12-6

walk-in closet

BED RM.
11-0 x 12-2

walk-in closet

bath

fireplace

GREAT RM.
18-0 x 19-4
(cathedral ceiling)

lin.

cl

FOYER
12-0 x 5-8

BED RM./ STUDY
12-0 x 12-0

cl

PORCH

DINING
12-0 x 13-8

MASTER BED RM.
13-0 x 18-8

master bath

walk-in closet

BRKFST.
12-0 x 8-4
skylights

KITCHEN
12-0 x 12-10

up

UTILITY
9-4 x 6-8

pd. rm.

d | w

GARAGE
25-8 x 20-0

storage

storage

© 1998 Donald A Gardner, Inc.

Width: 77'-4"
Depth: 62'-0"

attic storage

BONUS RM.
17-6 x 18-0

skylights

down

attic storage

Design HPT300240

Square Footage: 2,262
Bonus Room: 388 sq. ft.

◆ True tradition is exhibited in the brick and siding facade, hipped roof and keystone arches of this spacious four-bedroom home. Stately columns framing the front entry are repeated in the home's formal foyer. The generous great room boasts a fireplace with flanking built-ins. A dramatic cathedral ceiling enhances the space and is continued out into the adjoining screened porch. The nearby breakfast area is enriched by dual skylights. Three family bedrooms—two with walk-in closets—share an impressive hall bath. Secluded on the opposite side of the home, the master suite features rear-deck access, a walk-in closet and a private bath.

B. NATHAN

243

Design HPT300241

Square Footage: 2,137

◆ The grand balustrade and recessed entry are just the beginning of this truly spectacular home. A hip vaulted ceiling highlights the great room—a perfect place to entertain, made cozy by a massive fireplace and built-in cabinetry. An angled snack counter provides an uninterrupted interior vista of the living area from the gourmet kitchen. To the rear of the plan, French doors open to a spacious lanai—a beautiful spot for enjoying the harmonious sounds of the sea. On the lower level, separate bonus spaces easily convert to hobby rooms or can be used for additional storage. An additional storage area promises room for unused toys and furnishings.

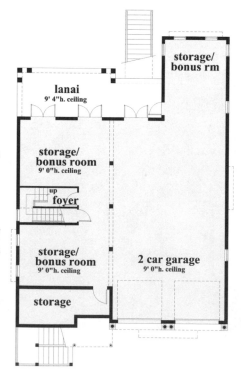

storage/
bonus rm

lanai
9' 4"h. ceiling

storage/
bonus room
9' 0"h. ceiling

up

foyer

storage/
bonus room
9' 0"h. ceiling

storage

2 car garage
9' 0"h. ceiling

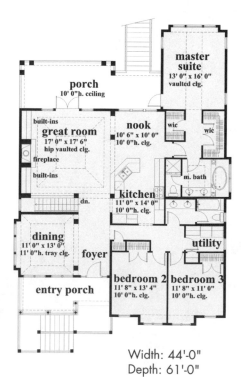

porch
10' 0"h. ceiling

master
suite
13' 0" x 16' 0"
vaulted clg.

built-ins

great room
17' 0" x 17' 6"
hip vaulted clg.

fireplace

built-ins

nook
10' 6" x 10' 0"
10' 0"h. clg.

wic

wic

m. bath

kitchen
11' 0" x 14' 0"
10' 0"h. clg.

dn.

dining
11' 0" x 13' 0"
11' 0"h. tray clg.

foyer

utility

bedroom 2
11' 8" x 13' 4"
10' 0"h. clg.

bedroom 3
11' 8" x 11' 0"
10' 0"h. clg.

entry porch

Width: 44'-0"
Depth: 61'-0"

One-Story Homes With a Country Flair

Design HPT300242
Square Footage: 1,675

Width: 63'-11"
Depth: 54'-8"

◆ A full porch of columns gives a relaxing emphasis to this country home. Inside, the great room includes a cozy fireplace framed by windows. An open floor plan connects the great room, dining room and kitchen. The island/snack bar adds to the available work space in the kitchen. Walk-in closets dominate this plan, with one in each of three bedrooms and one by the laundry room as well. The two-car garage contains a storage area for family treasures. The master bedroom boasts a private bath and a wonderful view of the rear yard. Please specify basement, crawlspace or slab foundation when ordering.

Bath
Master Bedroom 13-4x12-6
Porch 14-3x10-8
Storage 18-11x7-4
Laundry 9-0x7-5
Kitchen 13-4x11-5
Garage 21-6x21-4
©Larry James Designs
Bedroom 13-3x9-4
Bath
Dining 15-11x9-4
Greatroom 13-5x15-11
Bedroom 13-4x11-11
Foyer
Porch 34-5x6-0

Bedroom 13-3x9-4

Basement Stair Location

Design HPT3030013

Square Footage: 1,399
Bonus Room: 296 sq. ft.

◆ Open gables, a covered porch, and shuttered windows bring out the country flavor of this three-bedroom home. Inside, the great room enjoys a cathedral ceiling and a fireplace. Decorative columns set off the formal dining room, which is only steps away from the well-outfitted kitchen. Here, a window sink, a pantry, and a cooktop island overlooking the great room make an ideal food-preparation environment. Two family bedrooms located to the right of the plan share a full bath. The secluded master suite is highlighted by dual vanities, a compartmented shower and toilet, separate tub, walk-in closet, and cathedral ceiling.

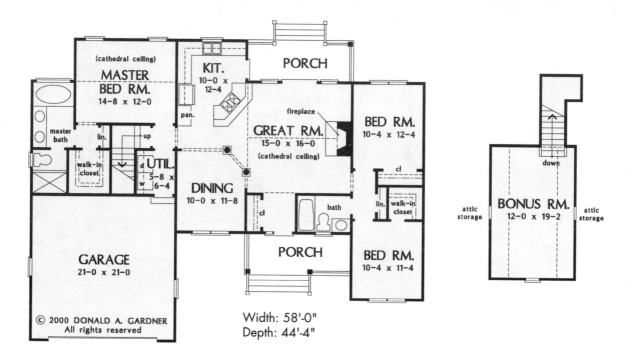

Width: 58'-0"
Depth: 44'-4"

246

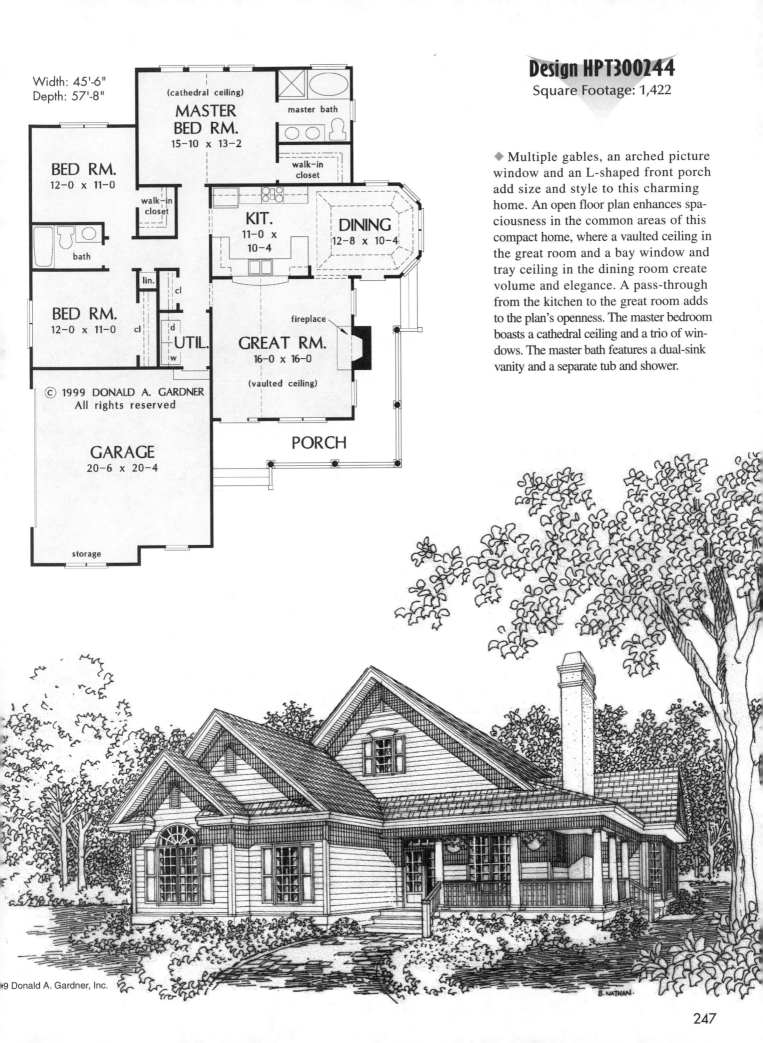

Width: 45'-6"
Depth: 57'-8"

(cathedral ceiling)

MASTER BED RM.
15-10 x 13-2

master bath

walk-in closet

BED RM.
12-0 x 11-0

walk-in closet

bath

KIT.
11-0 x 10-4

DINING
12-8 x 10-4

lin.

cl

BED RM.
12-0 x 11-0

cl

d

w

UTIL.

fireplace

GREAT RM.
16-0 x 16-0

(vaulted ceiling)

GARAGE
20-6 x 20-4

storage

PORCH

Design HPT300244
Square Footage: 1,422

◆ Multiple gables, an arched picture window and an L-shaped front porch add size and style to this charming home. An open floor plan enhances spaciousness in the common areas of this compact home, where a vaulted ceiling in the great room and a bay window and tray ceiling in the dining room create volume and elegance. A pass-through from the kitchen to the great room adds to the plan's openness. The master bedroom boasts a cathedral ceiling and a trio of windows. The master bath features a dual-sink vanity and a separate tub and shower.

B. NATHAN

Design HPT300245

Square Footage: 1,882
Bonus Room: 363 sq. ft.

◆ An arched window in a center front-facing gable lends style and beauty to the facade of this three-bedroom home. An open common area features a great room with a cathedral ceiling, a formal dining room with a tray ceiling, a functional kitchen and an informal breakfast area. The area separates the master suite from the secondary bedrooms for privacy. The master suite provides a dramatic vaulted ceiling, access to the back porch and abundant closet space. Access to a versatile bonus room is near the master bedroom.

BONUS RM.
14-0 x 21-0

attic storage   attic storage

down

Width: 61'-4"
Depth: 55'-0"

PORCH

BED RM.
11-4 x 11-0

(cathedral ceiling)

fireplace

GREAT RM.
16-0 x 18-8

cl

lin.

bath

BED RM.
14-0 x 11-4

FOYER
6-0 x 11-4

cl

cl

DINING
16-4 x 11-4

PORCH

BRKFST.
11-4 x 9-0

KIT.
11-4 x 11-8

UTIL.
6-0 x 9-0

w d

pd. rm.

up

storage

(vaulted ceiling)
MASTER BED RM.
14-8 x 16-8

cl

walk-in closet

master bath

GARAGE
21-0 x 21-0

© 1994 Donald A. Gardner Architects, Inc.

B. Nathan

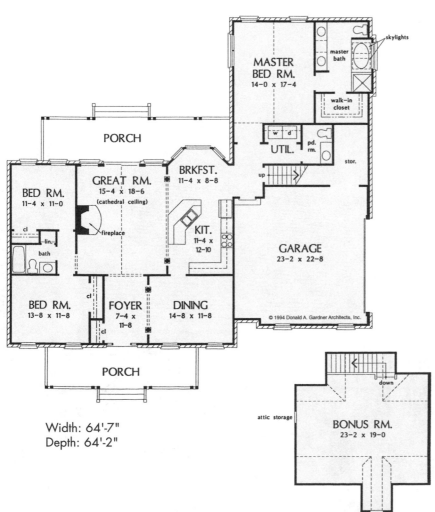

PORCH

MASTER BED RM.
14-0 x 17-4

master bath

skylights

walk-in closet

w d

pd. rm.

UTIL.

stor.

up

GREAT RM.
15-4 x 18-6
(cathedral ceiling)

BRKFST.
11-4 x 8-8

BED RM.
11-4 x 11-0

cl

lin.

bath

fireplace

KIT.
11-4 x 12-10

GARAGE
23-2 x 22-8

© 1994 Donald A. Gardner Architects, Inc.

BED RM.
13-8 x 11-8

cl

FOYER
7-4 x 11-8

cl

DINING
14-8 x 11-8

PORCH

Width: 64'-7"
Depth: 64'-2"

attic storage

down

BONUS RM.
23-2 x 19-0

Design HPT300246

Square Footage: 1,927
Bonus Room: 536 sq. ft.

◆ Sunlight takes center stage in this delightful country home. Each room has at least two windows to add warmth and radiance, and a clerestory window brightens the foyer. Two bedrooms and a full bath are to the left of the foyer. To the right is the dining room which leads into the L-shaped kitchen, featuring a peninsular cooktop and connecting bayed breakfast area. The central great room offers a cathedral ceiling, a fireplace and access to the rear porch. The master suite is separated for privacy and features a lovely display of windows, a large walk-in closet and a luxurious whirlpool bath with skylights. Additional storage space is available in the garage and in the attic.

249

Design HPT300247

Square Footage: 1,927
Bonus Room: 400 sq. ft.

◆ A beautiful Palladian window and enchanting front porch lend this cottage country charm. Built-in cabinets flank the fireplace in the vaulted great room. The master bedroom offers a full bath with two walk-in closets and private access to a covered rear porch. Two family bedrooms each provide a walk-in closet and share a bath that offers separate vanities. The kitchen contains built-in cabinets and a serving counter that allows access to the dining room. Notice the two-car garage that boasts a separate entrance and a compact storage area. Please specify basement, crawlspace or slab foundation when ordering.

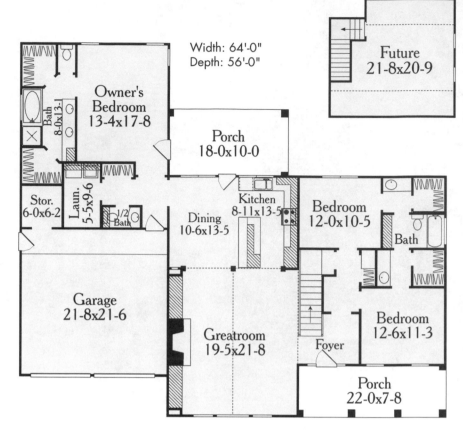

Width: 64'-0"
Depth: 56'-0"

Future
21-8x20-9

Bath
8-0x13-1

Owner's Bedroom
13-4x17-8

Porch
18-0x10-0

Kitchen
8-11x13-5

Bedroom
12-0x10-5

Bath

Stor.
6-0x6-2

Laun.
5-5x9-6

1/2 Bath

Dining
10-6x13-5

Garage
21-8x21-6

Greatroom
19-5x21-8

Foyer

Bedroom
12-6x11-3

Porch
22-0x7-8

Design HPT300248
Square Footage: 1,287

◆ This economical plan makes an impressive visual statement with its comfortable and well-proportioned appearance. The entrance foyer leads to all areas of the house. The great room, dining area and kitchen are all open to one another, allowing visual interaction. The great room and dining area share a dramatic cathedral ceiling and feature a grand fireplace flanked by bookshelves and cabinets. The master suite has a cathedral ceiling, walk-in closet and bath with double-bowl vanity, whirlpool tub and shower. Two family bedrooms and a full hall bath complete this cozy home.

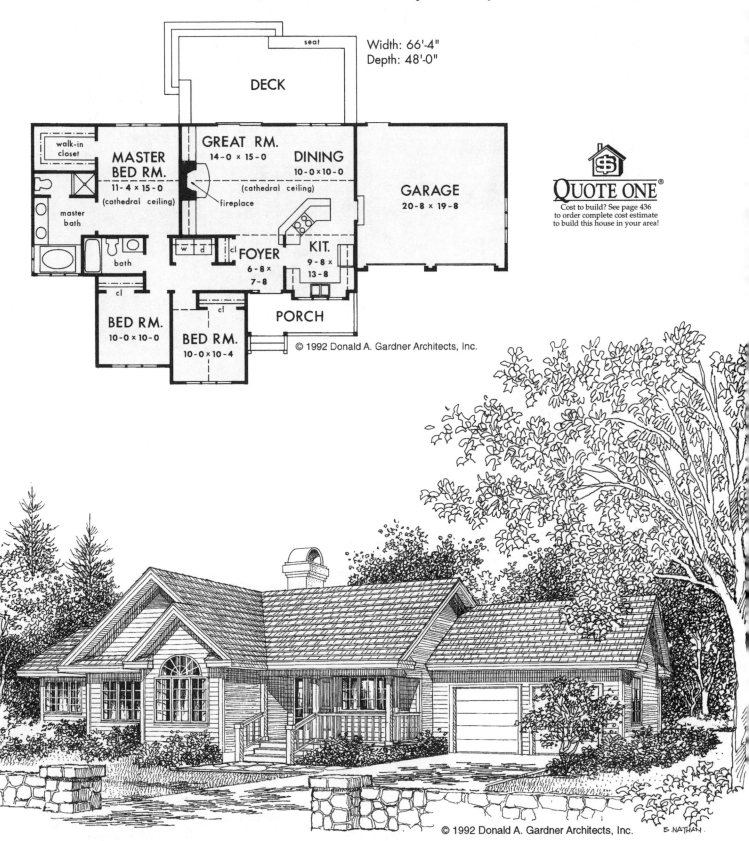

Width: 66'-4"
Depth: 48'-0"

seat

DECK

walk-in closet

MASTER BED RM.
11-4 × 15-0
(cathedral ceiling)

master bath

bath

cl

GREAT RM.
14-0 × 15-0

fireplace

(cathedral ceiling)

DINING
10-0 × 10-0

GARAGE
20-8 × 19-8

w d

cl

FOYER
6-8 ×
7-8

KIT.
9-8 ×
13-8

BED RM.
10-0 × 10-0

cl

BED RM.
10-0 × 10-4

PORCH

© 1992 Donald A. Gardner Architects, Inc.

Quote One®
Cost to build? See page 436 to order complete cost estimate to build this house in your area!

© 1992 Donald A. Gardner Architects, Inc.

E. NATHAN

Design HPT300249

Square Footage: 1,687
Bonus Room: 333 sq. ft.

◆ This traditional home blends characteristics of the folk houses of the national movement with the Cape Cod homes of the Colonial Revival period—note the shed-roofed porch that wraps from the foyer to the master suite at the rear. The formal dining room, to the left of the foyer, boasts a tray ceiling as does the master bedroom. A decorative column opens the dining room to the foyer and the great room where the majesty of the cathedral ceiling draws focus to the fireplace flanked by windows. The well-equipped kitchen serves the sunny breakfast nook and dining room with ease. Two family bedrooms, a shared full bath and the master suite complete the floor plan.

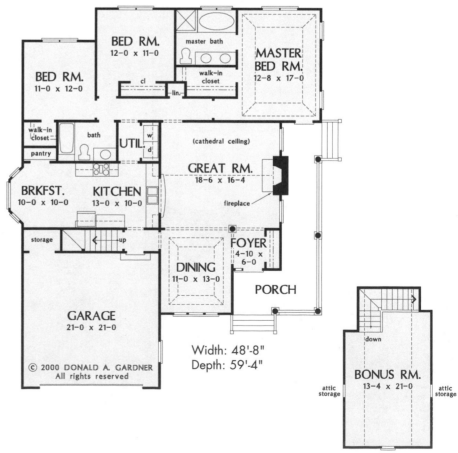

BED RM.
12-0 x 11-0

master bath

walk-in closet

MASTER BED RM.
12-8 x 17-0

BED RM.
11-0 x 12-0

cl

lin.

walk-in closet

bath

pantry

UTIL.

w
d

(cathedral ceiling)

GREAT RM.
18-6 x 16-4

fireplace

BRKFST.
10-0 x 10-0

KITCHEN
13-0 x 10-0

storage

up

FOYER
4-10 x 6-0

DINING
11-0 x 13-0

PORCH

GARAGE
21-0 x 21-0

Width: 48'-8"
Depth: 59'-4"

down

BONUS RM.
13-4 x 21-0

attic storage

attic storage

Width: 53'-4"
Depth: 66'-10"

DECK

BRKFST.
8-8 x 9-0

KIT.
10-8 x 10-0

GREAT RM.
17-0 x 16-10
(cathedral ceiling)

fireplace

MASTER BED RM.
13-0 x 17-0

pantry

bath

DINING
11-0 x 12-8

FOYER
5-6 x 10-0

cl

lin.

walk-in closet

master bath

BED RM.
11-0 x 12-0

cl

cl

BED RM.
11-0 x 12-0

w
d

PORCH

GARAGE
20-0 x 22-4

storage

Design HPT300250
Square Footage: 1,684

◆ This design offers a facade with nested gables, twin dormers and a welcoming covered entry with enough space to accommodate a porch swing for romantic interludes under the stars. The highlight of the interior is the magnificent great room where an intricate cathedral ceiling complements the window wall, that opens to the deck, and the fireplace that is framed by built-ins. Set to the right, the luxurious master suite offers privacy. To the left, the kitchen adjoins the breakfast nook. Two family bedrooms share a full bath on the far left where the hall leads past the laundry area and on to the two-car garage.

Design HPT300251
Square Footage: 1,652
Bonus Room: 367 sq. ft.

◆ A classic country exterior enriches the appearance of this economical home, while its front porch and two skylit back porches encourage weekend relaxation. The great room features a cathedral ceiling and a fireplace with adjacent built-ins. The master suite enjoys a double-door entry, back-porch access and a tray ceiling. The master bath has a garden tub set in the corner, a separate shower, twin vanities and a skylight. Loads of storage, an open floor plan and walls of windows make this three-bedroom plan very livable.

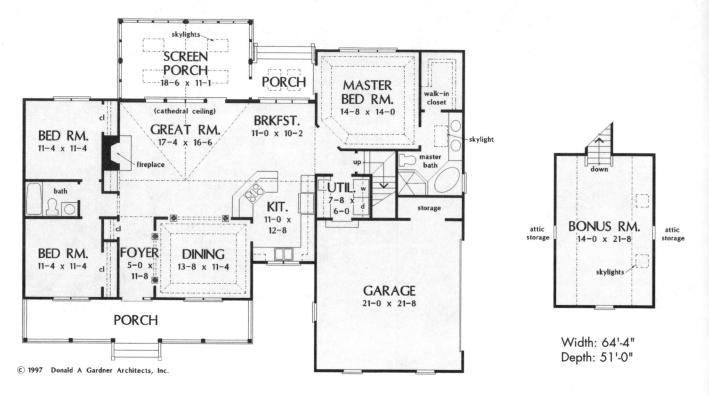

© 1997 Donald A Gardner Architects, Inc.

Width: 64'-4"
Depth: 51'-0"

© 1997 Donald A Gardner Architects

Design HPT300252

Square Footage: 1,864
Bonus Room: 420 sq. ft.

◆ Quaint and cozy on the outside with porches front and back, this three-bedroom country home surprises with an open floor plan featuring a large great room with a cathedral ceiling. A central kitchen with an angled counter opens to the breakfast and great rooms for easy entertaining. The privately located master bedroom has a cathedral ceiling and access to the deck. Two secondary bedrooms share a full hall bath. A bonus room makes expanding easy.

Width: 71'-0"
Depth: 56'-4"

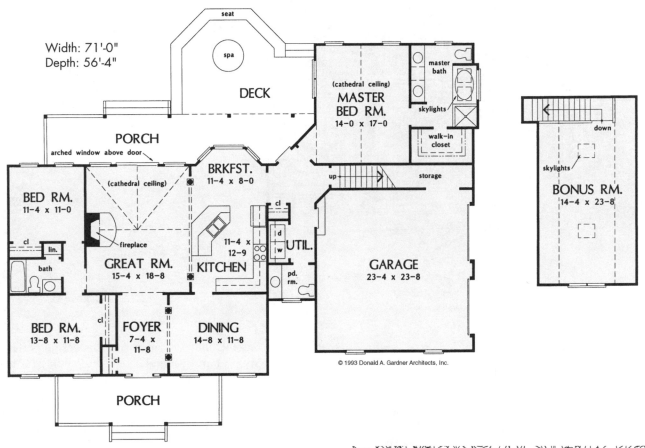

© 1993 Donald A. Gardner Architects, Inc.

B. NATHAN

93 Donald A. Gardner Architects, Inc.

B. NATHAN

Design HPT300253
Square Footage: 1,346

◆ A great room that stretches into the dining room makes this design perfect for entertaining. A cozy fireplace, stylish built-ins, and a cathedral ceiling further this casual yet elegant atmosphere. A rear deck extends living possibilities. The ample kitchen features an abundance of counter and cabinet space and an angled cook-top and serving bar that overlooks the great room. Two bedrooms, a hall bath and a handy laundry room make up the family sleeping wing while the master suite is privately located at the rear of the plan.

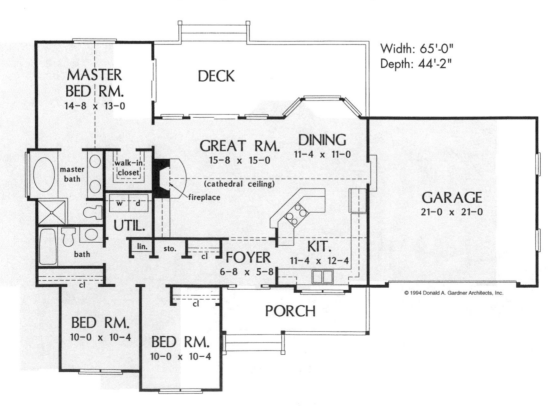

Width: 65'-0"
Depth: 44'-2"

MASTER BED RM.
14-8 x 13-0

DECK

GREAT RM.
15-8 x 15-0

DINING
11-4 x 11-0

master bath

walk-in closet

(cathedral ceiling)

fireplace

w | d

GARAGE
21-0 x 21-0

UTIL.

bath

lin. | sto.

cl

FOYER
6-8 x 5-8

KIT.
11-4 x 12-4

cl

BED RM.
10-0 x 10-4

cl

BED RM.
10-0 x 10-4

PORCH

© 1994 Donald A. Gardner Architects, Inc.

B. NATHAN

Design HPT300254

Square Footage: 2,207
Bonus Room: 435 sq. ft.

◆ This quaint four-bedroom home with front and rear porches reinforces its beauty with arched windows and dormers. The pillared dining room opens on the right, while a study that could double as a guest room is available on the left. Straight ahead lies the massive great room with its cathedral ceiling, enchanting fireplace and access to the private rear porch. Within steps of the dining room is the efficient kitchen and the sunny breakfast nook. The master suite enjoys a cathedral ceiling, rear-deck access and a master bath with a skylit whirlpool tub. Three additional bedrooms located at the opposite end of the house share a full bath.

Width: 76'-1"
Depth: 50'-0"

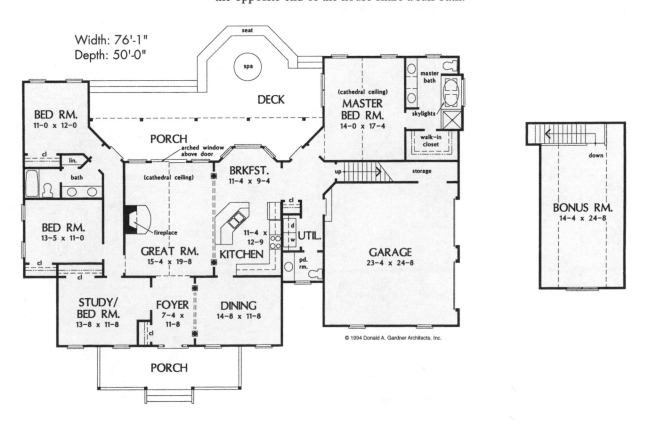

© 1994 Donald A. Gardner Architects, Inc.

Design HPT300255

Square Footage: 1,655

◆ Covered front porch dormers and arched windows welcome you to this modified version of one of our most popular country home plans. Interior columns dramatically open the foyer and the kitchen to the spacious great room. The drama is heightened by the great room's cathedral ceiling and fireplace. The kitchen, with its food-preparation island, easily serves the breakfast room and the formal dining room. The master bedroom boasts a tray ceiling and access to the rear deck. Added luxuries include a walk-in closet and a skylit master bath with a double vanity, garden tub and separate shower. Two generous bedrooms share the second bath.

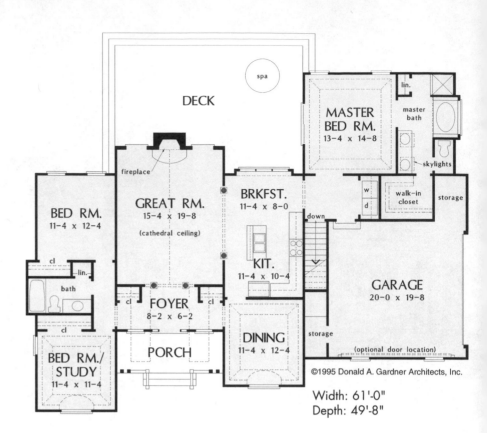

DECK

spa

MASTER BED RM.
13-4 x 14-8

lin.

master bath

skylights

storage

walk-in closet

w d

fireplace

GREAT RM.
15-4 x 19-8

(cathedral ceiling)

BRKFST.
11-4 x 8-0

down

BED RM.
11-4 x 12-4

cl

lin.

bath

KIT.
11-4 x 10-4

GARAGE
20-0 x 19-8

cl

FOYER
8-2 x 6-2

cl

cl

storage

(optional door location)

BED RM./ STUDY
11-4 x 11-4

PORCH

DINING
11-4 x 12-4

©1995 Donald A. Gardner Architects, Inc.

Width: 61'-0"
Depth: 49'-8"

Width: 59'-8"
Depth: 46'-8"

DECK

spa

MASTER BED RM.
13-4 x 13-8

master bath

skylights

fireplace

BRKFST.
11-4 x 7-4

BED RM.
11-4 x 11-4

GREAT RM.
15-4 x 16-10
(cathedral ceiling)

cl

bath

cl

BED RM./ STUDY
11-4 x 10-4

FOYER
8-2 x 6-2

cl

cl

PORCH

KITCHEN
11-4 x 10-0

DINING
11-4 x 11-4

w
d

walk-in closet

storage

GARAGE
20-0 x 19-8

Design HPT300256
Square Footage: 1,498

◆ This charming country home utilizes multi-pane windows, columns, dormers and a covered porch to offer a welcoming front exterior. Inside, the great room with a dramatic cathedral ceiling commands attention; the kitchen and breakfast room are just beyond a set of columns. The tier-ceilinged dining room presents a delightfully formal atmosphere for dinner parties or family gatherings. A tray ceiling in the master bedroom contributes to its pleasant atmosphere, as do the large walk-in closet and the gracious private bath with a garden tub and a separate shower. The secondary bedrooms are located at the opposite end of the house for privacy.

© 1993 Donald A. Gardner Architects, Inc.

Design HPT300257

Square Footage: 1,322

◆ Small doesn't necessarily mean boring in this well-proportioned, three-bedroom country home. A gracious foyer leads to the great room through a set of elegant columns. In this living area, a cathedral ceiling works well with a fireplace and skylights to bring the utmost livability to the homeowner. Outside, an expansive deck includes room for a spa. A handsome master suite has a tray ceiling and a private bath. Two additional bedrooms sit to the left of the plan. Each enjoys ample closet space, and they share a hall bath.

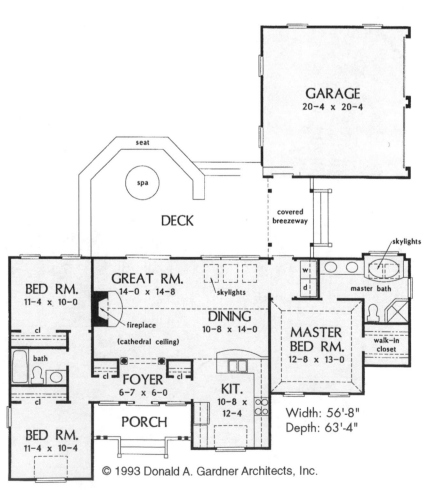

DECK

spa

MASTER BED RM.
13-4 x 14-8

lin.

master bath

skylights

fireplace

BRKFST.
11-4 x 7-10

w d

walk-in closet

storage

BED RM.
11-4 x 12-4

GREAT RM.
15-4 x 19-8
(cathedral ceiling)

cl

lin.

bath

KIT.
11-4 x 10-6

up

sto.

GARAGE
20-0 x 19-8

cl

FOYER
8-2 x 6-2

cl

cl

BED RM./ STUDY
11-4 x 11-4

PORCH

DINING
11-4 x 12-4

(optional door location)

Width: 64'-6"
Depth: 49'-8"

attic storage

BONUS RM.
20-0 x 13-0

down

attic storage

Design HPT300258
Square Footage: 1,699
Bonus Room: 336 sq. ft.

◆ An inviting front porch, dormers, gables and windows topped by half-rounds give this home curb appeal, while inside, an open floor plan with a split-bedroom design and a spacious bonus room steal the show. Two dormers add light and volume to the foyer, while a cathedral ceiling enlarges the open great room. Accent columns define the foyer, great room, kitchen and breakfast area. Both the dining room and the front bedroom/ study have tray ceilings that show off stunning picture windows with half-rounds. The private master suite with a tray ceiling accesses the rear deck through sliding glass doors, and the bath includes a garden tub, separate shower and two skylights over a double-bowl vanity.

Design HPT300259

Square Footage: 1,692
Bonus Room: 358 sq. ft.

◆ This cozy country cottage is enhanced with a front-facing planter box above the garage and a charming covered porch. The foyer leads to a vaulted great room, complete with a fireplace and radius windows. Decorative columns complement the entrance to the dining room, as does a decorative arch. On the left side of the plan resides the master suite, which is resplendent with amenities including a vaulted sitting room, tray ceiling, French doors to the vaulted full bath and an arched opening to the sitting room. On the right side, two additional bedrooms share a full bath. Please specify basement or crawlspace foundation when ordering.

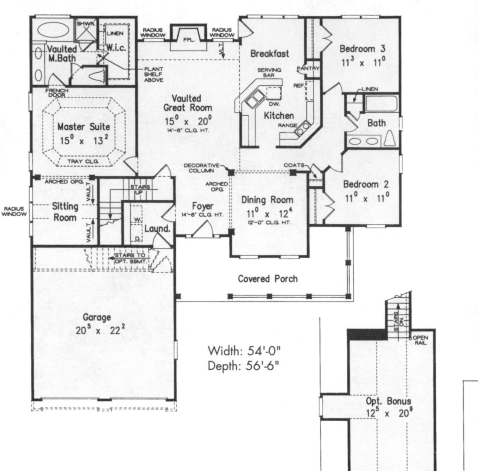

Width: 54'-0"
Depth: 56'-6"

Design HPT300260

Square Footage: 2,057
Bonus Room: 444 sq. ft.

◆ With its clean lines and symmetry, this home radiates grace and style. Inside, cathedral and tray ceilings add volume and elegance. The L-shaped kitchen includes an angled snack bar to the breakfast bay and great room. Secluded at the back of the house, the vaulted master suite includes a skylit bath. Of the two secondary bedrooms, one acts as a "second" master suite with its own private bath, and an alternate bath design creates a wheelchair-accessible option. The bonus room makes a great craft room, playroom, office or optional fourth bedroom with a bath. The two-car garage loads to the side.

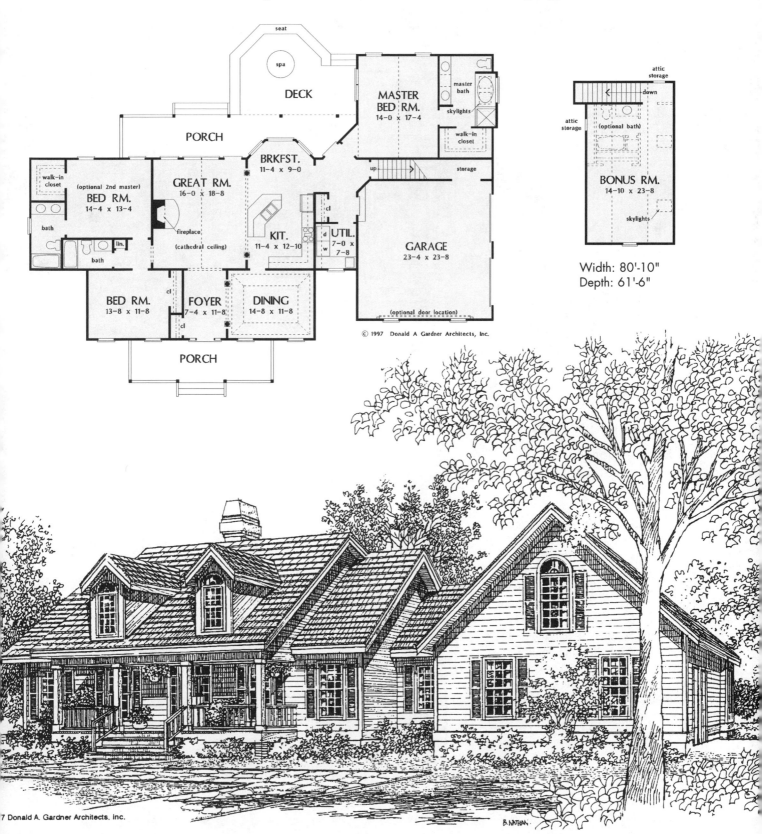

seat

spa

DECK

PORCH

MASTER BED RM.
14-0 x 17-4

master bath

skylights

walk-in closet

BRKFST.
11-4 x 9-0

GREAT RM.
16-0 x 18-8

walk-in closet

(optional 2nd master)

BED RM.
14-4 x 13-4

bath

fireplace

(cathedral ceiling)

KIT.
11-4 x 12-10

cl

up

storage

UTIL.
7-0 x 7-8

lin.

bath

BED RM.
13-8 x 11-8

cl

FOYER
7-4 x 11-8

cl

DINING
14-8 x 11-8

GARAGE
23-4 x 23-8

(optional door location)

© 1997 Donald A Gardner Architects, Inc.

PORCH

attic storage

attic storage

down

(optional bath)

BONUS RM.
14-10 x 23-8

skylights

Width: 80'-10"
Depth: 61'-6"

7 Donald A. Gardner Architects, Inc.

B. NATHAN

©1991 Donald A. Gardner Architects, Inc.

Design HPT300261

Square Footage: 1,541

◆ This traditional three-bedroom home with front and side porches, arched windows and dormers projects the appearance of a much larger home. The great room features a cathedral ceiling, a fireplace and an arched window above the sliding glass door to the expansive rear deck. Elegant round columns define the dining room. The master bedroom contains a pampering master bath with a whirlpool tub, separate shower, double-bowl vanity and walk-in closet. Two other bedrooms share a full bath that includes a double vanity.

Width: 71'-0"
Depth: 59'-0"

©1991 Donald A. Gardner Architects, Inc.

© 1992 Donald A. Gardner Architects, Inc.

GARAGE
22-0 × 21-4

Width: 70'-4"
Depth: 74'-0"

seat

spa

DECK

MASTER BED RM.
16-4 × 13-0

master bath

walk-in closet

GREAT RM.
15-4 × 18-10

fireplace

(cathedral ceiling)

BRKFST.
11-4 × 7-4

UTIL.
8-0 × 9-4

cl

w
d

KITCHEN
11-4 × 8-0

bath

BED RM.
11-0 × 10-4

cl

cl

DINING
11-4 × 12-0

cl

open to dormer above

FOYER
11-0 × 7-0

open to dormer above

cl

cl

BED RM.
13-0 × 12-0

PORCH

© 1992 Donald A. Gardner Architects, Inc.

Design HPT300262
Square Footage: 1,590

◆ The open floor plan of this country farmhouse packs in all of today's amenities in only 1,590 square feet. Columns separate the foyer from the great room with its cathedral ceiling and fireplace. Serving meals has never been easier—the kitchen makes use of direct access to the dining room as well as a breakfast nook overlooking the deck and spa. A handy utility room even has space for a counter and cabinets. Three bedrooms make this an especially desirable design. The master bedroom, off of the great room, provides private access to the deck. This design is flexible enough to be accommodated by a narrow lot if the garage is relocated.

Design HPT300263
Square Footage: 2,006
Bonus Room: 329 sq. ft.

BONUS RM.
14-4 x 19-10

attic storage

© 1996   Donald A Gardner Architects, Inc.

storage

GARAGE
22-0 x 23-4

up

Width: 76'-10"
Depth: 72'-2"

◆ Quaint and cozy on the outside, this country charmer offers an open floor plan with soaring open space as well as plenty of niches to nestle in. A cathedral ceiling and an extended-hearth fireplace highlight the grand great room. The formal dining room enjoys a bay of windows and is easily served by a spacious, U-shaped kitchen. A cathedral ceiling and relaxing bath amenities, such as a spa-style tub, highlight the secluded master suite. Two additional bedrooms—or make one a study—share a gallery hall that leads to a full bath and extra linen storage.

MASTER BED RM.
15-10 x 15-4
(cathedral ceiling)

master bath

walk-in closet

fireplace

PORCH

BRKFST.
10-4 x 9-4

KIT.
12-4 x 13-2

UTIL.
7-8 x 9-2

GREAT RM.
17-4 x 19-0
(cathedral ceiling)

bath

lin.

FOYER
8-8 x 8-0

DINING
12-4 x 12-8

BED RM.
12-2 x 12-4

BED RM./ STUDY
12-0 x 12-4

PORCH

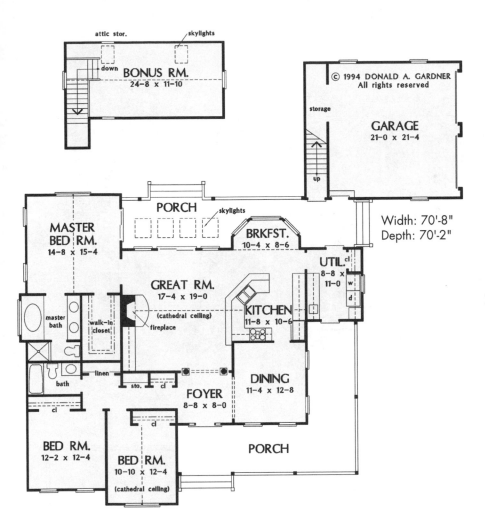

attic stor.   skylights

BONUS RM.
24-8 x 11-10

down

© 1994 DONALD A. GARDNER
All rights reserved

storage

GARAGE
21-0 x 21-4

up

PORCH   skylights

MASTER BED RM.
14-8 x 15-4

BRKFST.
10-4 x 8-6

UTIL. cl
8-8 x 11-0
w
d

GREAT RM.
17-4 x 19-0
(cathedral ceiling)

fireplace

master bath

walk-in closet

KITCHEN
11-8 x 10-6

linen

bath

cl

sto. cl

FOYER
8-8 x 8-0

DINING
11-4 x 12-8

cl

BED RM.
12-2 x 12-4

cl

BED RM.
10-10 x 12-4
(cathedral ceiling)

PORCH

Width: 70'-8"
Depth: 70'-2"

Design HPT300264

Square Footage: 1,815
Bonus Room: 336 sq. ft.

◆ Dormers, arched windows and covered porches lend this home its country appeal. Inside, the foyer opens to the dining room on the right and leads through a columned entrance to the great room warmed by a fireplace. Access is provided to the covered, skylit rear porch for outdoor livability. The open kitchen easily serves the great room, the bayed breakfast area and the dining room. A vaulted ceiling graces the master suite, which includes a walk-in closet and a private bath with a dual vanity and whirlpool tub. Two additional bedrooms share a full bath. A detached garage with a skylit bonus room is connected to the covered rear porch.

Quote One®
Cost to build? See page 436
to order complete cost estimate
to build this house in your area!

© 1994 Donald A. Gardner Architects, Inc.

B. NATHAN

267

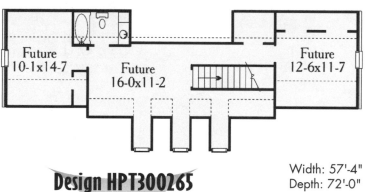

Design HPT300265
Square Footage: 1,722
Bonus Space: 819 sq. ft.

◆ Symmetry can be found in this design with three dormered windows, a covered porch and two complementary wings. The foyer opens to a long gallery hall to the sleeping areas or straight ahead to the great room. Skylights, a centered fireplace and open planning enhance the great room. The dining area enjoys rear-porch and patio access and is wonderfully convenient to the island kitchen. Two family bedrooms are spoiled with private baths. The master suite has great rear views with plenty of windows and enjoys a skylight in the full bath. Please specify basement, crawlspace or slab foundation when ordering.

Width: 57'-4"
Depth: 72'-0"

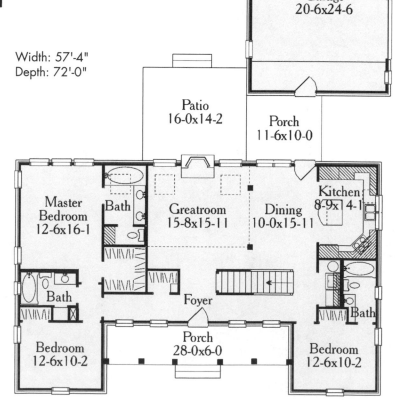

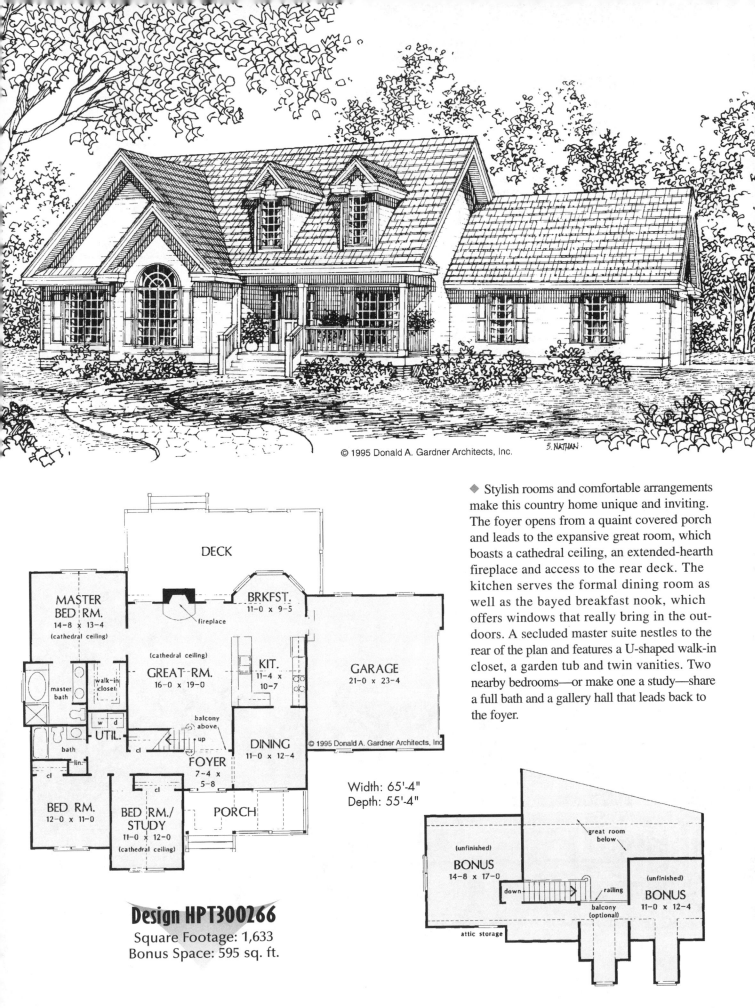

© 1995 Donald A. Gardner Architects, Inc.   S. NATHAN

DECK

MASTER BED RM.
14-8 x 13-4
(cathedral ceiling)

fireplace

BRKFST.
11-0 x 9-5

master bath

walk-in closet

(cathedral ceiling)

GREAT RM.
16-0 x 19-0

KIT.
11-4 x 10-7

GARAGE
21-0 x 23-4

w d

UTIL.

bath

balcony above
up

DINING
11-0 x 12-4

© 1995 Donald A. Gardner Architects, Inc

lin.

cl

cl

FOYER
7-4 x 5-8

BED RM.
12-0 x 11-0

BED RM./ STUDY
11-0 x 12-0
(cathedral ceiling)

cl

PORCH

Design HPT300266
Square Footage: 1,633
Bonus Space: 595 sq. ft.

◆ Stylish rooms and comfortable arrangements make this country home unique and inviting. The foyer opens from a quaint covered porch and leads to the expansive great room, which boasts a cathedral ceiling, an extended-hearth fireplace and access to the rear deck. The kitchen serves the formal dining room as well as the bayed breakfast nook, which offers windows that really bring in the outdoors. A secluded master suite nestles to the rear of the plan and features a U-shaped walk-in closet, a garden tub and twin vanities. Two nearby bedrooms—or make one a study—share a full bath and a gallery hall that leads back to the foyer.

Width: 65'-4"
Depth: 55'-4"

great room below

(unfinished)
BONUS
14-8 x 17-0

down

railing

balcony (optional)

(unfinished)
BONUS
11-0 x 12-4

attic storage

Design HPT300267

Square Footage: 2,090

LD

◆ This classic farmhouse enjoys a wrap-around porch that's perfect for enjoyment of the outdoors. To the rear of the plan, a sun terrace with a spa opens from the master suite and the morning room. A grand great room offers a sloped ceiling and a corner fireplace with a raised hearth. The formal dining room is defined by a low wall and by graceful archways set off by decorative columns. The tiled kitchen has a central island counter with a snack bar and adjoins a laundry area. Two family bedrooms reside to the side of the plan, and each enjoys private access to the covered porch. A secluded master suite nestles in its own wing and features a sitting area.

Width: 84'-6"
Depth: 64'-0"

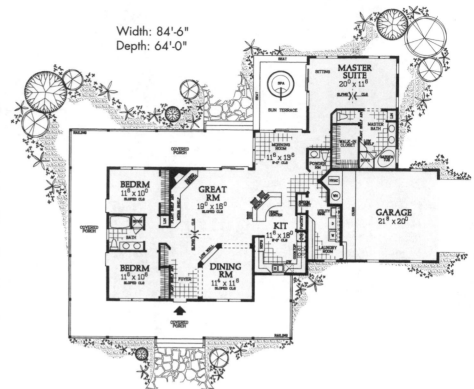

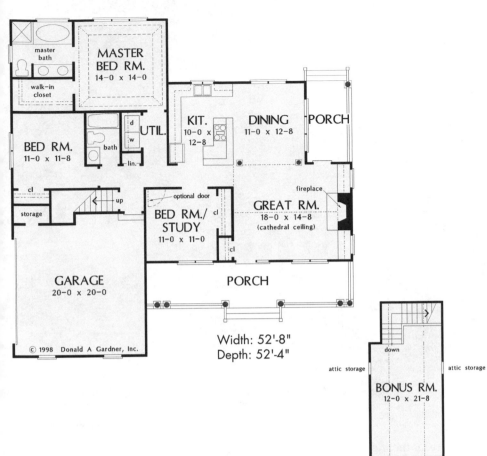

master bath

MASTER
BED RM.
14-0 x 14-0

walk-in
closet

BED RM.
11-0 x 11-8

bath

UTIL.

d

w

lin.

KIT.
10-0 x
12-8

DINING
11-0 x 12-8

PORCH

cl

storage

up

optional door

BED RM./
STUDY
11-0 x 11-0

cl

cl

fireplace

GREAT RM.
18-0 x 14-8
(cathedral ceiling)

GARAGE
20-0 x 20-0

PORCH

© 1998 Donald A Gardner, Inc.

Width: 52'-8"
Depth: 52'-4"

down

attic storage

attic storage

BONUS RM.
12-0 x 21-8

Design HPT3030014
Square Footage: 1,428
Bonus Room: 313 sq. ft.

◆ Stunning arched windows framed by bold front-facing gables add to the tremendous curb appeal of this modest home. Topped by a cathedral ceiling and with porches on either side, the great room is expanded further by its openness to the dining room and kitchen. Flexibility, which is so important in a home this size, is found in the versatile bedroom/study as well as the bonus room over the garage. The master suite is positioned for privacy at the rear of the home, with a graceful tray ceiling, walk-in closet, and private bath. An additional bedroom and a hall bath complete the plan.

© 1998 Donald A. Gardner, Inc.

©1994 Donald A. Gardner Architects, Inc.

Design HPT300269

Square Footage: 1,954
Bonus Room: 436 sq. ft.

◆ This beautiful brick country home offers style and comfort for an active family. Two covered porches and a rear deck with a spa invite enjoyment of the outdoors, while a well-defined interior provides places to gather and entertain. A cathedral ceiling soars above the central great room, warmed by an extended-hearth fireplace and by sunlight through an arch-top clerestory window. A splendid master suite enjoys its own secluded wing and offers a skylit whirlpool bath, cathedral ceiling and private access to the deck. Two family bedrooms share a full bath on the opposite side of the plan. The two-car garage features a storage area and a service entrance. A skylit bonus room may be developed later.

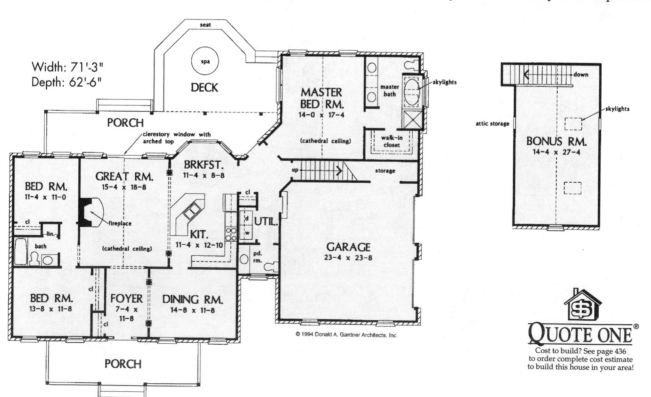

Width: 71'-3"
Depth: 62'-6"

© 1994 Donald A. Gardner Architects, Inc.

B. NATHAN

Design HPT300270

Square Footage: 2,136
Bonus Room: 405 sq. ft.

◆ An expansive front porch, three dormers and a score of windows all add to the charm and character of this country home. The spacious great room features built-in cabinets, a fireplace and a cathedral ceiling that continues into the adjoining screened porch. An island kitchen is conveniently grouped with the great room, the dining room and the skylit breakfast area for the cook who enjoys conversation while preparing meals. The master suite features a cathedral ceiling, a large walk-in closet and a relaxing private bath with a skylit whirlpool tub and separate shower. Two secondary bedrooms share a full bath.

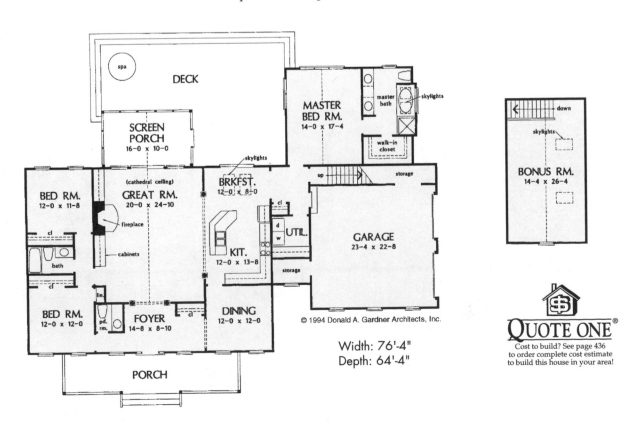

Width: 76'-4"
Depth: 64'-4"

Quote One®
Cost to build? See page 436
to order complete cost estimate
to build this house in your area!

Design HPT300271
Square Footage: 2,123
Bonus Room: 439 sq. ft.

◆ A covered porch and three dormer windows mark the facade of this country design. Inside the living is all on one level and completely commodious. The great room acts as the hub and is graced by a fireplace and cathedral ceiling. The kitchen features an angled counter and is set conveniently between a breakfast bay and a formal dining room. The master suite sits quietly behind the two-car garage. Its skylit bath features a separate tub and shower. Family bedrooms sit at the left side of the plan; one may become a study, if you prefer.

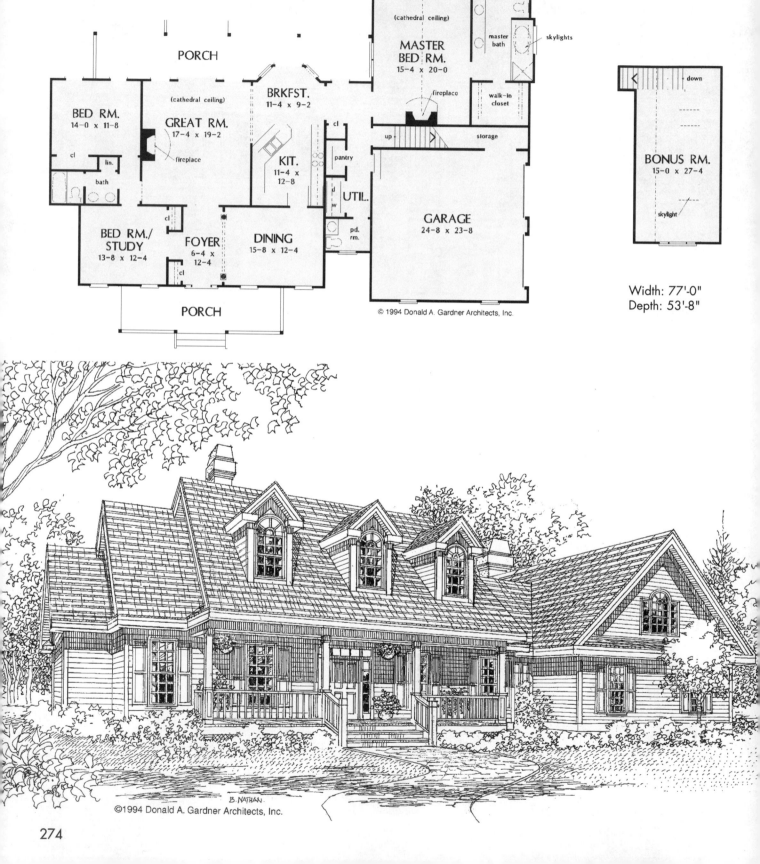

PORCH

BED RM.
14-0 x 11-8
cl
lin.
bath

GREAT RM.
17-4 x 19-2
(cathedral ceiling)
fireplace

BRKFST.
11-4 x 9-2

KIT.
11-4 x 12-8

pantry

cl

UTIL.

MASTER BED RM.
15-4 x 20-0
(cathedral ceiling)
fireplace
master bath
skylights
walk-in closet

up   storage

BED RM./ STUDY
13-8 x 12-4
cl

FOYER
6-4 x 12-4
cl

DINING
15-8 x 12-4

pd. rm.

GARAGE
24-8 x 23-8

PORCH

© 1994 Donald A. Gardner Architects, Inc.

BONUS RM.
15-0 x 27-4
down
skylight

Width: 77'-0"
Depth: 53'-8"

B. NATHAN
©1994 Donald A. Gardner Architects, Inc.

Design HPT300272

Square Footage: 2,192
Bonus Room: 390 sq. ft.

◆ Exciting volumes and nine-foot ceilings add elegance to this comfortable, open plan. There's also a tray ceiling in the front bedroom/study. Hosts whose guests always end up in the kitchen will enjoy entertaining here with only columns separating it from the great room. Children's bedrooms share a full bath that's complete with a linen closet. The master suite, located in a quiet wing, is highlighted by a tray ceiling and includes a skylit bath with a garden tub, private toilet, double-bowl vanity and spacious walk-in closet.

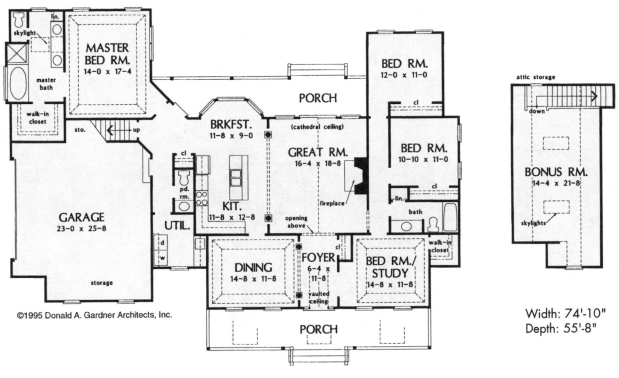

Width: 74'-10"
Depth: 55'-8"

©1995 Donald A. Gardner Architects, Inc.

©1995 Donald A. Gardner Architects, Inc.

B. NATHAN.

© 1995 Donald A. Gardner Architects, Inc.

B. NATHAN

Design HPT300273
Square Footage: 1,632

◆ This country home has a big heart in a cozy package. Special touches—interior columns, a bay window and dormers—add elegance. The central great room features a cathedral ceiling and a fireplace. A clerestory window splashes the room with natural light. The open kitchen easily serves the breakfast area and the nearby dining room. The private master bedroom, with a tray ceiling and a walk-in closet, boasts amenities found in much larger homes. The bath features a skylight and a whirlpool tub. Two additional bedrooms share a bath. The front bedroom features a walk-in closet and would make a nice study with an optional foyer entrance.

Width: 62'-4"
Depth: 55'-2"

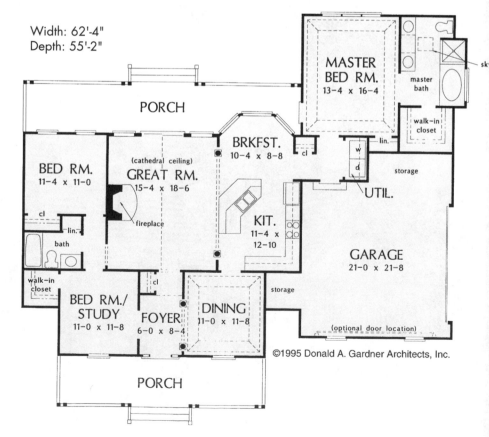

PORCH

MASTER BED RM.
13-4 x 16-4

master bath

sky

walk-in closet

lin.

BRKFST.
10-4 x 8-8

cl

storage

w
d

UTIL.

BED RM.
11-4 x 11-0

(cathedral ceiling)

GREAT RM.
15-4 x 18-6

fireplace

cl

lin.

bath

KIT.
11-4 x 12-10

GARAGE
21-0 x 21-8

walk-in closet

BED RM./ STUDY
11-0 x 11-8

FOYER
6-0 x 8-4

cl

DINING
11-0 x 11-8

storage

(optional door location)

©1995 Donald A. Gardner Architects, Inc.

PORCH

© 1995 Donald A. Gardner Architects, Inc.   B. BATMAN

Design HPT300274

Square Footage: 1,832
Bonus Room: 425 sq. ft.

◆ This plan boasts a cathedral ceiling in the great room. Dormer windows shed light on the foyer, which opens to a front bedroom or study and to the formal dining room. The kitchen is completely open to the great room and features a stylish snack-bar island and a bay window in the breakfast nook. The master suite offers a tray ceiling and a skylit bath. Two secondary bedrooms share a full bath. Bonus space over the garage may be developed in the future.

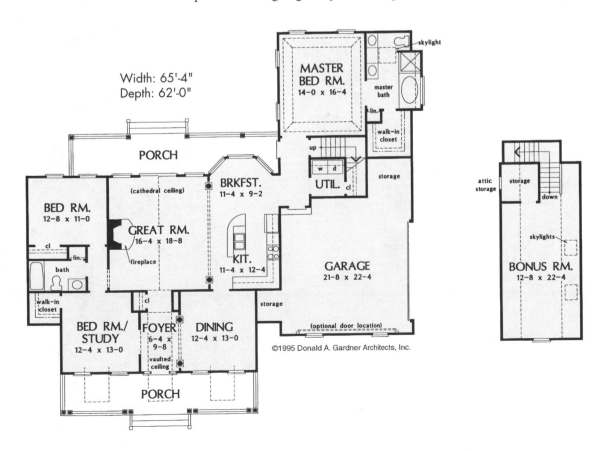

Width: 65'-4"
Depth: 62'-0"

©1995 Donald A. Gardner Architects, Inc.

MASTER BED RM. 14-0 x 16-4

PORCH

BRKFST. 11-4 x 9-2

UTIL.

BED RM. 12-8 x 11-0

GREAT RM. 16-4 x 18-8

KIT. 11-4 x 12-4

GARAGE 21-8 x 22-4

BED RM./STUDY 12-4 x 13-0

FOYER 6-4 x 9-8

DINING 12-4 x 13-0

(optional door location)

PORCH

BONUS RM. 12-8 x 22-4

Design HPT300275
Square Footage: 1,561

Width: 60'-10"
Depth: 51'-6"

◆ Combining the finest country details with the most modern livability, this one-story home makes modest budgets really stretch. The welcoming front porch encourages you to stop and enjoy the summer breezes. The entry foyer leads to a formal dining room defined by columns. Beyond it is the large great room with a cathedral ceiling and a fireplace. The kitchen and the breakfast room are open to the living area and include porch access. The master suite is tucked away in its own private space. It is conveniently separated from the family bedrooms, which share a full bath. The two-car garage contains extra storage space.

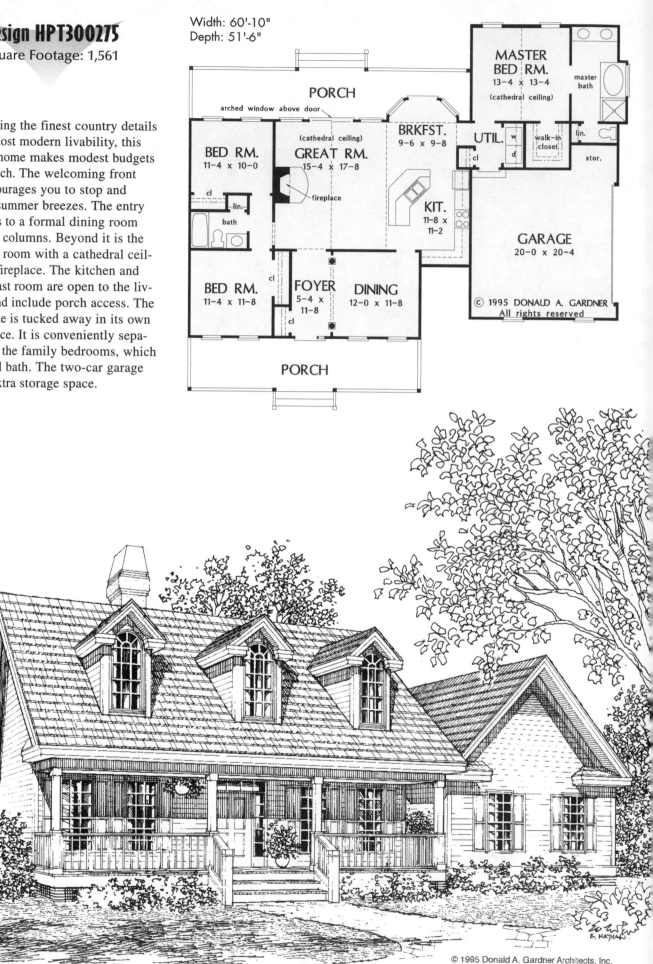

PORCH

arched window above door

MASTER BED RM.
13-4 x 13-4
(cathedral ceiling)

master bath

BED RM.
11-4 x 10-0

BRKFST.
9-6 x 9-8

UTIL.

cl

GREAT RM.
15-4 x 17-8
(cathedral ceiling)

fireplace

walk-in closet

lin.

stor.

bath

KIT.
11-8 x 11-2

GARAGE
20-0 x 20-4

BED RM.
11-4 x 11-8

cl

FOYER
5-4 x 11-8

DINING
12-0 x 11-8

PORCH

E. NATHAN

Floor Plan Labels

Second Floor (Future/Bonus):
- Future 16-9x14-11
- Future 20-2x7-6
- Future 22-6x14-11
- Future 31-5x9-2

Width: 69'-0"
Depth: 67'-4"

Main Floor:
- Storage 4-11x12-6
- Garage 21-7x21-5
- Porch 9-0x21-6
- Bath
- Desk
- Laun. 5-5x6-0
- Owner's Bedroom 14-3x15-11
- Greatroom 18-7x15-11
- Breakfast 12-7x10-1
- Bedroom 13-3x11-0
- Bath
- Kitchen 12-7x11-3
- Bath
- Bath
- Bonus Room 12-7x12-7
- Foyer
- Dining 12-7x11-2
- Bedroom 13-3x10-2
- Porch 32-8x6-0

Design HPT300276
Square Footage: 2,127
Bonus Space: 1,095 sq. ft.

◆ This home's facade employs an elegant balance of country comfort and traditional grace. Inside, the foyer opens to the formal dining room that features a coffered ceiling. Straight ahead, the great room offers a warm fireplace and open flow to the breakfast and kitchen areas. Two secondary bedrooms and a full bath can be found just off the kitchen. A bonus room, near the master suite, can be used as a nursery or den. The private master bath enjoys dual vanities, two walk-in closets and a compartmented toilet. Upstairs, unfinished space is ready for expansion. Please specify basement, crawl-space or slab foundation when ordering.

Design HPT300277

Square Footage: 1,822

◆ Country charm at its best and a design that suits your every need combine to create a very livable floor plan. French doors off the foyer open to a study/office with a walk-in closet. Across the hall is the living room with a fireplace and built-ins. The dining area is defined by columns and is easily served by the kitchen—which includes a breakfast nook. The master suite includes a walk-in closet and a private bath. The utility area is near the two-car garage. A full hall bath is available to the two family bedrooms; one of the bedrooms includes a walk-in closet.

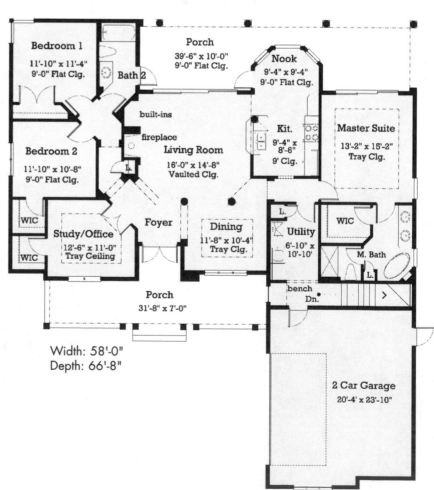

Width: 58'-0"
Depth: 66'-8"

© 1998 Donald A Gardner, Inc.

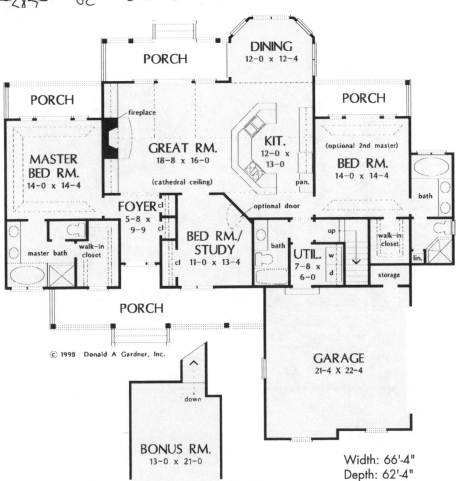

PORCH

DINING
12-0 x 12-4

PORCH

PORCH

fireplace

GREAT RM.
18-8 x 16-0

KIT.
12-0 x
13-0

(optional 2nd master)

BED RM.
14-0 x 14-4

(cathedral ceiling)

MASTER
BED RM.
14-0 x 14-4

pan.

bath

FOYER
5-8 x
9-9

cl

cl

optional door

master bath

walk-in
closet

BED RM./
STUDY
11-0 x 13-4

cl

bath

up

UTIL.
7-8 x
6-0

w
d

walk-in
closet

lin.

storage

PORCH

© 1998 Donald A Gardner, Inc.

down

BONUS RM.
13-0 x 21-0

attic storage

attic storage

GARAGE
21-4 X 22-4

Width: 66'-4"
Depth: 62'-4"

Design HPT300278

Square Footage: 1,792
Bonus Room: 338 sq. ft.

◆ Cedar shakes, siding and stone blend with the Craftsman details of a custom design in this stunning home. An open common area separates two suites, including an optional second master suite that would be great for guests or a roommate. Note the fireplace and direct porch access in the great room. Watch the glow of the fire from the kitchen's five-sided island. Enjoy the light-filled dining area for formal and informal dining situations. Added flexibility is found in the bedroom/study and bonus room.

Design HPT300279

Square Footage: 1,737

◆ Inviting porches are just the beginning of this lovely country home. To the left of the foyer, a columned entry supplies a classic touch to the spacious great room, which features a cathedral ceiling, built-in bookshelves and a fireplace that invites you to share its warmth. An octagonal dining room with a tray ceiling provides a perfect setting for formal occasions. The adjacent kitchen is designed to easily serve both formal and informal areas. The master suite, separated from two family bedrooms by the walk-in closet and utility room, offers privacy and comfort.

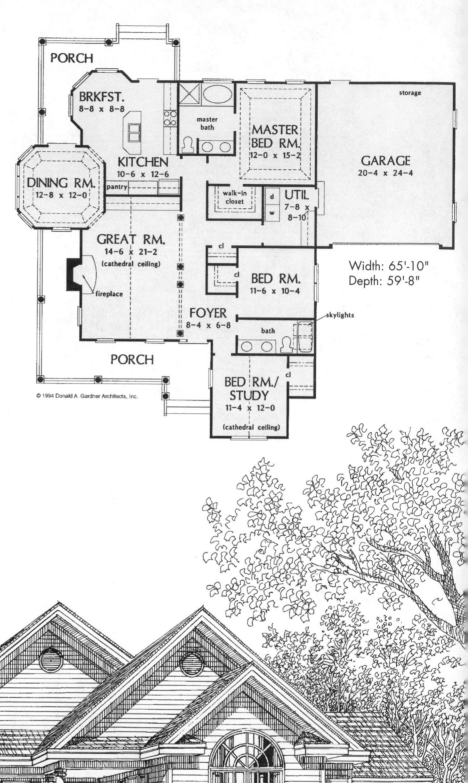

PORCH

BRKFST.
8-8 x 8-8

master bath

MASTER BED RM.
12-0 x 15-2

storage

GARAGE
20-4 x 24-4

KITCHEN
10-6 x 12-6

pantry

DINING RM.
12-8 x 12-0

walk-in closet

UTIL
7-8 x
8-10

d
w

GREAT RM.
14-6 x 21-2
(cathedral ceiling)

fireplace

cl

cl

cl

BED RM.
11-6 x 10-4

Width: 65'-10"
Depth: 59'-8"

FOYER
8-4 x 6-8

skylights

bath

PORCH

© 1994 Donald A. Gardner Architects, Inc.

BED RM./
STUDY
11-4 x 12-0

(cathedral ceiling)

cl

B. NATHAN

© 1994 Donald A. Gardner Architects, Inc.

Design HPT300280
Square Footage: 1,677

◆ This cozy three-bedroom home with arched windows and a wraparound porch displays a sense of elegance uncommon to a plan this size. Cathedral ceilings grace both the great room and the bedroom/study, while tray ceilings appear in the dining room and master suite. The open kitchen design allows for a serving island convenient to the breakfast area, dining room and rear porch. The master suite directly accesses the deck and also features a walk-in closet and bath with a double-bowl vanity, shower and whirlpool tub. A covered breezeway connects the garage to the house.

Width: 49'-10"
Depth: 89'-6"

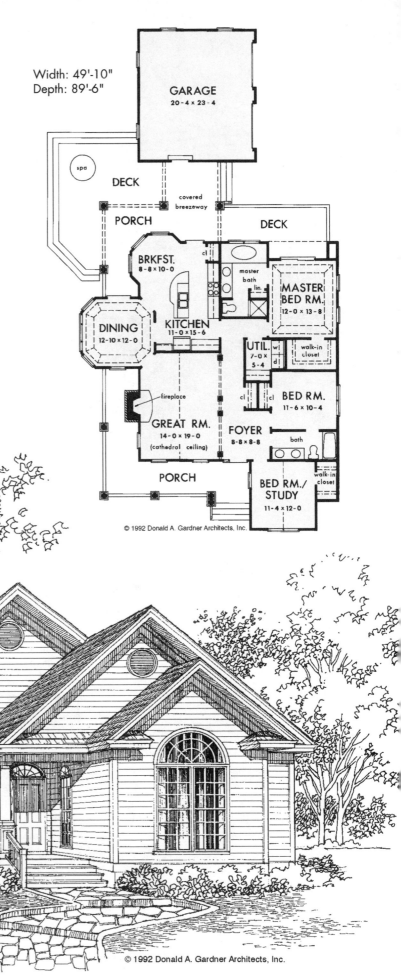

© 1992 Donald A. Gardner Architects, Inc.

© 1992 Donald A. Gardner Architects, Inc.

Design HPT300281
Square Footage: 1,302

◆ A spacious cathedral ceiling expands the open great room, dining room and kitchen. The versatile bedroom/study features a cathedral ceiling and shares a full skylit bath with another bedroom. The master bedroom is highlighted by a cathedral ceiling for extra volume and light. The private bath opens up with a skylight and includes a double-bowl vanity, garden tub and separately located toilet. A walk-in closet adjacent to the bedroom completes the suite.

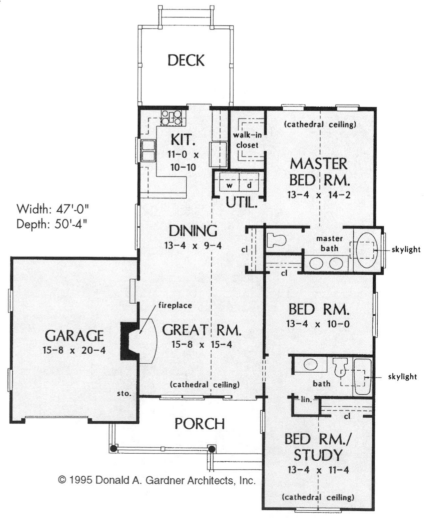

Width: 47'-0"
Depth: 50'-4"

DECK

master bath

MASTER BED RM.
13-4 x 15-6
(cathedral ceiling)

walk-in closet

cl

BED RM.
11-0 x 12-0

up

d UTIL.
w 6-0 x
8-4

storage

cl

GARAGE
21-0 x 21-0

fireplace

GREAT RM.
16-0 x 18-2

shelves

(cathedral ceiling)

BRKFST.
11-0 x 9-0

KIT.
11-0 x
11-4

pan.

bath

cl

cl

BED RM./ STUDY
11-4 x 12-0

FOYER
5-8 x
14-0

DINING
11-0 x 12-0

PORCH

Design HPT300282
Square Footage: 1,671
Bonus Room: 348 sq. ft.

◆ The front porch of this home offers sanctuary from the elements, while providing an entry to the foyer. To the right, the formal dining room features a tray ceiling and pocket-door access to the kitchen. To the left, a study or guest bedroom also features a tray ceiling and accesses a full bath. The great room sits at the center with a fireplace, built-ins, a cathedral ceiling and rear-deck access. With the breakfast area soaking up natural light from its many windows and the gourmet kitchen just steps away, the family will enjoy ease of service and a casual atmosphere. The master suite offers a cathedral ceiling, a spacious walk-in closet and a bath with dual vanities.

Width: 50'-8"
Depth: 52'-4"

down

BONUS RM.
14-0 x 21-0

attic storage

attic storage

Design HPT300283
Square Footage: 1,625

◆ This family-pleasing design is thoughtful, indeed. Living areas include a kitchen with an efficient work triangle, an adjoining breakfast room, a dining room with bay window and of course, the great room with fireplace and access to a rear porch. The master bedroom also has porch access, along with a walk-in closet and a lavish bath. Two family bedrooms include one featuring a half-round transom window, adding appeal to the exterior and interior. The laundry room is convenient to all three bedrooms.

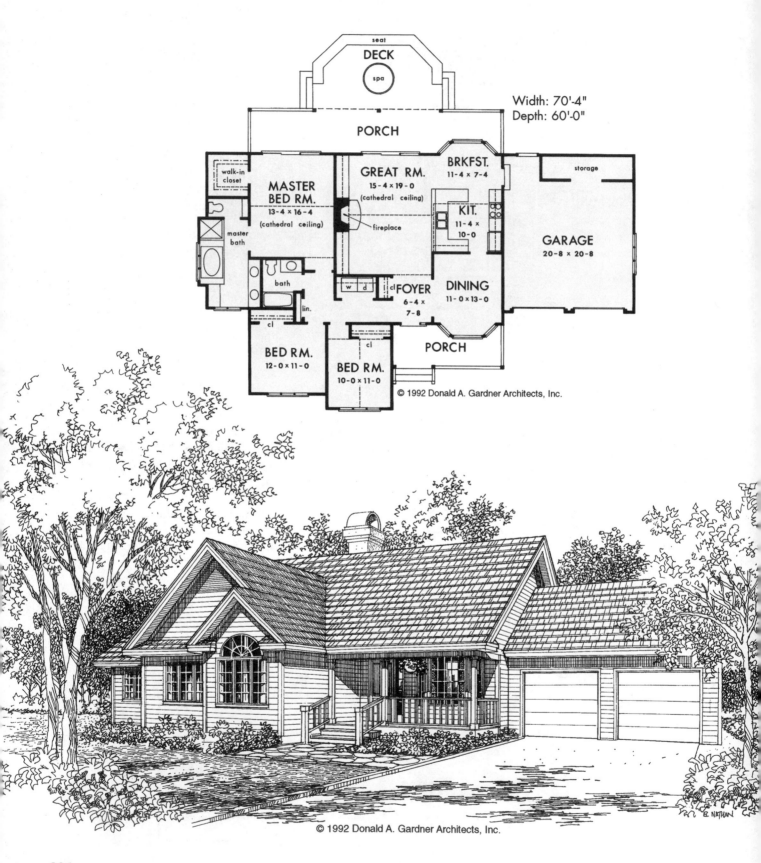

Width: 70'-4"
Depth: 60'-0"

© 1992 Donald A. Gardner Architects, Inc.

© 1992 Donald A. Gardner Architects, Inc.

Design HPT300284

Square Footage: 1,298

◆ This design has plenty of curb appeal. From its gable roof and covered front porch, to its large rear deck, this home will brighten any neighborhood. Inside, open planning is the theme in the dining room/great room area, with a cathedral ceiling combining the two areas into a comfortable unit. The kitchen contributes to the openness with its snack bar/work island. Three bedrooms complete this attractive second home. One of these bedrooms could easily be transformed into a study or library.

DECK

(optional two car garage)

(cathedral ceiling)

(cathedral ceiling)

walk-in closet

DINING
10-0 x 11-6

GREAT RM.
15-4 x 15-0

MASTER
BED RM.
12-4 x 15-0

GARAGE
13-4 x 20-4

fireplace

master bath

KIT.
9-8 x 11-2

FOYER
6-8 x
7-8

cl

w   d

UTIL.

bath

lin.

©1995 Donald A. Gardner Architects, Inc.

cl

Width: 59'-0"
Depth: 36'-0"

PORCH

cl

BED RM./
STUDY
10-0 x 10-0

BED RM.
12-4 x 10-0

(cathedral ceiling)

Design HPT300285

Square Footage: 1,246

◆ This one-story home offers tremendous curb appeal and many extras found only in much larger homes. A continuous cathedral ceiling in the great room, dining room and kitchen gives a spacious feel to an efficient plan. The kitchen, brightened by a skylight, features a pantry and a peninsula counter for easy preparation and service to the dining room and screened porch. The master suite opens up with a cathedral ceiling, walk-in and linen closets, and a private bath that includes a garden tub and a double-bowl vanity.

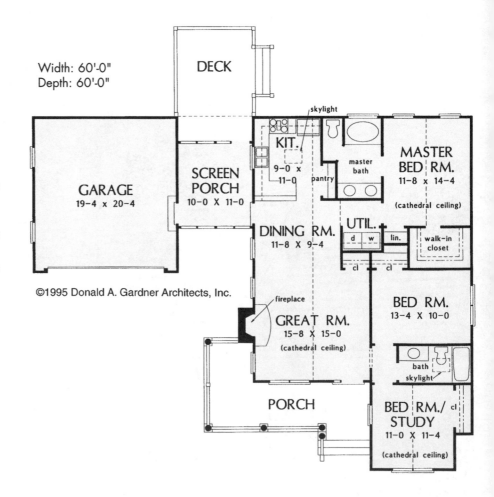

Width: 60'-0"
Depth: 60'-0"

DECK

GARAGE
19-4 x 20-4

SCREEN PORCH
10-0 X 11-0

KIT.
9-0 x 11-0

skylight

master bath

pantry

MASTER BED RM.
11-8 x 14-4
(cathedral ceiling)

DINING RM.
11-8 X 9-4

UTIL.
d w lin.

cl cl

walk-in closet

fireplace

GREAT RM.
15-8 X 15-0
(cathedral ceiling)

BED RM.
13-4 X 10-0

bath
skylight

PORCH

BED RM./
STUDY
11-0 X 11-4
(cathedral ceiling)

cl

© 1999 Donald A. Gardner, Inc.

B. NATHAN

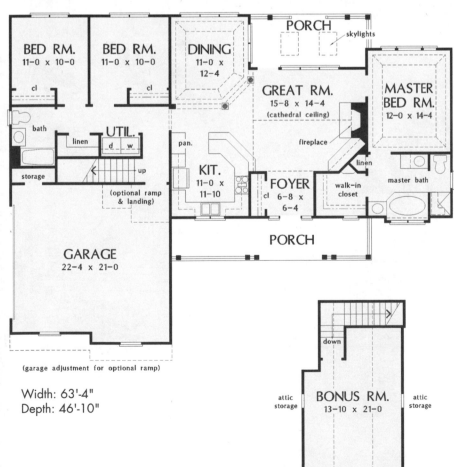

BED RM.
11-0 x 10-0

BED RM.
11-0 x 10-0

DINING
11-0 x 12-4

PORCH
skylights

cl

cl

bath

UTIL.
linen

d | w

GREAT RM.
15-8 x 14-4
(cathedral ceiling)

MASTER BED RM.
12-0 x 14-4

fireplace

storage

up

(optional ramp & landing)

pan.

linen

KIT.
11-0 x 11-10

FOYER
cl 6-8 x 6-4

walk-in closet

master bath

GARAGE
22-4 x 21-0

PORCH

(garage adjustment for optional ramp)

Width: 63'-4"
Depth: 46'-10"

down

attic storage

attic storage

BONUS RM.
13-10 x 21-0

Design HPT300286
Square Footage: 1,540
Bonus Room: 277 sq. ft.

◆ This country home features an open floor plan that works well for today's fast-paced families. A cathedral ceiling and fireplace grace the great room. The C-shaped kitchen has a separate pantry area and enjoys a close proximity to the dining room. Two family bedrooms are split from the master suite and share a bath. The master bedroom features a large bath and a walk-in closet. A bonus room with attic storage is available for future use—perfect for the growing family.

Design HPT300287

Square Footage: 1,594

◆ This home boasts transitional trends with its charming exterior. The entrance foyer with columns introduces the formal dining room and leads to the massive great room with a sloped ceiling and cozy fireplace. On the right, you will find French doors leading to a library/bedroom featuring built-in bookcases—another set of French doors accesses the rear deck. A family bedroom nearby shares a full bath. The gourmet kitchen enjoys an angled sink counter and a breakfast area with a bay window and built-in bench. The secluded master bedroom includes a walk-in closet, a full bath with dual vanities, and private access to the laundry room. This plan includes an optional layout for a third bedroom.

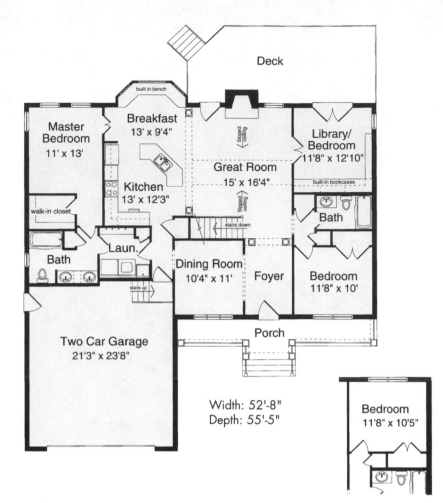

Deck

Breakfast
13' x 9'4"

Master Bedroom
11' x 13'

Sloped ceiling

Library/ Bedroom
11'8" x 12'10"

built-in bookcases

Great Room
15' x 16'4"

Kitchen
13' x 12'3"

walk-in closet

Sloped ceiling

Bath

built in bench

Bath

Laun.

stairs down

Bedroom
11'8" x 10'

Dining Room
10'4" x 11'

Foyer

stairs up

Two Car Garage
21'3" x 23'8"

Porch

Width: 52'-8"
Depth: 55'-5"

Bedroom
11'8" x 10'5"

Optional 3rd Bedroom

Design HPT300288

Square Footage: 1,937
Bonus Room: 414 sq. ft.

L

Width: 76'-4"
Depth: 73'-4"

SITTING 8'-0" CLG

MASTER SUITE 15'0 x 19'0
SLOPED CEILING

WALK-IN CLOSET

MASTER BATH

GARDEN TUB

PATIO DECK RETREAT

2-CAR GARAGE 23'0 x 25'6

OPTIONAL STAIR WHERE BONUS ROOM OCCURS

MORNING NOOK

KIT COOKTOP 19'0 x 13'0

LAUNDRY ROOM

GREAT ROOM 18'0 x 20'0 SLOPED CLG

REFG PANTRY

HALF WALL BELOW

DINING RM 12'2 x 10'0 8'-0" CLG

ENTRY

BEDRM 10'0 x 10'0 8'-0" CLG

BATH

COVERED PORCH

BEDRM 10'0 x 10'0 8'-0" CLG

OPT BONUS RM OVER GARAGE 14'0 x 22'0

◆ Country living in a unique floor plan makes this design the perfect choice for just the right family. The covered front porch opens to an angled foyer that leads to a large great room with a sloped ceiling and fireplace. To the right is the formal dining room, defined by columns and plenty of windows overlooking the porch. Two secondary bedrooms share a full bath at the front of the plan. Connecting to the two-car garage via a laundry area, the kitchen provides an island cooktop and a quaint morning room. The master suite offers a retreat with a sloped ceiling, walk-in closet and a bath with a whirl-pool tub.

QUOTE ONE®

Cost to build? See page 436 to order complete cost estimate to build this house in your area!

Design HPT300289
Square Footage: 1,606

◆ This ranch home enjoys a large covered front porch and a covered porch/patio in the rear, ready for the weekend barbecue. The great room set the stage with a fireplace flanked by windows. The breakfast nook is illuminated by natural lighting via two skylights. The adjoining kitchen is generous with its allowance of counter space. A split-bedroom plan places the master suite on the far right for privacy, with two family bedrooms sharing a full bath on the far left. Please specify basement, crawlspace or slab foundation when ordering.

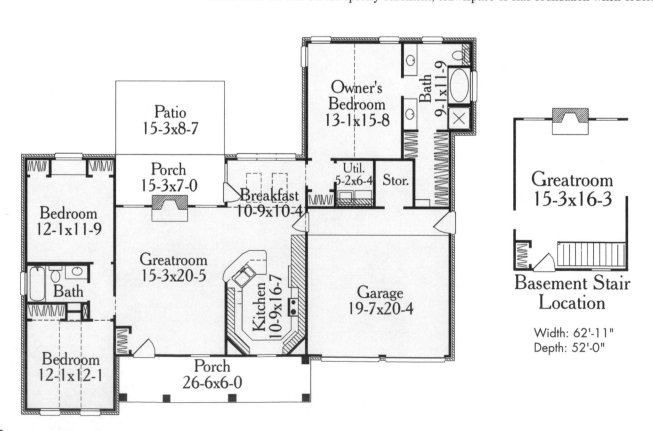

Patio
15-3x8-7

Porch
15-3x7-0

Owner's
Bedroom
13-1x15-8

Bath
9-1x11-9

Breakfast
10-9x10-4

Util.
5-2x6-4

Stor.

Bedroom
12-1x11-9

Bath

Greatroom
15-3x20-5

Kitchen
10-9x16-7

Garage
19-7x20-4

Greatroom
15-3x16-3

Basement Stair
Location

Bedroom
12-1x12-1

Porch
26-6x6-0

Width: 62'-11"
Depth: 52'-0"

Width: 50'-0"
Depth: 50'-0"

FUTURE
BR. 5
10/6 X 12/8

FUTURE
BR. 4
10/4 X 12/8

FUTURE
GAMES RM.
16/0 X 16/8 +

CRAWLSPACE

UP

CRAWLSPACE

Design HPT300290

Square Footage: 1,632
Finished Basement: 1,043 sq. ft.

DECK

VAULTED
MASTER
14/0 X 12/8

GREAT RM.
16/0 X 16/4
(11' CLG.)

NOOK
9/0 X 9/0
(9' CLG.)

NICHE

BR. 2
11/4 X 10/0
(9' CLG.)

LINEN

SHLVS

PAN   REF

DINING
11/4 X 12/2
(9' CLG.)

DN

GARAGE
19/8 X 21/8

DEN/BR. 3
11/6 X 10/4
(9' CLG.)

PORCH

SEAT

BENCH

◆ Lower-level space adds to the compact floor plan of this home and gives it future possibilities. The main level opens off a covered porch to a dining room on the right and a den or bedroom on the left. The great room with an attached nook opens to the rear deck. Note the amount of counter and cabinet space in the L-shaped kitchen. Two bedrooms—a master suite and a family bedroom—are on the left, as is a laundry alcove. The lower level has space for a game room, two additional bedrooms and a full bath.

Design HPT300291

Square Footage: 1,433

◆ This eye-catching three-bedroom ranch home is designed specifically for narrow lots. All the many features you've been looking for in a family home can be found here. The master bedroom includes a bath and a walk-in closet. A second bath is located between the two family bedrooms. The huge great room offers plenty of space for all your gatherings. The blueprints for this house show how to build both a basic, low-cost version and an enhanced, upgraded version.

Width: 35'-0"
Depth: 78'-0"

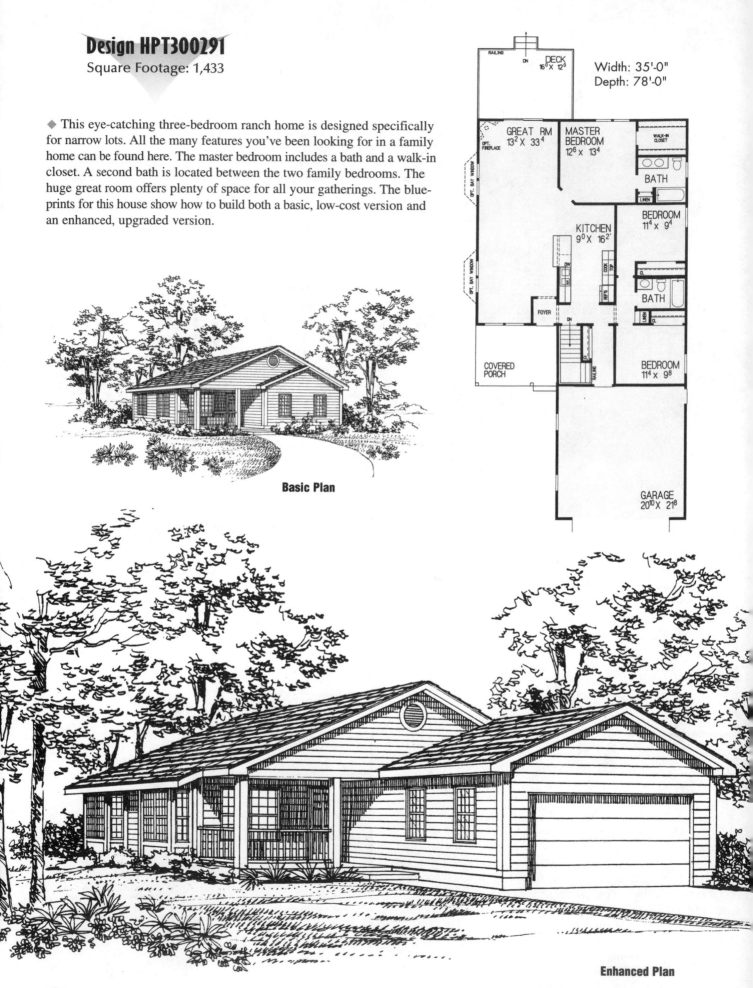

Basic Plan

Enhanced Plan

Design HPT300292
Square Footage: 1,648

BEDROOM
10⁴ x 10⁴

BEDROOM
10⁴ x 10⁴

DECK
13² x 9⁸

RAILING

GREAT RM
13² X 33⁴

OPT. FIREPLACE

BEDROOM
11⁴ x 10⁴

BATH

LINEN

KITCHEN
9² x 17¹⁰

OPT. BAY WINDOW

BATH

COOK TOP

DW

OPT. BAY WINDOW

WALK-IN CLOSET

LINEN

REFG

MASTER BEDROOM
11⁴ x 16⁰

FOYER

DN

COVERED PORCH

RAILING

GARAGE
20¹⁰ X 21⁸

Width: 35'-0"
Depth: 76'-0"

◆ If you have a narrow lot to build your home on, then this elegant ranch design is for you! The master bedroom includes a full-size bath and a walk-in closet, while a second full-size bath serves the remaining three bedrooms. A galley kitchen with an eat-in nook opens up to a huge great room that easily accommodates friends and family. This home is the wise choice for those who desire an affordable family plan. The house may be built with or without the two-car garage, rear deck, bay windows and fireplace. Blueprints include details for both the basic and the enhanced versions.

Basic Plan

Enhanced Plan

Design HPT300293
Square Footage: 1,118

L

◆ Compact and perfect for starters or empty-nesters, this is a wonderful single-level home. The beautiful facade is supplemented by a stylish and practical covered porch. Just to the left of the entry is a roomy kitchen with bright windows and convenient storage. The octagonal dining room shares a three-sided fireplace with the living room. A covered patio to the rear enhances outdoor living. A fine master suite enjoys a grand bath and is complemented by a secondary bedroom and full bath.

Quote One®

Cost to build? See page 436 to order complete cost estimate to build this house in your area!

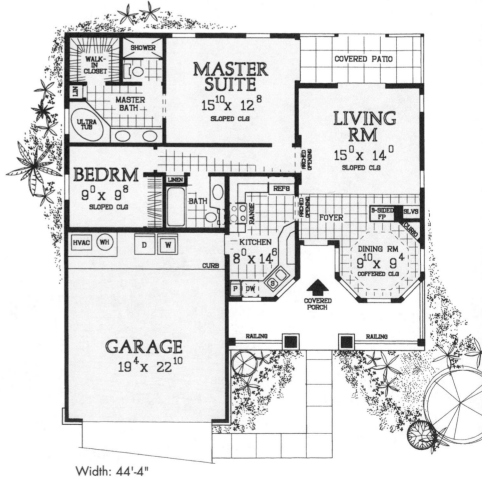

Width: 44'-4"
Depth: 47'-4"

Width: 52'-8"
Depth: 55'-5"

Deck

built in bench

Master Bedroom
11' x 13'

Breakfast
13' x 9'4"

Library/ Bedroom
11'8" x 12'10"

Sloped ceiling

Great Room
15' x 16'4"

built-in bookcases

walk-in closet

Kitchen
13' x 12'3"

Sloped ceiling

stairs down

Bath

Laun.

Bath

stairs up

Dining Room
10'4" x 11'

Foyer

Bedroom
11'8" x 10'

Two Car Garage
21'3" x 23'8"

Porch

Design HPT300294
Square Footage: 1,594

◆ This design is a traditional home. A covered porch, split bedrooms, formal and informal dining areas and sloped ceilings combine to create a delightful home in a moderate square footage. The large island in the kitchen brings definition to the space, while angled windows decorate the eating area. Split bedrooms allow privacy for the master bedroom, which offers a private bath and laundry-room access. Turn one of the family bedrooms into a library to create an exciting option. The open stairway to the full basement allows for easy expansion of the living area.

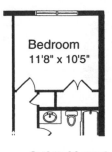

Bedroom
11'8" x 10'5"

Optional Layout

297

Design HPT300295
Square Footage: 1,408

◆ An eyebrow dormer and a large veranda give guests a warm country greeting outside, while vaulted ceilings lend a sense of spaciousness to this three-bedroom home inside. A bright country kitchen boasts an abundance of counter space and cupboards. The front entry is sheltered by a broad veranda. Built-in amenities adorn the interior, including a pot shelf over the entry coat closet, an art niche, a skylight, and a walk-in pantry and island workstation in the kitchen. A box-bay window and a spa-style tub highlight the master suite. The two-car garage provides a workshop area.

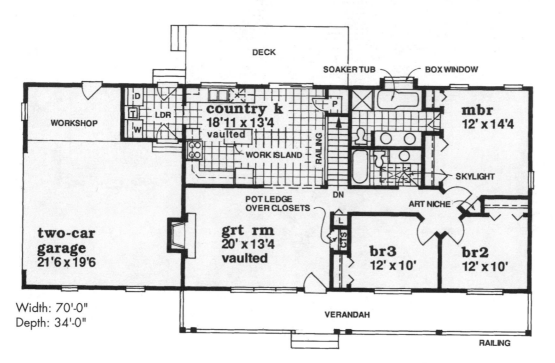

DECK

SOAKER TUB   BOX WINDOW

WORKSHOP

LDR

country k
18'11 x 13'4
vaulted

WORK ISLAND

RAILING

mbr
12' x 14'4

SKYLIGHT

POT LEDGE
OVER CLOSETS

DN

ART NICHE

two-car
garage
21'6 x 19'6

grt rm
20' x 13'4
vaulted

br3
12' x 10'

br2
12' x 10'

Width: 70'-0"
Depth: 34'-0"

VERANDAH

RAILING

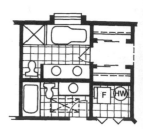

Optional Crawlspace Layout

Design HPT300296
Square Footage: 1,130

◆ Traditional charm is an apt description for this economical ranch home. The kitchen is designed to serve as an eat-in kitchen. The master bedroom offers a full bath plus ample closet space. A full-sized bath adjoins the other two bedrooms. Options include a one- or two-car garage, a front porch, a rear deck with railing, a box-bay window and a fireplace. The blueprints for this house show how to build both the basic, low-cost version and the enhanced, upgraded version.

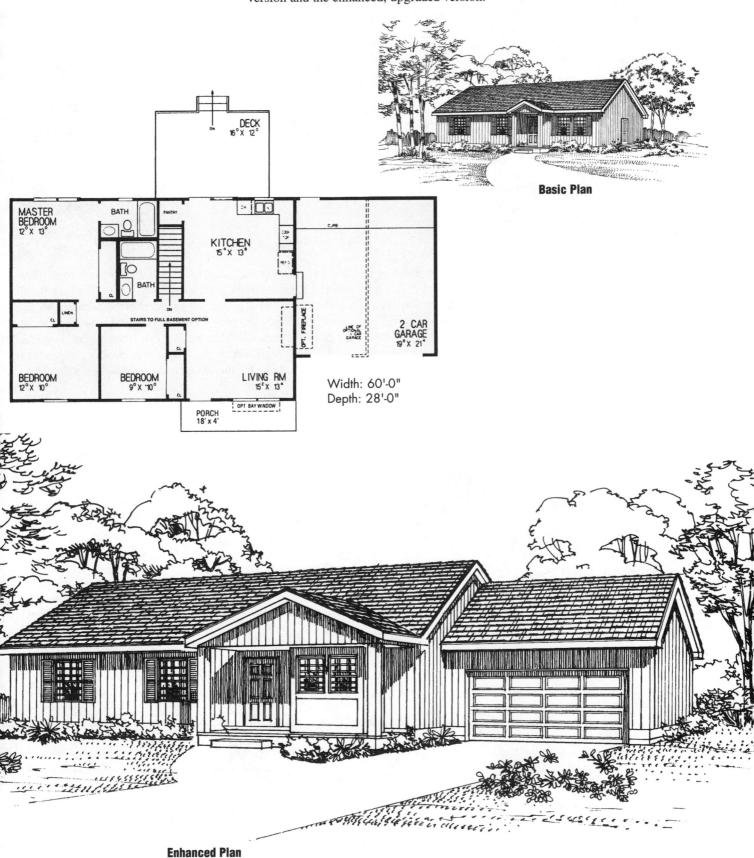

Basic Plan

DECK
16'0" X 12'0"

MASTER BEDROOM
12'0" X 13'0"

BATH

PANTRY

KITCHEN
15'4" X 13'8"

BATH

2 CAR GARAGE
19'8" X 21'4"

LINEN

CL

STAIRS TO FULL BASEMENT OPTION

OPT. FIREPLACE

BEDROOM
12'0" X 10'0"

BEDROOM
9'0" X 10'0"

CL

CL

LIVING RM
15'2" X 13'4"

PORCH
18' x 4'

OPT. BAY WINDOW

Width: 60'-0"
Depth: 28'-0"

Enhanced Plan

Enhanced Plan

Design HPT300297
Square Footage: 1,317

◆ All the charm of a traditional country home is wrapped up in this efficient, economical ranch design. The time-honored, three-bedroom plan can also serve as two bedrooms plus a study or playroom. The formal living room provides a warm welcome to guests, while the open kitchen and family-room combination offers plenty of space for active family gatherings. This functional interior is packaged in an exterior that features vertical siding, window and door shutters and a crisp brick ledge veneer. A one- or two-car garage may be attached. Other options include a front porch with railing, a bay window and a fireplace.

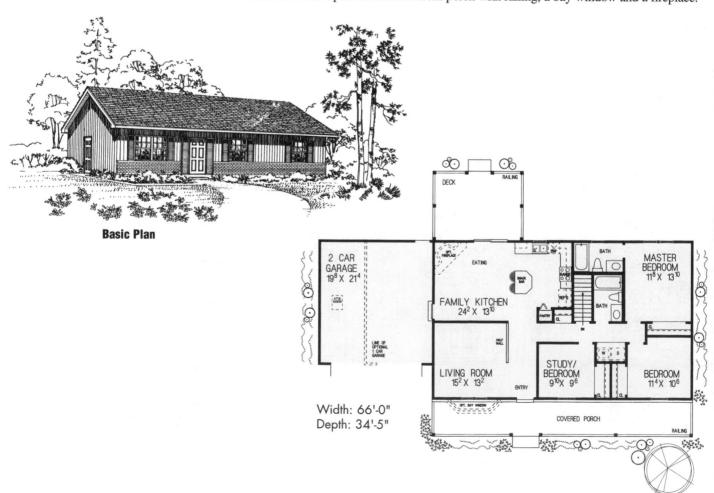

Basic Plan

Width: 66'-0"
Depth: 34'-5"

Design HPT300298
Square Footage: 1,800
L D

◆ Small but inviting, this ranch-style farmhouse is the perfect choice for a small family or empty-nesters. It's loaded with amenities even the most particular homeowner will appreciate. For example, the living room and dining room both have plant shelves, sloped ceilings and built-in cabinetry to enhance livability. The living room also sports a warming fireplace. The master bedroom contains a well-appointed bath with dual vanities and a walk-in closet. The additional bedroom has its own bath with linen storage. The kitchen is separated from the breakfast nook by a clever bar area. Access to the two-car garage is through a laundry area with washer/dryer hook-up space.

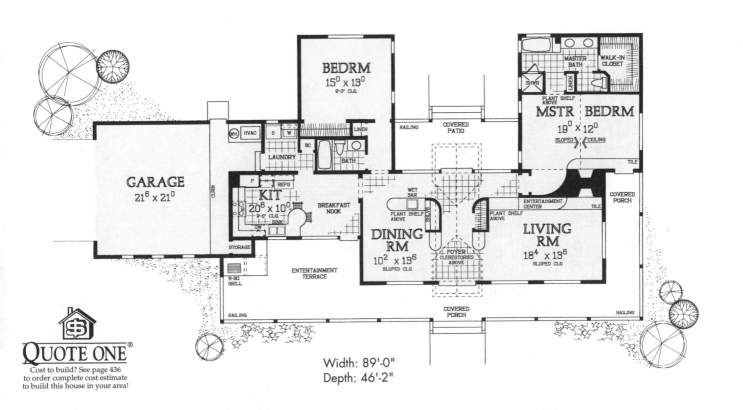

QUOTE ONE®
Cost to build? See page 436
to order complete cost estimate
to build this house in your area!

Width: 89'-0"
Depth: 46'-2"

Design HPT300299
Square Footage: 1,492

Basic Plan

◆ Comfort and charm combine in this very affordable ranch plan. A large dining area with a deck door joins the oversized kitchen. A master bedroom has a private bath; two additional bedrooms share a hall bath. Livability can be enhanced with the optional one- or two-car garage, rear deck with a railing, two angle-bay windows and a fireplace. The blueprints for this house show how to build both a basic, low-cost version and an enhanced, upgraded version.

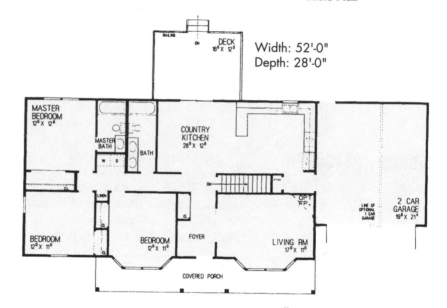

Width: 52'-0"
Depth: 28'-0"

DECK
16⁰ X 12⁰

MASTER BEDROOM
12⁸ X 12⁸

MASTER BATH

BATH

COUNTRY KITCHEN
28⁰ X 12⁸

2 CAR GARAGE
19⁸ X 21⁴

LINE OF OPTIONAL 1 CAR GARAGE

BEDROOM
12⁰ X 11⁰

LINEN

BEDROOM
12⁰ X 11⁰

FOYER

OPT. FP.

LIVING RM
17⁶ X 11⁰

COVERED PORCH

Enhanced Plan

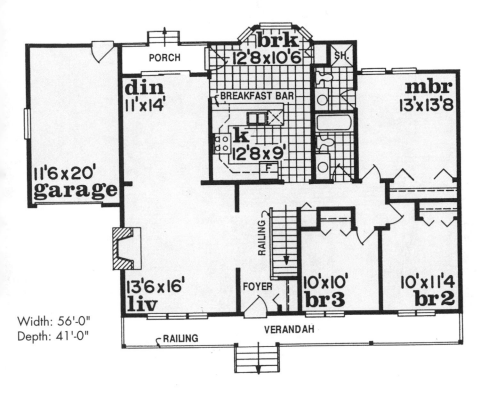

PORCH

brk
12'8x10'6

SH.

din
11'x14'

BREAKFAST BAR

mbr
13'x13'8

garage
11'6 x 20'

k
12'8x9'

F

RAILING

liv
13'6 x 16'

FOYER

RAILING

br3
10'x10'

br2
10'x11'4

Width: 56'-0"
Depth: 41'-0"

VERANDAH

RAILING

Design HPT300300
Square Footage: 1,456

◆ A covered veranda, spanning the width of this three-bedroom home, is a graceful and charming exterior detail. It leads to an entry foyer and the large living and dining space beyond. Here, a warming fireplace will act as a focal point. The dining room has a small covered porch beyond sliding glass doors. The U-shaped kitchen includes a breakfast bar and serves the dining room and sunny breakfast bay easily.

Design HPT300301
Square Footage: 2,415

◆ A covered porch, shutters and a centered dormer with an arched window dress up this country home with blue-ribbon style. To the left of the foyer, the family room features a built-in entertainment center and a bay window that provides a window seat overlooking the front yard. Nearby, the kitchen—angled for interest—contains a pantry and a snack bar that opens to the adjacent living room and dining room. From here, access is provided to the rear covered porch, supplying a spacious area for outdoor dining. Split planning places the restful master suite to the rear for privacy. Amenities include a large walk-in closet and a soothing master bath with a whirlpool tub, separate shower and double-bowl vanity.

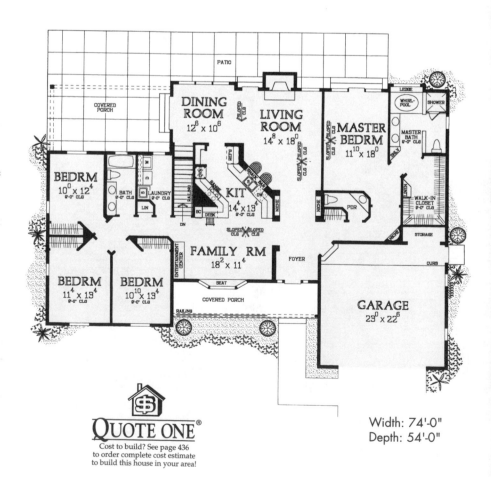

QUOTE ONE®
Cost to build? See page 436
to order complete cost estimate
to build this house in your area!

Width: 74'-0"
Depth: 54'-0"

Design HPT300302
Square Footage: 1,428

◆ This clever one-story ranch home features a covered veranda at the front to enhance outdoor livability. The entry opens to a foyer that leads to a vaulted living room on the left with a fireplace and a den or third bedroom on the right. The country kitchen is found at the back and is highlighted by a breakfast bar and French doors to the rear patio. The hallway contains an open-railed stairway to the basement and a laundry alcove, plus a coat closet. Bedrooms are large and have ample closet space. The master bedroom features a walk-in closet and a full, private bath. Family bedrooms share the use of a skylit bath.

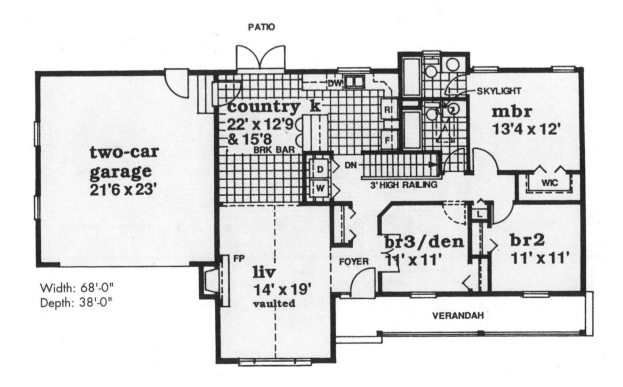

PATIO

two-car garage
21'6 x 23'

country k
22' x 12'9
& 15'8
BRK BAR

DW

SKYLIGHT

mbr
13'4 x 12'

DN

3' HIGH RAILING

WIC

D

W

FP

liv
14' x 19'
vaulted

FOYER

br3/den
11' x 11'

br2
11' x 11'

L

VERANDAH

Width: 68'-0"
Depth: 38'-0"

Design HPT300303

Square Footage: 2,549

L

◆ Covered porches to the front and rear will be the envy of the neighborhood when this house is built. The interior plan meets family needs perfectly in well-zoned areas. The sleeping wing has four bedrooms and two baths. The living zone has formal and informal gathering space. A work zone with a U-shaped kitchen shares space with the naturally-lit breakfast nook. The laundry and powder room are located in the far right corner of the plan. The two-car garage has a huge storage area.

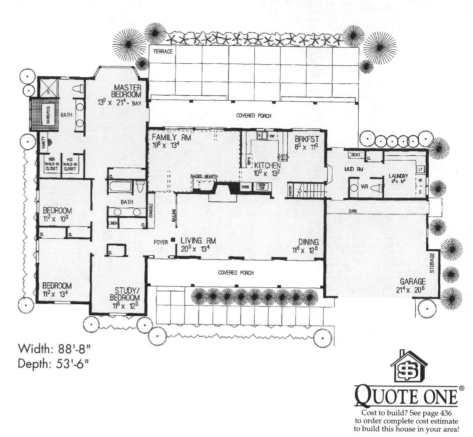

Width: 88'-8"
Depth: 53'-6"

QUOTE ONE®
Cost to build? See page 436
to order complete cost estimate
to build this house in your area!

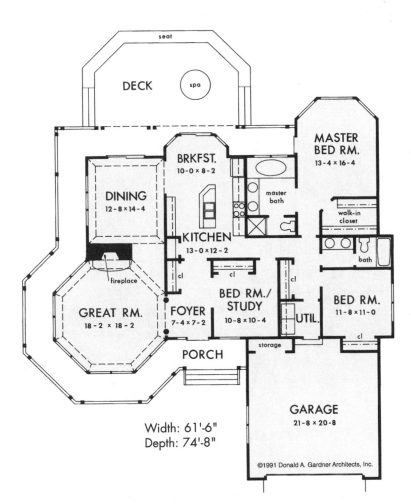

seat

DECK

spa

DINING
12-8 x 14-4

BRKFST.
10-0 x 8-2

master
bath

MASTER
BED RM.
13-4 x 16-4

walk-in
closet

KITCHEN
13-0 x 12-2

bath

cl

cl

cl

fireplace

GREAT RM.
18-2 x 18-2

FOYER
7-4 x 7-2

BED RM./
STUDY
10-8 x 10-4

UTIL.

BED RM.
11-8 x 11-0

cl

storage

PORCH

GARAGE
21-8 x 20-8

Width: 61'-6"
Depth: 74'-8"

©1991 Donald A. Gardner Architects, Inc.

Design HPT300304
Square Footage: 1,865

◆ This distinctive Victorian exterior conceals an open, contemporary floor plan. The entrance foyer with round columns offers visual excitement. The octagonal great room has a high tray ceiling and a fireplace. A generous kitchen with an angular island counter is centrally located, providing efficient service to the dining room, breakfast room and deck. The luxurious master bedroom suite has a large walk-in closet and a compartmented bath. Two additional bedrooms—one that would make a lovely study by including an entrance off the foyer—and a full hall bath round out this favorite plan.

Design HPT300305

Square Footage: 1,922

◆ Reminiscent of a Craftsman, this one-story home is enhanced by decorative brick detailing and muntin windows. The covered porch leads into the entry, flanked by the living room and formal dining room. The hearth-warmed family room enjoys views to the rear screened porch. The island kitchen provides plenty of counter space and a close proximity to the breakfast nook. All bedrooms reside on the left side of the plan. The master bedroom boasts a private covered patio and lavish full bath, while two family bedrooms share a full bath. A unique shop area attached to the two-car garage completes the plan.

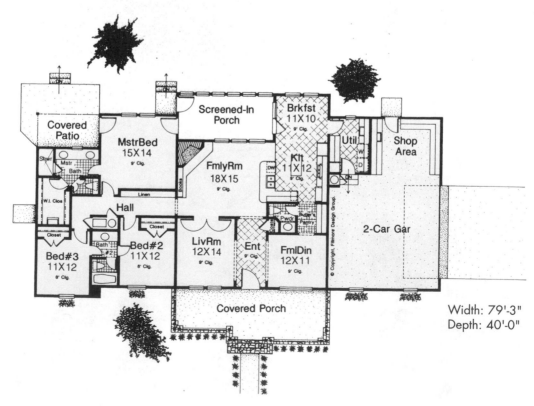

Width: 79'-3"
Depth: 40'-0"

Design HPT300306

Square Footage: 2,496
Bonus Room: 483 sq. ft.

◆ This countryside estate boasts a quaint rustic charm. Inside, the dining room and study can be found on either side of the entryway—both feature bayed windows. A gallery separates the formal rooms from the great room, which offers a country fireplace. The master suite is enhanced by a vaulted ceiling and features a private master bath. The right side of the home hosts two additional family bedrooms. Upstairs, an unfinished bonus room with a sloped ceiling is reserved for future use.

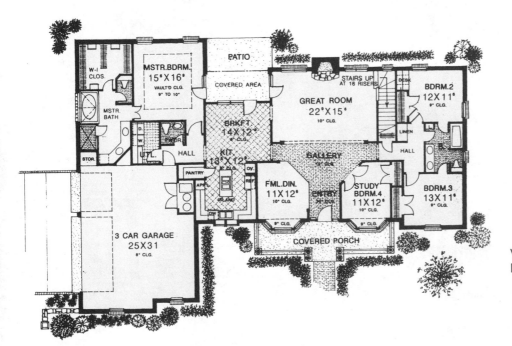

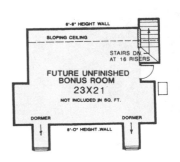

Width: 83'-4"
Depth: 57'-7"

Design HPT300307
Square Footage: 2,312

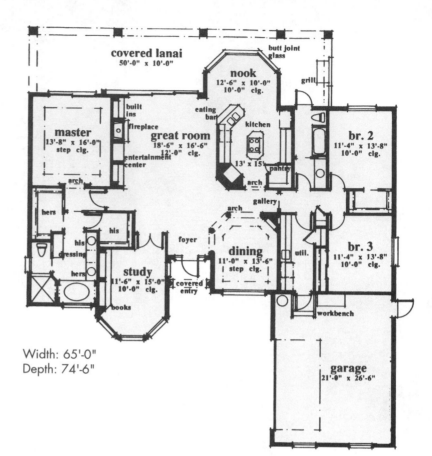

◆ From the street, the high-pitched rooflines, the raised dining room and stone detailing make this residence very elegant. The great room provides flexibility in a layout that can be great for entertaining or basic family living. The formal dining room is detailed by arches in columns. The oversized kitchen contains a walk-in pantry, an eating bar and an island cooktop. Two bedrooms have plenty of closet space and share a bath that accesses the lanai. The master wing consists of a study with built-ins, a nice suite with doors to the lanai, two walk-in closets, His and Hers vanity areas and a garden tub.

Width: 65'-0"
Depth: 74'-6"

Design HPT300308
Square Footage: 2,297

FamilyRm
16 x 14
Cathedral Ceiling

Covered Patio

Bed #2
12⁶ x 11³
8'-0" clg.

Walk-in Closet

Walk-in Closet

Bed #3
11 x 11⁶
8'-0" Clg.

Din
12⁶ x 10⁶
9'-0" Clg. Tile

Kit
10³ x 12
9'-0" Clg. Tile

D/W

Dbl Oven

Pantry

Linen

Pwdr

Linen

Books

Bed #4
11 X 11
8'-0" Clg.

Whirl-Pool

9'-0" Clg.

Walk-in Closet
9'-0" Clg.

Chest

Gallery
10'-0" Clg. Tile

Coats

Hall
8'-0" Clg.

Util

W

D

C/H

Walk-in Closet

MstrBed
15⁶ x 12⁶
9'-0" Clg.

Linen

Ent
10'-0" Clg. Tile

FmlDin
10⁶ x 13
10'-0" Clg.

Sitting Area
9'-0" Clg.

LivRm
13 x 13
10'-0" Clg.

8'-0" Clg.

Covered Porch

Gar
20 x 22
8'-4" Clg.

Stoop

Width: 60'-0"
Depth: 56'-1"

◆ Definitely European in nature, this home highlights the neighborhood with its brick and stone facade, hipped roof, arched and bay windows and dormer/gable ornamentations. The interior is equally exciting with bold angles created in the entry, living room and dining room. The family room, in the rear, enjoys a cathedral ceiling and a fireplace. Three bedrooms sit on the right with a full bath while the master suite resides on the left with a private bath, walk-in closet and sitting area for meditative and quiet moments. The sheltered patio in the rear is conveniently located near the kitchen—perfect for weekend barbecues.

Design HPT300309

Square Footage: 2,530
Bonus Room: 270 sq. ft.

◆ The side-loading three-car garage is set back and hidden from view, keeping this home's facade clean and fresh. The family room and study flank the study where it widens into the gallery. From here you enter the magnificent great room with its fireplace and patio beyond, or turn left to reach the lavish master suite. To the right, find the two family bedrooms with the shared full bath, or the diamond-shaped kitchen with the adjoining breakfast nook. The utility room is tucked behind the staircase that rises to the future bonus room.

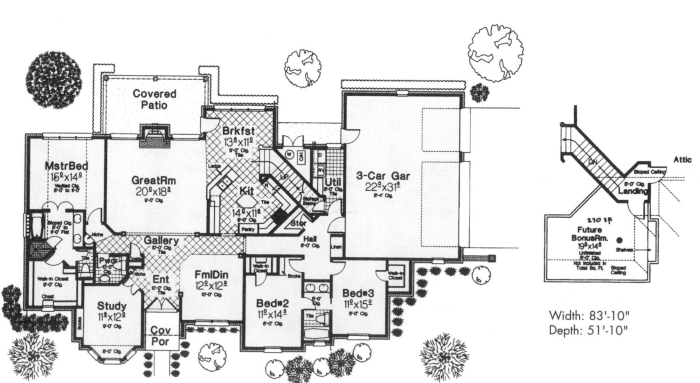

Width: 83'-10"
Depth: 51'-10"

Design HPT300310

Square Footage: 2,260

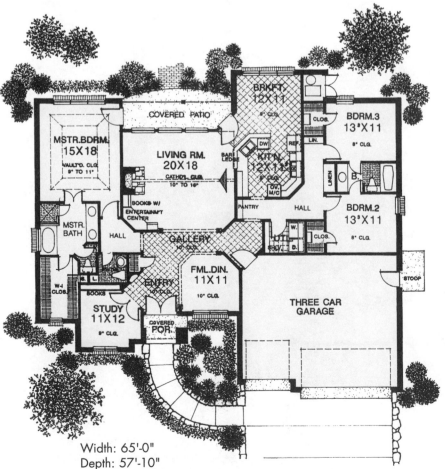

Width: 65'-0"
Depth: 57'-10"

◆ This home is reminiscent of those found in the French countryside with its hipped roof, keystone arches and rustic stone detailing. Inside, the floor plan offers all the modern conveniences. The family dining room is just steps from the kitchen which adjoins the sunny breakfast nook. The living room boasts a cathedral ceiling, fireplace and built-in entertainment center. A study to the left of the entry offers a quiet place to retreat as does the lavish master suite.

Design HPT300311

Square Footage: 2,329

◆ Rustic in nature, this charming home offers a refined interior that is accented by the multiple ceiling treatments throughout. The dining room and study flank the foyer and open to the great room where French doors lead to the rear property. Family bedrooms reside on the right and the master suite finds seclusion on the left with His and Hers walk-in closets and a lavish bath. The kitchen is smartly situated between the dining room and the breakfast nook which, in turn, opens to the covered rear porch.

Garage
23'-0" x 21'-0"

opt. Stairs to garage attic storage/bonus room

Porch
12'-4" x 22'-0"

Pwdr.

Nook
10'-8" x 12'-0"

Utility

Master Suite
14'-8" x 15'-0"
Tray Ceiling

built-in

Great Room
18'-10" x 17'-10"
Coffered Ceiling

Bedroom 2
12'-0" x 12'-4"

fireplace

Kitchen
11'-2" x 12'-11"

CL

built-in

P

Bath

Her WIC

His WIC

Dining
11'-0" x 11'-4"
Coffered Ceiling

L

Bench

Master Bath

Study
11'-10" x 11'-0"
Beamed Ceiling

Foyer

CL

Bedroom 1
12'-0" x 11'-0"

Porch
32'-0" x 6'-0"

Width: 72'-0"
Depth: 73'-4"

Design HPT300312

Square Footage: 1,854

◆ Country Craftsman architecture highlights the facade of this charming family
home. A combination of shingles and
stone graces the exterior, while interior
spaces offer tempting amenities. The foyer
leads to the great room, where plentiful
fixtures such as the fireplace flanked by
built-ins, a cathedral ceiling and sliding
glass doors to the rear porch offer entertainment options. The compact kitchen
serves the dining room with ease. The
right of the home provides a comfortable
master bedroom complete with a sitting
room, two walk-in closets and a dual-vanity bath. Two additional family bedrooms
share a hall bath—one bedroom converts
to a study. Finally, a utility room is placed
next to the two-car garage with storage.

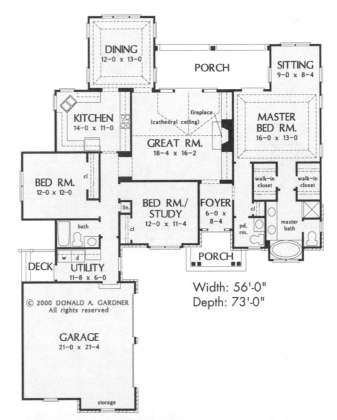

Width: 56'-0"
Depth: 73'-0"

© 1998   Donald A Gardner, Inc. B. NATHAN

Design HPT300313
Square Footage: 1,544
Bonus Room: 320 sq. ft.

◆ This home would look good in any neighborhood. From the covered front porch to the trio of gables, this design has a lot of appeal. Inside, the Craftsman styling continues with built-in shelves and a warming fireplace in the great room and plenty of windows to bring in the outdoors. The U-shaped kitchen offers easy access to the formal dining area. Expansion is possible with an optional bonus room, adding a second level. A tray ceiling adorns the master bedroom, along with His and Hers walk-in closets and a pampering bath complete with a twin-sink vanity and a separate shower and garden tub.

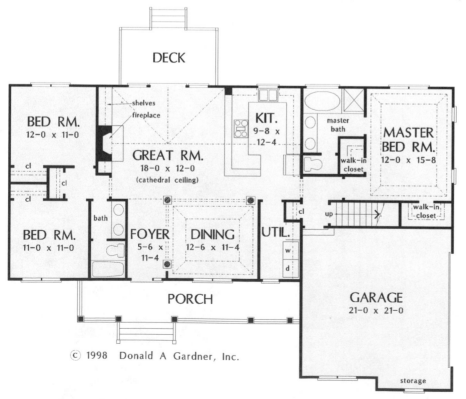

DECK

BED RM.
12-0 x 11-0

shelves
fireplace

KIT.
9-8 x
12-4

master
bath

MASTER
BED RM.
12-0 x 15-8

GREAT RM.
18-0 x 12-0
(cathedral ceiling)

walk-in
closet

cl

cl

cl

bath

BED RM.
11-0 x 11-0

FOYER
5-6 x
11-4

DINING
12-6 x 11-4

UTIL.

up

walk-in
closet

w
d

PORCH

GARAGE
21-0 x 21-0

storage

© 1998   Donald A Gardner, Inc.

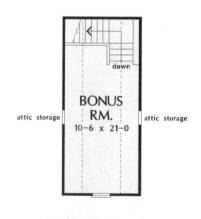

down

BONUS
RM.
10-6 x 21-0

attic storage

attic storage

Width: 63'-0"
Depth: 43'-0"

Design HPT300314
Square Footage: 1,411
Bonus Room: 330 sq. ft.

◆ This country-style one-story home is comfortable yet cozy. The covered front porch opens to a central foyer, divided from the great room by decorative columns. Bookcases flank a fireplace in the great room, while skylights add brightness. The vaulted kitchen serves a nearby dining room. Family bedrooms are on the left side of the plan, split from the master suite on the right. A large deck along the back of the plan contributes to outdoor fun.

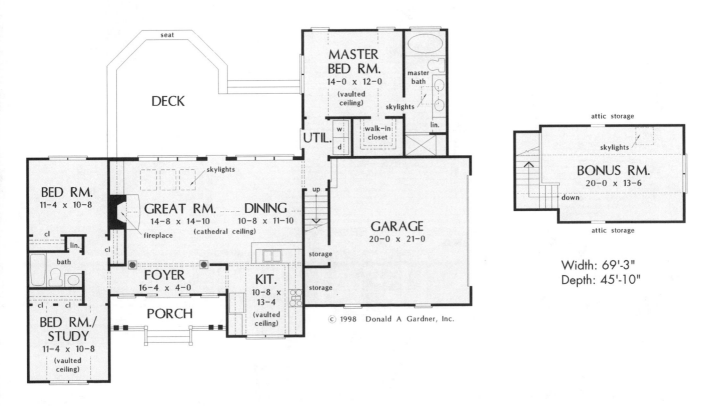

seat

DECK

MASTER BED RM.
14-0 x 12-0
(vaulted ceiling)

master bath

skylights

UTIL.

w
d

walk-in closet

lin.

skylights

up

BED RM.
11-4 x 10-8

cl
lin.

GREAT RM.
14-8 x 14-10
(cathedral ceiling)

fireplace

DINING
10-8 x 11-10

GARAGE
20-0 x 21-0

bath

cl

storage

FOYER
16-4 x 4-0

KIT.
10-8 x 13-4
(vaulted ceiling)

storage

BED RM./ STUDY
11-4 x 10-8
(vaulted ceiling)

cl   cl

PORCH

attic storage

skylights

BONUS RM.
20-0 x 13-6

down

attic storage

Width: 69'-3"
Depth: 45'-10"

Design HPT300315

Square Footage: 1,373

◆ A columned front porch and a steep gabled roofline punctuated with dormer windows give a traditional welcome to this family home. A vaulted ceiling tops the family and dining rooms, which are nicely accented with a fireplace and bright windows. An amenity-filled kitchen opens to the breakfast room. The master suite has a refined tray ceiling and a vaulted master bath. Two family bedrooms, a laundry center and a full bath—with private access from Bedroom 3—complete this stylish plan. Please specify basement or crawlspace foundation when ordering.

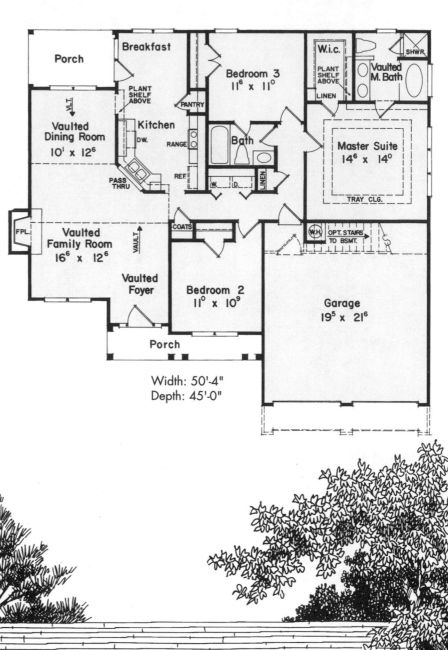

Porch

Breakfast

W.i.c.

PLANT SHELF ABOVE

SHWR.

Vaulted M. Bath

Bedroom 3
11⁶ x 11⁰

PANTRY

Vaulted Dining Room
10¹ x 12⁶

Kitchen

DW.

RANGE

Bath

LINEN

PLANT SHELF ABOVE

Master Suite
14⁶ x 14⁰

REF.

PASS THRU

W.   D.   LINEN

TRAY CLG.

FPL.

Vaulted Family Room
16⁶ x 12⁶

VAULT

COATS

W.H.

OPT. STAIRS TO BSMT.

Vaulted Foyer

Bedroom 2
11⁰ x 10⁹

Garage
19⁵ x 21⁶

Porch

Width: 50'-4"
Depth: 45'-0"

Design HPT300316

Square Footage: 1,520

Width: 38'-0"
Depth: 72'-0"

◆ Gables and a welcoming covered porch introduce this fine three-bedroom home and give it plenty of curb appeal. Inside, this charming cottage-style home offers a spacious living room with a focal-point fireplace and window transoms to let in the light. The dining room is served by a C-shaped kitchen with an angled double sink—directly under a corner window. A secluded master suite features a vaulted ceiling, a box-bay window, a lavish bath with a spa-style tub, and a walk-in closet. Two secondary bedrooms reside in the back of the plan. The two-car garage has rear-entry access—perfect for narrow lots.

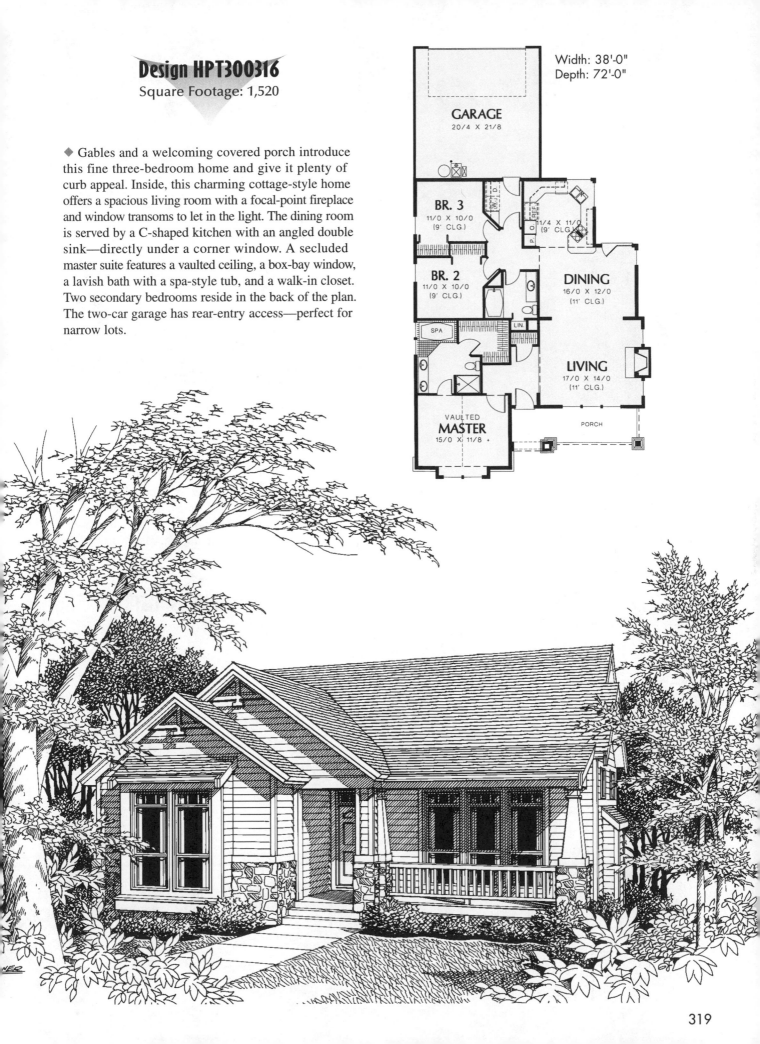

GARAGE
20/4 X 21/8

BR. 3
11/0 X 10/0
(9' CLG.)

BR. 2
11/0 X 10/0
(9' CLG.)

11/4 X 11/0
(9' CLG.)

SPA

LIN.

DINING
16/0 X 12/0
(11' CLG.)

LIVING
17/0 X 14/0
(11' CLG.)

VAULTED
MASTER
15/0 X 11/8 +

PORCH

♦ This cozy cottage features a front-facing office/guest suite, which provides privacy for the entry courtyard. With its separate entrance, it offers the perfect haven for a home office or for those with live-in parents. The remainder of the house is designed with the same level of efficiency. It contains a large living area with access to a covered patio and a three-sided fireplace that shares its warmth with a dining room featuring built-ins. A unique kitchen provides garage access. The bedrooms include a comfortable master suite with a whirlpool tub, a double-bowl vanity and twin closets.

Design HPT300317
Square Footage: 1,418

L

Design HPT300318
Square Footage: 1,414

L

QUOTE ONE®

Cost to build? See page 436 to order complete cost estimate to build this house in your area!

Width: 44'-8"
Depth: 54'-4"

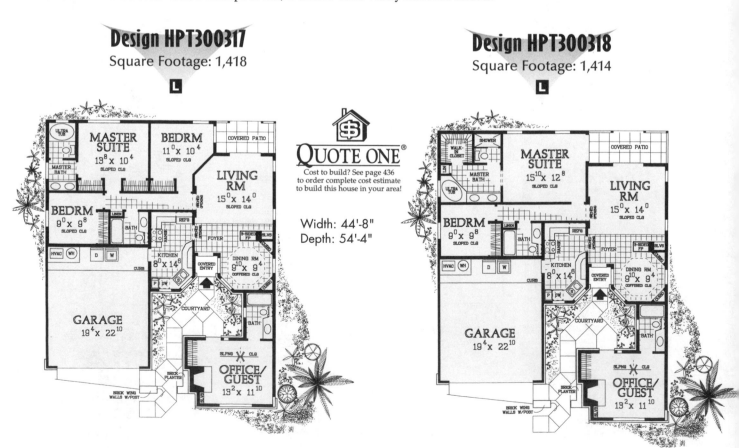

Width: 44'-0"
Depth: 52'-4"

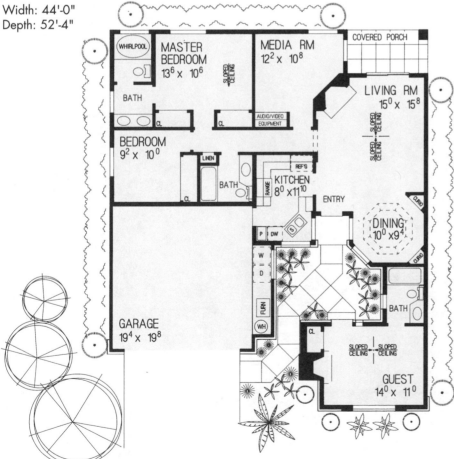

WHIRLPOOL

MASTER BEDROOM
13⁶ x 10⁶

SLOPED CEILING

MEDIA RM
12² x 10⁸

COVERED PORCH

BATH

CL

CL

AUDIO/VIDEO EQUIPMENT

LIVING RM
15⁰ x 15⁸

SLOPED CEILING · SLOPED CEILING

BEDROOM
9² x 10⁰

LINEN

REF'S

CL

BATH

RANGE

KITCHEN
8⁰ x 11¹⁰

ENTRY

CL/RD

DINING
10⁰ x 9⁴

CL/RD

P DW

S

W
D

BATH

FURN

GARAGE
19⁴ x 19⁸

WH

CL

SLOPED CEILING · SLOPED CEILING

GUEST
14⁰ x 11⁰

Design HPT300319
Square Footage: 1,375

L

◆ Here's a traditional design that will be economical to build and a pleasure to occupy. The front door opens into a spacious living room with a sloped ceiling, corner fireplace and sliding glass doors to the covered porch. This room also accesses the dining room with a coffered ceiling. The nearby L-shaped kitchen serves both areas easily. A few steps away is the cozy media room with built-in space for audiovisual equipment. Down the hall are two bedrooms and two baths; the master bedroom features a whirlpool tub and double vanities. The secondary bedroom has a full bath with a linen closet.

QUOTE ONE®
Cost to build? See page 436
to order complete cost estimate
to build this house in your area!

Design HPT300320
Square Footage: 1,267

LD

◆ Here is a charming early American adaptation that will serve as a picturesque and practical retirement home. Also, it will serve admirably those with a small family in search of an efficient, economically built home. The spacious living area is highlighted by the raised-hearth fireplace. The kitchen features eating space and easy access to the garage and basement. The dining room is adjacent to the kitchen and views the rear yard. The bedroom wing offers three bedrooms and two full baths. Don't miss the sliding doors to the terrace from the living room and the master bedroom.

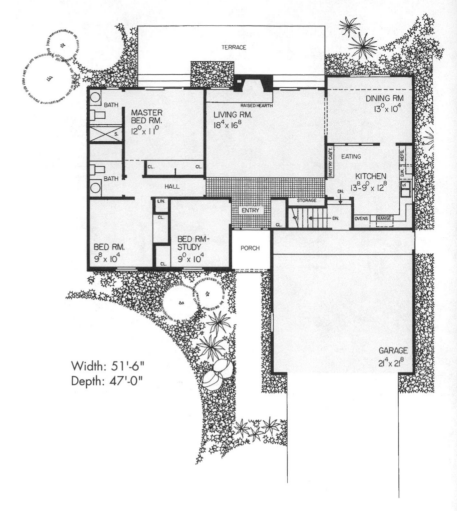

Width: 51'-6"
Depth: 47'-0"

Cost to build? See page 436
to order complete cost estimate
to build this house in your area!

Design HPT300321
Square Footage: 1,233

◆ A covered railed veranda, shuttered windows, siding and wood detailing and a Palladian window all lend their charm to this one-story ranch home. The living room shares a through-fireplace with the dining area and has a box-bay window at the front. A U-shaped kitchen is efficient and pleasant with a window to the backyard over the sink. Access the garage through the laundry room, where you will also find stairs to the basement. The three bedrooms are on the right side of the plan. The master suite contains two wall closets and a private bath. Two family bedrooms share a full hall bath.

Width: 54'-0"
Depth: 30'-0"

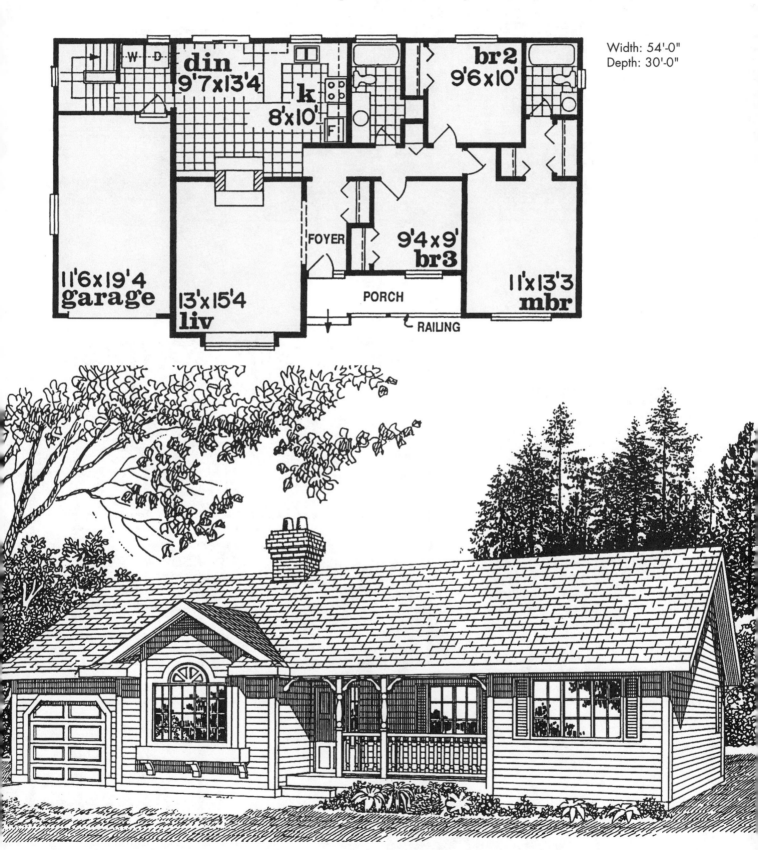

Design HPT300322
Square Footage: 1,495

◆ This three-bedroom starter home possess a practical layout and an appealing facade. A bay window, horizontal siding and a covered entry with turned post and wood railings are the first details you'll notice. The living room/dining room combination features a window seat in the bay window and a warming fireplace. The kitchen has a breakfast bar and a bay-windowed eating area and attaches to a family room with sliding glass doors to the rear patio. Three bedrooms include two family bedrooms sharing a full bath and a master suite with a private bath.

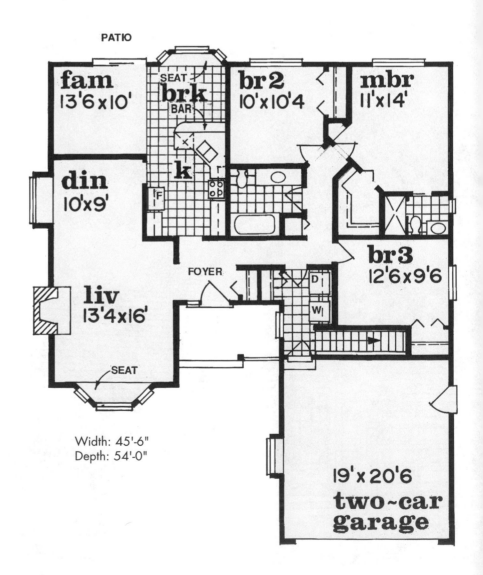

PATIO

fam
13'6 x 10'

SEAT
brk
BAR

br2
10' x 10'4

mbr
11' x 14'

din
10' x 9'

k

F

liv
13'4 x 16'

FOYER

br3
12'6 x 9'6

SEAT

D

W

19' x 20'6
two-car garage

Width: 45'-6"
Depth: 54'-0"

Design HPT300323

Square Footage: 1,647

◆ This floor plan is designed for a home that captures a view to the rear of the lot. French doors in the dining room, living room, master bedroom and breakfast room all lead out to the patio in the back. In the front, a skylit foyer is visually zoned from the living room by a plant shelf. Both the living room and dining room have vaulted ceilings and enjoy a warming fireplace set between them. The bedrooms are to the right and include two family bedrooms sharing a full bath. The vaulted master suite features a walk-in closet and a private bath with a separate tub and shower.

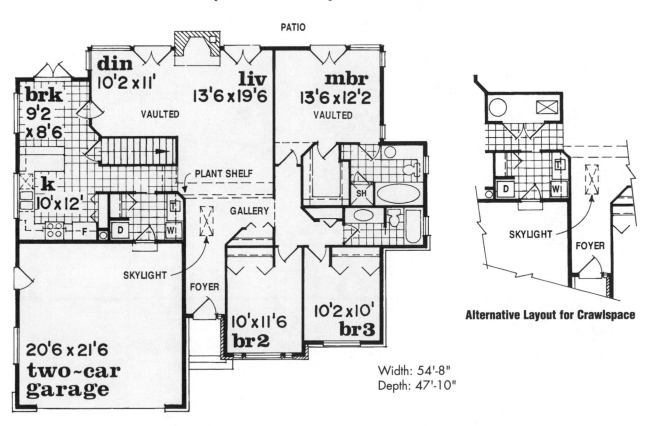

PATIO

din
10'2 x 11'

liv
13'6 x 19'6
VAULTED

mbr
13'6 x 12'2
VAULTED

brk
9'2
x 8'6

k
10'x 12'

VAULTED

PLANT SHELF

GALLERY

SH

br2
10'x 11'6

br3
10'2 x 10'

SKYLIGHT

FOYER

20'6 x 21'6
two-car
garage

SKYLIGHT

FOYER

Alternative Layout for Crawlspace

Width: 54'-8"
Depth: 47'-10"

325

Design HPT300324

Square Footage: 1,360

◆ Smaller in size, but big on livability, this one-story home has amenities and options usually found only in larger homes. Begin with the covered veranda and its entry to a central foyer. On the right is a vaulted living room with a central fireplace. The country kitchen lives up to its name—it features an open-railed stair to the basement, an L-shaped work counter, a breakfast snack island and a bayed breakfast nook with double-door access to the backyard. The two family bedrooms share a full bath, while the master suite has a private bath. A two-car garage sits to the side of the plan.

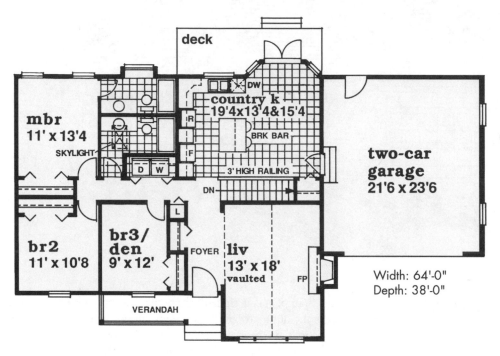

deck

mbr 11' x 13'4

SKYLIGHT

country k 19'4 x 13'4 & 15'4

BRK BAR

DW

3' HIGH RAILING

two-car garage 21'6 x 23'6

DN

D   W

br2 11' x 10'8

br3/ den 9' x 12'

L

FOYER

liv 13' x 18' vaulted

FP

VERANDAH

Width: 64'-0"
Depth: 38'-0"

Design HPT300325

Square Footage: 1,452

◆ This compact three-bedroom home is as economical to build as it is beautiful to behold. Its appeal begins right on the outside with a bay window, a half-circle window over the bay, and a railed front porch. The skylit entry foyer leads to a hallway that connects the living areas with the sleeping quarters. The vaulted living room features a fireplace, a built-in audiovisual center and a window seat in the bay window. The open dining room shares the vaulted ceiling. The kitchen, with ample work counters, has plenty of room for a breakfast table.

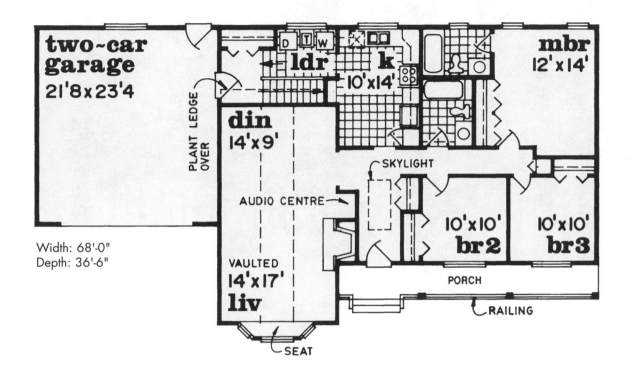

two-car garage
21'8 x 23'4

PLANT LEDGE OVER

ldr

k
10'x14'

mbr
12'x14'

din
14'x9'

SKYLIGHT

AUDIO CENTRE

10'x10'
br 2

10'x10'
br 3

VAULTED
14'x17'
liv

PORCH

RAILING

SEAT

Width: 68'-0"
Depth: 36'-6"

Design HPT3030015

Square Footage: 1,973
Bonus Room: 368 sq. ft.

◆ An inviting columned porch, flower-box window, and pinnacled cupola make this three-bedroom home a classic neighborhood charmer. Past the foyer, enter the great room, exquisite with a cathedral ceiling, built-in bookcase, and warming fireplace. The kitchen accesses the breakfast nook and dining room, each accented with bay windows. The secluded master suite features a walk-in closet and a luxurious bath with a whirlpool tub. Two bedrooms, a relaxing terrace, and a convenient utility room complete the plan.

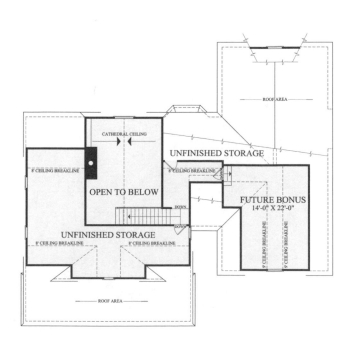

Width: 64'-10"
Depth: 58'-2"

This home, as shown in the photograph, may differ from the actual blueprints. For more detailed information, please check the floor plans carefully.

Design HPT3030016

Square Footage: 2,151
Bonus Space: 814 sq. ft.

◆ Country flavor is well established on this fine three-bedroom home. The covered front porch welcomes friends and family alike to the foyer, where the formal dining room opens off to the left. The vaulted ceiling in the great room enhances the warmth of the fireplace and wall of windows. An efficient kitchen works well with the bayed breakfast area. The secluded master suite offers a walk-in closet and a lavish bath; on the other side of the home, two family bedrooms share a full bath. Upstairs, an optional fourth bedroom is available for guests or in-laws and provides access to a large recreation room.

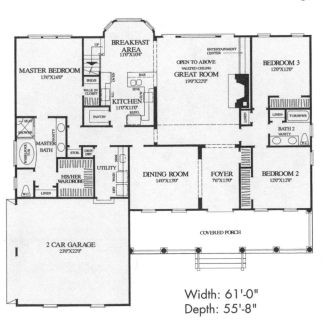

Width: 61'-0"
Depth: 55'-8"

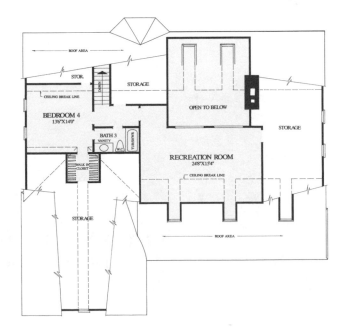

Design HPT300328

Square Footage: 1,295

L **D**

◆ Equally gracious outside and inside, this one- or two-bedroom cottage has a post-and-rail covered porch hugging one wing, with convenient access through double doors or pass-through windows in the dining room and kitchen. The columned entry foyer has a sloped ceiling and leads past a second bedroom or media room into a great room with another sloped ceiling, a fireplace and a low wall along the staircase that leads to the attic. The master suite fills the right wing and features a plant shelf in the bedroom and a garden tub in the master bath, plus a large walk-in closet and laundry facilities.

Quote One®

Cost to build? See page 436
to order complete cost estimate
to build this house in your area!

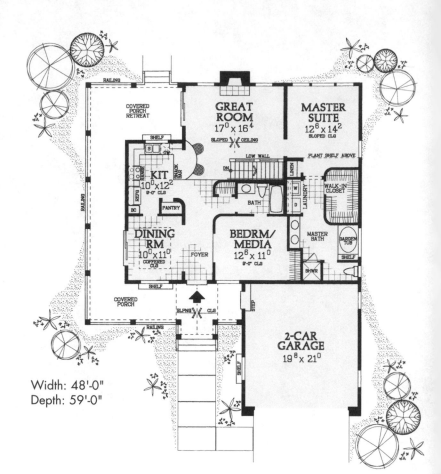

Width: 48'-0"
Depth: 59'-0"

Width: 40'-8"
Depth: 59'-0"

COVERED
RETREAT
PATIO
SLOPED CLG

RAILING

TILE
HEARTH

LIVING
RM
16⁸ x 14⁰
SLOPED CEILING

MASTER
SUITE
12⁶ x 14²
SLOPED CLG

PLANT SHELF ABOVE

LOW WALL

LINEN

KIT
10⁰ x 12²
9'-0" CLG

BREAKFAST
BAR

DN

WALK-IN
CLOSET

REFG

BATH

LAUNDRY

BC

PANTRY

OPT.
DOOR

MASTER
BATH

DINING
RM
10⁰ x 11⁰
TRAY CLG

FOYER

MEDIA/
BEDRM
12⁶ x 11⁰
9'-0" CLG

SHELF

SHWR

PLANTER

RAILING

COVERED
PORCH

SLPNG CLG

STEP

RAILING

RAILING

GARAGE
19⁸ x 21⁰

PLANTER

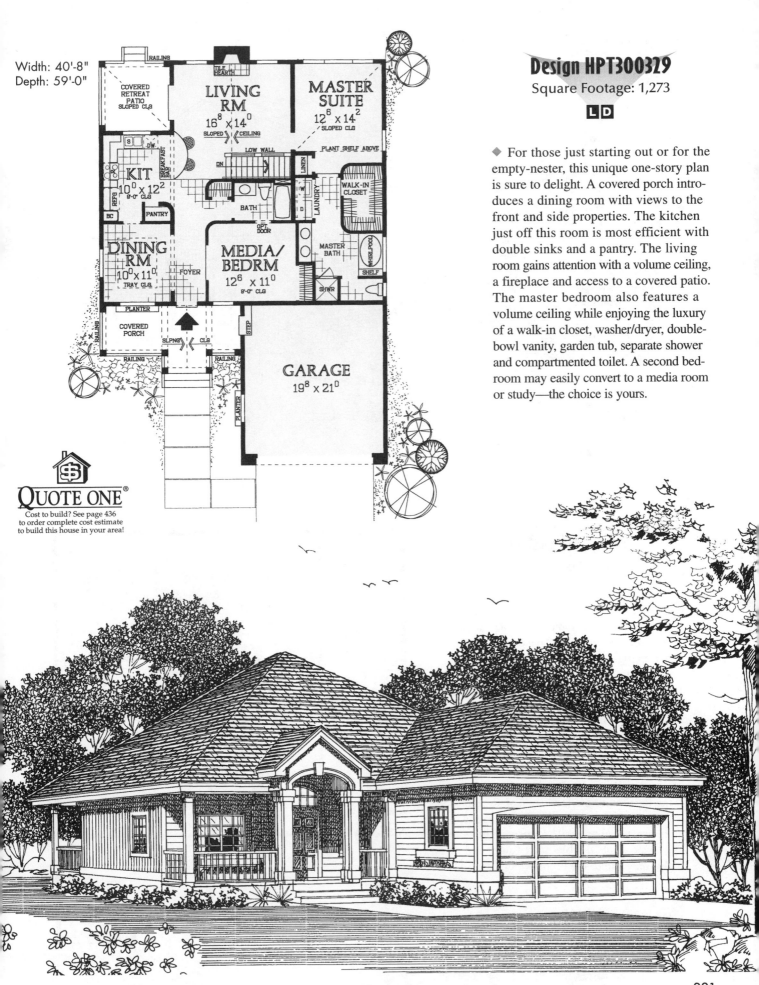

Design HPT300329
Square Footage: 1,273

L D

◆ For those just starting out or for the empty-nester, this unique one-story plan is sure to delight. A covered porch introduces a dining room with views to the front and side properties. The kitchen just off this room is most efficient with double sinks and a pantry. The living room gains attention with a volume ceiling, a fireplace and access to a covered patio. The master bedroom also features a volume ceiling while enjoying the luxury of a walk-in closet, washer/dryer, double-bowl vanity, garden tub, separate shower and compartmented toilet. A second bedroom may easily convert to a media room or study—the choice is yours.

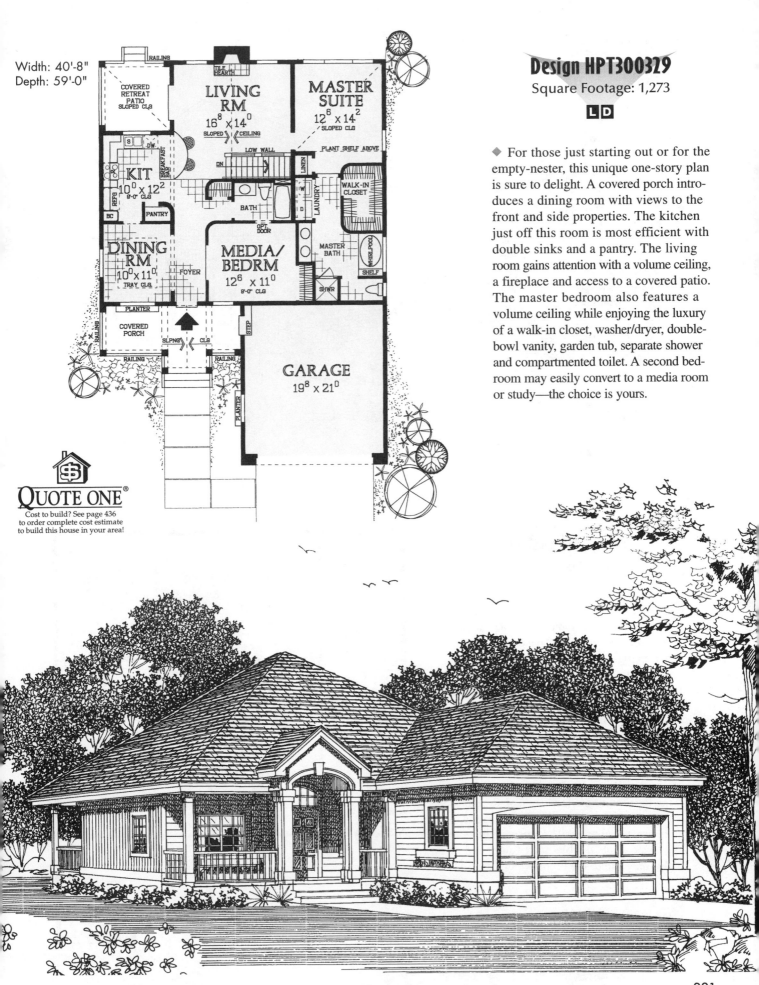

QUOTE ONE®
Cost to build? See page 436
to order complete cost estimate
to build this house in your area!

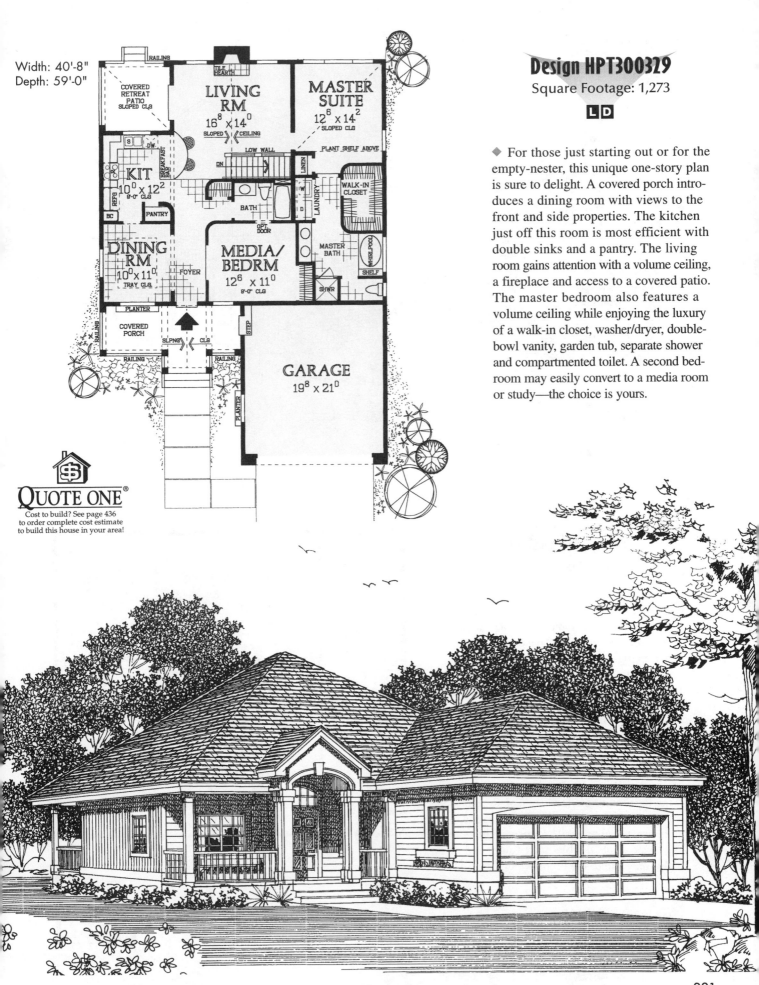

331

Design HPT300330

Square Footage: 1,861

◆ This one-story home offers step-saving convenience and large spaces for every-day living. A great room is placed to the rear of the home along with a formal dining room, a corner fireplace and glass doors overlooking the rear yard. A raised ceiling tops this area, adding volume and luxury. Open stairs to the lower level visually widen the entry. The large kitchen with a breakfast area generously attends to the daily needs of the family, while the location of the laundry isolates the work area. Two closets offer storage in the master suite, while a raised ceiling, whirlpool tub, double-bowl vanity and shower pamper the homeowner.

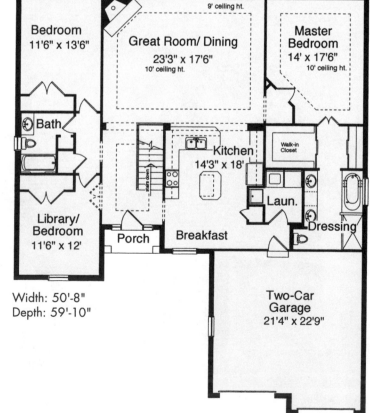

Deck

Bedroom
11'6" x 13'6"

Great Room/ Dining
23'3" x 17'6"
10' ceiling ht.

9' ceiling ht.

Master
Bedroom
14' x 17'6"
10' ceiling ht.

Bath

Walk-in
Closet

Kitchen
14'3" x 18'

Laun.

Library/
Bedroom
11'6" x 12'

Porch

Breakfast

Dressing

Width: 50'-8"
Depth: 59'-10"

Two-Car
Garage
21'4" x 22'9"

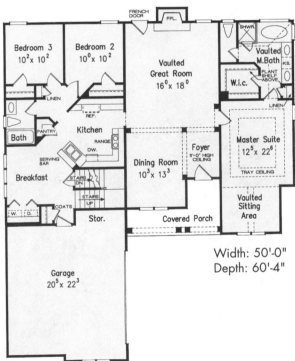

FRENCH DOOR   FPL.

Bedroom 3
10² x 10²

Bedroom 2
10⁰ x 10²

Vaulted
Great Room
16⁰ x 18⁰

SHWR.

Vaulted
M.Bath

LINEN

W.i.c.

PLANT SHELF ABOVE

K.S.

Bath

PANTRY

REF.

Kitchen

RANGE

LINEN

SERVING BAR

DW.

Foyer
11'-0" HIGH CEILING

Master Suite
12⁵ x 22⁶

Breakfast

STAIRS DN.

STAIRS UP

Dining Room
10³ x 13³

TRAY CEILING

W. D.

COATS

Stor.

Covered Porch

Vaulted
Sitting
Area

Garage
20⁵ x 22³

Width: 50'-0"
Depth: 60'-4"

Design HPT300331

Square Footage: 1,642
Bonus Space: 317 sq. ft.

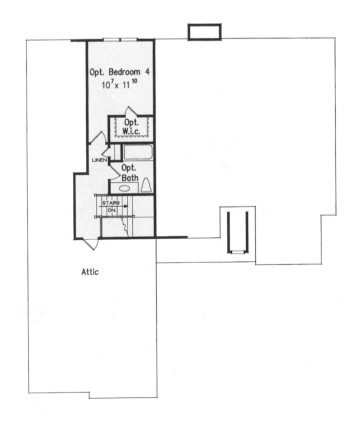

Opt. Bedroom 4
10⁷ x 11¹⁰

Opt.
W.i.c.

LINEN

Opt.
Bath

STAIRS DN.

Attic

◆ The stone and siding of this charming three-bedroom home is accented by flower boxes, shutters and keystone lintels. The foyer introduces a dining room and the hearth-warmed great room. To the right of the foyer is the sumptuous master suite. The master suite enjoys a tray ceiling and a vaulted bath with a walk-in closet, dual vanities and a compartmented toilet. A vaulted sitting bay completes this suite. Two family bedrooms share a full bath to the left, beyond the kitchen. The kitchen serves up both casual and formal meals with ease. The breakfast room is a lovely open area with plenty of natural light.

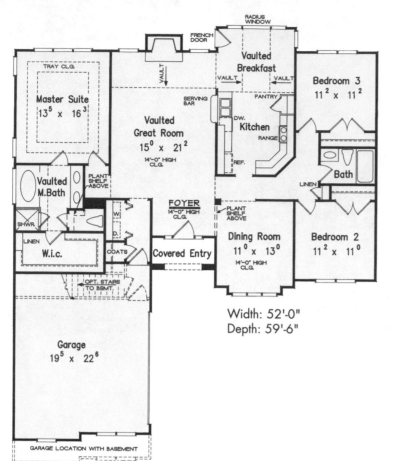

TRAY CLG.

Master Suite
13^5 x 16^3

Vaulted Breakfast

RADIUS WINDOW

FRENCH DOOR

VAULT

VAULT

VAULT

Bedroom 3
11^2 x 11^2

SERVING BAR

Vaulted Great Room
15^0 x 21^2
14'-0" HIGH CLG.

DW.

Kitchen

PANTRY

RANGE

REF.

Bath

LINEN

Vaulted M.Bath

PLANT SHELF ABOVE

SHWR.

LINEN

W.I.C.

W

D.

COATS

FOYER
14'-0" HIGH CLG.

PLANT SHELF ABOVE

Covered Entry

Dining Room
11^0 x 13^0
14'-0" HIGH CLG.

Bedroom 2
11^2 x 11^0

OPT. STAIRS TO BSMT.

Garage
19^5 x 22^6

GARAGE LOCATION WITH BASEMENT

Width: 52'-0"
Depth: 59'-6"

Design HPT300332
Square Footage: 1,696

◆ This three-bedroom home presents a fabulous European facade and welcomes family and visitors alike with its grand covered entrance. Inside, the foyer leads directly into the vaulted great room. Here, a warming fireplace, a serving bar from the kitchen and French-door access to the rear yard are sure to please. Meal times are easily handled by the large and efficient kitchen, whether they are held in the formal dining room or in the more casual breakfast room. Sleeping quarters are split for privacy. Please specify basement or crawlspace foundation when ordering.

Design HPT300333
Square Footage: 1,890

◆ This charming cottage home possesses a heart of gold with French folk style. A quartet of blended materials offers an ethereal elevation that's perfect for everyday living or a vacation retreat. In the living room a fireplace with an extended hearth is framed by built-in bookcases. A well-organized kitchen provides wrapping counters and a serving ledge, which overlooks the breakfast area. The formal dining room is highlighted by a coffered ceiling and enjoys easy service from the kitchen. The master suite features a private bath with a garden tub and a separate shower with a seat. Two additional family bedrooms share a full hall bath. Please specify crawlspace or slab foundation when ordering.

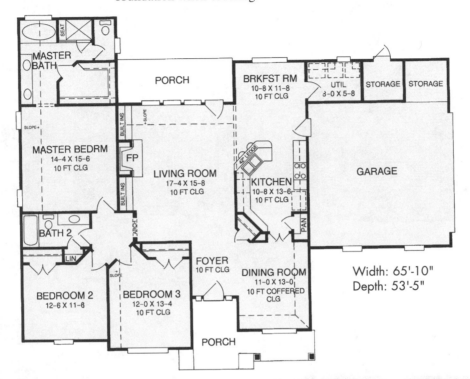

Width: 65'-10"
Depth: 53'-5"

Design HPT300334
Square Footage: 2,391

◆ An ultra-high roofline on the outside allows for soaring ceilings on the inside of this one-story home. A formal dining room lies just to the left of the entry and marks its boundaries with decorative columns. The entry to the great room is also adorned with columns, while the great room itself features a warming fireplace. The kitchen and breakfast room sit to the left of the great room, while the master suite is to the right. Family bedrooms are split from the master suite on the opposite side of the plan.

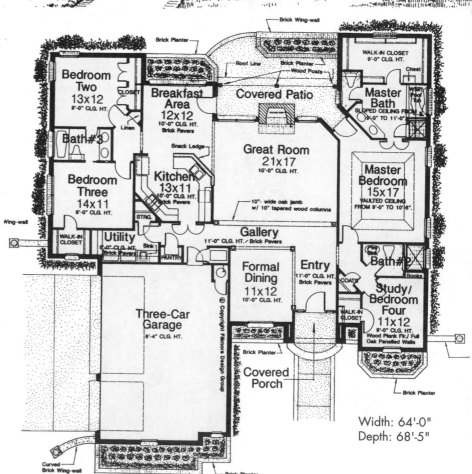

Width: 64'-0"
Depth: 68'-5"

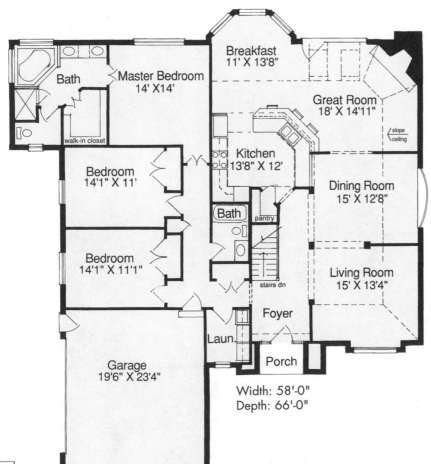

Breakfast 11' X 13'8"

Bath

Master Bedroom 14' X14'

walk-in closet

Great Room 18' X 14'11"

slope ceiling

Kitchen 13'8" X 12'

Bedroom 14'1" X 11'

Dining Room 15' X 12'8"

Bath

pantry

Bedroom 14'1" X 11'1"

stairs dn

Living Room 15' X 13'4"

Foyer

Laun.

Porch

Garage 19'6" X 23'4"

Width: 58'-0"
Depth: 66'-0"

Design HPT300335
Square Footage: 2,277

◆ Gables, brick quoins, a wing wall, sidelights and an arched transom at the entry combine to enhance the face of this one-level traditional home. Both the living and dining rooms are accentuated by a vaulted ceiling, columns and custom moldings. The excitement continues into the great room with a corner fireplace. A bar at the kitchen counter opens this area to the great room, and a pass-through to the dining room adds step-saving convenience. The master bedroom suite offers a whirlpool tub, double vanities, a separate shower stall and a walk-in closet, making this home attractive to the empty-nester or the move-up buyer.

Design HPT300336

Square Footage: 1,848

◆ This farmhouse is embellished with European touches. Fieldstone and stucco, arch-top windows and shutters invite a little bit of everything good into this design. The covered porch is a sweet treat for mild evenings. Inside, the dining room is graced with a stepped ceiling and defining column. The living room captures rear views through mulitple windows and rear-porch access. A master suite, to the right, is secluded for privacy. The country kitchen is a delight of casual space featuring interaction between the family room with a built-in entertainment center and the breakfast nook—all featuring vaulted ceilings. Two family bedrooms are found to the left and share a full bath.

Width: 58'-0"
Depth: 60'-0"

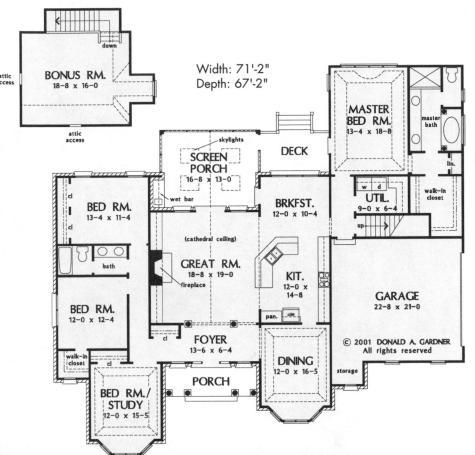

BONUS RM.
18-8 x 16-0

attic access

attic access

Width: 71'-2"
Depth: 67'-2"

BED RM.
13-4 x 11-4

bath

BED RM.
12-0 x 12-4

walk-in closet

BED RM./
STUDY
12-0 x 15-5

PORCH

FOYER
13-6 x 6-4

SCREEN PORCH
16-8 x 13-0

skylights

wet bar

GREAT RM.
18-8 x 19-0

fireplace

(cathedral ceiling)

DECK

BRKFST.
12-0 x 10-4

KIT.
12-0 x 14-8

pan.

DINING
12-0 x 16-5

MASTER BED RM.
13-4 x 18-8

master bath

lin.

UTIL.
9-0 x 6-4

w d

up

walk-in closet

GARAGE
22-8 x 21-0

storage

© 2001 DONALD A. GARDNER
All rights reserved

Design HPT300337

Square Footage: 2,461
Bonus Room: 397 sq. ft.

◆ Great outdoor living spaces define this plan—and comfortable amenities reside throughout the interior. An open foyer extends vistas and views through the great room to the screened porch and beyond. Family bedrooms share a hall bath on the left side of the plan. A flex room to the front of the plan converts to a study, guest room or home office. A garden tub and separate vanities highlight the master retreat. A bonus room is available for future use—perfect for an additional bedroom, storage or a playroom.

© 2001 Donald A. Gardner, Inc.

Design HPT300338
Square Footage: 2,555

◆ A striking pediment hovers above the columned porch and the glass-paneled entry of this home, introducing a well-planned interior. The foyer leads to a study and to the formal dining room. The great room offers a fireplace and a wall of French doors to the backyard. The island kitchen includes a nook and plenty of counter space. Two family bedrooms reside near the laundry and offer individual access to a full bath with dual vanities. The master bedroom provides His and Her closets and a lavish bath with a tub and a separate shower. A workbench is featured in the garage.

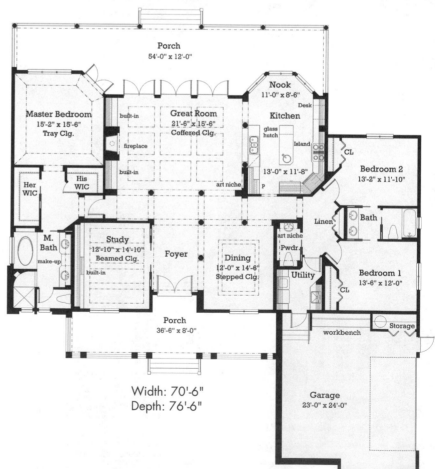

Width: 70'-6"
Depth: 76'-6"

Design HPT300339

Square Footage: 3,058
Bonus Second Level: 279 sq. ft.

L

◆ A centrally located interior atrium is just one of the interesting features of this Spanish design. The atrium has a built-in seat and will bring light to the adjacent living room, dining room and breakfast room. Beyond the foyer and down one step, a tiled reception hall includes a powder room. This area leads to the sleeping wing and up one step to the family room with its raised-hearth fireplace and sliding glass doors to the rear terrace. Overlooking the family room is a railed lounge that can be used for various activities. Sleeping areas include a deluxe master suite and three family bedrooms.

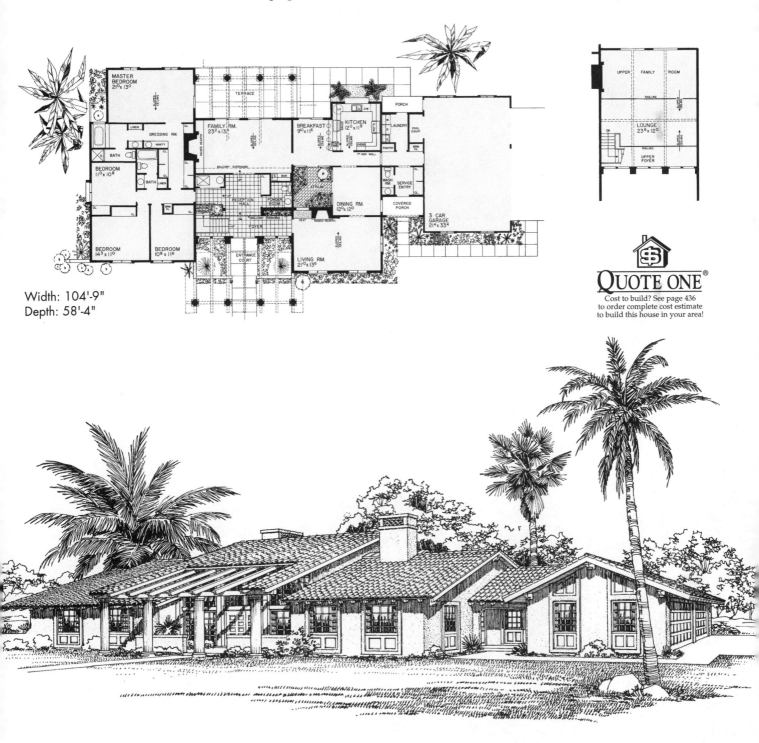

Width: 104'-9"
Depth: 58'-4"

QUOTE ONE®
Cost to build? See page 436
to order complete cost estimate
to build this house in your area!

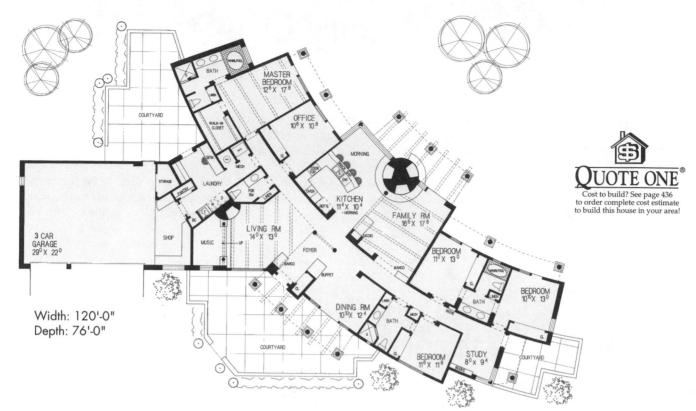

Quote One®
Cost to build? See page 436
to order complete cost estimate
to build this house in your area!

Width: 120'-0"
Depth: 76'-0"

◆ Projecting wood beams called vigas add a distinctive touch to this Santa Fe exterior. A private courtyard leads to the entryway of this radially planned home. To the left of the foyer rests a living room with a wood-beamed ceiling, music alcove and fireplace. Past the formal dining room on the right is the family room and large country kitchen with snack bar and morning room. The focal point of this casual living zone is the massive fireplace with three separate fire boxes—the center of the plan's radius. Three family bedrooms, two full baths and an open study with an adjoining courtyard round out the right wing.

Design HPT300340
Square Footage: 3,169
L

Design HPT300341
Square Footage: 3,262

L

◆ Reminiscent of the original low-slung ranch house from the Spanish Southwest, this is one wonderful one-story—from the magnificent double-door entryway, to the gargantuan gathering room (400 square feet and a mammoth fireplace), to the roomy master suite with a cozy private terrace. Other attractive features include an angular study and dining room, a large rear terrace off the gathering room, a spacious U-shaped kitchen with a prep island and a breakfast nook, and loads and loads of extra storage.

Width: 144'-8"
Depth: 71'-7"

QUOTE ONE®
Cost to build? See page 436
to order complete cost estimate
to build this house in your area!

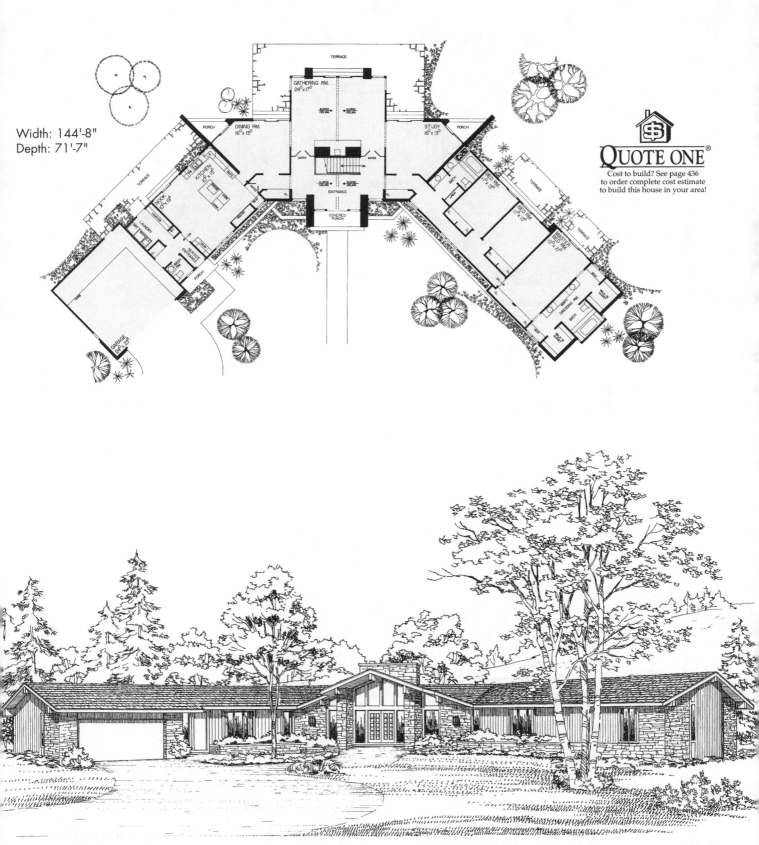

Design HPT300342
Square Footage: 4,282

Width: 88'-0"
Depth: 133'-0"

◆ This exciting exterior invites you in through its columned entry. Inside, the living room and dining room open to a covered rear lanai; built-ins line one wall of the adjacent study, which also opens to the lanai. A resplendent master suite occupies the left wing and provides a private garden, raised whirlpool tub, two walk-in closets and a sitting area. A leisure room to the rear of the plan features a fireplace and a built-in entertainment center. The gourmet kitchen shares an eating bar with the breakfast nook. Other special amenities include art display niches, a wet bar and a computer center.

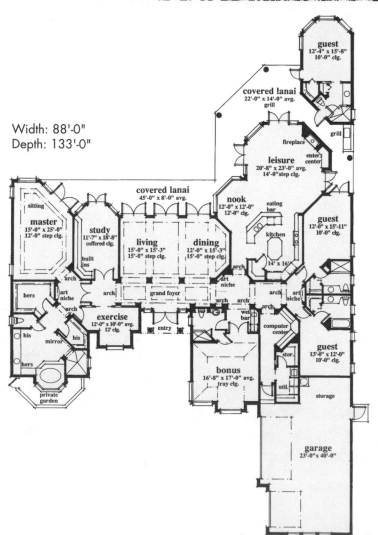

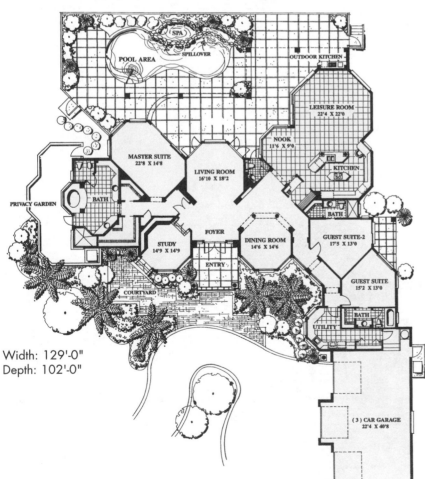

Width: 129'-0"
Depth: 102'-0"

POOL AREA

SPA

SPILLOVER

OUTDOOR KITCHEN

LEISURE ROOM
22'4 X 22'0

NOOK
11'6 X 9'0

KITCHEN

MASTER SUITE
22'8 X 14'8

LIVING ROOM
16'10 X 18'2

BATH

PRIVACY GARDEN

BATH

STUDY
14'9 X 14'9

FOYER

DINING ROOM
14'6 X 14'6

GUEST SUITE-2
17'5 X 13'0

ENTRY

GUEST SUITE
15'2 X 13'0

COURTYARD

BATH

UTILITY

(3) CAR GARAGE
22'4 X 40'8

Design HPT300343
Square Footage: 3,688

◆ Perfect for the California coast, this stucco design is an alluring masterpiece. The luxurious interior is introduced by a set of double doors, which open to the spacious foyer. The foyer is flanked by the study and the exquisite dining room shaped by elegant columns. Straight ahead, the formal living room opens through two sets of double doors to a rear terrace. The gourmet island kitchen overlooks the tiled nook and leisure room. An outdoor kitchen conveniently serves the pool area, which features a cozy spa and cascading spillover. The master suite indulges with enchanting style. Walk past two walk-in closets to the spacious master bath with whirlpool-tub luxury.

Design HPT300344

Square Footage: 3,273

L

◆ This house is in a class all its own. The entry gives way to an impressive living room with a dining room and study radiating from it. The master bedroom suite rests to one side of the plan and includes His and Hers walk-in closets and a luxury bath. A second full bath leads from the sitting area to the outdoors. At the other side of the house, informal living areas open with a kitchen, a breakfast nook and a family leisure area. Two bedrooms here share a full bath and will provide ample space for children or guests.

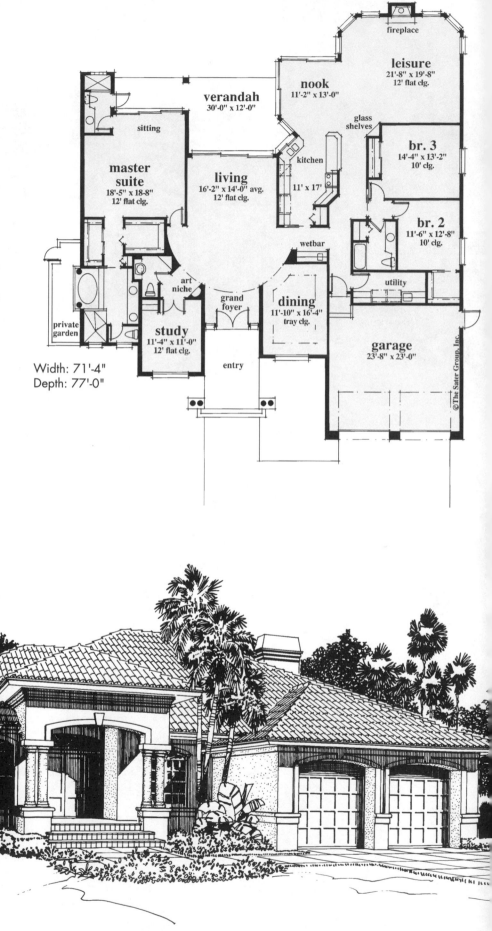

Width: 71'-4"
Depth: 77'-0"

fireplace

leisure
21'-8" x 19'-8"
12' flat clg.

nook
11'-2" x 13'-0"

verandah
30'-0" x 12'-0"

sitting

glass shelves

br. 3
14'-4" x 13'-2"
10' clg.

kitchen

master suite
18'-5" x 18'-8"
12' flat clg.

living
16'-2" x 14'-0" avg.
12' flat clg.

11' x 17'

br. 2
11'-6" x 12'-8"
10' clg.

wetbar

utility

art niche

dining
11'-10" x 16'-4"
tray clg.

study
11'-4" x 11'-0"
12' flat clg.

private garden

grand foyer

entry

garage
23'-8" x 23'-0"

©The Sater Group, Inc.

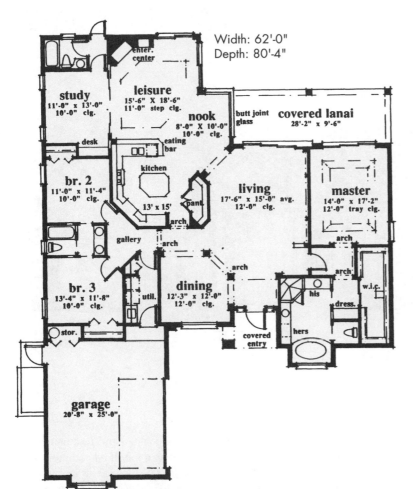

Width: 62'-0"
Depth: 80'-4"

study
11'-0" x 13'-0"
10'-0" clg.

enter. center

leisure
15'-6" X 18'-6"
11'-0" step clg.

desk

nook
8'-0" X 10'-0"
10'-0" clg.

butt joint glass

covered lanai
28'-2" x 9'-6"

br. 2
11'-0" x 11'-4"
10'-0" clg.

eating bar

kitchen

living
17'-6" x 15'-0" avg.
12'-0" clg.

master
14'-0" x 17'-2"
12'-0" tray clg.

13' x 15'

pant.

arch.

arch

gallery

arch

arch

w.i.c.

br. 3
13'-4" x 11'-8"
10'-0" clg.

util.

dining
12'-3" x 12'-0"
12'-0" clg.

arch

his

dress.

stor.

hers

covered entry

garage
20'-8" x 25'-0"

Design HPT300345
Square Footage: 2,802

◆ The facade of this home is clean and elegant with a mix of brick and stucco and high-pitched rooflines. The living room opens to a covered lanai facing the rear yard. The open kitchen, nook and leisure room focus toward the entertainment center. The two secondary bedrooms share a bath while the study has access to a pool. The master suite includes a tray ceiling and glass doors to the rear lanai. An oversized walk-in wardrobe closet, a dressing area, His and Hers vanities and a garden tub round out the luxurious bath.

Design HPT300346
Square Footage: 2,946
L

◆ This home's varying hipped-roof planes make a strong statement. Exquisite classical detailing includes delightfully proportioned columns below a modified pedimented gable and masses of brick punctuated by corner quoins. The central foyer, with its high ceiling, leads to interesting traffic patterns. This extremely functional floor plan fosters flexible living patterns. There are formal and informal living areas which are well defined by the living and family rooms. The suken family room is wonderfully spacious with its high, sloping ceiling. It contains a complete media-center wall and a fireplace flanked by doors to the entertainment patio. Occupying the isolated end of the floor plan, the master suite includes an adjacent office/den with a private porch.

Width: 94'-1"
Depth: 67'-4"

Quote One®
Cost to build? See page 436
to order complete cost estimate
to build this house in your area!

Design HPT300347

Square Footage: 3,317

◆ This wonderful ranch home features a sheltered entry and a towering brick chimney. Inside, the foyer leads to a short gallery that overlooks the living room and the formal dining area. The living room features a central fireplace that can be enjoyed from the dining room and a corner wet bar for entertaining. The kitchen provides plenty of room for multiple cooks and serves up casual meals to the breakfast area. A spacious recreation room and a bedroom—perfect as a guest room—complete the right wing. On the left, two secondary bedrooms share a full hall bath while the master suite is pampered by its own private bath.

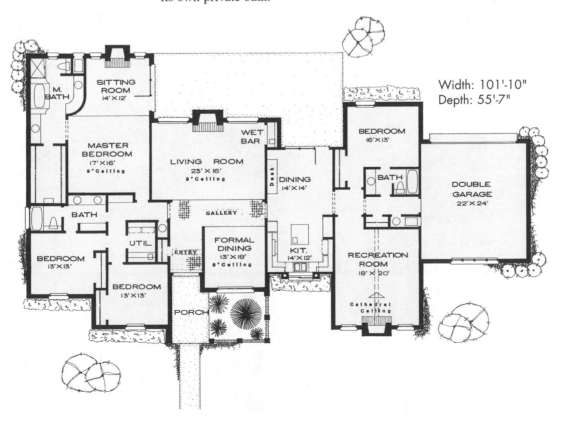

Width: 101'-10"
Depth: 55'-7"

Design HPT300348

First Floor: 2,563 sq. ft.
Second Floor: 552 sq. ft.
Total: 3,115 sq. ft.

L D

◆ This fine example of a rambling Cape Cod house illustrates how delightful this style of home can be. This plan delivers exceptional country-estate livability. Both formal and informal living are covered with a large living room with a fireplace and even larger family room with another fireplace, a wet bar and beamed ceiling. The kitchen and dining room are accented by a charming solarium, which also lights the master bedroom. A secondary bedroom or study opens off the foyer. Upstairs are two additional secondary bedrooms which share a full bath. The two-car garage connects to the main house via a convenient laundry room.

Width: 87'-8"
Depth: 68'-8"

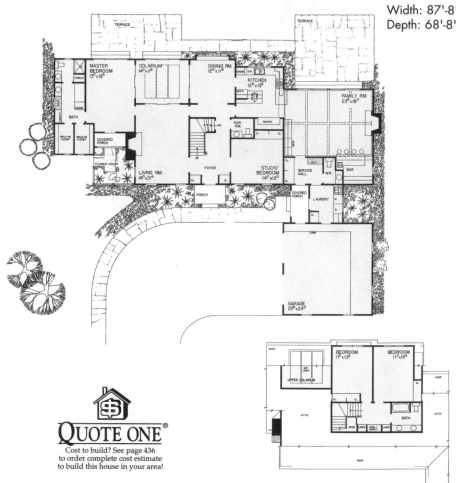

Quote One®

Cost to build? See page 436
to order complete cost estimate
to build this house in your area!

Photo by Andy Lautman, Lautman Photography

This home, as shown in the photograph, may differ from the actual blueprints. For more detailed information, please check the floor plans carefully.

Design HPT300349

First Floor: 3,215 sq. ft.
Second Floor: 711 sq. ft.
Total: 3,926 sq. ft.

L D

◆ Organized zoning makes this tradition-al design a comfortable home for living. A central foyer facilitates flexible traffic patterns. Quiet areas of the house encom-pass a media room and a luxurious master suite with a spacious closet space and a bath, as well as a lounge or writing area. Informal living areas include a sun room and a large country kitchen with an effi-cient food-preparation island. Formal liv-ing spaces are found in the living room and formal dining room. The second floor holds two bedrooms and a lounge.

Width: 97'-8"
Depth: 101'-4"

QUOTE ONE®
Cost to build? See page 436
to order complete cost estimate
to build this house in your area!

This home, as shown in the photograph, may differ from the actual blueprints.
For more detailed information, please check the floor plans carefully.

Photo by Laszlo Regos

351

Design HPT300350
Square Footage: 2,471

L

◆ Capstones, quoins and gentle arches lend an unpretentious spirit to this European-style plan. A vaulted entry reveals classic instincts and introduces an unrestrained floor plan designed for comfort. The tiled gallery opens to a sizable great room that invites casual entertaining and features a handsome fireplace with an extended hearth, framed with decorative niches. The kitchen features a cooktop island and a built-in desk, and opens to a windowed breakfast bay, which lets in natural light. For formal occasions, a great dining room permits quiet, unhurried evening meals. Relaxation awaits the homeowner in a sensational master suite, with an inner retreat and a private patio. Two family bedrooms share a private bath, and one room opens to a covered patio. A golf cart will easily fit into a side garage, which adjoins a roomy two-car garage.

Width: 86'-4"
Depth: 80'-2"

This home, as shown in the photograph, may differ from the actual blueprints. For more detailed information, please check the floor plans carefully.

Photo by Bob Greenspan

Width: 97'-0"
Depth: 102'-8"

QUOTE ONE®
Cost to build? See page 436
to order complete cost estimate
to build this house in your area!

Design HPT300351

First Floor: 3,067 sq. ft.
Second Floor: 648 sq. ft.
Total: 3,715 sq. ft.

L D

◆ This contemporary design has a great deal to offer. A fireplace opens up to both the living room and the country kitchen. The kitchen is a gourmet's delight, with a huge walk-in pantry and a deluxe island, which includes a snack bar. A media room has plenty of storage and offers access to the rear terrace. The first-floor master bedroom is away from the traffic of the house and features a dressing/exercise room, whirlpool tub and shower and spacious walk-in closet. Two more bedrooms and a full bath are on the second floor. The cheerful sun room adds 296 square feet to the total.

Design HPT300352

Square Footage: 2,713
Bonus Room: 324 sq. ft.

◆ Intricate rooflines along with a wide and varied assortment of windows add style and flair to this brick home, enhanced by a turret-style bay window. Inside, a coffered ceiling, a grand fireplace and radius windows create an elegant atmosphere in the family room, while the vaulted keeping room boasts a second fireplace and offers a cozy and intimate space in which to entertain. The master suite features His and Hers walk-in closets and a vaulted master bath for the private luxury of the homeowners. Family bedrooms on the opposite side of the home share a bath between them. A garage and laundry room complete this floor plan. Please specify basement or crawlspace foundation when ordering.

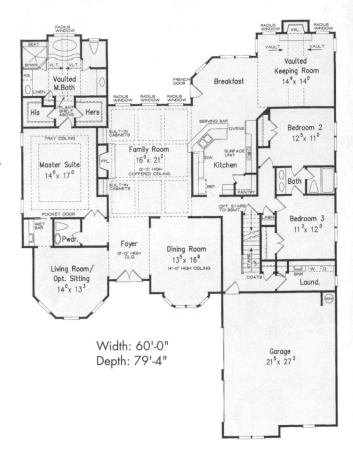

Width: 60'-0"
Depth: 79'-4"

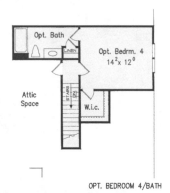

OPT. BEDROOM 4/BATH

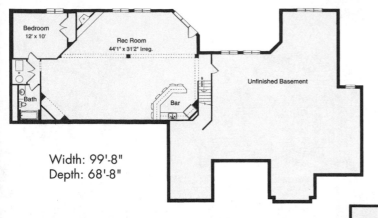

Width: 99'-8"
Depth: 68'-8"

Design HPT300353

Main Level: 3,793 sq. ft.
Lower Level: 1,588 sq. ft.
Total: 5,381 sq. ft.

◆ The richness of this home's exterior showcases an excellent Craftsman design. The wraparound foyer presents a luxurious entrance in addition to providing an efficient traffic flow. Columns at the entrance to the great room, dining room and kitchen combine to create a warm, inviting space. Split bedrooms provide privacy, while the master suite, with access to the rear deck, is complemented by a spacious dressing room and His and Hers walk-in closets. Various ceiling treatments throughout add to the enchanting atmosphere. Angled stairs lead to a finished lower level with a nine-foot ceiling height and a walkout to the rear yard.

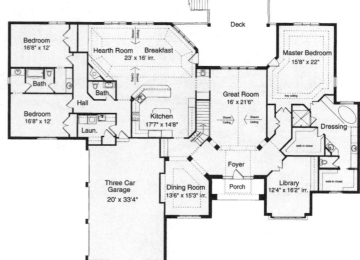

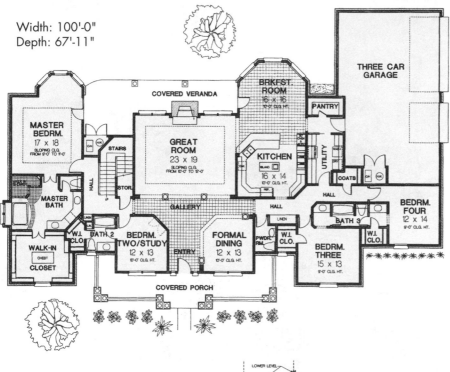

Width: 100'-0"
Depth: 67'-11"

Design HPT300354
Square Footage: 3,439
Bonus Room: 514 sq. ft.

◆ This gigantic country farmhouse features a beautiful facade, complete with a front covered porch. Inside, the entry is flanked by the study/ Bedroom 2 and the dining room. Across the gallery, the great room overlooking the rear veranda provides an impressive fireplace. The island kitchen opens to a bayed breakfast room. The right side of the home includes two family bedrooms that share a bath, a utility room and a three-car garage. The master wing of the home enjoys a bayed sitting area, a sumptuous bath and an enormous walk-in closet. The second-floor bonus room is cooled by a ceiling fan and is perfect for a guest suite.

Width: 83'-10"
Depth: 112'-0"

Design HPT3030017
Square Footage: 4,222
Bonus Room: 590 sq. ft.

◆ The striking facade of this magnificent estate is just the beginning of the excitement you will encounter inside. The foyer passes the formal dining room on the way to the columned gallery. The formal living room opens to the rear patio and has easy access to a wet bar. The contemporary kitchen has a work island and all the amenities for gourmet preparation. The family room will be a favorite for casual entertainment. The family sleeping wing begins with an octagonal vestibule and has three bedrooms with private baths. The master wing features a private garden and an opulent bath.

Design HPT300356
Square Footage: 2,777

◆ This distinctive ranch home features three open-facing gables. The foyer opens to the living room, which is enhanced by decorative columns, built-ins and two sets of French doors to the rear yard. The kitchen is convenient to the dining room and just a few steps from the breakfast bay and family room. A cozy fireplace and rear-porch access can be found in the family room. To the right, the master suite enjoys privacy and a full sumptuous bath. At the far left of the plan, two family bedrooms also enjoy privacy and share a full hall bath. Please specify slab or crawlspace foundation when ordering.

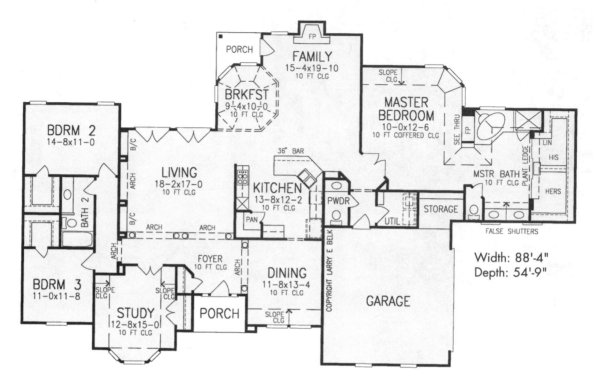

Width: 88'-4"
Depth: 54'-9"

COPYRIGHT LARRY E. BELK

Width: 94'-0"
Depth: 114'-0"

This home, as shown in the photograph, may differ from the actual blueprints.
For more detailed information, please check the floor plans carefully.

Design HPT3030018
Square Footage: 3,436
Bonus Room: 290 sq. ft.

◆ A striking front-facing pediment, bold columns, and varying rooflines set this design apart from the rest. An angled entry leads to the foyer, flanked on one side by the dining room with a tray ceiling and on the other by a lavish master suite. This suite is enhanced with a private bath, two large walk-in closets, a garden tub, a compartmented toilet and bidet, and access to the covered patio. The parlor also enjoys rear-yard views. The vaulted ceilings provide a sense of spaciousness from the breakfast nook and kitchen to the family room. A laundry room and roomy pantry are accessible from the kitchen area. Two family bedrooms reside on the right side of the plan; each has its own full bath and both are built at interesting angles. An upstairs, vaulted bonus room includes French doors opening to a second-floor sundeck.

Photo by Mark Englund

Design HPT300358
Square Footage: 4,825

◆ In this English country design, a series of hip roofs covers an impressive brick facade accented by fine wood detailing. You will entertain in style in formal living and dining rooms flanking the foyer and in the nearby media room, designed for home theater and surround sound. Fireplaces warm the living room and the family room, which also boasts a cathedral ceiling. The kitchen offers plenty of work space, a bright breakfast nook and two covered patios. All four bedrooms have private baths and walk-in closets. The master suite has the added luxury of a glass-enclosed sitting area.

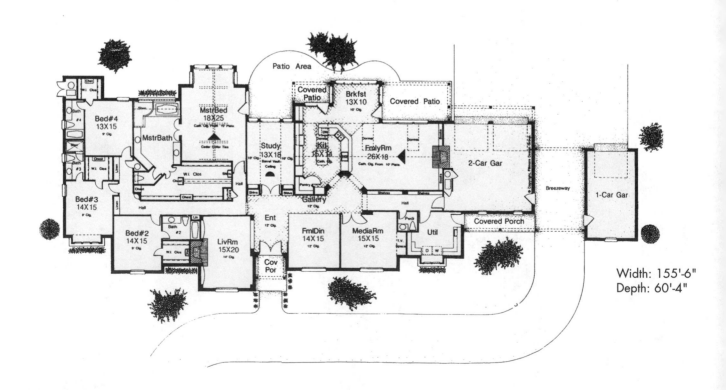

Width: 155'-6"
Depth: 60'-4"

Design HPT3030019
Square Footage: 2,791

◆ This stately country home is a quaint mix of Colonial style and romantic French flavor. Inside, formal living and dining rooms flank the entry foyer. Two sets of double doors open from the family room onto the rear patio. A romantic courtyard is placed to the far right of the plan, just beyond the family bedrooms. A three-car garage with an extra storage room offers plenty of space. The family game room is reserved for recreational fun. Please specify crawlspace or slab foundation when ordering.

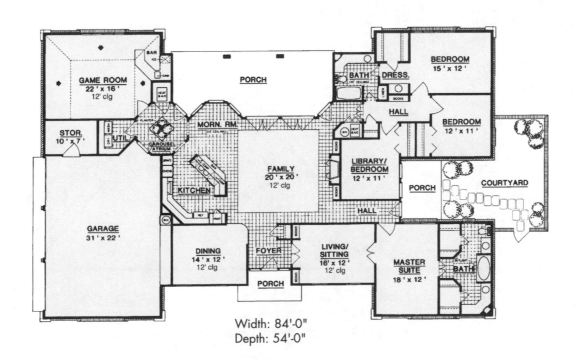

Width: 84'-0"
Depth: 54'-0"

Design HPT300360

Square Footage: 3,012
Bonus Room: 392 sq. ft.

◆ The European appeal of this spacious cottage plan features graceful elegance on the exterior, with abundant amenities found inside. The foyer is flanked by formal living and dining rooms. Straight ahead, double doors open to a study. The master suite features a sitting area with a fireplace and a private bath that extends into an enormous walk-in closet. The central island kitchen connects to the breakfast room, which is open to the great room at the rear of the plan. Three family bedrooms are located to the right. A future bonus room is available for additional expansion.

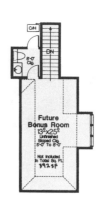

Width: 80'-0"
Depth: 72'-0"

Design HPT300361
Square Footage: 3,510

◆ Country manor style is reflected in this spacious one-story design. The tiled entry and gallery introduce the formal dining room, the great room with a warm fireplace and a quiet study with built-ins and a bay window. The kitchen opens up to the breakfast bay. Two family bedrooms just beyond the kitchen share a compartmented bath, and both enjoy walk-in closets. The master bedroom is split from the family bedrooms for privacy and features a sitting bay that looks out to the covered patio. A spacious walk-in closet and super-luxurious bath provide the master suite with supreme comfort.

Width: 91'-0"
Depth: 72'-10"

Design HPT300362
Square Footage: 3,162

◆ All the romance of Europe is found in this picturesque cottage, alive with the accents of timeless Old World architecture. Double doors open to a tiled foyer flanked by a formal dining room and a study warmed by a fireplace. A second fireplace is found in the great room, which also offers efficient built-ins. The island kitchen opens to a breakfast nook. The master suite is secluded to the left side of the plan for privacy and includes a sitting bay, private bath and roomy walk-in closet. This one-story elevation offers three additional family bedrooms on the right. The design is completed by a three-car garage with storage.

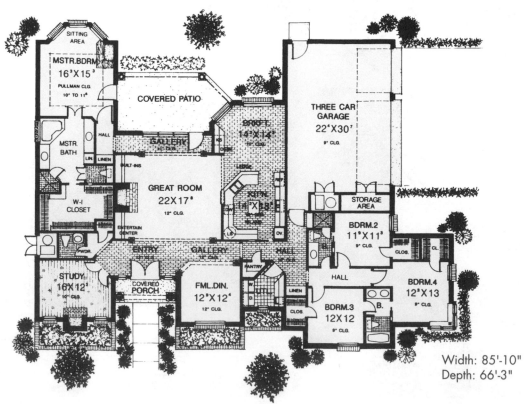

Width: 85'-10"
Depth: 66'-3"

Design HPT300363

Square Footage: 4,270
Bonus Room: 774 sq. ft.

◆ This grand European design lends a dignified presence to any neighborhood—old or new. Both formal and informal spaces grace the floor plan of this delightful one-story home. The master suite and one family bedroom sit on the left side of the plan, while two additional bedrooms reside on the right. The family room features a lovely beam ceiling and a cozy fireplace—a great spot for entertaining guests and family. Bonus space provides for future guest or maid's quarters.

Width: 112'-4"
Depth: 91'-3"

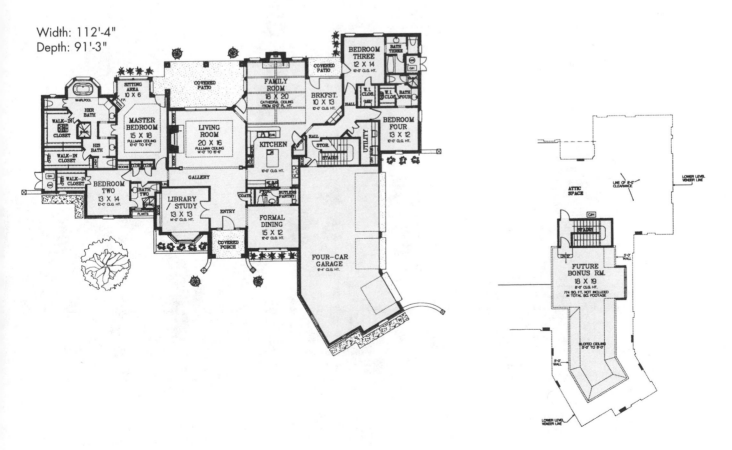

Design HPT300364
Square Footage: 3,818

◆ This sprawling traditional facade incorporates brick quoins and a cast-stone arched entry. The living room, with an eight-foot-wide fireplace, full-wall windows and a fourteen-foot ceiling, connects to the family room, which features yet another fireplace and an open wet bar. A study with another fourteen-foot ceiling and a bay window faces the front. The large kitchen is placed between the breakfast area and the formal dining room. A grand master suite includes His and Hers baths, each with a walk-in closet. Right next door, Bedroom 2 is perfect for a nursery. Bedrooms 3 and 4 on the right of the home are separated from the master suite and share a full bath.

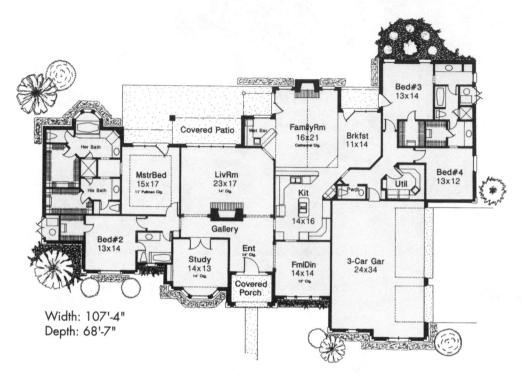

Width: 107'-4"
Depth: 68'-7"

One-Story Homes for Sun Country

Design HPT300365
Square Footage: 3,428

L

◆ An in-line floor plan follows the tradition of the original Santa Fe-style homes. The slight curve to the overall configuration lends an interesting touch. From the front courtyard, the plan opens to a formal living room and dining room, complemented by a family room and a kitchen with an adjoining morning room. The master suite is found to one side of the plan while family bedrooms share space at the opposite end. There's also a huge office and a bonus/study area for private times.

QUOTE ONE®
Cost to build? See page 436
to order complete cost estimate
to build this house in your area!

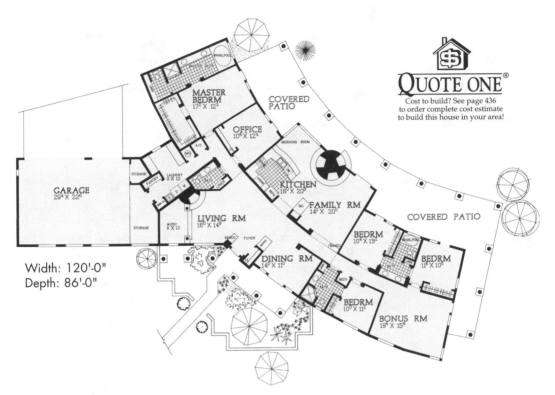

Width: 120'-0"
Depth: 86'-0"

Design HPT300366
Square Footage: 2,966

L

◆ Here's a rambling Santa Fe home with a unique configuration. Massive double doors at the front entrance are sheltered by the covered porch. This well-zoned plan offers exceptional one-story livability for the active family. The central foyer routes traffic effectively while featuring a feeling of spaciousness. The interesting angular living room has a commanding corner fireplace with a raised hearth, a wall of windows, a doorway to the huge rear covered porch and a pass-through to the kitchen. At the opposite end of the plan from the family bedrooms, and guaranteed its full measure of privacy, is the large master suite. The master bedroom, with its high ceiling, enjoys direct access to the rear porch.

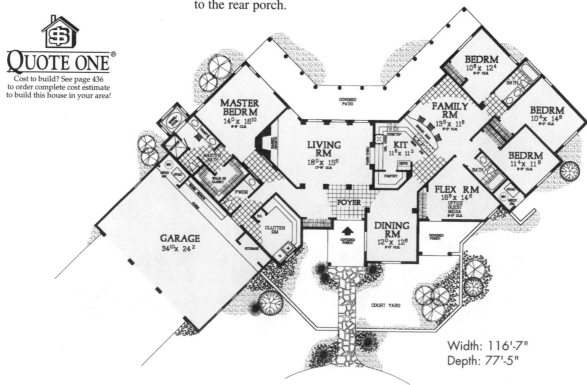

Width: 116'-7"
Depth: 77'-5"

Design HPT300367
Square Footage: 2,226

L

◆ The impressive double-door entry to the walled courtyard sets the tone for this Santa Fe masterpiece home. The expansive great room shows off its casual style with a centerpiece fireplace and abundant windows. The large gourmet kitchen has an eat-in snack bar and joins the family room to create a warm atmosphere for casual entertaining. Extras in the family room include a fireplace, entertainment built-ins and double doors to the front courtyard. Just off the family room are the two large family bedrooms, which share a private bath. The relaxing master suite is located off the great room and has double doors to the back patio.

Width: 103'-1"
Depth: 71'-11"

Design HPT300368
Square Footage: 2,000

◆ This classic stucco design provides a cool retreat in any climate. From the covered porch, enter the skylit foyer to find an arched ceiling leading to the central gathering room with its raised-hearth fireplace and terrace access. A connecting corner dining room is conveniently located near the amenity-filled kitchen. The large master suite includes terrace access and a private bath with a whirlpool tub, a separate shower and plenty of closet space. A second bedroom and a study that can be converted to a bedroom complete this wonderful plan.

Width: 75'-0"
Depth: 55'-0"

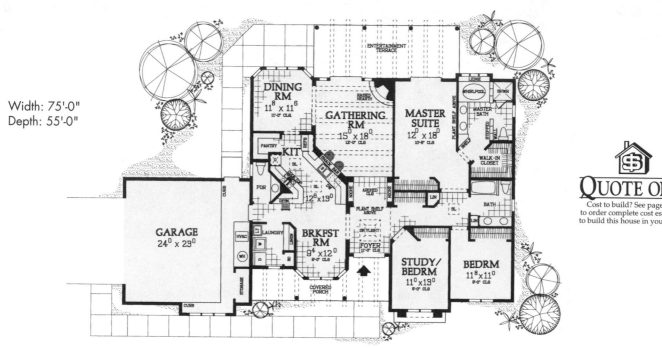

QUOTE ONE®
Cost to build? See page 436
to order complete cost estimate
to build this house in your area!

Design HPT300369
Square Footage: 2,945

Width: 73'-0"
Depth: 68'-10"

◆ Flat roofs, soft curved wall lines, masses of stucco, exposed rafter tails, an arched privacy wall, carriage lamps and a court-yard are the distinguishing features of this pueblo-style ranch house. Inside, twin archways provide access to the beam-ceilinged family room. The modified U-shaped kitchen and breakfast area are open to the family room. The kitchen will be a delight in which to work with its island, pantry and fine counter space. Down the hall are four bedrooms and two baths. Each of the three sizable bedrooms for the children is convenient to the main bath with double lavatories. The master suite is outstanding with a view of the patio as well as direct access to it.

QUOTE ONE®
Cost to build? See page 436
to order complete cost estimate
to build this house in your area!

371

Design HPT300370

Square Footage: 2,539

L

◆ Exposed rafter tails, arched porch detailing, massive paneled front doors and stucco exterior walls enhance the western character of this U-shaped ranch house. Double doors open to a spacious slope-ceilinged art gallery. The quiet sleeping zone is comprised of an entire wing. The extra room at the front of this wing may be used for a den or an office. The family dining and kitchen activities are located at the opposite end of the plan. Indoor/outdoor living relationships are outstanding. The master suite has a generous sitting area, a walk-in closet, twin lavatories, a whirlpool tub and a stall shower.

Width: 75'-2"
Depth: 68'-8"

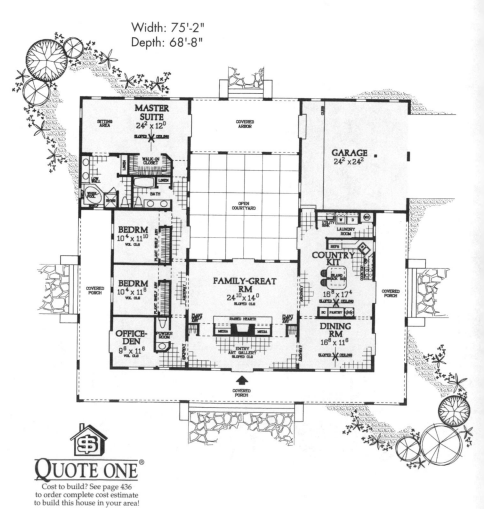

QUOTE ONE®

Cost to build? See page 436
to order complete cost estimate
to build this house in your area!

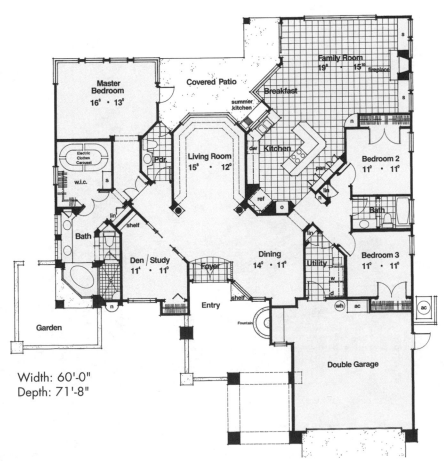

Master Bedroom
16⁸ · 13⁰

Covered Patio

Family Room
19⁸ · 15⁹⁸ fireplace

Breakfast

summer kitchen

Kitchen

Electric Clothes Carousel

w.i.c.

Pdr.

Living Room
15⁸ · 12⁰

dw

ref

Bedroom 2
11⁰ · 11⁰

Bath

shelf

Bath

Den / Study
11⁴ · 11⁰

Foyer

Dining
14⁰ · 11⁰

Utility

Bedroom 3
11⁰ · 11⁰

Entry

shelf

Fountain

w
d

wh ac

ac

Garden

Double Garage

Width: 60'-0"
Depth: 71'-8"

Design HPT300371
Square Footage: 2,397

◆ Low-slung hipped rooflines and an abundance of glass enhance the unique exterior of this sunny one-story home. Inside, the use of soffits and tray ceilings heighten the distinctive style of the floor plan. To the left, double doors lead to the private master bedroom, which is bathed in natural light. Convenient planning of the gourmet kitchen places everything at minimal distances and serves the outdoor summer kitchen, breakfast nook and family room with equal ease.

Design HPT300372

Square Footage: 2,656

◆ A graceful design sets this charming home apart from the ordinary and transcends the commonplace. From the foyer, the dining room branches off the sunny living room, setting a lovely backdrop for entertaining. Casual living is the focus in the oversized family room, where sliding doors open to the patio and the eat-in gourmet kitchen is open for easy conversation. Two family bedrooms and a cabana bath are just off the family room. The master suite has a cozy fireplace in the sitting area, and twin closets and a compartmented bath. A large covered patio adds to the living area.

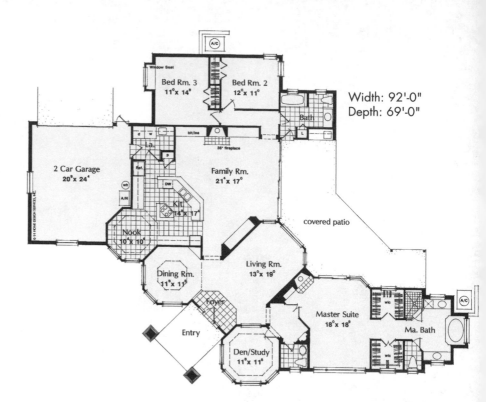

Width: 92'-0"
Depth: 69'-0"

Bed Rm. 3
11⁰ x 14⁰

Bed Rm. 2
12⁰ x 11⁰

Bath

2 Car Garage
20⁰ x 24⁴

Family Rm.
21⁴ x 17⁰

covered patio

Kit.
14⁴ x 17

Nook
10' x 10'

Living Rm.
13⁰ x 19⁰

Dining Rm.
11⁸ x 11⁵

Foyer

Master Suite
18' x 18'

Ma. Bath

Entry

Den/Study
11⁸ x 11⁸

Design HPT300373

Square Footage: 2,319

◆ The tiled foyer of this Sun Country design invites guests into a gathering room with a fireplace and views of the rear grounds. Half-walls define the formal dining area, which offers rear-patio access. The kitchen is equipped to serve formal and informal occasions, and includes a snack counter for meals on the go. An office or guest room has a sunny bay window and an adjacent powder room. The outstanding master suite contains twin walk-in closets, a whirlpool tub, a sit-down vanity and a stylish doorless shower. Two secondary bedrooms share a bath.

Width: 97'-2"
Depth: 57'-4"

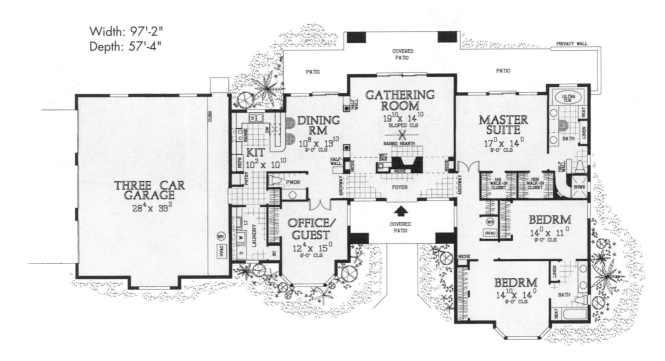

Design HPT300374

Square Footage: 2,986

L

◆ Tropical living takes off in this super one-story home. Double doors lead to a lovely formal living area consisting of a living room, dining room and study. Through an archway, a gallery adds an air of distinction. The kitchen is open to a sunny nook and a bright leisure area for delightful dining and relaxing. A playroom opens off this area and is sure to please the kids of the house. A full bath here leads outside. Two bedrooms nearby each sport a walk-in closet and utilize a full bath in between. The master bedroom suite enjoys a private bath with a whirlpool tub, dual sinks, a large walk-in closet and a compartmented toilet and shower.

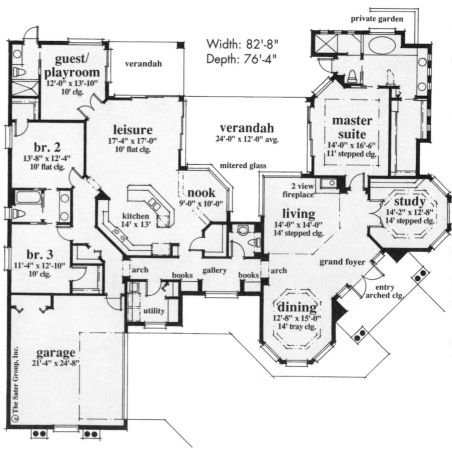

Width: 82'-8"
Depth: 76'-4"

private garden

guest/playroom
12'-0" x 13'-10"
10' clg.

verandah

master suite
14'-0" x 16'-6"
11' stepped clg.

leisure
17'-4" x 17'-0"
10' flat clg.

verandah
24'-0" x 12'-0" avg.

br. 2
13'-8" x 12'-4"
10' flat clg.

mitered glass

nook
9'-0" x 10'-0"

2 view fireplace

study
14'-2" x 12'-8"
14' stepped clg.

kitchen
14' x 13'

living
14'-0" x 14'-0"
14' stepped clg.

br. 3
11'-4" x 12'-10"
10' clg.

arch

books

gallery

books

arch

grand foyer

entry arched clg.

utility

dining
12'-8" x 15'-0"
14' tray clg.

garage
21'-4" x 24'-8"

© The Sater Group, Inc.

376

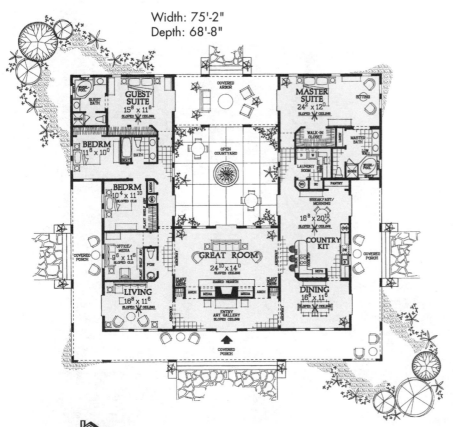

Width: 75'-2"
Depth: 68'-8"

Design HPT300375
Square Footage: 3,163

L

◆ An open courtyard takes center stage in this home, providing a happy marriage of indoor/outdoor relationships. Art collectors will appreciate the gallery that enhances the entry and showcases their favorite works. The formal dining room accommodates special occasions with style, while casual mealtimes are enjoyed in the adjacent country kitchen conveniently designed with an island snack bar and a large pantry. The centrally located great room supplies the nucleus for formal and informal entertaining. A raised-hearth fireplace flanked by built-in media centers adds a special touch. The master suite provides a private retreat where you may relax—try the sitting room or retire to the private bath for a pampering soak in the corner whirlpool tub.

Design HPT300376
Square Footage: 2,978

◆ This home is designed to be a home-owner's dream come true. A formal living area opens from the gallery foyer through graceful arches and looks out to the veranda, which hosts an outdoor grill and service counter. The leisure room offers a private veranda, a cabana bath and a wet bar just off the gourmet kitchen. The master suite opens to the rear property through French doors and boasts a lavish bath. An art niche off the gallery hall, a private dressing area and a secluded study complement the master suite. Two family bedrooms occupy the opposite wing of the plan and share a full bath and private hall.

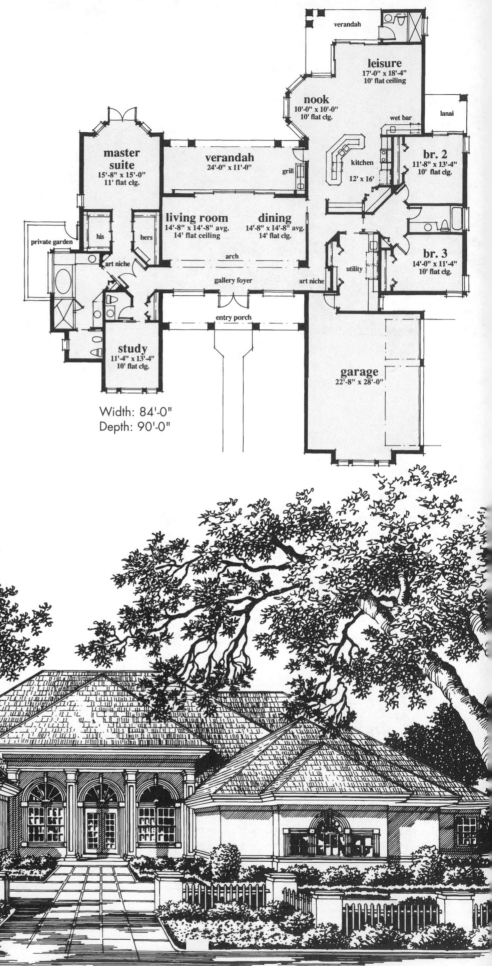

verandah

leisure
17'-0" x 18'-4"
10' flat ceiling

nook
10'-0" x 10'-0"
10' flat clg.

wet bar

lanai

master suite
15'-8" x 15'-0"
11' flat clg.

verandah
24'-0" x 11'-0"

grill

kitchen
12' x 16'

br. 2
11'-8" x 13'-4"
10' flat clg.

his

hers

living room
14'-8" x 14'-8" avg.
14' flat ceiling

dining
14'-8" x 14'-8" avg.
14' flat clg.

private garden

art niche

arch

utility

br. 3
14'-0" x 11'-4"
10' flat clg.

gallery foyer

art niche

entry porch

study
11'-4" x 13'-4"
10' flat clg.

garage
22'-8" x 28'-0"

Width: 84'-0"
Depth: 90'-0"

Width: 84'-0"
Depth: 77'-0"

Design HPT300377
Square Footage: 2,831

L

◆ Besides great curb appeal, this home has a wonderful floor plan. The foyer features a fountain that greets visitors and leads to a formal dining room on the right and a living room on the left. A large family room at the rear has a built-in entertainment center and a fireplace. The U-shaped kitchen is perfectly located for servicing all living and dining areas. To the right of the plan, away from the central entertaining spaces, are three family bedrooms sharing a full bath. On the left side, with solitude and comfort for the master suite, are a large sitting area, an office and an amenity-filled bath. A deck with a spa sits outside the master suite.

Design HPT300378
Square Footage: 2,467

L

◆ This is it! The home you've been looking for—a stately stucco one-story home with a soaring entrance. With a large family, four bedrooms may not be quite enough, perhaps five is just right. For added flexibility, the guest room located to the front of the plan can be used as a home office. The floor plan is open and provides a hub of formal space that won't interfere with private quarters. This design offers room for a golf cart—or make it a storage space. The master bedroom offers privacy and a luxurious retreat featuring a sitting bay surrounded by windows.

QUOTE ONE®

Cost to build? See page 436
to order complete cost estimate
to build this house in your area!

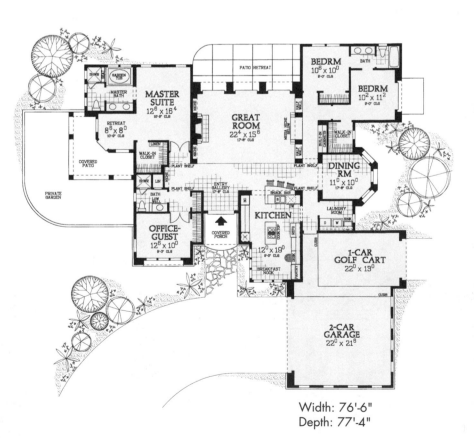

Width: 76'-6"
Depth: 77'-4"

Design HPT300379

Square Footage: 3,034

L

◆ A grand entry enhances the exterior of this elegant stucco home. The office located at the front of the plan makes this design ideal for a home-based business. Formal areas combine to provide lots of space for entertaining. The kitchen, complete with a snack bar and a breakfast nook, opens to the family room which connects to the media room. The private master suite includes two retreats—one is a multi-windowed sitting area, the other contains a spa for outdoor enjoyment. A walk-in closet and a luxurious bath complete this area. Two family bedrooms share a full bath.

Width: 112'-0"
Depth: 74'-6"

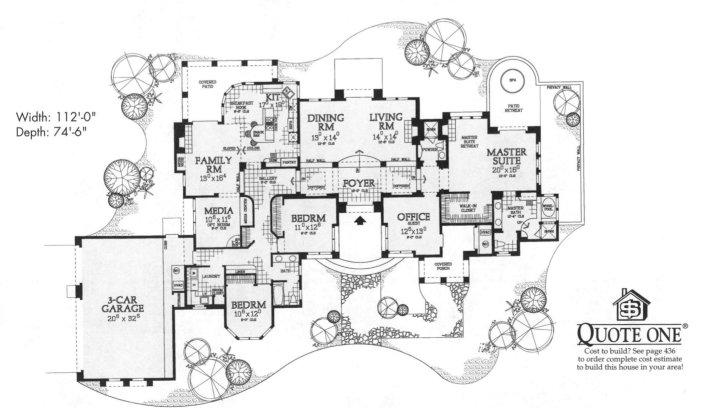

Quote One®

Cost to build? See page 436 to order complete cost estimate to build this house in your area!

Design HPT300380
Square Footage: 2,962

◆ Enter the formal foyer of this home and you are greeted with a traditional split living room/dining room layout. But the family room is where the real living takes place. It expands onto the outdoor living space, which features a summer kitchen. The ultimate master suite contains coffered ceilings, a "boomerang" vanity and angular mirrors that reflect the bayed soaking tub and shower. Efficient use of space creates a huge closet with little center space.

Master Bedroom
18⁰ · 16⁰

see-thru fireplace

Master Bath

w.i.c.

Utility
w   d

tray ceiling

Covered Patio

summer kitchen

Breakfast Nook
vaulted ceiling

dw

Kitchen
rng

desk

pantry

ref

shelves

wh

ac

Family Room
vaulted ceiling
16⁰ · 23⁸

fireplace

shelves

Bedroom 2
14⁰ · 11⁰

Bath 2

lin   lin

Bedroom 3
11⁸ · 12⁰

linen

Bath 3

Bedroom 4
12⁰ · 11⁰

planter

3 Car Garage

shelves

Dining
vaulted ceiling
11⁰ · 12⁰

Foyer

Entry

Living Room
vaulted ceiling
12⁰ · 13⁰

Width: 70'-0"
Depth: 76'-0"

planter

J. N. HANSEN P.T.L.

Design HPT300381
Square Footage: 2,691

Width: 78'-6"
Depth: 73'-10"

Family Rm.
20⁸ · 14⁰
10' CLG.

Brk. Nook
18⁸ · 11⁸
10' CLG.

Bed Rm. 3
11⁸ · 12⁰
10' CLG.

covered patio
10' CLG.

Master Suite
19⁸ · 14⁰
10' CLG.

Bath

Living Rm.
16⁰ · 13⁰
12' CLG.

Kit.
12⁴ · 14⁰

Ba.

Ba.

Ma. Bath

Bed Rm. 2
11⁸ · 12⁰
10' CLG.

Laun.

Den/Bed Rm.
11⁰ · 12⁰
12' CLG.

Foyer
14' CLG.

Dining Rm.
14² · 14⁸
12' CLG.

Double Garage

Entry
14' CLG.

◆ Italianate lines add finesse to the formal facade of this home. Strong symmetry, a soaring portico and gentle rooflines are the prized hallmarks of this relaxed, yet formal design. To the right of the foyer, columns and a stepped ceiling offset the dining room. A plant shelf heralds the living room, which also has a twelve-foot ceiling. An angled cooktop counter adds flair to the kitchen, which also has a desk and walk-in pantry and serves the breakfast nook. A corner fireplace, high ceiling and patio enhance the family room. An arch opens the entry to the lavish master suite. Two additional bedrooms come with separate entries to a full bath.

R. BRADSHAW

Design HPT300382
Square Footage: 2,373

◆ This unique design takes the concept of open floor planning a step further. The formal living and dining space holds a warm fireplace and sliding glass doors to the covered patio. The kitchen, with a giant island work center, separates these formal areas from the more casual family room. The attached breakfast nook overlooks the patio. A corner fireplace in the family room acts as a focal point. Built-ins and double doors to the patio further enhance its appeal. Family bedrooms on the left side of the plan share a full bath. The master bedroom has double-door access to the patio and a bath with a huge walk-in closet, double sinks and a separate tub and shower.

Width: 63'-4"
Depth: 64'-8"

Family Room
19⁸ · 15⁸

Breakfast

shelf

Bedroom 3
12⁰ · 10⁸

Kitchen

dw

Covered Patio

pass-thru

Master Bedroom
21⁰ · 13⁰

Pdr.

lin

Living Room
13⁰ · 11⁸

ref

lin

Bath

shelf

pan

Bedroom 2
12⁰ · 10⁸

w

Utility

d

wh   ac

Dining
12⁰ · 11⁶

Foyer

Bedroom/Study
11⁴ · 11⁰

Bath

seat

Double Garage

Entry

w.i.c.

Alternate Elevation

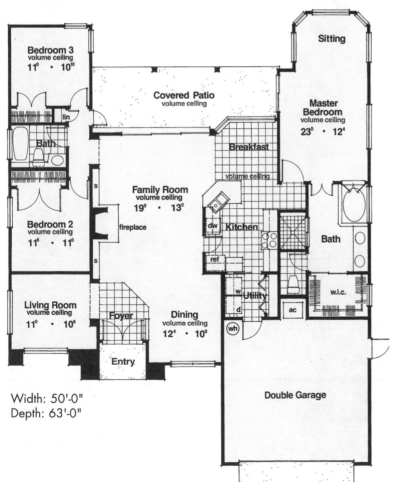

Bedroom 3
volume ceiling
11⁰ · 10¹⁰

Covered Patio
volume ceiling

Sitting

Master Bedroom
volume ceiling
23⁰ · 12⁴

Bath

Breakfast

volume ceiling

Bath

Family Room
volume ceiling
19⁰ · 13⁰

Kitchen

dw

ref

Bedroom 2
volume ceiling
11⁶ · 11⁰

fireplace

w.i.c.

Living Room
volume ceiling
11⁰ · 10⁸

Foyer

Dining
volume ceiling
12⁴ · 10⁰

w
d

Utility

ac

wh

Entry

Double Garage

Width: 50'-0"
Depth: 63'-0"

Design HPT300383
Square Footage: 1,817

◆ First impressions make a grand statement in this volume-look home. A traditional split entry finds the living room on the left and the dining room on the right. The latter shares a large open space with the family room, made more impressive with its volume ceiling. The tiled kitchen and breakfast room are the height of charm and efficiency. On one side of the plan, the master bedroom boasts a private sitting space and a lavish bath with shutter doors at the soaking tub and a nearly room-size walk-in closet. At the other side of the house, two family bedrooms each afford ample closet space and room to grow.

Design HPT300384
Square Footage: 2,517

L

◆ Though distinctly Southwestern in design, this home has some features that are universally appealing. Note, for instance, the central gallery, perpendicular to the raised entry hall, running almost the entire width of the house. An L-shaped angled kitchen serves the breakfast room and family room in equal fashion. Sleeping areas are found in four bedrooms, including an optional study and a exquisite master suite. With a sitting area, twin walk-in closets, dual vanities and a compartmented toilet, the master suite pampers the homeowners.

QUOTE ONE®
Cost to build? See page 436
to order complete cost estimate
to build this house in your area!

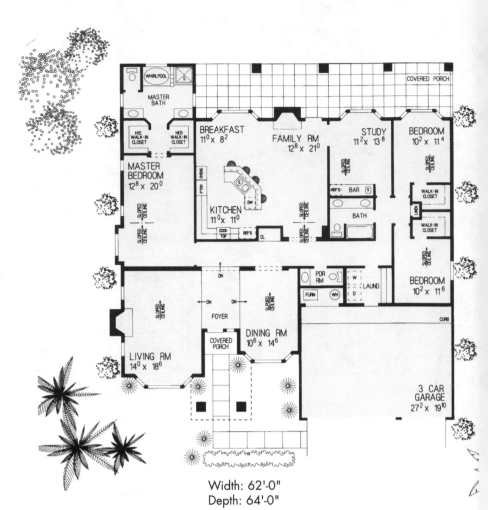

Width: 62'-0"
Depth: 64'-0"

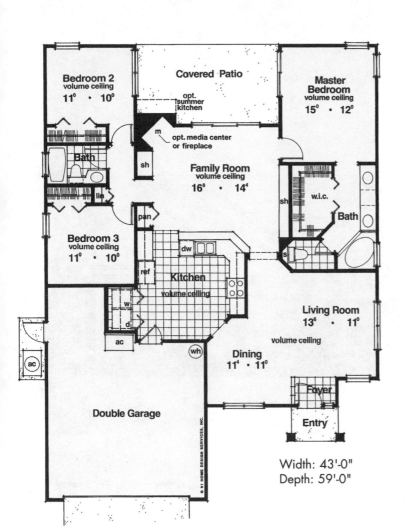

Bedroom 2
volume ceiling
11⁰ · 10⁰

Bath

Bedroom 3
volume ceiling
11⁰ · 10⁰

pan

Covered Patio

opt. summer kitchen

m   opt. media center or fireplace

sh

Family Room
volume ceiling
16⁸ · 14⁴

Master Bedroom
volume ceiling
15⁰ · 12⁰

sh   w.i.c.

Bath

dw

Kitchen
volume ceiling

ref

w

d

ac

wh

ac

Double Garage

Living Room
13⁶ · 11⁰
volume ceiling

Dining
11⁴ · 11⁰

Foyer

Entry

© 91 HOME DESIGN SERVICES, INC.

Width: 43'-0"
Depth: 59'-0"

Design HPT300385
Square Footage: 1,550

◆ Enjoy resort-style living in this striking Sun Country home. Guests will always feel welcome when entertained in the formal living and dining areas, but the eat-in country kitchen overlooking the family room will be the center of attention. Enjoy casual living in the large family room and out on the patio with the help of an optional summer kitchen and a view of the fairway. Built-in shelves and an optional media center provide decorating options. The master suite features a volume ceiling and a spacious master bath.

Alternate Elevation

Design HPT300386

Square Footage: 2,931

◆ The brick French-door entrance, corner quoins and keystone windows are just a few of this home's beautiful finishing touches. Inside, rich tile flows throughout for beautiful accent. The foyer opens to a large living room with a vaulted ceiling. The wonderful kitchen with a walk-in pantry opens up to the windowed breakfast area and an immense family room with built-in shelves and a fireplace. The large covered patio with a summer kitchen is perfect for cookouts and entertaining and is accessible through the breakfast area, living room and master suite. His and Hers walk-in closets, twin sinks, a compartmented toilet and a windowed tub make the master suite.

Width: 70'-8"
Depth: 83'-0"

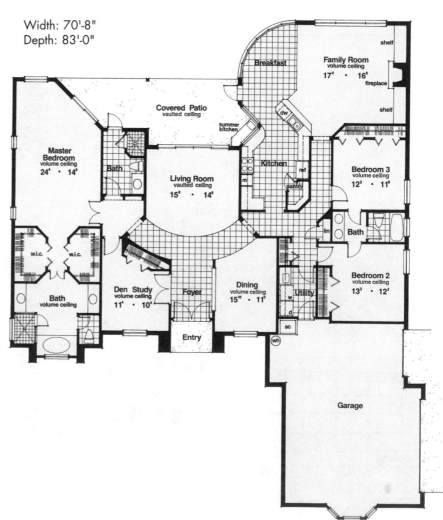

Width: 66'-0"
Depth: 73'-4"

Covered Patio

Master Bedroom
18⁰ • 13⁰

Bath

lin

w.l.c.

sh

s

s

Bath

up

Study/
Bedroom 4
12⁰ • 10⁰

Foyer

Entry

Living Room
volume ceiling
15⁸ • 14⁴

Dining
12⁰ • 11⁰

pan

Kitchen

ref

dw

linen

volume ceiling

Nook

fireplace

Family Room
volume ceiling
19⁰ • 14⁰

Bedroom 3
12⁰ • 11⁰

Bath

Utility

w

d

Bedroom 2
12⁰ • 10¹⁰

ac

wh

ac

Double Garage

planter

Design HPT300387
Square Footage: 2,258

◆ Columns add the finishing touches to this dazzling plan. The double-door entry opens to the foyer, which leads to the vaulted living room with sliding glass doors to the covered patio. The kitchen is open to both the living room and the bayed nook. A bow window and a fireplace define the family room. The master bedroom features access to the covered patio and provides dual walk-in closets and a spa tub. Two additional bedrooms share a full bath that has a bay window.

Alternate Elevation

Design HPT300388
Square Footage: 2,125

◆ A luxurious master suite is just one of the highlights offered in this stunning plan—an alternate plan for this suite features a sitting room, wet bar and fireplace. Two family bedrooms to the right of the plan share a full bath that includes a dual vanity, and a gallery hall that leads directly to the covered patio. Tile adds interest to the living area and surrounds the spacious great room, which offers a fireplace and access to the rear patio. A formal dining room and a secluded den or study flank the foyer.

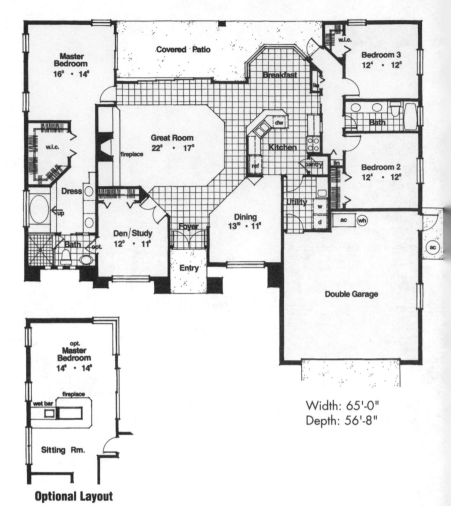

Optional Layout

Width: 65'-0"
Depth: 56'-8"

Design HPT300389
Square Footage: 2,287

Bedroom 4
13⁰ · 11⁰

Family Room
18⁸ · 14⁰

fireplace

Covered Patio

Bath

lin

lin

dw

Kitchen

ref

Breakfast

Living Room
16⁰ · 14⁰

Master Bedroom
18⁸ · 15⁰

w.i.c.

w.i.c.

Bedroom 3
13⁰ · 11⁰

Utility

pantry

w

d

ac

wh

Dining
12⁸ · 10⁸

Pdr.

Bath

lin

up

Double Garage

Foyer

Entry

Den/ Bedroom 2
12⁸ · 11⁸

lin

Width: 63'-4"
Depth: 62'-4"

◆ Low-pitched roofs and a grand columned entry introduce a floor plan that's designed for the 21st Century. Ceramic tiles lead from the foyer to the breakfast area and roomy kitchen, which offers an angled wrapping counter and overlooks the family room. French doors open off the foyer to a secluded den or guest suite, which complements the nearby master suite. A gallery hall off the breakfast nook leads to family sleeping quarters, which share a full bath.

© 91 HOME DESIGN SERVICES, INC.

Design HPT300390

Square Footage: 2,145

L

◆ Split-bedroom planning makes the most of a one-story design. In this case, the master suite is on the opposite side of the house from two family bedrooms. Gourmets can rejoice at the abundant work space in the U-shaped kitchen and will appreciate the natural light afforded by the large bay window in the breakfast room. A formal living room has a sunken conversation area with a cozy fireplace as its focus. The rear covered porch can be reached through sliding glass doors in the family room.

Quote One®

Cost to build? See page 436
to order complete cost estimate
to build this house in your area!

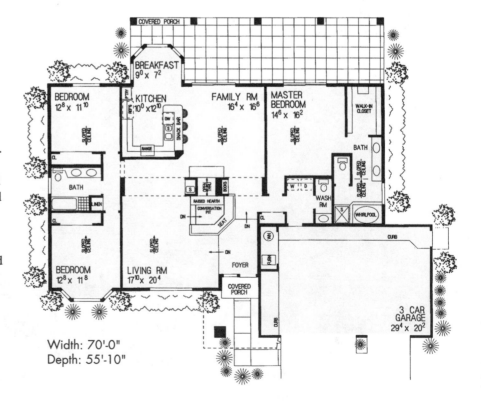

Width: 70'-0"
Depth: 55'-10"

Design HPT300391
Square Footage: 2,678

L

◆ The home you've been looking for—a stately stucco one-story home with a spellbinding entrance. With five bedrooms, this plan is sized just right. For added flexibility, the guest room located to the front of the plan can be used as a home office. The great room will accommodate any size gathering and will do so with the charm of a fireplace, built-ins and extensive rear-patio access. The dining room sits in a bay that looks out to the side yard and is easily served by the spacious hardworking kitchen. Another bedroom, just off the laundry room, provides more space for guests or even a second office space.

Width: 76'-6"
Depth: 77'-4"

MASTER SUITE 12⁸ x 16⁴

GREAT ROOM 22⁴ x 15⁶

BEDRM 10⁸ x 10⁰

BEDRM 10² x 11²

RETREAT 8⁶ x 8⁰

DINING RM 11⁰ x 10⁰

OFFICE-GUEST 12⁸ x 10⁰

KITCHEN 12⁰ x 19⁰

BEDRM 11⁴ x 11⁴

2-CAR GARAGE 22⁰ x 22⁰

QUOTE ONE®

Design HPT300392
Square Footage: 2,480

Width: 67'-4"
Depth: 70'-8"

◆ This Florida contemporary home is a best seller among families who insist on formal and casual living spaces. The master retreat, with a bay sitting area, is secluded away from the family area for quiet and solitude. The master bath includes a sumptuous soaking tub, shower for two, His and Hers vanities and a huge walk-in closet. The secondary bedrooms share a split bath, designed for dual use as well as privacy. The kitchen, nook and family room all provide magnificent views of the outdoor living space. Note the media wall in the family area—a must for today's sophisticated buyers.

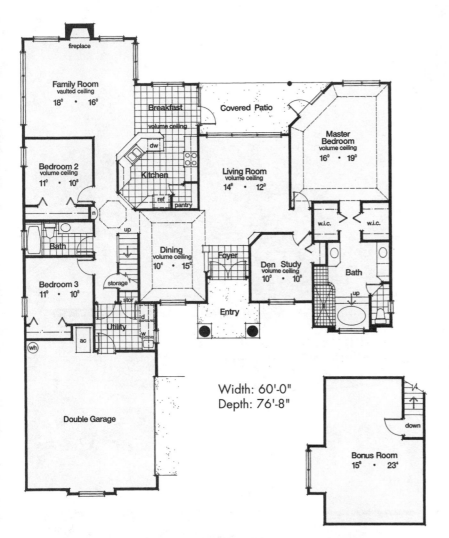

Family Room
vaulted ceiling
18⁰ • 16⁰

fireplace

Breakfast
volume ceiling

Covered Patio

Master Bedroom
volume ceiling
16⁰ • 19⁰

dw

Kitchen

ref   pantry

Living Room
volume ceiling
14⁶ • 12⁰

Bedroom 2
volume ceiling
11⁰ • 10⁸

Bath

up

w.i.c.   w.i.c.

Dining
volume ceiling
10⁴ • 15⁰

Foyer

Den Study
volume ceiling
10⁰ • 10⁰

Bath

Bedroom 3
11⁰ • 10⁸

storage

stor

Entry

up

d

Utility

w

ac

wh

Double Garage

Width: 60'-0"
Depth: 76'-8"

down

Bonus Room
15⁸ • 23⁴

Design HPT300393

Square Footage: 2,322
Bonus Room: 370 sq. ft.

◆ Grand Palladian windows create a classic look for this sensational stucco home. A magnificent view from the living room provides unlimited vistas of the rear grounds through a wall of glass. The kitchen, breakfast nook and family room comprise the family wing, coming together to form the perfect place for casual gatherings. Two secondary bedrooms share a bath and provide complete privacy to the master suite located on the opposite side of the plan. The master bedroom sets the mood for relaxation, and the lavish master bath impresses with a soaking tub flanked by a step-down shower and a compartmented toilet.

J.N. HANSEN P.T.L.

Design HPT300394
Square Footage: 2,005

◆ Vaulted and volume ceilings soar above well-designed living areas in this spectacular move-up home. An elegant dining room, defined by columns, offers views to the front property through multi-level muntin windows. To the left of the foyer, an extensive living room offers plans for an optional fireplace. The great room opens to the breakfast room with patio access and to the kitchen with its angled counter. Two family bedrooms, each with a volume ceiling, and a bath with twin lavatories complete the right side of the plan. The master bedroom enjoys its own bath with a whirlpool tub, separate shower, dual vanity and compartmented toilet.

Width: 58'-0"
Depth: 60'-0"

Design HPT300395
Square Footage: 1,750

◆ Though small in square footage, this home feels large because of volume ceilings. The expanded ceilings begin in the formal living and dining areas just off the entry. Centered between the formal areas and the casual family room, the L-shaped kitchen features a pantry and eat-in breakfast area. Split-bedroom planning puts the master suite on one side of the home, separate from two family bedrooms. The master suite sports a large bath area with a double vanity, separate tub and shower and huge walk-in closet. The blueprint package includes both elevations.

Bedroom 2
volume ceiling
11⁰ · 10⁴

Family Room
volume ceiling
19⁰ · 16⁶

Master Bedroom
volume ceiling
15⁰ · 12⁰

Bath

w
d

lin

dw

Bath

Kitchen
volume ceiling

ref

Bedroom 3
volume ceiling
11⁰ · 10⁴

Breakfast

pan

w.i.c.

ac

wh

ac

Double Garage

volume ceiling

Dining
11² · 11⁰

Living Room
17⁴ · 11²

Foyer

Entry

Width: 42'-6"
Depth: 55'-8"

Alternate Elevation

Design HPT300396
Square Footage: 2,577

◆ This spacious Southwestern home will be a pleasure to come home to. With a soaring entry enhanced by open beams and tall windows, the welcome is elegant and warm. Immediately off the foyer are the dining room and step-down living room with a bay window. The highlight of the four-bedroom sleeping area is the master suite with porch access and a whirlpool tub. The informal living area features an enormous family room with a fireplace, and the bay-windowed kitchen and breakfast room.

Width: 72'-0"
Depth: 57'-4"

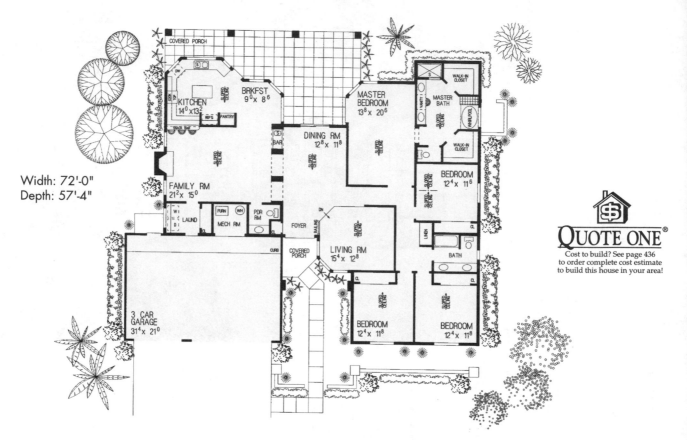

Quote One®
Cost to build? See page 436 to order complete cost estimate to build this house in your area!

Design HPT300397
Square Footage: 2,612
L

BEDRM
12⁰ x 12⁴
9'-0" CLG

BEDRM
10⁴ x 13⁴

BEDRM
10⁴ x 12⁰

COVERED PATIO

COVERED PATIO

COVERED PATIO

MASTER BEDRM
14⁸ x 14⁸
COFFERED CLG

KIT
10⁰ x 14⁴
9'-0" CLG

FAMILY RM
19⁰ x 17¹⁰
9'-0" CLG

MASTER BATH

SHOWER

GARDEN TUB

WALK-IN CLOSET

BATH

LIN

PANT

OVEN

LAUNDRY

STORAGE

DINING
13⁶ x 10⁸
COFFERED CLG

FOYER

PDR RM

MEDIA/OFFICE
14⁸ x 14⁸
9'-0" CLG

COVERED PORCH

GARAGE
21⁰ x 23⁸

Width: 93'-7"
Depth: 74'-10"

Quote One®
Cost to build? See page 436
to order complete cost estimate
to build this house in your area!

◆ Spanish architecture meets modern livability in this fine one-story home. High rooflines and a columned entry add a sense of grand proportions. The family room holds court at the hub of the plan and features a corner fireplace and covered patio access. A media room or home office offers a more secluded space just across the foyer from the formal dining room. The master bedroom is split away from family bedrooms and features a walk-in closet fit for the largest wardrobes. The island kitchen has access to a private dining porch. Family bedrooms share a full bath on the left side of the home.

Design HPT300398

Square Footage: 2,551
Bonus Room: 287 sq. ft.

Width: 69'-8"
Depth: 71'-4"

◆ Shutters and multi-pane windows dress up the exterior of this lovely stucco home. Formal and informal areas flow easily, beginning with the dining room sized to accommodate large parties and function with the adjacent living room. A gourmet kitchen is complete with a walk-in pantry and a cozy breakfast nook. Double doors lead to the spacious master suite. The lavish master bath features His and Hers walk-in closets, a tub framed by a columned archway, and an oversized shower. Off the angular hallway are two bedrooms that share a Pullman-style bath and a study desk. A bonus room over the garage provides additional space.

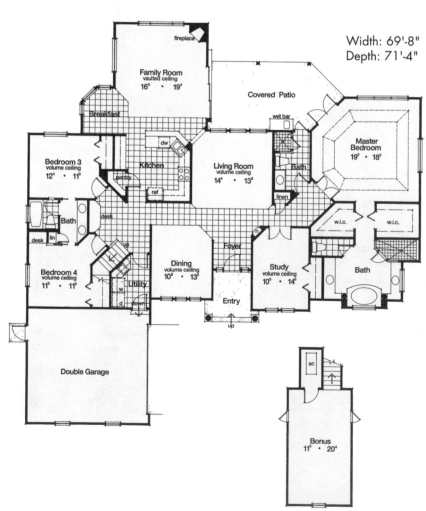

Design HPT300399
Square Footage: 3,866

L D

◆ This modern home adds a contemporary twist to the typical ranch-style plan. The turret study and bayed dining room add a sensuous look from the streetscape. The main living areas open up to the lanai and offer broad views to the rear through large expanses of glass and doors. The family kitchen, nook and leisure room focus on the lanai, the entertainment center and an ale bar. The guest suites have separate baths and also access the lanai. The master bath features a curved-glass shower, whirlpool tub, and private toilet and bidet room. Dual walk-in closets and an abundance of light further the appeal of this suite.

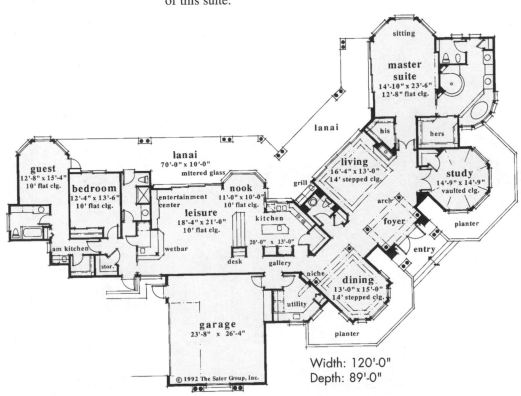

Width: 120'-0"
Depth: 89'-0"

© 1992 The Sater Group, Inc.

Design HPT300400

Square Footage: 1,932

L

◆ This is a superb home-building candidate for those with a narrow building site. Trim, hipped roofs with wide overhangs result in expansive and interesting roof planes. The covered porch, with its railing, provides shelter for the entryway. Separate formal and informal dining areas are achieved through the incorporation of a breakfast bar. The modified, U-shaped kitchen will be a joy in which to work—it looks out to the covered rear patio. The spacious living room features a sloped ceiling, a central fireplace and cheerful windows. The master suite has a sloped ceiling and delights with a high shelf for plants or other decor items. The media room easily converts to form a second bedroom.

QUOTE ONE®

Cost to build? See page 436
to order complete cost estimate
to build this house in your area!

Width: 50'-0"
Depth: 68'-0"

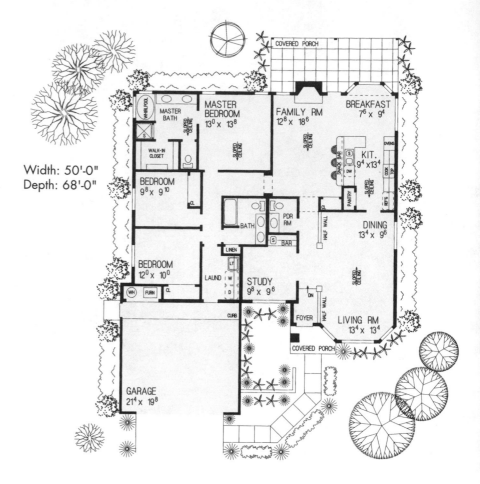

BRKFST RM 11⁸ X 7⁸

COVERED PORCH

MASTER BEDROOM 14⁸ X 15¹⁰

WHIRLPOOL

UP BATH

KITCHEN 11⁸ X 11⁸

REFG RANGE DW

DINING 7⁸ X 10⁰

LIVING RM 12² X 15⁸

WALK-IN CLOSET

SNACK BAR

BEDROOM 10⁶ X 10⁰

BATH

FAMILY RM 19⁴ X 13⁰

LEDGE

LIN CL

FOYER CL CL

CURB

PORCH

WASH RM

COVERED PORCH

BEDROOM 9¹⁰ X 10¹⁰

BEDROOM 10⁶ X 11⁴

W D

LAUND/ MECH

WH FURN

GARAGE 19⁴ X 20⁰

Width: 56'-0"
Depth: 56'-0"

◆ By combining the well-defined look of Floridian styling with just a hint of Tudor detailing, we've created a truly unique exterior that works well in any area—but was designed for the Florida lifestyle. The day-to-day living spaces in this home are kept to the left of the plan: large family room with fireplace, hard-working kitchen, and breakfast room. Formal areas are focused at the center of the plan and overlook the rear covered porch. Four bedrooms (in such a modest square footage!) are all to the right of the home. The master suite has a hexagonal bath with a compartmented shower and toilet and a whirlpool tub. The family bedrooms access a good-sized bath in the hall.

Design HPT300402
Square Footage: 3,265

◆ A turret study and a raised entry add elegance to this marvelous stucco home. A guest suite includes a full bath, porch access and a private garden entry, making it perfect for use as an in-law suite. Secondary bedrooms share a full bath. The master suite has a foyer with a window seat overlooking another private garden and fountain area; the private master bath holds dual closets, a garden tub and a curved-glass shower.

Width: 80'-0"
Depth: 103'-8"

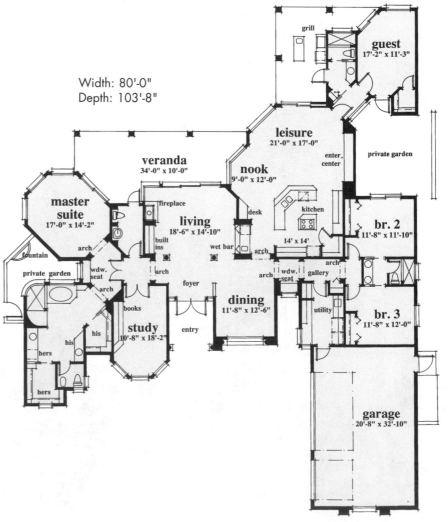

grill

guest
17'-2" x 11'-3"

leisure
21'-0" x 17'-0"

enter. center

private garden

veranda
34'-0" x 10'-0"

nook
9'-0" x 12'-0"

kitchen

master suite
17'-0" x 14'-2"

fireplace

living
18'-6" x 14'-10"

desk

14' x 14'

br. 2
11'-8" x 11'-10"

arch

arch

wet bar

arch

fountain

built ins

arch

arch

wdw. seat

gallery

private garden

wdw. seat

arch

foyer

arch

utility

arch

his

books

his

study
10'-8" x 18'-2"

entry

dining
11'-8" x 12'-6"

br. 3
11'-8" x 12'-0"

hers

hers

garage
20'-8" x 32'-10"

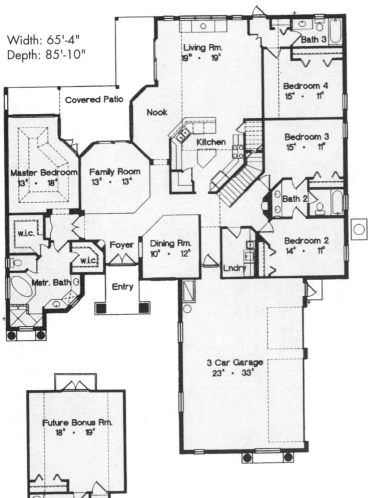

Width: 65'-4"
Depth: 85'-10"

Covered Patio

Living Rm.
19⁶ • 19⁹

Bath 3

Bedroom 4
15⁴ • 11⁰

Nook

Kitchen

Master Bedroom
13⁵ • 18⁰

Family Room
13⁰ • 13⁴

Bedroom 3
15⁴ • 11⁰

w.i.c.

Bath 2

w.i.c.

Foyer

Dining Rm.
10⁰ • 12⁰

Bedroom 2
14⁴ • 11⁰

Mstr. Bath

Entry

Lndry

3 Car Garage
23⁴ • 33⁰

Future Bonus Rm.
18⁰ • 19⁴

Design HPT300403
Square Footage: 2,774
Bonus Room: 493 square feet

◆ This very efficient plan minimizes the use of enclosed hallways, creating a very open feeling of space and orderliness. As you enter the foyer you have a clear view through the spacious living room to the covered patio beyond. The formal dining area is to the right and the master wing is to the left. The master bedroom boasts a sitting area, access to the patio, His and Hers walk-in closets, dual vanities, walk-in shower and compartmented toilet. A large island kitchen overlooks the nook and living room, which has a built-in media/fireplace wall. Three additional bedrooms and two full baths complete the plan.

Design HPT300404
Square Footage: 2,761

◆ Dramatic rooflines dominate this three-bedroom Sun Country design. Interior space begins with a double-door entrance leading directly through the vaulted foyer to a sunken living room with a vaulted ceiling and fireplace. The dining room reaches to the kitchen through a butler's pantry. In the kitchen, snack counters and an attached breakfast room with a bay window make casual dining easy. A sunken family room just beyond is warmed by a fireplace and offers double-door access to a rear patio. Bedrooms include a master suite with a hearth-warmed sitting room, lanai access, and a bath with a walk-in closet and whirlpool tub.

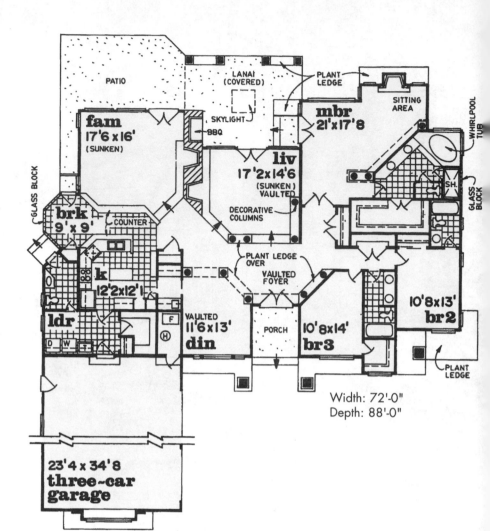

PATIO

LANAI (COVERED)

PLANT LEDGE

fam 17'6 x 16' (SUNKEN)

SKYLIGHT

BBQ

mbr 21' x 17'8

SITTING AREA

WHIRLPOOL TUB

GLASS BLOCK

brk 9' x 9'

COUNTER

liv 17'2 x 14'6 (SUNKEN) VAULTED

DECORATIVE COLUMNS

SH.

GLASS BLOCK

k 12'2 x 12'1

PLANT LEDGE OVER

VAULTED FOYER

10'8 x 13' **br2**

ldr

D W

F

H

VAULTED 11'6 x 13' **din**

PORCH

10'8 x 14' **br3**

PLANT LEDGE

Width: 72'-0"
Depth: 88'-0"

23'4 x 34'8 **three-car garage**

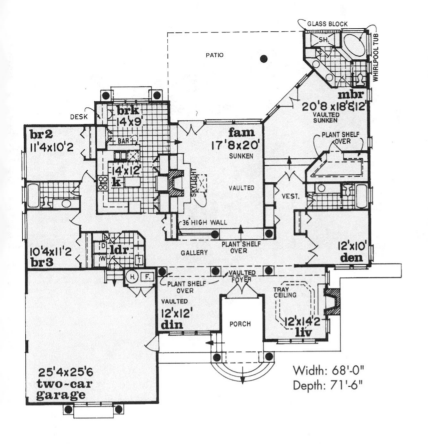

br2
11'4x10'2

DESK

brk
14x9

BAR

14x12
k

br3
10'4x11'2

ldr

D
W

H F.

PATIO

GLASS BLOCK

SH.

WHIRLPOOL TUB

mbr
20'8 x18'6|12'
VAULTED
SUNKEN

fam
17'8x20'
SUNKEN

VAULTED

SKYLIGHT

PLANT SHELF
OVER

VEST.

36" HIGH WALL

PLANT SHELF
OVER

GALLERY

PLANT SHELF
OVER

12'x10'
den

VAULTED
FOYER

PLANT SHELF OVER

VAULTED
12'x12'
din

PORCH

TRAY
CEILING

12'x14'2
liv

25'4x25'6
two-car
garage

Width: 68'-0"
Depth: 71'-6"

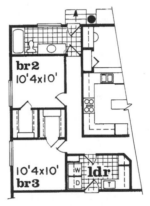

br2
10'4x10'

10'4x10'
br3

W
D

ldr
T

Optional Layout

◆ Elegant arched windows, a portico entry and low-maintenance stucco distinguish this California design. Flanking the foyer are the formal living and dining rooms—defined by decorative columns and plant shelves. The living room boasts a tray ceiling and a fireplace. A sunken family room is graced by double doors to the patio, a fireplace, a vaulted ceiling and a skylight. Two steps up is the U-shaped kitchen with an island and attached breakfast room, separated by a snack-bar counter. The master suite contains access to the patio and a bath with a whirlpool tub, double-bowl vanity and separate shower.

Design HPT300406

Square Footage: 2,086

L

◆ A majestic facade creates magnificent curb appeal with this lovely Sun Country home. An open arrangement of the interior allows dual-use space in the wonderful sunken sitting room and media area. The kitchen has a breakfast bay and looks over the snack bar to the sunken family area. A few steps from the kitchen, the formal dining room functions well with the upper patio. Two family bedrooms share a full bath. The private master suite includes a sitting area and French doors that open to a private covered patio.

Width: 82'-0"
Depth: 58'-4"

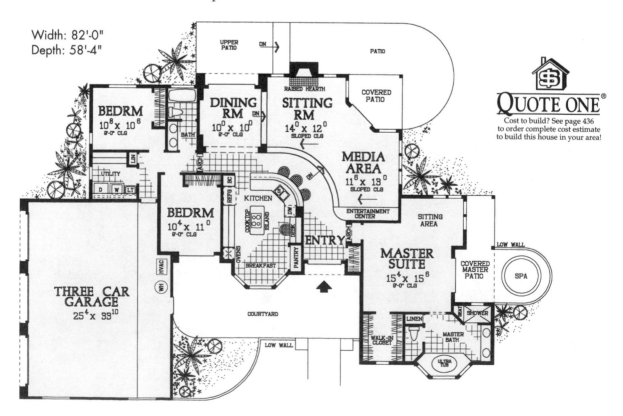

QUOTE ONE®
Cost to build? See page 436
to order complete cost estimate
to build this house in your area!

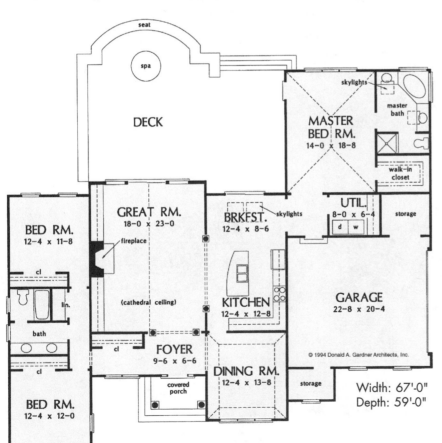

seat

spa

DECK

skylights

MASTER
BED RM.
14-0 x 18-8

master
bath

walk-in
closet

GREAT RM.
18-0 x 23-0

BRKFST.
12-4 x 8-6

skylights

UTIL.
8-0 x 6-4

storage

BED RM.
12-4 x 11-8

fireplace

d | w

cl

(cathedral ceiling)

lin.

KITCHEN
12-4 x 12-8

GARAGE
22-8 x 20-4

bath

cl

FOYER
9-6 x 6-6

BED RM.
12-4 x 12-0

covered
porch

DINING RM.
12-4 x 13-8

storage

Width: 67'-0"
Depth: 59'-0"

Design HPT300407
Square Footage: 2,090

◆ This exciting Southwestern design is enhanced by the use of arched windows and an inviting arched entrance. The large foyer opens to a massive great room with a fireplace and built-in cabinets. The kitchen features an island cooktop and a skylit breakfast area. The master suite has an impressive cathedral ceiling and a walk-in closet as well as a luxurious bath that boasts separate vanities, a corner whirlpool tub and a separate shower. Two additional bedrooms are located at the opposite end of the home for privacy and share a full bath.

Design HPT300408
Square Footage: 3,018

◆ Two distinct exteriors can be built from the details for this plan—both are perfect as Sun Country designs. The grand entry allows for a twelve-foot ceiling in the entry foyer. Open planning calls for columns to separate the formal living and dining rooms from the foyer and central hall. Both rooms have tray ceilings, and the living room has a fireplace and double-door access to the skylit lanai. The modified U-shaped kitchen opens to an attached breakfast room and steps down to the family room with its fireplace and optional wet bar. A lovely octagonal foyer introduces family bedrooms and their private baths. Separated from family bedrooms, the master suite offers double-door access to the rear yard, a walk-in closet and a full bath with a whirlpool tub, double vanity, compartmented toilet and separate shower.

Width: 74'-0"
Depth: 82'-0"

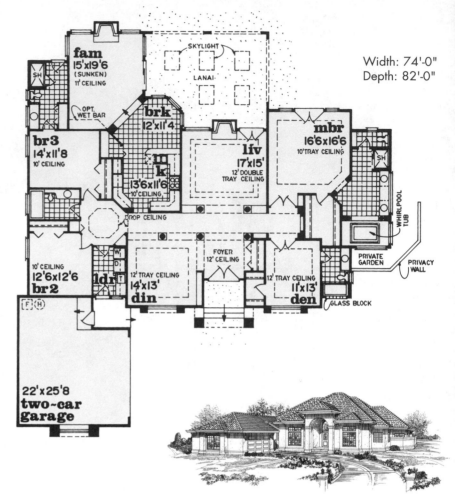

Alternate Elevation

Design HPT300409
Square Footage: 2,520

L

PATIO RETREAT

COVERED PATIO

MASTER SUITE
14⁴ x 15⁸
SLOPED CEILING

WALK-IN CLOSET

MASTER BATH

WHIRLPOOL

SHOWER

MORNING RM
11⁰ x 10⁴
13'-0" CLG

BEDRM
10⁰ x 11¹⁰
9'-0" CLG

BATH

KIT
12¹⁰ x 14⁰
13'-0" CLG

COOK TOP

ISLAND

DW

HALF WALL

OVN

REFS

FAMILY RM
15⁸ x 14⁰
13'-0" CLG

ARCHED OPENING

OFFICE/DEN
10² x 10⁶
9'-0" CLG

COVERED PORCH

RAILING

HALF WALL

PNTRY

9'-0" CLG

BEDRM
12⁰ x 11²
9'-0" CLG

BUILT-IN

D

LAUNDRY

POWDER

BC

HVAC

WH

PLANT SHELVES ABOVE

HALF WALL

DINING RM
14⁰ x 10⁴

FOYER
13'-0" CLG

LIVING RM
12⁴ x 14⁰
13'-0" CLG

HALF WALL

9'-0" CLG

CURB

GARAGE
28⁴ x 22⁰

STORAGE/WORKSHOP

CURB

COVERED PORCH

RAILING

Width: 70'-0"
Depth: 67'-4"

◆ This lovely one-story home fits right into sunny regions. Its stucco exterior with easily accessed outdoor living areas makes it an all-time favorite. Inside, the floor plan accommodates empty-nester lifestyles. There is plenty of room for both formal and informal entertaining: living room, dining room, family room and morning room. A quiet study or media room provides a getaway for more intimate occasions. Sleeping areas are split with the master bedroom and bath on one side and two secondary bedrooms and a bath on the other. Other special features include a warming hearth in the family room, a private porch off the study and a grand rear deck.

QUOTE ONE®

Cost to build? See page 436
to order complete cost estimate
to build this house in your area!

B. NATHAN

Design HPT300410
Square Footage: 1,315

◆ Southwestern influences are evident in this design, from the tiled roof to the warm stucco exterior. A covered porch leads indoors where the great room gains attention. A cathedral ceiling, a fireplace and built-ins enhance this area. The dining room remains open to this room. In the kitchen, a pass-through cooktop counter allows the cook to converse with family and friends. Three bedrooms include two family bedrooms that share a hall bath and a master suite with skylights, a walk-in closet and a private bath.

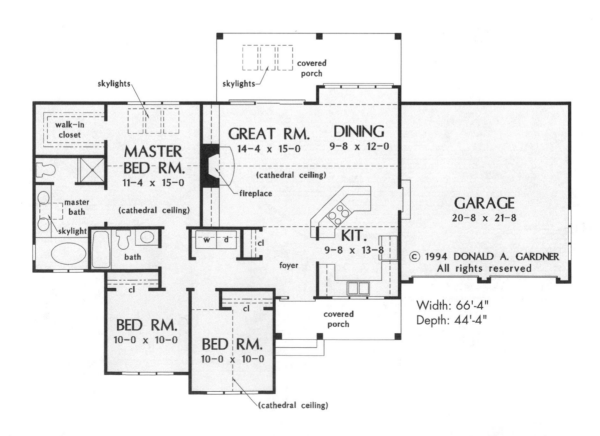

skylights

covered porch

skylights

walk-in closet

GREAT RM.
14-4 x 15-0

DINING
9-8 x 12-0

MASTER BED RM.
11-4 x 15-0

(cathedral ceiling)

fireplace

(cathedral ceiling)

GARAGE
20-8 x 21-8

master bath

skylight

bath

w d

cl

KIT.
9-8 x 13-8

foyer

cl

BED RM.
10-0 x 10-0

cl

BED RM.
10-0 x 10-0

covered porch

Width: 66'-4"
Depth: 44'-4"

(cathedral ceiling)

© '91 HOME DESIGN SERVICES, INC.

Design HPT300411

Square Footage: 1,868

◆ This innovative plan takes advantage of an angled entry into the home, maximizing visual impact and making it possible to include four bedrooms. The joining of the family and dining space makes creative interior decorating possible. The master suite also takes advantage of angles in creating long vistas into this private environment. The master bath is designed with all the amenities usually found in much larger homes. The kitchen and breakfast nook overlook the outdoor living space where you can even have an outdoor kitchen area—a great design for entertaining.

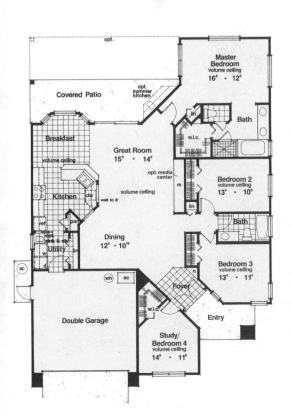

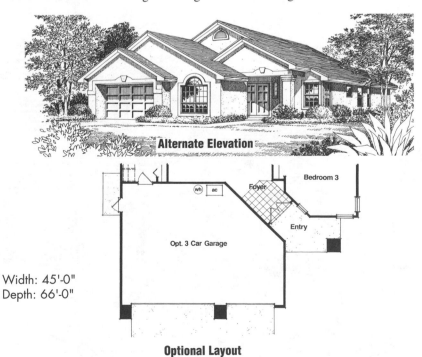

Alternate Elevation

Width: 45'-0"
Depth: 66'-0"

Optional Layout

Design HPT300412
Square Footage: 1,707

◆ Mediterranean and French influences brighten this country home, which offers a covered front porch and a deck in the rear. The foyer opens to the great room, with marvelous views, and the formal dining room. The angled kitchen adjoins the breakfast nook. Two family bedrooms sit at the front sharing a full bath. The master suite, with a large walk-in closet and private bath, is tucked behind the garage for privacy.

Width: 56'-6"
Depth: 45'-8"

DECK

GREAT RM.
17-0 x 18-0
fireplace
shelves

BRKFST.
11-0 x 8-0

KIT.
11-0 x 10-0

MASTER BED RM.
13-8 x 15-0

walk-in closet

lin.

master bath

UTIL.
5-8 x 6-4
d w

BED RM./ STUDY
11-0 x 12-0

bath

cl

cl

FOYER
5-8 x 14-4

DINING
11-0 x 13-0

GARAGE
21-0 x 21-0

BED RM.
11-0 x 12-0

PORCH

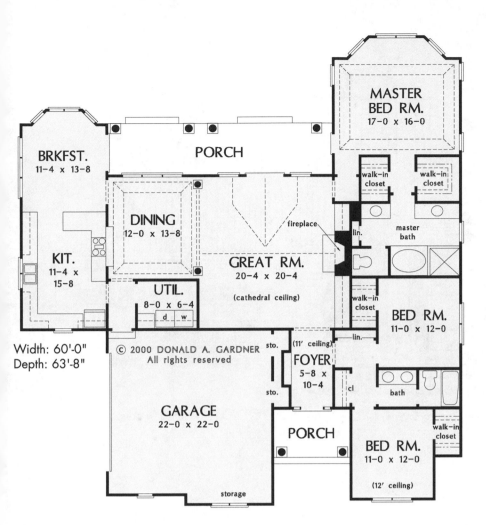

BRKFST.
11-4 x 13-8

PORCH

MASTER
BED RM.
17-0 x 16-0

walk-in
closet

walk-in
closet

DINING
12-0 x 13-8

fireplace

master
bath

lin.

KIT.
11-4 x
15-8

GREAT RM.
20-4 x 20-4

(cathedral ceiling)

UTIL.
8-0 x 6-4

d   w

walk-in
closet

BED RM.
11-0 x 12-0

lin.

Width: 60'-0"
Depth: 63'-8"

© 2000 DONALD A. GARDNER
All rights reserved

sto.

(11' ceiling)

FOYER
5-8 x
10-4

sto.

cl

bath

GARAGE
22-0 x 22-0

PORCH

BED RM.
11-0 x 12-0

walk-in
closet

storage

(12' ceiling)

Design HPT300413
Square Footage: 2,098

◆ This three-bedroom home fits nicely into any neighborhood, with its complex hipped roof and stucco facade offering a European/Mediterranean flair. The vaulted great room, with a fireplace, built-ins and a window wall that opens to the covered porch, adjoins the elegant dining room where decorative columns and a tray ceiling set a formal tone. The rear porch can be accessed as well by the breakfast nook, which enjoys a sunny location abutting the kitchen, and the master bedroom.

Design HPT300414
Square Footage: 1,831

◆ This one-story, three-bedroom design takes its inspiration from the French and Neo-French Eclectic periods, with the steeply pitched hipped roof and the entry's elevated arch. Very modern in design, the interior boasts an efficient arrangement of private and social areas. The hub of social activities is definitely the great room, which adjoins the dining room and opens to the rear porch while enjoying a pass-through to the kitchen. Tray ceilings grace the formal dining room and the master suite that includes two walk-in closets, double-sink vanity, a tub and compartmented shower and toilet.

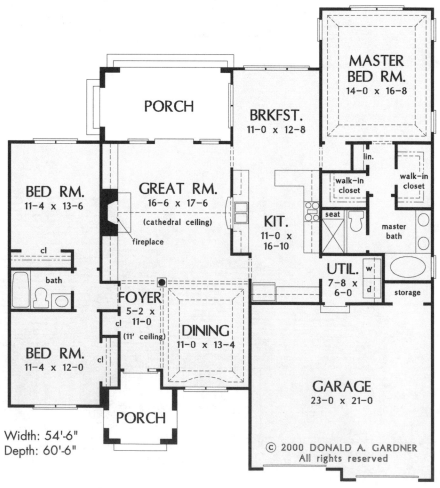

MASTER BED RM. 14-0 x 16-8

PORCH

BRKFST. 11-0 x 12-8

lin.

walk-in closet

walk-in closet

BED RM. 11-4 x 13-6

GREAT RM. 16-6 x 17-6

(cathedral ceiling)

fireplace

KIT. 11-0 x 16-10

seat

master bath

cl

bath

UTIL. 7-8 x 6-0

w

d

storage

FOYER 5-2 x 11-0

(11' ceiling)

cl

DINING 11-0 x 13-4

BED RM. 11-4 x 12-0

cl

GARAGE 23-0 x 21-0

PORCH

Width: 54'-6"
Depth: 60'-6"

Design HPT300415

Square Footage: 2,300
Finished Basement: 1,114 sq. ft.

◆ Looking for all the world like a one-story plan, this elegant hillside design has a surprise on the lower level. The main level is reached through an arched, recessed entry that opens to a twelve-foot ceiling. The formal dining room is on the right, next to a cozy den or Bedroom 3. Columns decorate the hall and separate it from the dining room and great room, which contains a tray ceiling and a fireplace flanked by built-ins. The breakfast nook and kitchen are just steps away, on the left. Lower-level space includes another great room with built-ins and two family bedrooms sharing a full bath.

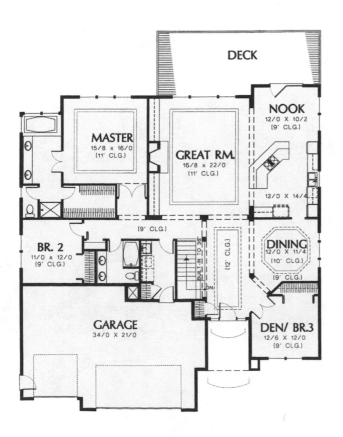

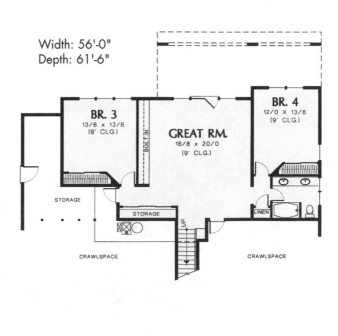

Width: 56'-0"
Depth: 61'-6"

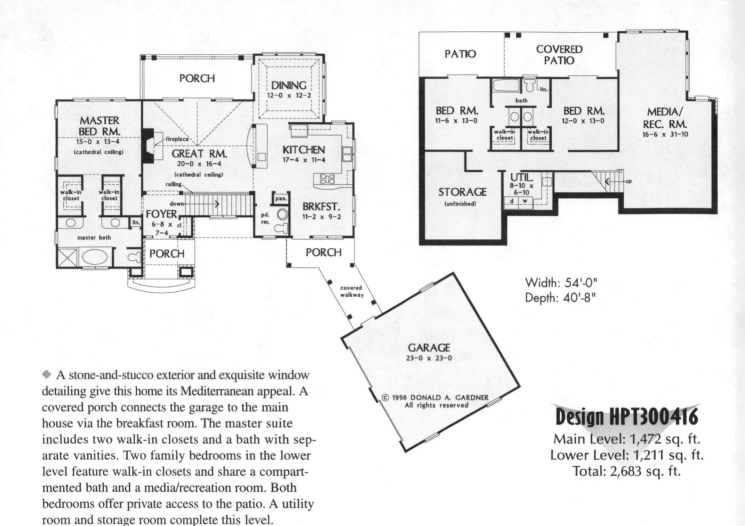

PORCH

DINING
12-0 x 12-2

MASTER
BED RM.
15-0 x 13-4
(cathedral ceiling)

fireplace

GREAT RM.
20-0 x 16-4
(cathedral ceiling)

KITCHEN
17-4 x 11-4

walk-in closet

walk-in closet

railing

master bath

lin.

FOYER
6-8 x cl 7-4

down

pan.

pd. rm.

BRKFST.
11-2 x 9-2

PORCH

PORCH

covered walkway

PATIO

COVERED PATIO

BED RM.
11-6 x 13-0

bath

lin.

BED RM.
12-0 x 13-0

MEDIA/
REC. RM.
16-6 x 31-10

walk-in closet

walk-in closet

STORAGE
(unfinished)

UTIL.
8-10 x 6-10

d   w

up

Width: 54'-0"
Depth: 40'-8"

GARAGE
23-0 x 23-0

◆ A stone-and-stucco exterior and exquisite window detailing give this home its Mediterranean appeal. A covered porch connects the garage to the main house via the breakfast room. The master suite includes two walk-in closets and a bath with separate vanities. Two family bedrooms in the lower level feature walk-in closets and share a compartmented bath and a media/recreation room. Both bedrooms offer private access to the patio. A utility room and storage room complete this level.

Design HPT300416
Main Level: 1,472 sq. ft.
Lower Level: 1,211 sq. ft.
Total: 2,683 sq. ft.

One-Story Vacation And Second Homes

Design HPT300417
Square Footage: 1,404
Loft: 256 sq. ft.

◆ This rustic Craftsman-style cottage provides an open interior with good outdoor flow. The front covered porch invites casual gatherings, while inside, the dining area is set for both everyday and planned occasions. A centered fireplace in the great room shares its warmth with the dining room. A rear hall leads to the master suite and a secondary bedroom, while an upstairs loft has space for computers.

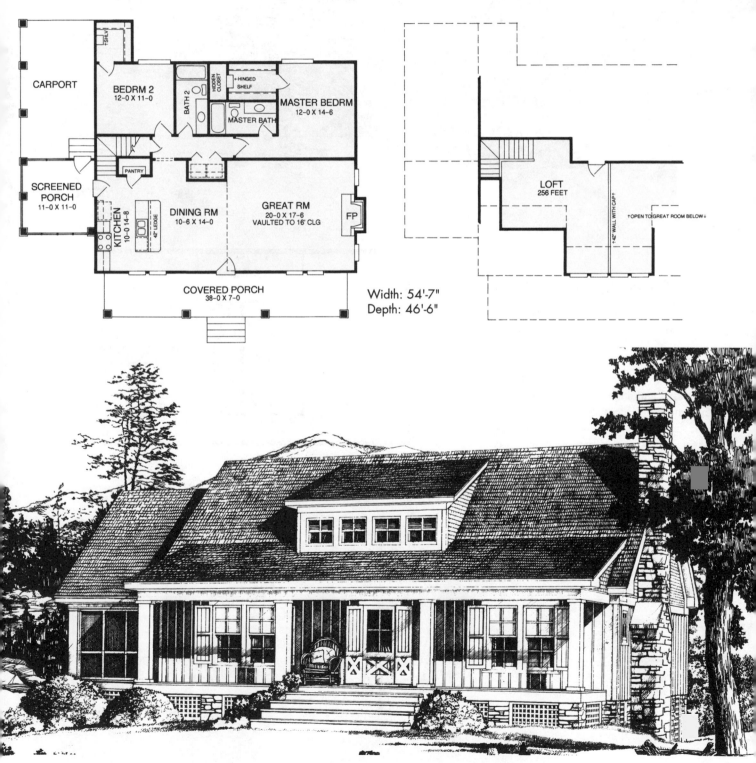

CARPORT

BEDRM 2
12-0 X 11-0

BATH 2

HIDDEN CLOSET

↓HINGED SHELF

MASTER BEDRM
12-0 X 14-6

MASTER BATH

PANTRY

SCREENED PORCH
11-0 X 11-0

KITCHEN
10-0 14-8

DINING RM
10-6 X 14-0

42" LEDGE

GREAT RM
20-0 X 17-6
VAULTED TO 16' CLG

FP

COVERED PORCH
38-0 X 7-0

Width: 54'-7"
Depth: 46'-6"

LOFT
256 FEET

↑42" WALL WITH CAP↑

↑OPEN TO GREAT ROOM BELOW↓

Design HPT300418

Square Footage: 1,320
Finished Basement: 1,320 sq. ft.

◆ Good things come in small packages!
The size and shape of this design will
help hold down construction costs without sacrificing livability. The enormous
great room is a multi-purpose living space
with room for a dining area and several
seating areas. Also notice the sloped
ceilings. Sliding glass doors provide
access to the wraparound deck and
sweeping views of the outdoors. The
well-equipped kitchen includes a pass-
through and a pantry. Two bedrooms, each
with sloped ceilings, and a compartmented
bath round out the plan.

QUOTE ONE®

Cost to build? See page 436
to order complete cost estimate
to build this house in your area!

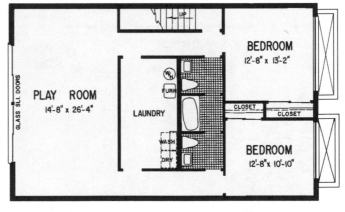

Width: 52'-0"
Depth: 36'-0"

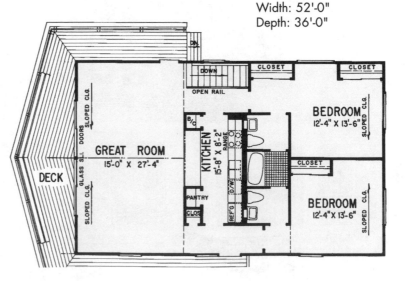

420

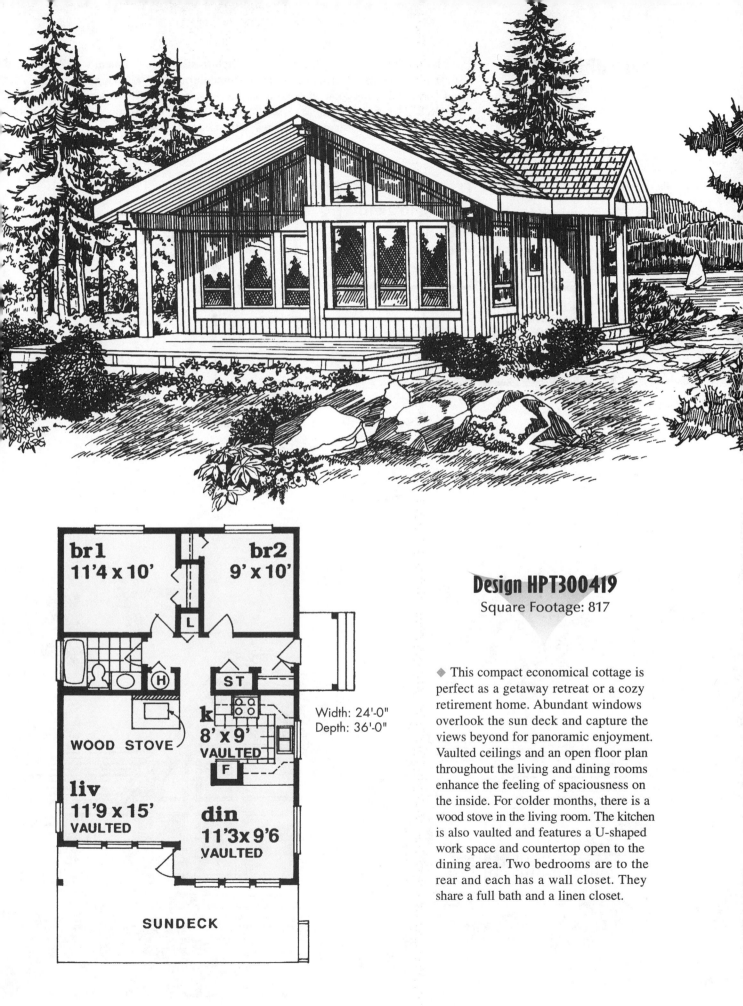

br1
11'4 x 10'

br2
9' x 10'

L

ST

H

WOOD STOVE

k
8' x 9'
VAULTED

F

liv
11'9 x 15'
VAULTED

din
11'3 x 9'6
VAULTED

SUNDECK

Width: 24'-0"
Depth: 36'-0"

Design HPT300419
Square Footage: 817

◆ This compact economical cottage is perfect as a getaway retreat or a cozy retirement home. Abundant windows overlook the sun deck and capture the views beyond for panoramic enjoyment. Vaulted ceilings and an open floor plan throughout the living and dining rooms enhance the feeling of spaciousness on the inside. For colder months, there is a wood stove in the living room. The kitchen is also vaulted and features a U-shaped work space and countertop open to the dining area. Two bedrooms are to the rear and each has a wall closet. They share a full bath and a linen closet.

Design HPT300420
Square Footage: 1,495

◆ This three-bedroom cottage has just the right rustic mix of vertical wood siding and stone accents. High vaulted ceilings are featured throughout the living room and master bedroom. The living room also has a fireplace and full-height windows overlooking the deck. The dining room accesses the deck through double doors. A convenient kitchen includes a U-shaped work area with storage space.

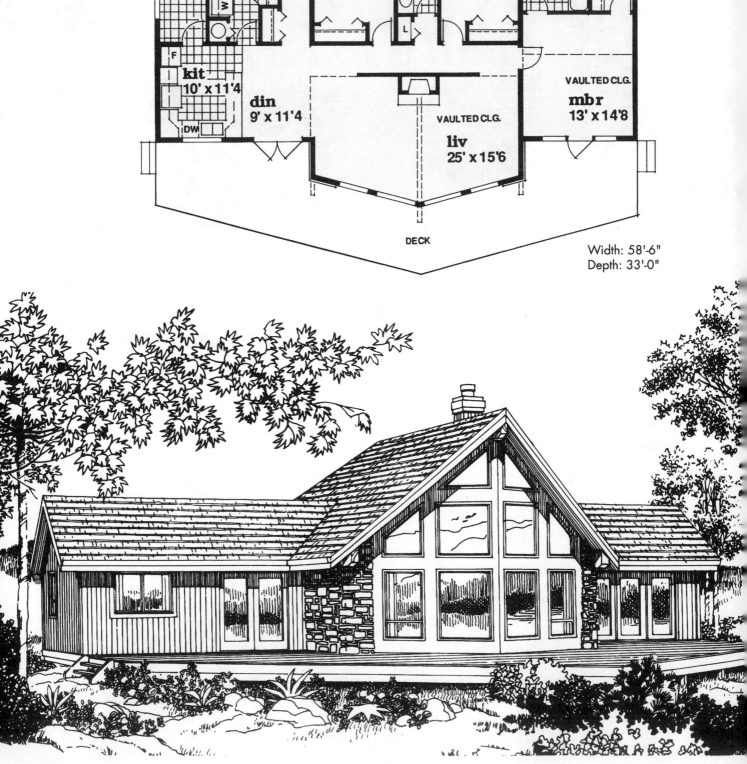

stor

br2
10'2 x 10'

br3
9' x 10'

kit
10' x 11'4

din
9' x 11'4

VAULTED CLG.

liv
25' x 15'6

VAULTED CLG.

mbr
13' x 14'8

DECK

Width: 58'-6"
Depth: 33'-0"

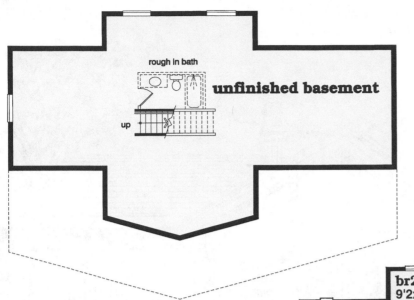

rough in bath

unfinished basement

up

This is a grand vacation or second home, designed for views and the outdoor lifestyle. The full-width deck complements the abundant windows in rooms facing its way. The living room is made for gathering with a vaulted ceiling, a fireplace and full-height windows overlooking the deck. Open to this living space is the dining room with sliding glass doors to the outdoors and a pass-through counter to the U-shaped kitchen. Two family bedrooms sit in the middle of the plan and share a full bath. The master suite features a private bath and deck views.

Design HPT300421
Square Footage: 1,296
Basement: 1,296 sq. ft.

Width: 55'-6"
Depth: 33'-0"

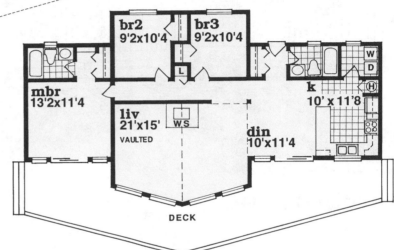

br2
9'2x10'4

br3
9'2x10'4

mbr
13'2x11'4

liv
21'x15'
VAULTED

W.S

din
10'x11'4

k
10' x 11'8

W
D
H

L

DECK

Design HPT300422

Square Footage: 1,405

◆ This three-bedroom leisure home is perfect for the family that spends casual time out of doors. An expansive wall of glass gives a spectacular view to the great room and accentuates the high vaulted ceilings throughout the design. The great room is also warmed by a wood stove and is open to the dining room and L-shaped kitchen. A triangular snack bar graces the kitchen and provides space for casual meals. Bedrooms are split, with the master bedroom on the right side of the plan and family bedrooms on the left.

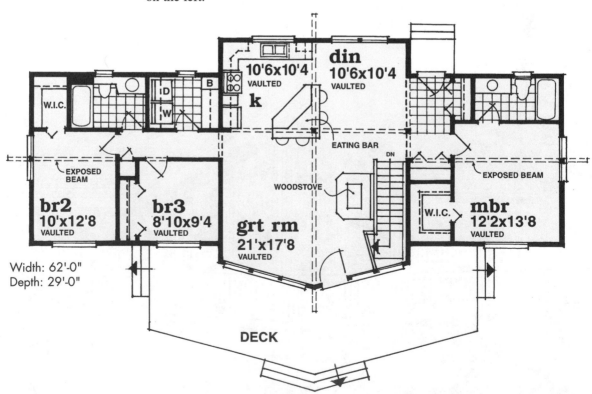

Width: 62'-0"
Depth: 29'-0"

W.I.C.

D
W
B

10'6x10'4
VAULTED

k

din
10'6x10'4
VAULTED

EATING BAR

EXPOSED BEAM

EXPOSED BEAM

WOODSTOVE

DN

W.I.C.

br2
10'x12'8
VAULTED

br3
8'10x9'4
VAULTED

grt rm
21'x17'8
VAULTED

mbr
12'2x13'8
VAULTED

DECK

Design HPT300423
Square Footage: 1,292

◆ The casual living space of this cozy home offers room to kick off your shoes or put on a bash, and is highlighted by a wood stove and a vaulted ceiling. A wraparound deck provides space to enjoy the great outdoors, while tall windows bring plenty of natural light inside. A tiled kitchen offers plenty of counter space and a snack counter. The master suite nestles to the left of the living area and boasts a walk-in closet. Two secondary bedrooms allow space for guests and family members.

Width: 52'-0"
Depth: 34'-0"

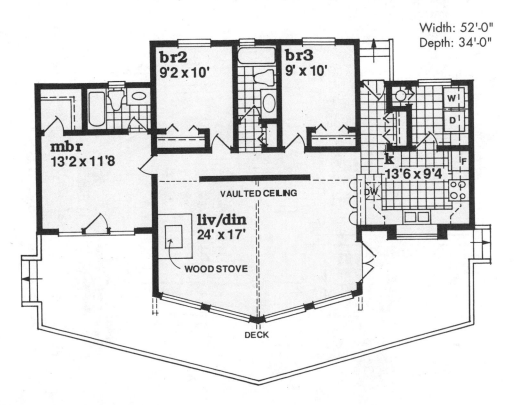

br2
9'2 x 10'

br3
9' x 10'

W
D

mbr
13'2 x 11'8

k
13'6 x 9'4

DW

F

VAULTED CEILING

liv/din
24' x 17'

WOOD STOVE

DECK

Design HPT300424

Square Footage: 2,190
Bonus Room: 875 sq. ft.

◆ A dramatic set of stairs leads to the entry of this home. The foyer opens to an expansive grand room with a fireplace and built-in bookshelves. For formal meals, a front-facing dining room offers plenty of space and a bumped-out bay. The kitchen serves this area easily as well as the breakfast nook. A study and three bedrooms make up the rest of the floor plan. The two secondary bedrooms share a full bath. The master suite contains two walk-in closets and a full bath.

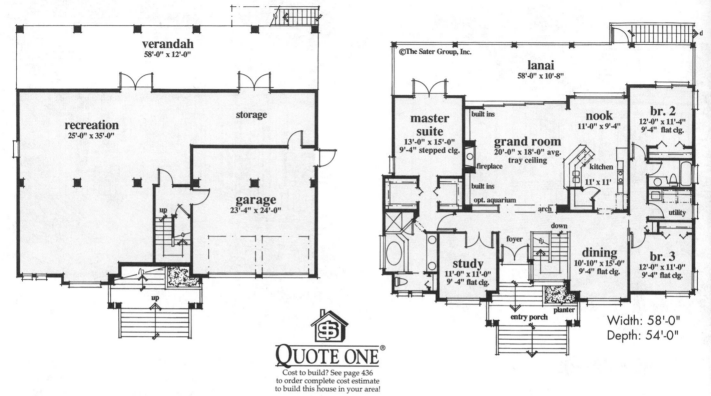

verandah
58'-0" x 12'-0"

recreation
25'-0" x 35'-0"

storage

garage
23'-4" x 24'-0"

up

up

©The Sater Group, Inc.

lanai
58'-0" x 10'-8"

master suite
13'-0" x 15'-0"
9'-4" stepped clg.

built ins

nook
11'-0" x 9'-4"

br. 2
12'-0" x 11'-4"
9'-4" flat clg.

grand room
20'-0" x 18'-0" avg.
tray ceiling

fireplace

built ins

opt. aquarium

kitchen
11' x 11'

arch

utility

down

study
11'-0" x 11'-0"
9'-4" flat clg.

foyer

dining
10'-10" x 15'-0"
9'-4" flat clg.

br. 3
12'-0" x 11'-0"
9'-4" flat clg.

planter

entry porch

Width: 58'-0"
Depth: 54'-0"

QUOTE ONE®
Cost to build? See page 436
to order complete cost estimate
to build this house in your area!

Width: 44'-0"
Depth: 63'-0"

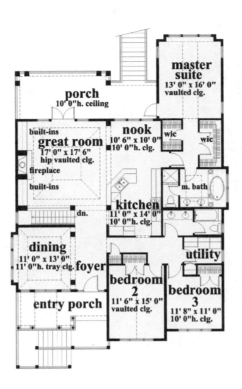

lanai
9' 4"h. ceiling

**storage/
bonus room**
9' 0"h. ceiling

foyer
up

**storage/
bonus room**
9' 0"h. ceiling

**storage/
bonus rm**

2 car garage
9' 0"h. ceiling

storage

porch
10' 0"h. ceiling

**master
suite**
13' 0" x 16' 0"
vaulted clg.

great room
17' 0" x 17' 6"
hip vaulted clg.
built-ins
fireplace
built-ins

nook
10' 6" x 10' 0"
10' 0"h. clg.

wic

wic

m. bath

kitchen
11' 0" x 14' 0"
10' 0"h. clg.

dn.

dining
11' 0" x 13' 0"
11' 0"h. tray clg.

foyer

utility

**bedroom
2**
11' 6" x 15' 0"
vaulted clg.

**bedroom
3**
11' 8" x 11' 0"
10' 0"h. clg.

entry porch

◆ This raised Tidewater design is well suited for many building situations, with comfortable outdoor areas that encourage year-round living. A vaulted hipped ceiling highlights the great room, made comfy by a centered fireplace, extensive built-ins and French doors that let in fresh air and sunlight. The formal dining room opens from the entry hall and features a triple-window view of the side property. Family members will gather in the morning nook or at the snack counter in the kitchen. The master suite features a sitting area with a wide window and a door to a private area of the rear porch. Each of two secondary bedrooms has a triple window and an ample wardrobe.

Design HPT300426
Square Footage: 2,385

◆ This cabin is the ideal vacation home for a retreat to the mountain lake. Inside, beyond the covered front porch, the foyer steps lead up to the formal living areas on the main floor. The study is enhanced by a vaulted ceiling and double doors, which open to the front balcony. The vaulted central great room overlooks the rear deck. The island kitchen is open to an adjacent breakfast nook. The master suite is thoughtfully placed on the left side of the plan for privacy and offers two walk-in closets and a pampering master bath with a whirlpool tub.

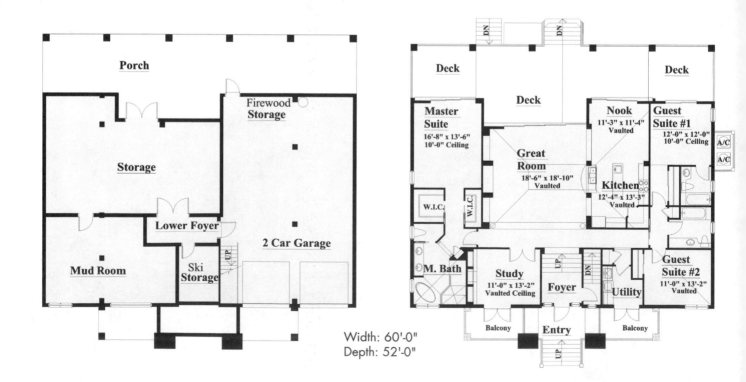

Width: 60'-0"
Depth: 52'-0"

Design HPT300427

Square Footage: 2,430

◆ With a rugged blend of stone and siding, an inviting mix of details creates the kind of comfortable beauty that every homeowner craves. Massive stone columns support a striking pediment entry. A spacious formal dining room complements a gourmet kitchen designed to serve any occasion and equipped with a walk-in pantry and a nearby powder room. The morning nook boasts a wall of glass that allows casual diners to kick back and be at one with nature. Separate sleeping quarters thoughtfully place the master suite to the right of the plan, in a wing of the home that includes a private porch. Guest suites on the opposite side of the plan share a hall and a staircase that leads to a lower-level mudroom, porch and ski storage.

Width: 70'-2"
Depth: 53'-0"

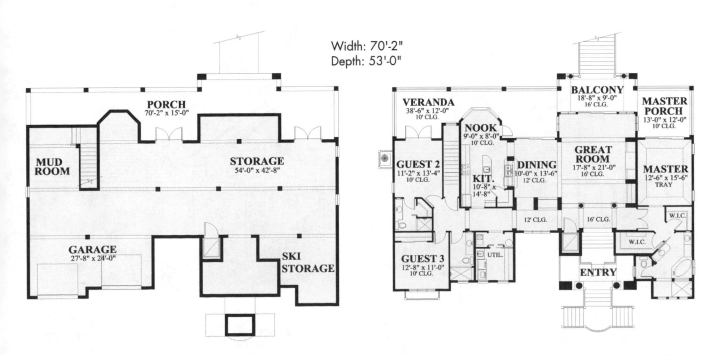

Design HPT300428

Square Footage: 1,862

◆ Stone and brick, accented with keystone-arched windows and classic shutters, make a fine statement on the outside of this home. Inside, the layout is commodious and convenient. A large open living area with a fireplace and built-ins adjoins a dining room and kitchen. A snack-bar counter defines the kitchen's space. Three bedrooms line the front of the home: a master suite and two family bedrooms. The master bath is grand, with a walk-in closet, spa tub and compartmented toilet. A double garage sits to the back of the plan.

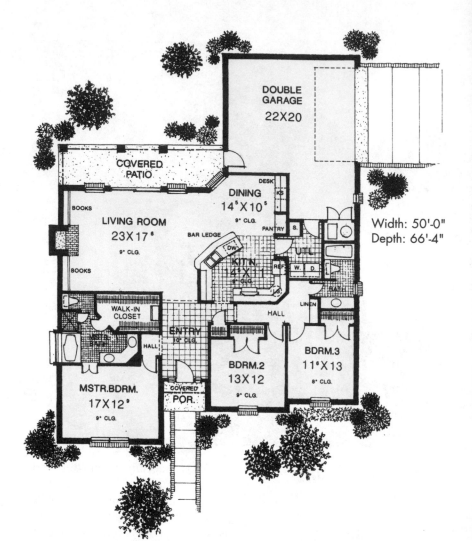

DOUBLE GARAGE 22X20

COVERED PATIO

DINING 14⁵ X 10⁵

LIVING ROOM 23 X 17⁶

BOOKS

KIT'N

MSTR.BDRM. 17 X 12⁹

WALK-IN CLOSET

ENTRY

BDRM.2 13X12

BDRM.3 11⁶ X 13

COVERED POR.

Width: 50'-0"
Depth: 66'-4"

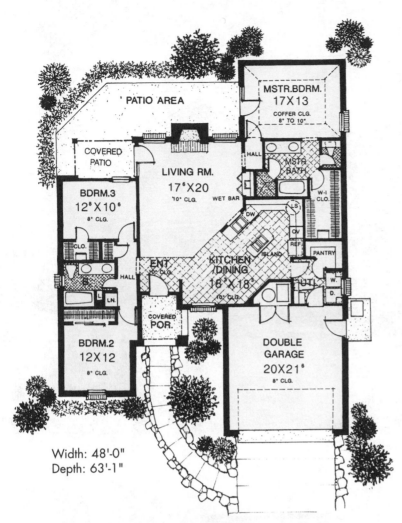

PATIO AREA

COVERED PATIO

MSTR.BDRM.
17X13
COFFER CLG.
8" TO 10"

HALL

LIVING RM.
17⁶X20
10" CLG.

MSTR.
BATH

WET BAR

W-I
CLO.

BDRM.3
12⁸X10⁶
8" CLG.

CLO.

DW

OV
REF

PANTRY

ENT
10' CLG.

HALL

KITCHEN
/DINING
18⁸X18³
10" CLG.

ISLAND

UTIL

W.
D.

COVERED
POR.

BDRM.2
12X12
8" CLG.

DOUBLE
GARAGE
20X21⁶
8" CLG.

Width: 48'-0"
Depth: 63'-1"

Design HPT300429
Square Footage: 1,673

◆ Quaint country charm pervades the facade of this one-story cottage plan. The living room is at the heart of the floor plan and features a fireplace and ten-foot ceiling. The island kitchen and dining area are nearby. A covered patio to the back leads to an even larger patio area, accessible from the living room and the master bedroom. Note the coffered ceiling and fine bath that are part of the master suite. Twin family rooms share a bath that includes double sinks in the left wing of the home.

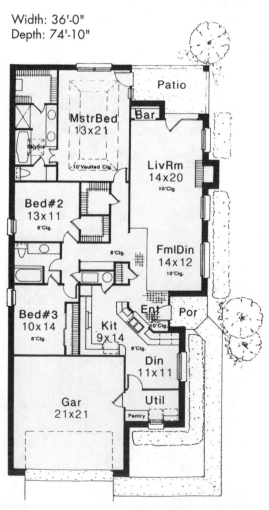

Width: 36'-0"
Depth: 74'-10"

Design HPT300430
Square Footage: 1,888

◆ This narrow-lot home features a side entry that opens to a dazzling layout. The angled kitchen leads to the informal dining area where the utility room accesses the garage. The formal dining/living room are barrier-free, creating a large living area with a wet bar, fireplace and access to the rear patio. The master suite, with a private bath and generous walk-in closet, rests at back of the floor plan. Two family bedrooms share a full bath at the end of the second leg of the hall.

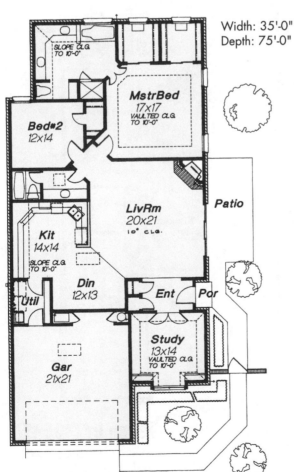

Width: 35'-0"
Depth: 75'-0"

Design HPT300431
Square Footage: 1,943

◆ This traditional-style home begins with a private side entrance and a covered entry porch. A large living room with a corner fireplace opens to the patio area. A laundry area is nestled between the garage, the U-shaped kitchen and the skylit dinette. Both the study and the master suite feature tray ceilings. The master suite also enjoys a double-sink vanity, a tub and separate shower, and two walk-in closets. A second bedroom features a walk-in closet and accesses a full hall bath.

◆ Classic shutters and delightful dormers adorn the facade of this cottage farmhouse. Inside, there's plenty of space for the family and for entertaining, even though the footprint is smaller. Guests and family occupy two bedrooms at the front of the plan, while the master suite is to the back. A covered porch opens from the great room and the dining area; note the stepped ceilings in both these rooms. Over the garage, a bonus room features a private bath. Develop this space later, if you like. This home is designed with a crawlspace foundation.

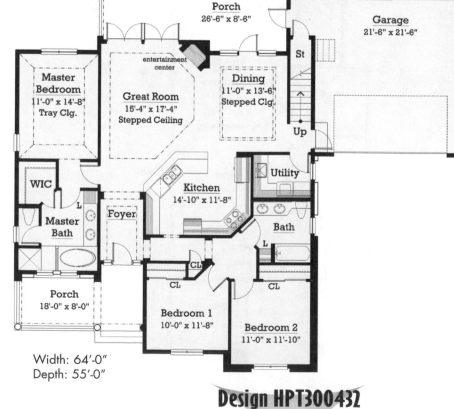

Width: 64'-0"
Depth: 55'-0"

Design HPT300432
Square Footage: 1,616
Bonus Space: 362 square feet

LET US SHOW YOU OUR HOME BLUEPRINT PACKAGE

BUILDING A HOME? PLANNING A HOME?

OUR BLUEPRINT PACKAGE HAS NEARLY EVERYTHING YOU NEED TO GET THE JOB DONE RIGHT,

whether you're working on your own or with help from an architect, designer, builder or subcontractors. Each Blueprint Package is the result of many hours of work by licensed architects or professional designers.

QUALITY

Hundreds of hours of painstaking effort have gone into the development of your blueprint plan. Each home has been quality-checked by professionals to insure accuracy and buildability.

VALUE

Because we sell in volume, you can buy professional quality blueprints at a fraction of their development cost. With our plans, your dream home design costs substantially less than the fees charged by architects.

SERVICE

Once you've chosen your favorite home plan, you'll receive fast, efficient service whether you choose to mail or fax your order to us or call us toll free at 1-800-521-6797. After you have received your order, call for customer service toll free 1-888-690-1116.

SATISFACTION

Over 50 years of service to satisfied home plan buyers provide us unparalleled experience and knowledge in producing quality blueprints.

ORDER TOLL FREE 1-800-521-6797

After you've looked over our Blueprint Package and Important Extras, call toll free on our Blueprint Hotline: 1-800-521-6797, for current pricing and availability prior to mailing the order form on page 445. We're ready and eager to serve you. After you have received your order, call for customer service toll free 1-888-690-1116.

Each set of blueprints is an interrelated collection of detail sheets which includes components such as floor plans, interior and exterior elevations, dimensions, cross-sections, diagrams and notations. These sheets show exactly how your house is to be built.

SETS MAY INCLUDE:

FRONTAL SHEET
This artist's sketch of the exterior of the house gives you an idea of how the house will look when built and landscaped. Large floor plans show all levels of the house and provide an overview of your new home's livability, as well as a handy reference for deciding on furniture placement.

FOUNDATION PLANS
This sheet shows the foundation layout including support walls, excavated and unexcavated areas, if any, and foundation notes. If slab construction rather than basement, the plan shows footings and details for a monolithic slab. This page, or another in the set, may include a sample plot plan for locating your house on a building site.

DETAILED FLOOR PLANS
These plans show the layout of each floor of the house. Rooms and interior spaces are carefully dimensioned and keys are given for cross-section details provided later in the plans. The positions of electrical outlets and switches are shown.

HOUSE CROSS-SECTIONS
Large-scale views show sections or cut-aways of the foundation, interior walls, exterior walls, floors, stairways and roof details. Additional cross-sections may show important changes in floor, ceiling or roof heights or the relationship of one level to another. Extremely valuable for construction, these sections show exactly how the various parts of the house fit together.

INTERIOR ELEVATIONS
Many of our drawings show the design and placement of kitchen and bathroom cabinets, laundry areas, fireplaces, bookcases and other built-ins. Little "extras," such as mantelpiece and wainscoting drawings, plus molding sections, provide details that give your home that custom touch.

EXTERIOR ELEVATIONS
These drawings show the front, rear and sides of your house and give necessary notes on exterior materials and finishes. Particular attention is given to cornice detail, brick and stone accents or other finish items that make your home unique.

IMPORTANT EXTRAS TO DO THE JOB RIGHT!

*INTRODUCING IMPORTANT PLANNING AND CONSTRUCTION
AIDS DEVELOPED BY OUR PROFESSIONALS TO HELP YOU
SUCCEED IN YOUR HOME-BUILDING PROJECT*

MATERIALS LIST

(Note: Because of the diversity of local building codes, our Materials List does not include mechanical materials.)

For many of the designs in our portfolio, we offer a customized materials take-off that is invaluable in planning and estimating the cost of your new home. This Materials List outlines the quantity, type and size of materials needed to build your house (with the exception of mechanical system items). Included are framing lumber, windows and doors, kitchen and bath cabinetry, rough and finish hardware, and much more. This handy list helps you or your builder cost out materials and serves as a reference sheet when you're compiling bids. Some Materials Lists may be ordered before blueprints are ordered, call for information.

SPECIFICATION OUTLINE

This valuable 16-page document is critical to building your house correctly. Designed to be filled in by you or your builder, this book lists 166 stages or items crucial to the building process. It provides a comprehensive review of the construction process and helps in choosing materials. When combined with the blueprints, a signed contract, and a schedule, it becomes a legal document and record for the building of your home.

QUOTE ONE®

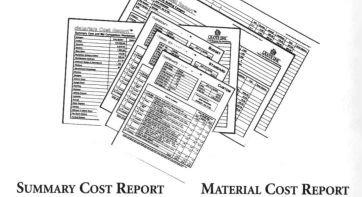

SUMMARY COST REPORT   **MATERIAL COST REPORT**

A product for estimating the cost of building select designs, the Quote One® system is available in two separate stages: The Summary Cost Report and the Material Cost Report.

The **Summary Cost Report** is the first stage in the package and shows the total cost per square foot for your chosen home in your zip-code area and then breaks that cost down into various categories showing the costs for building materials, labor and installation. The report includes three grades: Budget, Standard and Custom. These reports allow you to evaluate your building budget and compare the costs of building a variety of homes in your area.

Make even more informed decisions about your home-building project with the second phase of our package, our **Material Cost Report.** This tool is invaluable in planning and estimating the cost of your new home. The material and installation (labor and equipment) cost is shown for each of over 1,000 line items provided in the Materials List (Standard grade), which is included when you purchase this estimating tool. It allows you to determine building costs for your specific zip-code area and for your chosen home design. Space is allowed for additional estimates from contractors and subcontractors, such as for mechanical materials, which are not included in our packages. This invaluable tool includes a Materials List. A Material Cost Report cannot be ordered before blueprints are ordered. Call for details. In addition, ask about our Home Planners Estimating Package.

If you are interested in a plan that is not indicated as Quote One®, please call and ask our sales reps. They will be happy to verify the status for you. To order these invaluable reports, use the order form.

CONSTRUCTION INFORMATION

IF YOU WANT TO KNOW MORE ABOUT TECHNIQUES— and deal more confidently with subcontractors — we offer these useful sheets. Each set is an excellent tool that will add to your understanding of these technical subjects. These helpful details provide general construction information and are not specific to any single plan.

PLUMBING

The Blueprint Package includes locations for all the plumbing fixtures, including sinks, lavatories, tubs, showers, toilets, laundry trays and water heaters. However, if you want to know more about the complete plumbing system, these Plumbing Details will prove very useful. Prepared to meet requirements of the National Plumbing Code, these fact-filled sheets give general information on pipe schedules, fittings, sump-pump details, water-softener hookups, septic system details and much more. Sheets also include a glossary of terms.

ELECTRICAL

The locations for every electrical switch, plug and outlet are shown in your Blueprint Package. However, these Electrical Details go further to take the mystery out of household electrical systems. Prepared to meet requirements of the National Electrical Code, these comprehensive drawings come packed with helpful information, including wire sizing, switch-installation schematics, cable-routing details, appliance wattage, doorbell hook-ups, typical service panel circuitry and much more. A glossary of terms is also included.

CONSTRUCTION

The Blueprint Package contains information an experienced builder needs to construct a particular house. However, it doesn't show all the ways that houses can be built, nor does it explain alternate construction methods. To help you understand how your house will be built—and offer additional techniques—this set of Construction Details depicts the materials and methods used to build foundations, fireplaces, walls, floors and roofs. Where appropriate, the drawings show acceptable alternatives.

MECHANICAL

These Mechanical Details contain fundamental principles and useful data that will help you make informed decisions and communicate with subcontractors about heating and cooling systems. Drawings contain instructions and samples that allow you to make simple load calculations, and preliminary sizing and costing analysis. Covered are the most commonly used systems from heat pumps to solar fuel systems. The package is filled with illustrations and diagrams to help you visualize components and how they relate to one another.

THE HANDS-ON HOME FURNITURE PLANNER

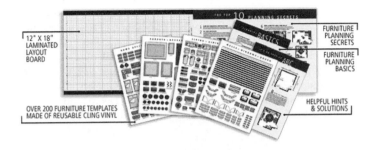

Effectively plan the space in your home using The **Hands-On Home Furniture Planner**. It's fun and easy—no more moving heavy pieces of furniture to see how the room will go together. And you can try different layouts, moving furniture at a whim.

The kit includes reusable peel and stick furniture templates that fit onto a 12" x 18" laminated layout board—space enough to layout every room in your home.

Also included in the package are a number of helpful planning tools. You'll receive:

- ✓ Helpful hints and solutions for difficult situations.
- ✓ Furniture planning basics to get you started.
- ✓ Furniture planning secrets that let you in on some of the tricks of professional designers.

The **Hands-On Home Furniture Planner** is the one tool that no new homeowner or home remodeler should be without. It's also a perfect housewarming gift!

To Order, Call Toll Free
1-800-521-6797

After you've looked over our Blueprint Package and Important Extras on these pages, call for current pricing and availability prior to mailing the order form. We're ready and eager to serve you. After you have received your order, call for customer service toll free 1-888-690-1116.

THE FINISHING TOUCHES...

THE DECK BLUEPRINT PACKAGE

Many of the homes in this book can be enhanced with a professionally designed Home Planners Deck Plan. Those homes marked with a **D** have a complementary Deck Plan, sold separately, which includes a Deck Plan Frontal Sheet, Deck Framing and Floor Plans, Deck Elevations and a Deck Materials List. A Standard Deck Details Package, also available, provides all the how-to information necessary for building *any* deck. Our Complete Deck Building Package contains one set of Custom Deck Plans of your choice, plus one set of Standard Deck Building Details, all for one low price. Our plans and details are carefully prepared in an easy-to-understand format that will guide you through every stage of your deck-building project. This page shows a sample Deck layout to match your favorite house. See Blueprint Price Schedule for ordering information.

THE LANDSCAPE BLUEPRINT PACKAGE

For the homes marked with an **L** in this book, Home Planners has created a front-yard Landscape Plan that is complementary in design to the house plan. These comprehensive blueprint packages include a Frontal Sheet, Plan View, Regionalized Plant & Materials List, a sheet on Planting and Maintaining Your Landscape, Zone Maps and Plant Size and Description Guide. These plans will help you achieve professional results, adding value and enjoyment to your property for years to come. Each set of blueprints is a full 18" x 24" in size with clear, complete instructions and easy-to-read type. A sample Landscape Plan is shown below. See Blueprint Price Schedule for ordering information.

CONTEMPORARY LEISURE DECK
Deck ODA021

CAPE COD COTTAGE
Landscape OLA003

REGIONAL ORDER MAP

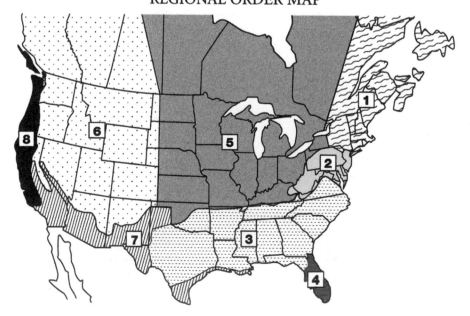

Most Landscape Plans are available with a Plant & Materials List adapted by horticultural experts to 8 different regions of the country. Please specify the Geographic Region when ordering your plan. See Blueprint Price Schedule for ordering information and regional availability.

Region	1	Northeast
Region	2	Mid-Atlantic
Region	3	Deep South
Region	4	Florida & Gulf Coast
Region	5	Midwest
Region	6	Rocky Mountains
Region	7	Southern California & Desert Southwest
Region	8	Northern California & Pacific Northwest

BLUEPRINT PRICE SCHEDULE

TIERS	1-SET STUDY PACKAGE	4-SET BUILDING PACKAGE	8-SET BUILDING PACKAGE	1-SET REPRODUCIBLE*
P1	$20	$50	$90	$140
P2	$40	$70	$110	$160
P3	$70	$100	$140	$190
P4	$100	$130	$170	$220
P5	$140	$170	$210	$270
P6	$180	$210	$250	$310
A1	$440	$490	$540	$660
A2	$480	$530	$580	$720
A3	$530	$590	$650	$800
A4	$575	$645	$705	$870
C1	$625	$695	$755	$935
C2	$670	$740	$800	$1000
C3	$715	$790	$855	$1075
C4	$765	$840	$905	$1150
L1	$870	$965	$1050	$1300
L2	$945	$1040	$1125	$1420
L3	$1050	$1150	$1240	$1575
L4	$1155	$1260	$1355	$1735
SQ1				.35/SqFt

* Requires a fax number

OPTIONS FOR PLANS IN TIERS A1–L4
Additional Identical Blueprints
in same order for "A1–L4" price plans ....$50 per set
Reverse Blueprints (mirror image)
with 4- or 8-set order for "A1–L4" plans...........................$50 fee per order
Specification Outlines...$10 each
Materials Lists for "A1–C3" plans ....$70 each
Materials Lists for "C4–SQ1" plans ....$70 each

OPTIONS FOR PLANS IN TIERS P1–P6
Additional Identical Blueprints
in same order for "P1–P6" price plans.....................................$10 per set
Reverse Blueprints (mirror image) for "P1–P6" price plans ....$10 fee per order
1 Set of Deck Construction Details ....$14.95 each
Deck Construction Package ....**add $10 to Building Package price**
(includes 1 set of "P1–P6" plans, plus 1 set Standard Deck Construction Details)

IMPORTANT NOTES
SQ one-set building package includes one set of reproducible vellum construction drawings plus, one set of study blueprints.
The 1-set study package is marked "not for construction."
Prices for 4- or 8-set Building Packages honored only at time of original order.
Some foundations carry a $225 surcharge.
Right-reading reverse blueprints, if available, will incur a $165 surcharge.
Additional identical blueprints may be purchased within 60 days of original order.

TO USE THE INDEX, refer to the design number listed in numerical order (a helpful page reference is also given). Note the price tier and refer to the Blueprint Price Schedule above for the cost of one, four or eight sets of blueprints or the cost of a reproducible drawing. Additional prices are shown for identical and reverse blueprint sets, as well as a very useful Materials List for some of the plans. Also note in the Plan Index those plans that have Deck Plans or Landscape Plans. Refer to the schedules above for prices of these plans. The letter "Y" identifies plans that are part of our Quote One® estimating service and those that offer Materials Lists.

TO ORDER, Call toll free 1-800-521-6797 for current pricing and availability prior to mailing the order form. FAX: 1-800-224-6699 or 520-544-3086.

PLAN INDEX

DESIGN	PRICE	PAGE	MATERIALS LIST	QUOTE ONE®	DECK	DECK PRICE	LANDSCAPE	LANDSCAPE PRICE	REGIONS
HPT300001	A4	4							
HPT300002	A2	5							
HPT300003	A2	6	Y						
HPT300004	A2	7	Y						
HPT300005	A2	8	Y						
HPT300006	A2	9	Y						
HPT300007	A2	10	Y						
HPT300008	A2	11	Y						
HPT300009	A2	12	Y						
HPT300010	A3	13	Y						
HPT300011	A3	14	Y						
HPT300012	A3	15	Y						
HPT300013	A2	16	Y						
HPT300014	A2	17	Y						
HPT300015	A2	18							
HPT300016	A2	19							
HPT300017	A2	20	Y	Y	ODA014	P2	OLA027	P3	12345678
HPT300018	A2	21	Y						
HPT300019	A2	22	Y						
HPT300021	A2	24	Y						
HPT300022	A2	25	Y						
HPT300023	A2	26	Y						
HPT300024	A3	27	Y	Y			OLA022	P3	123568
HPT300025	A2	28							
HPT300026	A3	29	Y						
HPT300027	A3	30							
HPT300028	A2	31	Y						
HPT300030	A3	33	Y						
HPT300031	A2	34	Y						
HPT300032	A3	35							
HPT300033	A4	36	Y						
HPT300034	A3	37	Y						
HPT300035	A3	38	Y		ODA019	P2	OLA026	P3	1234568
HPT300036	A3	39	Y	Y	ODA015	P2	OLA006	P3	123568
HPT300037	C1	40	Y	Y	ODA013	P2			
HPT300038	A3	41	Y						
HPT300039	A3	42	Y						
HPT300040	A3	43							
HPT300041	C1	44			ODA019	P2	OLA033	P3	47
HPT300042	A4	45	Y	Y			OLA001	P3	123568
HPT300043	C2	46	Y				OLA021	P3	123568
HPT300044	A3	47	Y						
HPT300045	A3	48			ODA019	P2	OLA021	P3	123568
HPT300046	A3	49	Y		ODA014	P2	OLA021	P3	123568
HPT300047	A3	50					OLA001	P3	123568
HPT300048	A3	51	Y				OLA001	P3	123568
HPT300049	A3	52							
HPT300050	A4	53	Y						
HPT300051	A3	54	Y						

BEFORE FILLING OUT

THE ORDER FORM,

PLEASE CALL US ON

OUR TOLL-FREE

BLUEPRINT HOTLINE

1-800-521-6797.

YOU MAY WANT TO

LEARN MORE ABOUT

OUR SERVICES AND

PRODUCTS. HERE'S

SOME INFORMATION

YOU WILL FIND HELPFUL.

OUR EXCHANGE POLICY

With the exception of reproducible plan orders, we will exchange your entire first order for an equal or greater number of blueprints within our plan collection within 90 days of the original order. The entire content of your original order must be returned before an exchange will be processed. Please call our customer service department for your return authorization number and shipping instructions. If the returned blueprints look used, redlined or copied, we will not honor your exchange. Fees for exchanging your blueprints are as follows: 20% of the amount of the original order...plus the difference in cost if exchanging for a design in a higher price bracket or less the difference in cost if exchanging for a design in a lower price bracket. **(Reproducible blueprints are not exchangeable or refundable.)** Please call for current postage and handling prices. Shipping and handling charges are not refundable.

ABOUT REPRODUCIBLES

When purchasing a reproducible you may be required to furnish a fax number. The designer will fax documents that you must sign and return to them before shipping will take place.

ABOUT REVERSE BLUEPRINTS

Although lettering and dimensions will appear backward, reverses will be a useful aid if you decide to flop the plan. See Price Schedule and Plans Index for pricing.

REVISING, MODIFYING AND CUSTOMIZING PLANS

Like many homeowners who buy these plans, you and your builder, architect or engineer may want to make changes to them. We recommend purchase of a reproducible plan for any changes made by your builder, licensed architect or engineer. As set forth below, we cannot assume any responsibility for blueprints which have been changed, whether by you, your builder or by professionals selected by you or referred to you by us, because such individuals are outside our supervision and control.

ARCHITECTURAL AND ENGINEERING SEALS

Some cities and states are now requiring that a licensed architect or engineer review and "seal" a blueprint, or officially approve it, prior to construction due to concerns over energy costs, safety and other factors. Prior to application for a building permit or the start of actual construction, we strongly advise that you consult your local building official who can tell you if such a review is required.

ABOUT THE DESIGNS

The architects and designers whose work appears in this publication are among America's leading residential designers. Each plan was designed to meet the requirements of a nationally recognized model building code in effect at the time and place the plan was drawn. Because national building codes change from time to time, plans may not comply with any such code at the time they are sold to a customer. In addition, building officials may not accept these plans as final construction documents of record as the plans may need to be modified and additional drawings and details added to suit local conditions and requirements. We strongly advise that purchasers consult a licensed architect or engineer, and their local building official, before starting any construction related to these plans.

LOCAL BUILDING CODES AND ZONING REQUIREMENTS

At the time of creation, our plans are drawn to specifications published by the Building Officials and Code Administrators (BOCA) International, Inc.; the Southern Building Code Congress (SBCCI) International, Inc.; the International Conference of Building Officials (ICBO); or the Council of American Building Officials (CABO). Our plans are designed to meet or exceed national building standards. Because of the great differences in geography and climate throughout the United States and Canada, each state, county and municipality has its own building codes, zone requirements, ordinances and building regulations. Your plan may need to be modified to comply with local requirements regarding snow loads, energy codes, soil and seismic conditions and a wide range of other matters. In addition, you may need to obtain permits or inspections from local governments before and in the course of construction. Prior to using blueprints ordered from us, we strongly advise that you consult a licensed architect or engineer—and speak with your local building official—before applying for any permit or beginning construction. We authorize the use of our blueprints on the express condition that you strictly comply with all local building codes, zoning requirements and other applicable laws, regulations, ordinances and requirements. Notice: Plans for homes to be built in Nevada must be re-drawn by a Nevada-registered professional. Consult your building official for more information on this subject.

TOLL FREE
1-800-521-6797

REGULAR OFFICE HOURS:
8:00 a.m.-9:00 p.m. EST, Monday-Friday

If we receive your order by 3:00 p.m. EST, Monday-Friday, we'll process it and ship within **two business days**. When ordering by phone, please have your credit card or check information ready. We'll also ask you for the Order Form Key Number at the bottom of the order form.

By FAX: Copy the Order Form on the next page and send it on our FAX line: 1-800-224-6699 or 520-544-3086.

Canadian Customers
Order Toll Free 1-877-223-6389

ORDER FORM

*CALL FOR CURRENT PRICING & AVAILABILITY
PRIOR TO MAILING THIS ORDER FORM.*

DISCLAIMER

The designers we work with have put substantial care and effort into the creation of their blueprints. However, because they cannot provide on-site consultation, supervision and control over actual construction, and because of the great variance in local building requirements, building practices and soil, seismic, weather and other conditions, WE CANNOT MAKE ANY WARRANTY, EXPRESS OR IMPLIED, WITH RESPECT TO THE CONTENT OR USE OF THE BLUEPRINTS, INCLUDING BUT NOT LIMITED TO ANY WARRANTY OF MERCHANTABILITY OR OF FITNESS FOR A PARTICULAR PURPOSE. **ITEMS, PRICES, TERMS AND CONDITIONS ARE SUBJECT TO CHANGE WITHOUT NOTICE. REPRODUCIBLE PLAN ORDERS MAY REQUIRE A CUSTOMER'S SIGNED RELEASE BEFORE SHIPPING.**

TERMS AND CONDITIONS

These designs are protected under the terms of United States Copyright Law and may not be copied or reproduced in any way, by any means, unless you have purchased Reproducibles which clearly indicate your right to copy or reproduce. We authorize the use of your chosen design as an aid in the construction of one single family home only. You may not use this design to build a second or multiple dwellings without purchasing another blueprint or blueprints or paying additional design fees.

HOW MANY BLUEPRINTS DO YOU NEED?

Although a standard building package may satisfy many states, cities and counties, some plans may require certain changes. For your convenience, we have developed a Reproducible plan which allows a local professional to modify and make up to 10 copies of your revised plan. As our plans are all copyright protected, with your purchase of the Reproducible, we will supply you with a Copyright release letter. The number of copies you may need: 1 for owner; 3 for builder; 2 for local building department and 1-3 sets for your mortgage lender.

 ORDER TOLL FREE!

**For information about
any of our services
or to order call
1-800-521-6797**

**Browse our website:
www.eplans.com**

**BLUEPRINTS ARE
NOT REFUNDABLE
EXCHANGES ONLY**

**For Customer Service,
call toll free
1-888-690-1116.**

HOME PLANNERS, LLC wholly owned by Hanley-Wood, LLC
3275 WEST INA ROAD, SUITE 220 • TUCSON, ARIZONA • 85741

THE BASIC BLUEPRINT PACKAGE
Rush me the following (please refer to the Plans Index and Price Schedule in this section):
___ Set(s) of reproducibles*, plan number(s) _____ $_____
    indicate foundation type _____ surcharge (if applicable): $_____
___ Set(s) of blueprints, plan number(s) _____ $_____
    indicate foundation type _____ surcharge (if applicable): $_____
___ Additional identical blueprints (standard or reverse) in same order @ $50 per set $_____
___ Reverse blueprints @ $50 fee per order. Right-reading reverse @ $165 surcharge $_____

IMPORTANT EXTRAS
Rush me the following:
___ Materials List: $70 (Must be purchased with Blueprint set.) $_____
___ **Quote One®** Summary Cost Report @ $29.95 for one, $14.95 for each additional,
    for plans _____ $_____
    Building location: City _____ Zip Code _____
___ **Quote One®** Material Cost Report @ $130
    for plan _____ (Must be purchased with Blueprints set.) $_____
    Building location: City _____ Zip Code _____
___ Specification Outlines @ $10 each $_____
___ Detail Sets @ $14.95 each; any two $22.95; any three $29.95; all four for $39.95 (save $19.85) $_____
    ❏ Plumbing ❏ Electrical ❏ Construction ❏ Mechanical
___ Home Furniture Planner @ $15.95 each $_____

DECK BLUEPRINTS
(Please refer to the Plans Index and Price Schedule in this section)
___ Set(s) of Deck Plan _____. $_____
___ Additional identical blueprints in same order @ $10 per set. $_____
___ Reverse blueprints @ $10 fee per order. $_____
___ Set of Standard Deck Details @ $14.95 per set. $_____
___ Set of Complete Deck Construction Package (Best Buy!) Add $10 to Building Package.
    Includes Custom Deck Plan _____ Plus Standard Deck Details

LANDSCAPE BLUEPRINTS
(Please refer to the Plans Index and Price Schedule in this section.)
___ Set(s) of Landscape Plan _____ $_____
___ Additional identical blueprints in same order @ $10 per set $_____
___ Reverse blueprints @ $10 fee per order $_____
Please indicate appropriate region of the country for Plant & Material List. Region _____

POSTAGE AND HANDLING *SIGNATURE IS REQUIRED FOR ALL DELIVERIES.*	1–3 sets	4+ sets
DELIVERY		
No CODs (Requires street address—No P.O. Boxes)		
•Regular Service (Allow 7–10 business days delivery)	❏ $20.00	❏ $25.00
•Priority (Allow 4–5 business days delivery)	❏ $25.00	❏ $35.00
•Express (Allow 3 business days delivery)	❏ $35.00	❏ $45.00
OVERSEAS DELIVERY	fax, phone or mail for quote	

Note: All delivery times are from date Blueprint Package is shipped.

POSTAGE (From box above) $_____
SUBTOTAL $_____
SALES TAX (AZ & MI residents, please add appropriate state and local sales tax.) $_____
TOTAL (Subtotal and tax) $_____

YOUR ADDRESS (please print legibly)
Name _____

Street _____

City _____ State _____ Zip _____

Daytime telephone number (required) (_____) _____

* Fax number (required for reproducible orders) _____
TeleCheck® Checks By Phone℠ available
FOR CREDIT CARD ORDERS ONLY
Credit card number _____ Exp. Date: (M/Y) _____

Check one ❏ Visa ❏ MasterCard ❏ American Express

Order Form Key

HPT303

Signature (required) _____
Please check appropriate box: ❏ Licensed Builder-Contractor ❏ Homeowner

 **ORDER TOLL FREE!**
1-800-521-6797

BY FAX: Copy the order form above and send it on
our FAXLINE: 1-800-224-6699 OR 520-544-3086

445

1 BIGGEST & BEST

1001 of our best-selling plans in one volume. 1,074 to 7,275 square feet. 704 pgs $12.95 1K1

2 ONE-STORY

450 designs for all lifestyles. 800 to 4,900 square feet. 384 pgs $9.95 OS

3 MORE ONE-STORY

475 superb one-level plans from 800 to 5,000 square feet. 448 pgs $9.95 MO2

4 TWO-STORY

443 designs for one-and-a-half and two stories. 1,500 to 6,000 square feet. 448 pgs $9.95 TS

5 VACATION

430 designs for recreation, retirement and leisure. 448 pgs $9.95 VS3

6 HILLSIDE

208 designs for split-levels, bi-levels, multi-levels and walkouts. 224 pgs $9.95 HH

7 FARMHOUSE

300 Fresh Designs from Classic to Modern. 320 pgs. $10.95 FCP

8 COUNTRY HOUSES

208 unique home plans that combine traditional style and modern livability. 224 pgs $9.95 CN

9 BUDGET-SMART

200 efficient plans from 7 top designers, that you can really afford to build! 224 pgs $8.95 BS

10 BARRIER-FREE

Over 1,700 products and 51 plans for accessible living. 128 pgs $15.95 UH

11 ENCYCLOPEDIA

500 exceptional plans for all styles and budgets—the best book of its kind! 528 pgs $9.95 ENC

12 ENCYCLOPEDIA II

500 completely new plans. Spacious and stylish designs for every budget and taste. 352 pgs $9.95 E2

13 AFFORDABLE

300 Modest plans for savvy homebuyers. 256 pgs. $9.95 AH2

14 VICTORIAN

210 striking Victorian and Farmhouse designs from today's top designers. 224 pgs $15.95 VDH2

15 ESTATE

Dream big! Eighteen designers showcase their biggest and best plans. 224 pgs $16.95 EDH3

16 LUXURY

170 lavish designs, over 50% brand-new plans added to a most elegant collection. 192 pgs $12.95 LD3

17 EUROPEAN STYLES

200 homes with a unique flair of the Old World. 224 pgs $15.95 EURO

18 COUNTRY CLASSICS

Donald Gardner's 101 best Country and Traditional home plans. 192 pgs $17.95 DAG

19 COUNTRY

85 Charming Designs from American Home Gallery. 160 pgs. $17.95 CTY

20 TRADITIONAL

85 timeless designs from the Design Traditions Library. 160 pgs $17.95 TRA

21 COTTAGES

245 Delightful retreats from 825 to 3,500 square feet. 256 pgs. $10.95 COOL

22 CABINS TO VILLAS

Enchanting Homes for Mountain Sea or Sun, from the Sater collection. 144 pgs $19.95 CCV

23 CONTEMPORARY

The most complete and imaginative collection of contemporary designs available anywhere. 256 pgs. $10.95 CM2

24 FRENCH COUNTRY

Live every day in the French countryside using these plans, landscapes and interiors. 192 pgs. $14.95 PN

25 SOUTHERN

207 homes rich in Southern styling and comfort. 240 pgs $8.95 SH

26 SOUTHWESTERN

138 designs that capture the spirit of the Southwest. 144 pgs $10.95 SW

27 SHINGLE-STYLE

155 Home plans from Classic Colonials to Breezy Bungalows. 192 pgs. $12.95 SNG

28 NEIGHBORHOOD

170 designs with the feel of main street America. 192 pgs $12.95 TND

29 CRAFTSMAN

170 Home plans in the Craftsman and Bungalow style. 192 pgs $12.95 CC

30 GRAND VISTAS

200 Homes with a View. 224 pgs. $10.95 GV

Home Planners wants your building experience to be as pleasant and trouble-free as possible.
That's why we've expanded our library of do-it-yourself titles to help you along.

31 DUPLEX & TOWNHOMES

115 Duplex, Multiplex &
Townhome Designs. 128 pgs.
$17.95 MFH

32 WATERFRONT

200 designs perfect for your
waterside wonderland.
208 pgs $10.95 WF

33 NATURAL LIGHT

223 Sunny home plans for all
regions. 240 pgs. $8.95 NA

34 NOSTALGIA

100 Time-Honored designs
updated with today's features.
224 pgs. $14.95 NOS

35 STREET OF DREAMS

Over 300 photos showcase
54 prestigious homes.
256 pgs $19.95 SOD

36 NARROW-LOT

250 Designs for houses
17' to 50' wide. 256 pgs.
$9.95 NL2

37 SMALL HOUSES

Innovative plans for
sensible lifestyles.
224 pgs. $8.95 SM2

38 GARDENS & MORE

225 gardens, landscapes,
decks and more to
enhance every home.
320 pgs. $19.95 GLP

39 EASY-CARE

41 special landscapes
designed for beauty and
low maintenance.
160 pgs $14.95 ECL

40 BACKYARDS

40 designs focused solely on
creating your own specially
themed backyard oasis. 160
pgs $14.95 BYL

41 BEDS & BORDERS
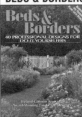
40 Professional designs
for do-it-yourselfers
160 pgs. $14.95 BB

42 BUYER'S GUIDE

A comprehensive look at 2700
products for all aspects of
landscaping & gardening.
128 pgs $19.95 LPBG

LANDSCAPE DESIGNS

43 OUTDOOR

74 easy-to-build designs,
lets you create and build
your own backyard oasis.
128 pgs $9.95 YG2

44 GARAGES

145 exciting projects from
64 to 1,900 square feet.
160 pgs. $9.95 GG2

45 DECKS

A brand new collection
of 120 beautiful and
practical decks. 144 pgs.
$9.95 DP2

46 HOME BUILDING

Everything you need to know
to work with contractors and
subcontractors. 212 pgs
$14.95 HBP

47 RURAL BUILDING

Everything you need to know
to build your home in the
country. 232 pgs.
$14.95 BYC

48 VACATION HOMES

Your complete guide to
building your vacation
home. 224 pgs.
$14.95 BYV

PROJECT GUIDES

Book Order Form

To order your books, just check the box of the book numbered below and complete the coupon. We will process
your order and ship it from our office within two business days. Send coupon and check (in U.S. funds).

YES! Please send me the books I've indicated:

❏ 1:1K1 ....$12.95	❏ 17:EURO...$15.95	❏ 33:NA..........$8.95
❏ 2:OS............$9.95	❏ 18:DAG $17.95	❏ 34:NOS $14.95
❏ 3:MO2.........$9.95	❏ 19:CTY......$17.95	❏ 35:SOD $19.95
❏ 4:TS $9.95	❏ 20:TRA......$17.95	❏ 36:NL2........$9.95
❏ 5:VS3..........$9.95	❏ 21:COOL...$10.95	❏ 37:SM2.......$8.95
❏ 6:HH............$9.95	❏ 22:CCV......$19.95	❏ 38:GLP.....$19.95
❏ 7:FCP.......$10.95	❏ 23:CM2.....$10.95	❏ 39:ECL.....$14.95
❏ 8:CN............$9.95	❏ 24:PN........$14.95	❏ 40:BYL.....$14.95
❏ 9:BS............$8.95	❏ 25:SH.........$8.95	❏ 41:BB.......$14.95
❏ 10:UH $15.95	❏ 26:SW.......$10.95	❏ 42:LPBG ...$19.95
❏ 11:ENC.......$9.95	❏ 27:SNG $12.95	❏ 43:YG2.......$9.95
❏ 12:E2 ....$9.95	❏ 28:TND $12.95	❏ 44:GG2 ......$9.95
❏ 13:AH2........$9.95	❏ 29:CC........$12.95	❏ 45:DP2.......$9.95
❏ 14:VDH2 ...$15.95	❏ 30:GV........$10.95	❏ 46:HBP.....$14.95
❏ 15:EDH3 ...$16.95	❏ 31:MFH.....$17.95	❏ 47:BYC.....$14.95
❏ 16:LD3......$12.95	❏ 32:WF.......$10.95	❏ 48:BYV.....$14.95

Canadian Customers Order Toll Free 1-877-223-6389

Books Subtotal $_____
ADD Postage and Handling (allow 4–6 weeks for delivery) $ 4.00
Sales Tax: (AZ & MI residents, add state and local sales tax.) $_____
YOUR TOTAL (Subtotal, Postage/Handling, Tax) $_____

YOUR ADDRESS (PLEASE PRINT)

Name _____

Street _____

City _____ State _____ Zip _____

Phone (_____) _____ — _____

YOUR PAYMENT

TeleCheck® Checks By Phone℠ available

Check one: ❏ Check ❏ Visa ❏ MasterCard ❏ American Express
Required credit card information:

Credit Card Number _____

Expiration Date (Month/Year)_____ / _____

Signature Required _____

Home Planners, LLC
3275 W. Ina Road, Suite 220, Dept. BK, Tucson, AZ 85741

HPT303

HEAT-N-GLO
1-888-427-3973
WWW.HEATNGLO.COM

No one builds a better fire

Heat-N-Glo offers quality gas, woodburning and electric fireplaces, including gas log sets, stoves, and inserts for preexisting fireplaces. Now available gas grills and outdoor fireplaces. Send for a free brochure.

Ideas for your next project. Beautiful, durable, elegant low-maintenance millwork, mouldings, balustrade systems and much more. For your free catalog please call us at 1-800-446-3040 or visit www.stylesolutionsinc.com.

ARISTOKRAFT
ONE MASTERBRAND CABINETS DRIVE
JASPER, IN 47546
(812) 482-2527
WWW.ARISTOKRAFT.COM

Cabinetry

Great Ideas
Made Easy

Aristokraft offers you superb value, outstanding quality and great style that fit your budget. Transform your great ideas into reality with popular styles and features that reflect your taste and lifestyle. $5.00

THERMA-TRU DOORS
1687 WOODLANDS DRIVE
MAUMEE, OH 43537
1-800-THERMA-TRU
WWW.THERMATRU.COM

THERMA TRU
DOORS

THE DOOR SYSTEM YOU CAN BELIEVE IN

The undisputed brand leader, Therma-Tru specializes in fiberglass and steel entry doors for every budget. Excellent craftsmanship, energy efficiency and variety make Therma-Tru the perfect choice for all your entry door needs.

---

225 GARDEN, LANDSCAPE
AND PROJECT PLANS
TO ORDER, CALL
1-800-322-6797

225 Do-It-Yourself designs that help transform boring yards into exciting outdoor entertainment spaces. Gorgeous gardens, luxurious landscapes, dazzling decks and other outdoor amenities. Complete construction blueprints available for every project. Only $19.95 (plus $4 shipping/handling).

HAVE WE GOT PLANS FOR YOU!

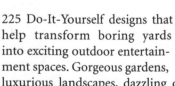

Stop dreaming. Start building.

Your online source for home designs and ideas. Find thousands of plans from the nation's top designers...all in one place. Plus, links to the best known names in building supplies and services.